# In the Wake of the Goddesses

# In the Wake of the Goddesses

## Women, Culture, and the Biblical Transformation of Pagan Myth

## Tikva Frymer-Kensky

THE FREE PRESS
*A Division of Macmillan, Inc.*
NEW YORK

Maxwell Macmillan Canada
TORONTO

Maxwell Macmillan International
NEW YORK   OXFORD   SINGAPORE   SYDNEY

The Free Press
A Division of Macmillan, Inc.
866 Third Avenue, New York, N.Y. 10022

Maxwell Macmillan Canada, Inc.
1200 Eglinton Avenue East
Suite 200
Don Mills, Ontario M3C 3N1

Macmillan, Inc. is part of the Maxwell Communication
Group of Companies

Printed in the United States of America

printing number
1   2   3   4   5   6   7   8   9   10

Library of Congress Cataloging-in-Publication Data

Frymer-Kensky, Tikva Simone.
    In the wake of the goddesses : women, culture, and the biblical
transformation of pagan myth / Tikva Frymer-Kensky.
        p.    cm.
    Includes bibliographical references and index.
    ISBN 0-02-910800-4
    1. Goddesses.   2. God (Judaism)   3. Women in the Bible.   4. Sex in
the Bible.   I. Title.
BL473.5.F78   1992
220.92—dc20                                                    91-21860
                                                                  CIP

# Contents

Preface     vii

1. Introduction    *On the Nature of Monotheism*    1

### PART I
## The World of the Goddesses

2. The Pantheon    9

3. "Godwomen"    *Goddesses, Women, and Gender*    14

4. The Wisdom of Women    *Goddesses and the Arts of Civilization*    32

5. In the Body of the Goddess    *Goddesses and Nature*    45

6. Bridges to the Gods    *Love, War, and the Goddess Inanna/Ishtar*    58

7. The Marginalization of the Goddesses    70

### PART II
## In the Absence of Goddesses
### *Biblical Transformations*

8. Israel and the Master of the Universe    83

9. But in Ourselves    100

10. *Homo Sapiens*    108

11. Gender and Its Image  *Women in the Bible*               118

12. The Wanton Wife of God                                   144

13. Asherah and Abundance                                    153

14. Our Father and Our Mother                                162

15. Zion, the Beloved Woman                                  168

16. Wisdom, the Lover of Man                                 179

PART III

# Sex and Gender
## *The Unfinished Agenda*

17. Sex in the Bible                                         187

18. Sex and the People  *The Myth of Orgy*                   199

19. Gifts of the Greeks                                      203

    Epilogue  *Religion in the Wake of the Goddesses*        213

    Appendix  *The Goddesses of Sumer*                       221

    Abbreviations                                            225

    Notes                                                    229

    Index                                                    283

# Preface

I began this book eight years ago, while teaching a course on women and religion at the University of Michigan. As histories and theologies of "the Goddess" appeared, I became increasingly disturbed. A scholar of ancient Near Eastern religions, I had read many texts written for and about goddesses, and had formed some clear impressions of the goddesses of the ancient world. This modern literature on the Goddess was alien to my understanding of the worship of these ancient deities. There was not one Goddess, there were many goddesses; they were not enshrined in a religion of women, but in the official religion of male-dominated societies; they were not evidence of ancient mother-worship, but served as an integral part of a religious system that mirrored and provided the sacred underpinnings of patriarchy. My first reaction was scholarly bemusement: how could people write about goddesses when they couldn't read any of the ancient literature? This soon passed into a form of territorial protectiveness: goddesses, after all, were my turf: when nonscholars wrote about such matters, not only did they invade my turf, but they excavated with a steam shovel, confusing the issues and making it harder to discern the delicate vestiges of the past. In doing so, they also trivialized and invalidated my area of expertise: if you could discover all you needed to know about the Goddess from inside your soul and your mind, why should anyone study Sumerian and Akkadian? Should not knowledge of the ancient texts be the authoritative ground from which to analyze and critique modern theories about the Goddess? I began to get angry: why wasn't anyone listening to the scholars? But the anger became directed at myself as I realized that scholars weren't writing much that was pertinent. It is not sufficient to criticize others and point out where their theories are disproved by facts. The issues raised by the new Goddess writings are real issues, and if current beliefs seemed wrong, then it was up to me to study these ancient deities in as exacting and responsible way as I could. The subject is vast and mostly unexplored, and I chose to study the myths in order to concentrate on the function of these goddesses. What is it that goddesses do in a religious system? What does the femaleness of the deity indicate about that deity, and what does the existence of both male and female deities suggest about the nature of humanity and the cosmos? The results of my study constitute the first part of this book, "The World of the Goddesses."

I could not stop there. Neither do people reconstruct or reinvent ancient paganism out of antiquarian curiosity, nor is the modern interest in the Goddess purely academic. Rather, it stems from a desire to remedy the results of millennia of misogyny and marginalization in the monotheist religions. The Goddess is an alternative to aspects of monotheism that are now perceived as painful to women and dangerous to the earth. The study of ancient goddesses has important implications for our understanding of monotheism, and should illuminate aspects of it that have been ignored or covered over when viewed from other perspectives. Once we realize that the goddesses of ancient pagan religion were not vestigial remnants of a romantic female past, that they had real functions within their religious systems, then we must ask: what happens to those functions when the goddesses are no more? If goddesses represent certain elements in the conceptualization of culture, how does the absence of goddesses affect this conceptualization? If the interplay between gods and goddesses determines the working of the cosmos, how does the lack of this interplay influence our understanding of the world? And if the world of the gods and goddesses exemplifies gender relations and gender ideology, does the concept of gender change when there is only one god? As I studied the ancient polytheist literature, I turned to the Bible with new eyes and asked these questions. The transformations that biblical monotheism brought in the way human beings look at themselves and at the universe are described in the second part of this book, "In the Absence of Goddesses: Biblical Transformations."

The picture of biblical monotheism that emerges is significantly different from that of later monotheist religions, and one must ask: how did we get from there to here? If biblical monotheism transformed the way we look at everything, why did it not stay the dominant vision? What were the problems within biblical monotheism that made it unstable? What were the questions it left unanswered, and what was unsatisfactory in the answers it provided? Part III of this book, "The Unfinished Agenda," considers some of the changes from biblical monotheism in the development of postbiblical Western religion. After studying these issues, I have become convinced that biblical monotheism has much to say to us today, and in the epilogue, I add my voice to current theological discussion.

Part of the scholarly ferment in recent years has been the realization that the reader is always present in the reading of texts, and that the present is always part of the interpretation of the past. There is no such thing as the totally objective recovery of history, for something informs our choice of questions to ask and our selection of data that seems significant to us. There is also no such thing as one true reading of a piece of literature—even the author's own explanation of the meaning of a work could not encompass the totality of what the work means. Gone is the naïve assumption that knowledge is absolute and absolutely attainable. Instead, we work in a sophisticated universe in which we try to be faithful to the data, knowing full well that we are part of the interpretation of this data. But, if total objectivity is a chimera, how does one distinguish between free interpretative speculations and responsible scholarship? After all, pure subjectivity is an artistic enterprise, not a scholarly one. The answers to this problem are still being articulated, but one working principle is that if the reader is crucial to the interpretation, then the reader should be revealed. If I am the reader of these ancient texts, then my readers in turn should know who I am, what consciously informs my vision, and what might inadvertently affect my judgment. I therefore feel that it is important to introduce myself.

By training, I am an Assyriologist/Sumerologist, which means I spend a large part of my life studying the literatures from ancient Sumer, Babylon, and Assyria. My interests are in religion, law, and literature, and my studies in these areas have only served to reinforce the commitment that brought me into the field: the sense that these ancient religious systems are serious examples of the human quest for understanding, that these ancient cultures are dignified and significant and worthy of respect.

I am also a biblicist, spending my time studying and pondering the one great book left by ancient Israel. I find the Hebrew Bible to be endlessly fascinating in the intensity of its message, the multiplicity of its meanings, the many ramifications of its thinking, and the impact, past and present, of its existence.

I am also a late-twentieth-century postmodern American feminist Jew, with all that this implies about love of tradition in general combined with desire for free inquiry; love of community with assertion of self; universal sense of humanity with appreciation of the need for closer associations; and love of my own traditions in particular with a deeply pluralistic understanding of the religious quest. Such seeming contradictions form the dynamic tensions within which I understand my universe and from which I draw my creativity.

In all my efforts, I am a scholar. After months of deciphering, decoding, and interpreting, I am happy when I read the literature on my topic and find that no one before me has seen my questions, has studied the data in quite the same way. But I also feel validated when I work out something carefully and painstakingly from primary data and later discover that someone else had the same insight and published the results in some obscure place or language that had escaped me. Above all, my scholarship makes me extremely reluctant to make assumptions or to draw conclusions that are too facile, too easily arrived at.

I am, as well, a teacher, eager to impart my knowledge, always looking for the text that brings the ancient world alive and the issue that causes the modern person to relate directly to the testimonies of the ancients. I have tried to learn to be a writer, to focus on the line of argument of this book, and not to include many discoveries that I have made that branch out and digress into other fascinating and curious byways in the areas of ancient Near Eastern and biblical religions. And, finally I have learned to be a "person-who-has-written," to overcome my sense of all that there is yet to explore long enough to share with others what I have already learned.

I have worked alone. The rewards of collaboration have so far eluded me, and I look forward to the day when I can work on a project with a colleague who is close enough in both interests and place to make such collaboration feasible. But I have never worked in isolation. By and large, Assyriologists and biblical scholars in America have a considerable feeling of fellowship for each other. If there are deep personal antagonisms and feuds in my fields, I have remained naïvely and blissfully unaffected by them. Everyone I have talked to has been supportive of me, even when initially suspicious of the possibility of scholarly work on goddesses. I have benefited greatly from my conversations with scholarly colleagues during the years that I have been studying these issues, and would especially like to thank Ann Guinan, Peter Machinist, and Jeffrey Tigay for taking the time to let me talk through some thorny questions as they have arisen. In addition, David Noel Freedman and Moshe Greenberg read and commented on the first drafts of several chapters in the Bible section of this book, Bendt Alster read an early draft on the Sumerian section, Sally Humphreys and Elizabeth Castelli read the section on the Greeks, Neil Danzig, David Goldenberg, and Allan Kensky read the rabbinic materials. As the work progressed, one of my students, Seth Riemer, read chapters in progress and helped improve their clarity and accessibility, as did Diane Sharon and Sasha Golomb. Later, Phyllis Trible and Sarah Japhet read the first complete manuscript and offered valuable comments. I would also like to thank my two editors at The Free Press, Laura Wolff and Gioia Stevens. Laura Wolff encouraged me in the initial stages, helping me refine my ideas. When Laura left The Free Press, Gioia Stevens patiently saw me through the writing stages and demanded focus and readability. Finally, in the end stages of preparation of this manuscript, when eight years of labor did not prevent the mad last-minute rush to tie up loose ends, I was ably assisted by Etty Lassman, secretary at the Annenberg Research Institute.

I have also been very fortunate as to place. I began in Ann Arbor, but during the years that I have worked on this book, I have lived in Jerusalem, Ann Arbor, and Philadelphia. Everywhere, there were colleagues to talk to and wonderful libraries to use: the École Biblique and Hebrew University in Jerusalem; the University of Michigan Library in Ann Arbor; the Jewish Theological Seminary and Union Theological Seminary in New York; the Annenberg Research Institute, Eastern Baptist Seminary, Lutheran Theological Seminary, Reconstructionist Rabbinical College, and the University of Pennsylvania in Philadelphia. I have been particularly fortunate in the past few years as a professor at the Reconstructionist Rabbinical College, a warm, supportive, pluralist environment eager to participate in the development of new ideas, and as a fellow at the Annenberg Research Institute, a taste of scholar's heaven on earth, where scholars are made to feel like the apex of the enterprise of learning instead of the drones.

I have not published this book in preliminary form, but I have lectured on the issues that many chapters raise. Wherever I have spoken, whether to scholars or to lay people, the audience response has been unfailingly positive. The interest that people have shown in my questions and their enthusiasm about my answers have supported me during the darkest, most arduous days of study and writing. I thank all who have learned and caused me to learn, and I dedicate this book to all those involved in the transmissions of tradition and learning: to my teachers and my parents; to my students and my children, and to my husband Allan Kensky, who is my teacher and my student, my colleague and my friend.

# 1

## Introduction

### On the Nature of Monotheism

Religion is on people's minds these days. Fundamental religious questions are being asked. Liberalism versus fundamentalism, orthodoxy and reconstructionism, tradition and revision, immanentism and trancendentalism, rationalism and mysticism are all being debated. Prominent in these discussions are disputes about polytheism and monotheism. The ancient battles between YHWH and the gods,* between pagans and Christians, are being played out again in our time. In their dissatisfaction with the manifestations of monotheism in Judaism and particularly in Christianity, many modern thinkers, particularly feminists, have turned again to polytheistic religions, and in particular to the idea of "The Goddess." Earth-centered, immanent, and immediate, the Goddess of modern neopaganism serves as a refuge from, and counterbalance to, what many consider the remote and punitive god of Western religions.

"Paganism," once a term of scorn, is no longer derogatory. In an ironic twist, the traditional Judeo-Christian view of paganism is often unquestioned. Now however, this paganism is appreciated as body-and-life-affirming. Frequently, now, it is monotheism that is under attack. But the "monotheism" attacked as world-denying, body-deprecating and woman-hating has little to do with monotheism as it first appeared in biblical Israel. And the traditional Judeo-Christian view of paganism is very unlike the polytheism reflected in ancient documents. When we

---

*The letters YHWH stand for the tetragrammaton, the four-letter name of God. The name was most probably pronounced *Yahweh*. However, in Jewish tradition this is not pronounced, and the four letters are pronounced *Adonay* ("God"). In deference to this tradition, I transcribe YHWH and readers can read it as they will.

1

let the ancient texts speak for themselves, we begin to understand the nature of the monotheist revolution and the promise of our belief-systems.

The age-old questions about monotheism and paganism can be answered today in a new way because of our recovery of the great civilizations of ancient Mesopotamia. The archaeological excavations in Iraq and the decipherment of the cuneiform tablets have revealed the ancient Mesopotamian civilizations: Sumer and Akkad, and the cultures that later developed from them, Babylon and Assyria. These were the mother-cultures of a large area that extended through Syria to the Mediterranean coast, and greatly influenced the many nations that emerged in the "fertile crescent," including Canaan and Israel. The ancient Mesopotamian people have given us a great legacy in the cuneiform tablets that they left behind, tablets that contain the records of the actions and thoughts of the people in Iraq from 2500 B.C.E. until after the beginning of the common era.[1] Not only do they provide an exciting new perspective on the ancient world, they also revolutionize our appreciation of ancient civilization.

These Mesopotamian tablets include the prayers, hymns and the myths of the people of Mesopotamia. They provide a window into ancient religion, for the authors of these tablets were not writing for us: they wrote for their own cultic and ceremonial occasions, and for their own edification. We do not have to glean our information from the writings of later polemicists who might be interested in proving the worth—or lack of worth—of Mesopotamian beliefs or customs. Instead, we can read tablets inscribed by people who believed what they were writing, texts that are a direct reflection of the thoughts, feelings, and concepts of the ancient authors and the people who heard their words. These are not the beliefs of the common people, of course, for "folk" religion usually has its own characteristics, but it is the religion of the scribes, priests, courtiers, and intelligentsia of an ancient world.

If we study the literature of the ancient Babylonians and Sumerians, we can no longer believe the description of "pagan" religion that has long been part of Western tradition and is still often found in modern religious writing. Instead of capricious gods acting only in pursuit of their own desires, we meet deities concerned with the proper ordering of the universe and the regulation of history. Instead of divine cruelty and arrogance, we find deliberation and understanding. Instead of lawlessness and violence, we see a developed legal system and a long tradition of reflective jurisprudence. Instead of immoral attitudes and behavior, we find moral deliberation, philosophical speculation, and penitential prayer. Instead of wild orgiastic rites, we read of hymns, processions, sacrifices, and prayers. Instead of the benighted paganism of the Western imagination, cuneiform literature reveals to us an ethical polytheism that commands serious attention and respect.

But this new valuation of paganism creates its own dilemmas and awakens new questions. If the Bible is not the first dawn of enlightenment in a world of total darkness, then what is it? If polytheism was not the dark disaster that our cultural tradition has imagined it to be, why was it abandoned in Israel and replaced by biblical monotheism? If the old religions swept away by our own monotheist tradition were not grossly deficient, how can we find the precise significance of one God as opposed to the many? How does a monotheistic religion develop? Did the god of Israel simply absorb all the functions and attributes of the pagan gods, essentially changing nothing? Or did monotheism represent a radical break with the past after all, a break not as simply defined and immediately apparent as has been believed, but no less revolutionary?

The discovery of advanced polytheism poses a central theological issue: if polytheism can have such positive attributes, what is the purpose of monotheism? Did the Bible simply substitute another system, one that represented no advance towards a better understanding of the universe and a more equitable way of living? Indeed, were there some aspects of paganism lost in the transition that present, in fact, a more positive way of living in the world? The immediacy of these issues makes imperative an analysis of the nature of paganism and the precise nuances and essential messages of the monotheist revolution of the Bible. We cannot build our spiritual quest on prejudiced assumptions and polemical attributions. We must attain a profound knowledge of ancient polytheism and a sophisticated reading of the biblical texts informed by this knowledge. Thanks to the discovery of ancient Near Eastern literature, we have the ability to study these questions, understand our own past religious development, and make informed contributions to our future.

Among the many elements of our civilization that are first recorded in Sumer is writing itself, invented in Sumer in the early third millennium B.C.E. There are few natural resources (other than petroleum) in southern Iraq, where these civilizations emerged. There is little stone and little wood, practically nothing but clay and reeds. The Sumerians mixed clay with reeds to make bricks for their building, and they pressed the reeds into the clay for their writing. Their writing was not always intended for posterity, but because of the durable nature of the clay, it has nevertheless survived. Sun-hardened clay tablets may shatter, and break, but they often survive. When these tablets were fired, either intentionally or through the burning of the buildings in which they were housed, they became even harder and longer lasting. It is due to the durability of clay that so many documents have survived to reveal the culture of the ancient Mesopotamians.

Not only are the antiquity and authenticity of the cuneiform tablets exciting; they enable us to pose far more detailed and sophisticated questions about the ideas of the ancients than any we might attempt to answer by interpreting nonliterary cultural artifacts. Through careful reading and analysis of these texts, we can reconstruct the past and trace the origins of many of our cultural institutions as far back as the beginning of writing. This is a fascinating and tantalizing enterprise, but it entails many difficulties and a sometimes elusive goal. Many problems in the study of ancient civilization need to be understood and stated at the outset. First, we have to be aware of the incomplete nature of our data base. Our information is sporadic, for despite the abundance of cuneiform documents, we are nowhere near to having a complete record of Mesopotamia. We cannot fully select which tablets we can study—the availability of evidence depends on the accident of archeological discovery. We have not dug up all the tablets waiting in the sands of Iraq, we have not copied and studied all the tablets that are sitting in our museums, we have not yet assembled and edited all the literature that these tablets contain. We are not even aware of what it is that we do not yet know. This fact is somewhat intimidating, for it is dangerous to argue from silence, and we are constantly aware that carefully worked-out conclusions might be invalidated by a newly discovered tablet. Nevertheless, enough tablets have been excavated so that we can at least begin the reconstruction of ancient ideas.

It is exciting to hold in our hands something written four thousand years ago and to read from it the words of the ancients. The clay tablet is an authentic message from an ancient author. However, deciphering the message can be difficult. Tablets are frequently incomplete and hard to read. They are often broken, sometimes so badly that we cannot follow the exact sequence of events. They are almost always chipped, particularly at the edges, which, for Sumerian, means at the subject or verb of the sentence. Thus, the meaning is often elusive and tantalizing, and our restorations and translations may be inadequate. Stories and hymns are frequently pieced together from several broken copies of the same text, as we use one to help read the others.

Even when the tablets are perfectly preserved, they are not always clear. These tablets are written in two ancient languages, Sumerian and Akkadian. Akkadian, a Semitic language, was deciphered almost one hundred and fifty years ago. It can be read with a certain degree of fluency, but there are still troublesome passages where two equally possible translations yield very different meanings. The study of Sumerian is a twentieth-century discipline. Sumerian is neither Semitic nor Indo-European, and cannot be studied by means of grammatical or lexical similarity to other languages. In the last fifty years, there have been enormous advances in our knowledge of the language, and we can read and understand the myths of the Sumerians. Nevertheless, our translations of key passages in Sumerian literature are still somewhat tentative. It is important not to infer too much from any single passage, particularly one whose translation is difficult and problematic. We may also be thwarted in our attempts to interpret meaning and reconstruct ideas, for the tablets tell us only what they tell us, not always the answers to what we ask. In the language of anthropology, these tablets are our native informants, but they are dead. The enterprise is complex, frequently tedious and frustrating, but no difficulties and problems can overshadow the excitement of reading this ancient literature. Rich and fascinating, these texts illuminate the ancient world and our own.

The central question asked by this book is: what happens in the Bible to central ideas of polytheism, and to the functions and roles once played by goddesses? We focus on goddesses for several reasons. There have been several studies of the relationship of the God of Israel to pagan gods, particularly the Canaanite gods El and Ba'al. But a study of goddesses provides a new perspective that reveals aspects of biblical monotheism that have not otherwise been noticed. In addition, we could expect the essentially masculine God of Israel to be able to absorb the attributes of the various male gods, but it might not be as easy for this deity to absorb the functions and attributes of female goddesses. Some of the attributes of these goddesses *are*, clearly, absorbed by YHWH. But others cannot be, and the absence of goddesses causes major changes in the way the Bible—compared with the ancient texts—looks at humanity, culture, society, and nature.

We begin by examining the goddesses of Sumer, despite the fact that the Sumerian tablets were written a millennium before the time of biblical Israel. The reason is quite simple. Goddesses are present and active in Sumerian mythology. Later during the second millennium, information about the goddesses is much harder to glean from the texts. The myths record the exploits and relationship of male gods, and the goddesses have been marginalized. The religion of Israel's contemporaries was not one in which gods and goddesses had equal roles and import. There was no longer possible a choice between monotheism and the goddesses, but rather one between monotheism and a male-dominated polytheism.

But in these later religions, the functions that the goddesses of Sumer had performed had to be addressed in some fashion. By the first millennium, the male gods of polytheism had usurped many of these functions, and the goddesses were invoked to perform whatever remaining functions the male gods had not fully taken over. Biblical monotheism did not have this option. Gender had disappeared from the divine, and there are no more "male" and "female" functions. What the "female" functions had been, how the Bible reorganized its world view in the absence of gender, the ramifications of the absence of goddesses in the Bible, and the transformations it entailed are subjects we will consider in the chapters to come.

# PART I

## The World of the Goddesses

# 2

## The Pantheon

The pantheon of a complex civilization like Sumer was not simple. There were many components to the identity of a god: natural, political, cultural, and familial. In part, gods represented the power felt in the universe. They ordered, regulated, and controlled the natural elements: the sky, sun, moon, storms, and stars. In this way, all aspects of the cosmos that were significant to the life of humans were supervised and determined. Because of the gods' supervision, the world was not chaotic. Those same gods that controlled nature also supervised the polis. Each city-state of ancient Sumer had its own pantheon, headed by the chief god or goddess of that city. The sun-god Utu was the god of Sippar, the moon-god Nanna was the god of Ur, and so forth. These gods were charged with the patronage and oversight of their respective towns, and were celebrated in the city-cults of these cities. In the earliest historical periods of Sumer, the god (through its temple representatives) was probably the chief landholder and major employer of the city, and worship of the god was an effective and meaningful way to mobilize the community. Throughout Sumerian history, the city-god was believed to oversee the well-being of that city, to provide peace and prosperity, and to maintain a special relationship with the city's ruler. This concept of city-god expressed a sense of the community as an organic whole. The city was not simply a coincidental assemblage of people who happened to live in the same place. It was an entity that had unity, integrity, and power—it was a locus of divinity.

Another axis of divine identity was that of the "personal god." Each family understood itself to be under the patronage of a specific god and goddess, who protected the family members and helped insure health, prosperity, and success. In addition, every individual, no matter how small, had his/her own gods. The rank of these personal gods in the pantheon was commensurate with the importance of the individual. Ordinary private people had gods whose names they knew, but which have rarely come down to us. The mighty of Sumer had the great cosmic gods as their personal deities.[1]

Because the city-states were not isolated from each other, the gods of the various city-states had to be brought into some relationship with each other. Throughout the first thousand years of recorded history, there were two contrary forces in Mesopotamia: one, allegiance to one's city and the rivalry between cities that this produced, and, on the other hand, a drive for peace through confederation into national governments.[2] There were such periods of regional unification as the Sargonic (the "Akkadian period," circa 2300–2100 B.C.E.)* and Ur III (the Neo-Sumerian period, circa 2100–2000 B.C.E.); there were such periods of local dominance as the Isin-Larsa (the "Early Old Babylonian period," circa 2000–1800 B.C.E.). These historical periods came and went, and the relative power of the city-gods of Mesopotamia rose and fell. Gods were harmonized with each other; gods were identified with each other and/or were brought into family relationships with each other. Rival theologies developed, such as those clustering around Enlil and Enki, but then later harmonized with each other in the creation of national pantheons.

There is yet another factor that increases the complexity of the Mesopotamian pantheon. Two distinct peoples lived in southern Iraq from the beginning of history: the Sumerians and the Akkadians. As far as we can tell, there were no ethnic conflicts between them. Nor were their cultures kept separate. Despite the fact that these peoples spoke two very different languages, Akkadian-speakers participated fully in what we call Sumerian civilization. Various linguistic clues indicate pretty conclusively that writing was developed to write Sumerian. But writing was not the exclusive property of the Sumerian-speaking peoples. The tablets of Abu Salabikh, written in Sumerian soon after the dawn of writing, were often inscribed by people who signed their obviously Akkadian names. At the same time, the people of Ebla, in central Syria, who also spoke a Semitic language, wrote beautiful Sumerian tablets. By the beginning of recorded history, there was already a considerable amount of cultural intermingling or syncretism between Semites (Akkadians) and Sumerians.[3]

*B.C.E. ("before the Christian Era" or "before the Common Era") and C.E. ("Common Era" or "Christian Era") are non-Christocentric ways of referring to the time periods sometimes denoted as B.C. and A.D.

As history progresses, the relationship between Semites and Sumerians gets even more complicated. The first successful unification of the cities of southern Mesopotamia (that we know of) was by Sargon, king of Akkad, around 2350 B.C.E. The royal inscriptions of Sargon were in Akkadian (our first Akkadian literature), but under his reign his daughter Enheduanna, the En priestess of Ur, composed beautiful and extensive hymns in Sumerian. The great flowering of Sumerian literature occurred in what we call the Neo-Sumerian period, the time of the kings of the third dynasty of Ur (circa 2111—2000 B.C.E.) and of the kings of the dynasties of Isin and Larsa that followed (the Early Old Babylonian period). But there is a body of evidence to show that the people of the Ur III period no longer spoke Sumerian.[4] This great flowering was happening while Sumerian was a scholarly language, a position it was to maintain to some extent even after much religious literature was written in Akkadian. By the Old Babylonian period, an Akkadian literature was developing, but even then, Sumerian religious texts were not only still being copied and studied but also composed.

By the beginning of the second millennium, a new ethnic element entered the picture. A large extensive migration of West Semites, people from the area of Syria, Lebanon, and Israel, immigrated into Mesopotamia and were absorbed. Some of these people became the ruling dynasts of major southern cities. The religious texts written at this time (called the Early Old Babylonian Period), whatever language they are written in, are clearly in the Mesopotamian tradition, but are nevertheless an amalgam of the Mesopotamian (Old Akkadian or Sumerian) ideas and those brought by the West Semites.

In addition to these historical and ethnic factors, the pantheon constantly changed in response to different economic systems and new socioeconomic realities. All this made for a rich and varied pantheon, fascinating even as it is overwhelming. It is, of course, confusing to us who are unfamiliar with such a plethora of powers. Even the Mesopotamians themselves felt a need to give some sort of order to this assemblage of gods. Already in the early periods of Sumerian writing, at Abu Salabikh, it is clear that the scribes (theologians) of ancient Sumer had the urge to put the gods into some kind of system. One of these very early Abu Salabikh texts is a god list.[5] The god list put the plethora of gods into an intellectually comprehensible relationship to each other. This job of compiling god lists continued throughout Mesopotamian history, and culminated in the great god list An-anum, the modern edition of which is still in preparation.[6] This is not the place to create a thorough study of the gods of Mesopotamia; however, in order to make some sense of the gods, I offer a small goddess list of the major personae of the Sumerian pantheon in an appendix.

The complex pantheon of Sumer sorts itself immediately into two easily recognizable categories: male gods and female gods. Goddess worship was not a separate religion, and goddesses as well as gods were an integral part of Sumerian religion and thought. The stories about goddesses do not come from any separatist women's cult and are neither female fantasies nor women's mythmaking. They are mainstream literature, the high culture of ancient Sumer. The authors of most of these compositions, male or female, are anonymous; but the earliest great poems of Sumer were written by a woman, Enheduanna, who was both En priestess of the god Nanna in the city of Ur and daughter of King Sargon of Akkad. She was the Shakespeare of ancient Sumerian literature in that her beautiful compositions were studied, copied, and recited for more than half a millennium after her death. These poems were not shared only with the women of ancient Sumer. On the contrary, we know these poems, as we know most of the literature of ancient Sumer, from copies that were made by students in the ancient Sumerian schools. Most, if not all, of these students were male. The poems of Enheduanna, and the other myths and hymns about goddesses whose authors (male or female) are unknown, were part of the curriculum of these schools, studied and taught by males. Men as well as women discussed and worshiped the goddesses of ancient Sumer.

This two-gendered pantheon mirrors the duality of nature, in which humans and other animals, and even some plants, occur as masculine and feminine. In some cases, the sex of a god makes no real difference to its function. In their control of cities, goddesses and gods play equivalent roles. The god of the city could be either male or female. In most cases, this deity also had a spouse who was less important to the well-being of the city than the deity itself. It was not always the male partner who was the major god. Either configuration was possible: the goddess could be the major deity, with her male spouse less significant than she; the male god could be chief deity, with a wife secondary to him.

However, in most conceptual realms, the sex division in the Sumerian divine world is not incidental. The sex of a god was crucial to that god's role and function in the thought system. Gods and goddesses are not interchangeable: the god Enlil could not be the goddess Ninlil, his spouse. The goddess Inanna could not be the god Utu, her brother. The femaleness of a goddess is essential. In the following chapters, we look at Sumerian thought concerning four different conceptual realms: society, culture, nature, and history. In each, goddesses play a role that is quintessentially female. As we shall see, the goddesses define the "female" in family, culture, cosmos, and polis. The stories create an organic picture of the significance and complexity that the concept of "female" could have in an ancient thought system. They also reveal the importance of the male-female dichotomy in polytheistic thinking.

# 3

## "Godwomen"

### Goddesses, Women, and Gender

Goddesses are the "women" of the divine world and behave much as women are expected to behave. They are not role models that women devised for themselves, nor are they purely female self-perceptions, for the mythic images of goddesses-as-women had to make sense to the men who were reading and teaching the texts. By the same token, the contributions of Enheduanna and other women show that these goddesses were not solely male projections about the nature of women. These portrayals of goddesses are the cultural projections of the whole society and reflect what that culture believed that women are and should be. They served an important social purpose for both men and women: Through these stories, men could think about the social reality of women, and women could see divine modeling for their own roles in life. The goddesses provided a way for society to discuss the roles and nature of women. Furthermore, the fact that goddesses play the roles of women in the divine realm reinforces cultural stereotypes about women and makes these stereotypes sacred.

When the goddesses portray and represent women in society, they are women writ large, with the same positions in the god-world that women have in the human world. They appear in well-known familial relationships to men and are the archetypes of woman-in-the family. They exemplify the Sumerian understanding of that particular social role for women, their beliefs about how women behave in those roles. A classic example of this paradigmatic role of the goddesses is the goddess Amageshtinanna, the sister of the god Dumuzi and the perfect example of sisterly devotion. Amageshtinanna plays an important role in the myth and cult of Dumuzi and Inanna. In these poems she has one dominant characteristic: she shows her brother unselfish love and undying loyalty. This love manifests itself after the death of Dumuzi, when his sister Amageshtinanna offers long and unceasing laments. The very endlessness of her lamenting made her an effective intercessor: Her cries were such an effective irritant to the gods that they listened to her pleas. They granted her the right to replace Dumuzi in the netherworld for part of each year. Every year, when Amageshtinanna went down to the netherworld, Dumuzi was resurrected to begin again his cycle of love and death. There were other, similar death-and-renewal cults in Sumer showing sisters concerned about, lamenting, and even journeying to their dead brothers. In these myths, sisters have no other role. The essence of their identity is their sisterhood, and its essence is intense devotion to the brother. Similarly, goddesses are found in all the major social roles of women: mother, mother-in-law, queen, wife, daughter, and sister.

Many goddesses are shown in the role of mother. Myths such as that of Enki and Ninmah and of Enki and Ninhursag focus attention on the biological role of procreation. Other myths concern the social role of the mother, her relationship to her noninfant children. The close relationship between the mother Ninlil and her son Ninurta is the subject of an important episode in the epic myth, Lugal-e.[1] In this text, Ninurta has attacked Azag, a mountain monster who was about to attack Sumer. After considerable time and effort, Ninurta succeeds in killing Azag and then acts to improve life in Sumer by controlling the flood waters of the Tigris River by building a levee of stones, the **hursag** (the "foothills"), to direct and control the waters. These two accomplishments, the great military adventure against Azag and his major contribution to the fertility of the land, establish Ninurta's reputation among the gods, who praise Ninurta to his father Enlil.

At this point Ninurta's mother, Ninlil, enters the story.[2] Unable to sleep because of her worry about her son, she decides to go out to the mountains to see him. Ninurta is delighted at her arrival, "casts his life-giving eye upon her," and rewards her for coming to the battle zone by making her the queen of this new foothill region. By taking on responsibility for the foothills (the **hursag**), she thus becomes *Ninhursag*, "mistress of the hursag," and Ninurta declares that status equal to his. This name change identifies Ninlil with the well-known mother-goddess Ninhursag. By having Ninurta confer this new name and high status upon her, the author of the myth makes Ninlil/Ninhursag's prominence secondary to and dependent upon Ninurta.[3] He also reinforces the closeness and mutuality expected between mother and son.

The love that a son has for his mother is also shown in an unusual literary composition, the letter of Ludingirra to his mother, in which the poet describes her in the most laudatory terms. He extols her as beauty, joy, and fertility, to such hyperbolic extent that we do not know if the mother described was Ludingirra's actual mother, or a goddess to whom he claimed sonship:

> My mother is like a bright light on the horizon,
>    active in the mountains.
> A morning star (shining even) at noon
> A precious carnelian-stone, a topaz from Marhasi
> A treasure for the brother of the king, full of
>    charm.[4]

The goddess-mother is also shown as being close to her daughter, to whom she gives advice and who is directly accountable to her. From these tales, we can see that it was the responsibility of the mother to safeguard the pubescent girl and deliver her safely to marriage. In a Dumuzi-Inanna courtship song, when Dumuzi urges Inanna to dally with him in the moonlight, Inanna's reply clearly indicates to whom she is accountable: "What lies should I tell my mother?"[5] In two major mythical texts, the Myth of Enlil and Ninlil and the Myth of Enki and Ninhursag, the mother figure cautions her daughter in proper sexual strategy. In the Myth of Enlil and Ninlil, Nunbarshegunu, the mother of Ninlil, advises her to go bathe in the pure canal.[6] The reason for this instruction is for Enlil to see her, kiss her, and impregnate her. In much the same way, in the Myth of Enki and Ninhursag, it is the grand mother-goddess Nintur who counsels Uttu not to give in to Enki as Enki sees her from the marsh and wishes to sleep with her. These texts have many layers, and are not intended solely as exemplars of human marital and familial behavior, but such modeling is certainly one aspect of their significance.

The love and loyalty of children for their mother is mutual, grounded in the loyalty that the mother gives them as she champions her children's cause. The primordial mother Nammu plays this role in the opening scene of the Myth of Enki and Ninmah, when the laboring gods come to Enki weeping for relief. As Enki is asleep, they dare not rouse him; whereupon Nammu, the mother of Enki, takes the tears of the gods to her son and begs him to arise and use his ingenuity to relieve them from their digging. The classic example of motherly compassion is in an Akkadian text, the Babylonian state epic Enuma Elish. Here

Tiamat, the mother of all, denied her own husband Apsu in favor of her children. Apsu sought her support to forcefully quiet the active creative gods who were disturbing their sleep. But she refused, arguing, "Shall we destroy that which we have created? Their ways are truly troublesome, but let us be patient and kind."[7] It is only later, after Apsu has been slain, that Tiamat prepares for battle against the active pantheon. This new willingness to fight comes about only after other gods, who are also her children, plead for rest from the tumult caused by the heavenly gods. The Enuma Elish myth is from a different time, at least half a millenium after the Sumerian texts we are discussing. By that later period, many of the former functions of goddesses had been taken over by male gods.[8] Nevertheless, the basic concept of the mother and therefore of the mother-goddess did not change, and the portrayal of the mother Tiamat's concern for her children would have been equally at home in the much earlier Enki and Ninmah myth.

The mother's devotion and loyalty to her children is her dominant, perhaps even her defining, characteristic. This attachment does not stop even with the death of the child, for it is, above all, the mother who mourns the death of her child. The very act of lamenting was particularly associated with women. The goddesses of ruined cities lament their loss, and the goddess-mothers of dead sons weep bitterly, continuing to mourn inconsolably beyond any practical expectation of reward for their efforts. These songs of lamentation are ritual laments, sung as part of the cult of dying gods such Damu.[9] In such lamenting, the mother shows a fierce unchanging loyalty and love for her son who is no more, a love that can expect no reciprocation.

But mother is not a simple figure in our imagination. The child's experience of a mother is not all one of compassion and love. The mythology also reflects the child's awareness of a mother's power and anger. There are two myths, that of Enki and Ninmah, and that of Enki and Ninhursag,[10] in which the mother either despairs or becomes very angry at Enki. Each myth concerns the mother's role in procreation, and shows the mother as jealous of her prerogatives. In the Myth of Enki and Ninmah,[11] these two gods have a banquet altercation about their relative importance in the creation of human lives. Ninmah claims that she is the one who determines whether a human will have a good mode of being, while Enki replies that he can mitigate the destiny—good or bad—of the newborn. Ninmah thereupon creates characters who are clearly defective, such as palsied or blind men, and Enki mitigates their handicaps by finding an appropriate place for them in society.

Since Ninmah has not been able to prove her superiority over Enki, it is now Enki's turn to show his superior abilities. He tries to mold a creature on his own, without the help of the mother goddess. He discharges his semen, but summons no female to bring the fetus to full and proper gestation. The resulting (and possibly premature) creature is born helpless. It cannot eat or drink, and Ninmah cannot care for it or assign a role for it. Enki has done what Ninmah could not do: he has created a creature for which Ninmah can find no use. Ninmah takes this as her total defeat, but at this point, Enki magnanimously admits that the very uselessness of the creature he has made is an acknowledgment of the absolute indispensability of Ninmah in the making of fully formed creatures. Ninmah's reaction conforms to the social belief that the ability to procreate is essential to a woman's self-esteem, and that her appreciation of reproduction as "woman's power" greatly increases her own sense of self-worth. It is even more understandable in the light of religious history, for it is clear that the figure of Enki enlarged and grew more important at the expense of the mother-goddess by usurping some of her roles and functions.[12] This ongoing transformation of the role of the mother-goddess must have been known to the people who told and listened to the myth, even though such a historical perspective would never be openly expressed in the narrative of myths. The historic competition between father-god and mother-goddess lies beneath the surface of the myth, informs it (and possibly generates it), and heightens the drama of the competition between Enki and Ninmah. Here, the historical background (the real world) enters into the heart of the mythic structure, and makes the reader (ancient and modern) acutely aware of Ninmah's problem.

The Myth of Enki and Ninhursag[13] also shows Enki and the mother-goddess at loggerheads, and also indicates that the relative importance of the mother and the father, of creator-goddess and creator-god, was an issue in Sumerian religion. In this story, Ninhursag has had to remove Enki's seed from Uttu's womb and plant it within the earth. Enki appropriates and eats the plants that grow from this seed, whereupon Ninhursag, in a rage, curses him with a terrible oath, vowing "Never will I look upon him with life-giving eye until he is dying." Despite this oath, the compassion of the mother Ninhursag eventually overwhelms her anger. When Enki becomes ill from these semen-plants (which continue to develop inside him) "Ninhursag came running." She has the Anunnaki-gods ritually release her from her curse, and she comes to the aid of Enki by placing him in her vulva, thus delivering the goddesses who had developed from the plants that he ate.

In these portrayals of the mother, it is her *relational* aspect that is most important. The mother is close to her children: she shows devotion and loyalty to them, and they show consideration and respect for her. In procreation, the mother and the father must interact. They may have a rivalrous alliance, but the mother's powers are necessary in the creation of children, and are formally recognized by the males. Both the Son (Ninurta in the myth, Lugale-e) and the father (Enki in the Myth of Enki and Ninmah, also see The Marriage of Sud below) acknowledge the generative powers of the mother. In child-rearing and supervision, on the other hand, father and mother neither cooperate nor conflict. The mother/child axis is distinct from the husband/wife relationship. The relationship of mother to her child is completely separate from any relationship that the child might have to its father. The child's experience of its mother, unmediated by any agents, is both direct and complex. The texts focus, not on the goddess-mother as a person with individual desires and personality traits, but on the goddess as "mother." Nevertheless, the mother is not pasteboard or unidimensional. The goddess-mother is a stereotype of the concept of "mother" in Sumer, but the concept is rich and multifaceted. The very complexity of the portrayal of mother-goddess, with its love, loyalty, rage, and compassion, is rooted in our own experience of human mothers.

## Ninlil, the Queenly Wife

In the Myth, Lugal-e, the god Ninurta gave his mother Ninlil the foothills (the **hursag**) so that she became Ninhursag, "mistress of the hursag" which is a name of the mother-goddess.[14] Another myth makes this same identification between Ninlil, city-goddess of Nippur, and the mother-goddess Ninhursag. This is the myth of marriage of Enlil and Ninlil, known as Enlil and Ninlil: The Marriage of Sud. In this story, Enlil sees the young girl Sud in the street in front of her mother Nisaba's house. He assumes that she is readily available because she is out in the street, and he makes advances to her. She, however, does not take kindly to such disrespectful behavior. Enlil then sends a proper declaration of marriage intentions, with bridal gifts, to the girl's mother. He asks to have Sud come to the Kiur (the sacred precinct of the city of Nippur, the forecourt of the temple of Enlil) and the Ekur (the temple of Enlil in Nippur). She will thereupon be named "Ninlil," the counterpart of Enlil, whose name is to spread throughout the countries. Moreover, upon her marriage to Enlil, he makes Sud/Ninlil the mother-goddess, decreeing her name to be "Nintu, the Lady-who-gives-birth" and "Lady-of-the-open-legs,"[15] and placing her in charge of all the secrets pertaining to women. Like her mother, the grain goddess Nisaba, Sud/Ninlil will also be a fertility goddess, will be identified with wheat, and will have a role in the scribal arts similar to that of her mother Nisaba.[16]

The identification of Ninlil with the great mother-goddess Ninhursag accomplishes several theological purposes. Ninhursag, originally separate from Ninlil, was one of the triad of great gods An, Enlil, and Ninhursag. Identifying Ninlil with Ninhursag elevates Ninlil to the company of the greatest of the gods, and cuts Ninhursag down to size at the same time. Ninhursag is brought fully within the circle and household of Enlil, the god of Nippur and the chief executive of the council of the gods of the national pantheon, thus increasing the power of Enlil. In addition, it situates the powerful goddess within a household dominated by a male god, thus diminishing her independent authority. In fact, even her mother-powers are said to be bestowed upon her by her husband Enlil and her son Ninurta. As in the case of the Myth, Enki and Ninmah, this mythical point can be read on two levels. In human terms, it is a reminder that the mother who looms so powerfully in the life and emotions of her children is also a wife whose relationship to her husband forms a major component of her social identity and status. At the same time, it is an expression of the increasing diminution of the mother-goddess. As in the Enki and Ninmah myth, historical factors have entered into the dynamics of the myth itself, coloring the plot and conditioning the reader's reaction to it.

Another myth about the marriage of Enlil and Ninlil, the Myth of Enlil and Ninlil, relates how Ninlil became an important goddess-mother, the mother of the major gods Nanna, Ninurta, and Ninazu. The myth begins at the meeting of Enlil and Ninlil, when Enlil approaches and propositions her after she has come to walk along the pure canal. She demurs, explaining that she is very young and innocent, and that her parents would be displeased. Nevertheless, Enlil perseveres, sleeps with her, and impregnates her. Such behavior cannot be tolerated, and the gods in Nippur pronounce him "unclean" and banish him from the city.[17] Despite the impropriety of Enlil's advances, Ninlil is determined to be with him and to bear his childen. She sets out to follow Enlil to the netherworld, and meets him in his three successive disguises: as man of the city gate, man of the river, and Silulim the ferryman. The story does not relate that Ninlil recognizes him, but nevertheless, she sleeps with him in all these disguises and thereby conceives several of the major gods of the netherworld and of fertility-bringing water.

Ninlil's behavior seems peculiar to us. She is devoted to someone who has abused her by impregnating her without proper marriage (statutory, if indeed not actual, rape). And then, despite this devotion, she is willing to sleep with all these seducers without knowing that they are Enlil. The myth neither remarks upon nor censures this behavior, but rather ends with praise to mother Ninlil and with a celebration of Enlil as bringer of fertility. After all, these acts of Ninlil created some of the most important gods of the pantheon. This acceptance of Ninlil's behavior may indicate that Ninlil acted precisely the way that Sumerians expected young women to behave. In this conceptualization, young women are vulnerable to seduction. It is the job of society, with its protocols of marriage and adultery, to intervene. Enlil acts contrary to social mores, and is indeed banished from civilized society. When Ninlil voluntarily follows him, she too leaves civilization and its constraints upon sexuality.

Because of her prominence as wife of Enlil and mother of these gods, Ninlil is not the model of an average wife. Even though her name is a feminine by-form of Enlil,[18] she never fades into the woodwork. She is the wife of the master and shares his power, often being called mistress and queen.[19] She shares Enlil's role and his functions. In The Marriage of Sud, when Enlil proposed to Sud, he promised her that she too would decree destinies. The temple hymn to the temple of Ninlil relates how Ninlil sits at the side of Enlil in the Kiur (The forecourt of the Ekur temple) during the New Year's Festival.[20] There she decides the fates with him.[21] In the Ekur, noted for its role in justice, Ninlil as well as Enlil is often noted as counselor and judge: "She, for her part too, dwells with you on a holy throne dais, next to the pure throne dais. She advises with you, ponders with you, makes with you the decisions at the place of sunrise."[22] Ninlil is a perceptive and wise counselor.[23] She consults, gives advice, and makes great decisions in her lofty place.[24] Far from being an insignificant consort, Ninlil is an august queen who wields power along with her husband, Lord Enlil.

Ninlil is prominent because she is the wife of the king. In Sumerian times, royal women wielded considerable power, both in the court and in the larger political and economic system. Queens, governors' wives, and royal princesses participated actively in the public life of Sumer.[25] These women led lives vastly different from those of ordinary women—

lives of prominence, power, and influence. Ninlil is the divine paradigm of queens as Uttu models the role of ordinary women.

## The Domestic Woman: Uttu the Weaver

The average wife was no queen. Far from participating in literary or political life, she was fully occupied with the rearing of children and the multiple economic functions that women performed for their households. She was not insignificant, for her contributions were essential to the survival and well-being of her family. But her activities were all in the private sphere; she wielded little or no power outside the family. The Myth of Enki and Ninhursag presents one view of the origins of marital relationships, of the domestication of male and female. In this myth, Enki has copulated freely first with Ninhursag, then with the daughter of that union (Ninnisiga), the daughter of the second union (Ninkurra), and the daughter of the third union (Ninimma). Things begin to change with Ninimma's daughter Uttu. As Uttu reaches puberty, Ninhursag intervenes to give Uttu the advice that when Enki wishes to sleep with her, she should ask first for the gift of fruits. Enki gets these fruits, which in this context represent the gifts that a husband gives his bride, and comes formally bearing the gifts to Uttu's house. Uttu thereupon opens the door (a formal act of marriage), Enki comes in, gives her the gifts, and consummates their "marriage."

In this myth, as in so many myths of origins, social reality is given a history, by which institutions of society are shown to have evolved from an earlier, unsatisfactory, state. In the Myth Enki and Ninhursag, marriage has come because of sexual reticence, and Uttu is now a properly married woman. But marriage is not a simple institution. For this reason, the myth presents one unexpected and unpleasant consequence of domestication. Enki's partners before Uttu, from Ninhursag though Ninimma, had all been instantly responsive to Enki's sexual overtures. They had sex readily, conceived easily, underwent pregnancies which lasted nine days rather then nine months, and then gave birth effortlessly ("like sweet butter and juniper oil"). "Easy in, easy out": no part of their reproduction had any hesitation, delay, or difficulty. By contrast, Uttu, who was not instantly available, has difficulty in pregnancy. Enki has to woo her, first bringing bride gifts and coming to her home, then making her ready for the marriage act by plying her with beer before having sex with her.[26] Uttu then has trouble bearing a child. Quite unlike her predecessors among Enki's sexual partners, this first "properly married" woman is in such agony early in her pregnancy that

Ninhursag has to intervene to remove the seed from her womb. The story of Uttu connects marriage and domesticity with difficulty in childbirth. This combination might seem strange, but a similar juxtaposition of marriage and difficult childbearing is known to us from the story of Adam and Eve. In Genesis, after the expulsion from the garden, the lot of Eve is twofold: to be subordinate to the husband she desires, and to have great difficulty in childbirth. The very human and civilized institution of marriage is part of the differentiation of humans from animals, which also give birth so much more easily than human women. In the Enki and Ninhursag myth, the contrast between Uttu and the premarital sexual partners of Enki may also represent a belief, found also in the Bible[27] and some of our own folk beliefs, that cultured, civilized women do not give birth with the same ease as "natural" women. The domestication of women makes them more "civilized," farther removed from animals and nature, and as a result they no longer are able to perform the "natural" function of childbirth with ease.

In this myth, the goddess Uttu is the first wife, the paradigm of a married woman. In other myths, she appears as the divine weaver. In the Myth of Enki and the World Order, Enki organizes the cosmos, and gives Uttu charge over "everything pertaining to women," specifically, the weaving of clothing.[28] Uttu also appears as the weaver in another composition, the philosophical disputation "Lahar and Ašnan" ("Ewe and Grain"). This dispute begins with a glimpse of proto-time, a time when Ewe (the archetype of wool-bearing animals) and Wheat had not yet been created, and Uttu herself had not yet been born. As a result, there was no cloth to wear, and people went around naked and eating grass. The gods acted to better the condition of humanity, and by so doing make humans more able to feed and clothe the gods. They created Ewe and Wheat and gave them to humanity.[29] Then, in a dinner-altercation, Ewe boasts that she possesses all the yarns of Uttu.[30] Uttu according to this composition, is the weaver of the cloth of royalty.[31] A bilingual Sumerian and Akkadian book of incantations and rituals for the release of problems, "Šurpu," contains a ritual of first tying and then releasing the sufferer. The incantation for this act invokes Uttu as the spinner who spins the great multicolored thread.[32] Uttu's prowess in spinning and weaving gives her the titles of **munus dím.ma** ("skillful woman") and **munus-zi** ("faithful woman").[33]

Uttu's role as divine weaver is not separate from her role as paradigm of wife. In producing cloth, she shares with human wives their basic economic task, their most important and characteristic nonprocreative function. The importance of women's spinning and weaving in early economic life cannot be overestimated. It has survived in our language in such words as "distaff" (originally a spinning device) and "spinster." In the ancient world, women were often depicted as holding a hand-spindle and a whorl, and these serve as the characteristic symbol of femininity.[34]

There is yet another way in which Uttu mirrors and models the life of a Sumerian wife. Nothing is known of her beyond her marriage, her difficulty in childbirth, and her cloth making. She is not a major figure of the pantheon; she takes no part in any adventures or deliberations of the gods. Uttu appears in the literature only as weaver or as first wife. But her nonparticipation in the public activities of the gods is not mere absence. The silence screams out at us, for her nonpresence in public life is essential to her modeling of wifehood. Invisibility and anonymity are precisely the attributes of nonroyal wives, for they had little role to play in the public sphere. In that which she does not do as well as in that which she does, Uttu is the model of a Sumerian wife.


In all these roles, the goddesses model women-in-the-family. They exemplify sociological positions familiar to the people of Sumer. They reflect what the Sumerians thought about women as they lived out these socially approved roles; they model how the Sumerians expected these women to act. These goddesses are more generic figures than individual personalities and convey images appropriate to many women rather than to themselves alone. There is little individuation, little speculation about the personality of these goddesses beyond their archetypical characteristics. But this "stereotype" function does not necessarily make them unidimensional or static figures. Some of these roles are indeed characterized by their dominant attribute: the mother-in-law is wise; the daughter, desirable and innocent; the sister, loyal; the queen, perceptive and powerful; and the ordinary wife, invisible. But other portrayals are more complex: the young woman is also vulnerable to being seduced; the mother shows anger and despair as well as compassion and loyalty. The multifaceted nature of these goddesses is itself part of their paradigmatic character. These unexpected, sometimes self-contradictory aspects of their personalities arise from the paradoxical position of woman in Sumerian society. Women are powerful within the household and powerless in the political sphere; mothers are figures of leadership and authority to their children, but must accommodate to their husbands. The different demands placed on women also result in ambiguous attitudes of society towards women, particularly mothers. The stories display the many aspects of society's expectations about women's roles and reveal the tightrope which women walk.

In this mythic depiction of women-in-the-family, social roles are not portrayed by *human* women, whether legendary or real. They are modeled by goddesses, figures whose importance in the universe is known and revered by their worshippers. The fact that these potent deities play the same roles in the divine realm that women are expected to play in society gives a powerful seal of approval to these family roles. When modeling is done by the divine, the modeling does not simply illustrate; it authorizes and approves what it models. This is a powerful two-edged sword. On the one hand, divine modeling for women's family roles gives women esteem within these roles so that these roles become a source of self-satisfaction and nourishment. On the other hand, this same divine modeling makes cultural attitudes and stereotypes part of the realm of the sacred, lending powerful support to these attitudes and inhibiting change.

## Inanna, the Nondomesticated Woman

One portrayal of a goddess as woman-in-society reveals basic Sumerian conceptions about the nature and characteristics of women apart from their family functions. This is the goddess Inanna (called also by the Semitic name Ishtar), who serves the important function of modeling a role that women were not expected to fill and that was not considered socially desirable. She represents the nondomesticated woman, and exemplifies all the fear and attraction that such a woman elicits. She is the exception to the rule, the woman who does not behave in societally approved ways, the goddess who models the crossing of gender lines and the danger that this presents. Because of her anomalous position, Inanna is the goddess who receives the most attention in these Sumerian myths, and appears as a most richly developed character.

In the poems about Inanna and Dumuzi,[35] Inanna, the young maiden, sets out on the path of womanly domestication. She does all the things that young girls are supposed to do, and yet comes out very differently, as an undomesticated woman. In her courtship, she behaves like a proper young lady, worrying about the niceties and legalities of the social interaction between the sexes. When Dumuzi comes after her, she fears that it is without the permission of her mother, grandmother, father, or brother.[36] After she meets him, she trembles with love.[37] The protocol of male-female courtship was clear in Sumerian society. The Sumerian laws indicate that the sexual consent of a young girl was almost immaterial: if the parents had not consented, the action was improper. Despite her love for Dumuzi, Inanna does not violate social convention. When he wants her to tarry with him in the moonlight, she exclaims, "What lies could I tell my mother?" and refuses to learn the stories that Dumuzi calls "the women-lies." She does not mean to reject Dumuzi, for when he declares himself ready to come to the gate of her mother (to ask for her hand), Inanna is overjoyed.[38] She preserves her innocence and irreproachability until her wedding. Inanna is known in Sumerian literature as the goddess of sexual attractiveness and desire. Nevertheless, when she appears in her aspect of the young sexually desirable girl, she is a sexual innocent:

> I am one who knows not that which is
>     womanly—copulating,
> I am one who knows not that which is
>     womanly—kissing
> I am one who knows not copulating,
> I am one who knows not kissing.[39]

Inanna is the paradigm of the betrothed maiden. As such, she may act in ways that contradict her functions as goddess of sex or of power in agricultural abundance. Like some human brides, and like Uttu in the Myth of Enki and Ninhursag, Inanna is interested in wedding gifts, particularly in the provision of food. When we consider Inanna's function in the provision of fertility and abundance, it might seem strange that she has to look to Dumuzi for sustenance. Her social role as bride-to-be causes Inanna to want Dumuzi to fulfill the bridegroom's role of providing food. Inanna prepares for her wedding by washing herself, anointing herself with oil, putting on kohl (eyeliner), dressing her hair, and adorning herself with jewelry. For his part, Dumuzi promises to bring the food that she wishes.[40] The sense of husband as giver of food is found even in a lament for the dead Dumuzi in which Inanna mourns the loss of her provider, wailing, "the one who gave me food will no longer give me food; the one who gave me water will no longer give me water."[41]

Despite many similarities between Inanna and young girls about to be brides, she is drastically different. When she marries, she never takes on the jobs of wives. In the first place, Inanna weds without assuming any of the economic duties of a wife. Uttu the wife makes cloths, Inanna does not. Before she agrees to marry, she and Utu (her brother) have a conversation about the making of linen sheets. When he offers to bring her the green flax, she declines to ret, spin, dye, weave, or bleach it.[42] The treatment of flax and the creation of linen is an archetypical work of women; Inanna's ignorance and refusal of these tasks are a denial of the production role of women. Similarly, at her wedding, Inanna may tell Dumuzi (the text is broken) that she does not know how to use a loom. It is clear that he replies to her with assurances that "I have not carried you off into servitude . . . O, my bride, cloth you will not weave for me/ O Inanna, yarn you will not spin for me/ O my bride, fleece you will not ravel for me."[43]

At their wedding, Dumuzi makes Inanna another unique stipulation. She is to eat at the splendid table at which he himself eats. His own mother and sister do not have this privilege, but Inanna will do so, and will not have to perform any of the domestic duties of ordinary wives.[44] There is only one wifely job that Dumuzi anticipitates that she will do: he expects that she will bear children. At their wedding, he brings Inanna to the chapel of his personal god and prays that she give birth to a son.[45] But, despite this wish of Dumuzi, and quite unlike queen Ninlil, Inanna does not turn into a maternal figure. In some texts, Inanna is the mother of Šara and Lulal, two relatively insignificant gods, but they seem ancillary and irrelevant to her persona and identity. She is not "mother": having neither maternal nor domestic economic duties, Inanna remains without any of the usual roles and functions of the ordinary married woman. Released from all such duties, she has nothing to tie her down, nothing to occupy her time, and, at the same time, nothing to make her conscious of her marital status. She is the unencumbered woman, the wife whose domestic status is so nebulous that it cannot possibly domesticate her.

Inanna is, in essence, unattached. She is married to Dumuzi, and celebrates the wedding at the New Year's festival. But without children or economic function, she has no true niche in society. This makes her, despite her prominence, an essentially marginal figure. In the Myth of Enki and the World Order, Inanna herself complains of this marginality. After Enki has apportioned among the gods the various roles and positions in the universe, Inanna points out that the mother-goddess has her functions, that Uttu the weaver, Ninmug the smith, and Nisaba the scribe all have clear roles in society, but that she herself does not. Enki's reply only emphasizes her anomalous nature, for he reminds her of her role in war, and of her ability to transcend and reverse boundaries.[46] Inanna has enormous power, and in some sense has control over heaven, earth, and lordship, in addition to her role in war,[47] but her great power and authority are ill-defined. Having a great variety of powers and roles, she nevertheless does not fit any of the niches that society has provided for its women.

This anomalous condition of Inanna makes her restless and power-hungry. In the Myth, Inanna and the Mes, Inanna comes to visit Enki in Eridu, a very successful journey in which she returns to her own city having received from a tipsily magnanimous Enki the great **mes**, aspects of divine essence which thereafter belong to her.[48] Another myth, The Descent of Inanna to the Netherworld, relates a far less successful journey. Inanna sets her face to the netherworld, an action perceived by the denizens of the netherworld as an attempt to wrest power over the land of the dead out of the hands of her sister Ereshkigal. Inanna is killed and trapped in the netherworld, and has to be rescued and resuscitated before she can leave there.

As an unencumbered woman, Inanna, is not tied down. She is frequently on the move, going or walking about. As Uttu and Ninlil had done before, the young maiden Inanna walks along the canal.[49] But marriage doesn't change Inanna's behavior. In the Myth of Inanna and Ebih, Inanna sings the refrain "as I walk along the land"; in yet another text, [50] she chants "as I go out, as I go out"; and in Inanna and Sukalletuda, she sings "I go around heaven and earth."[51] An Akkadian-language hymn to Nana/Inanna also records this strange behavior: "They call me the daughter of Ur, the queen of Ur, daughter of princely Sin. She who goes around and enters every house."[52] Inanna's role as goddess of the morning and evening stars (which seem to change place in the sky through the seasons) may account in part for the mobility of Inanna/Ishtar, but this restless nature also fits her societal role as the unencumbered wife.

Such peripatetic movement is not what one expects from proper married women, who are expected to remain mostly at home and to leave their houses only on legitimate errands. Reflecting this social expectation, the Old Babylonian laws of Hammurabi state that if a woman wants a divorce, the court investigates the situation. If she was good and her husband was not, she gets her divorce; but if she was a *wasi'at* (literally, "one who goes out and about") she is to be thrown into the river.[53]

Society was not at ease with the idea of freely roaming women. In the Inanna-Ninegalla Hymn,[54] Inanna is said to go from house to house and street to street;[55] this very phrase is used in later literature in descriptions of demons.[56] Such female roaming is demonic, and Inanna's epithet *sahiratu*, "the one who roams about," is also an epithet of the dreaded baby-stealing she-demon Lamashtu, who also can enter houses at will.[57]

There were, of course, women in the streets. The death of her master and mistress could force a slave girl to roam the streets,[58] but this was tragic and unusual. Young girls might be found in the streets, perhaps despite society's disapproval and always with the possibility of rape.[59] To some extent, the girl in the street was fair game, and thus Enlil, meeting Sud, automatically assumes the worst.[60] Most often, it is the prostitute who might be met in the street. Restless, roaming Inanna is the model of a prostitute. She is called **kar-kid**, and *harimtu* ("prostitute"),[61] and indulges in the activity of a prostitute. She sits in the door of the tavern,[62] and, wearing the beads of a prostitute around her neck, she takes a man.[63] As the incipit of an incantation states, "the beautiful girl standing in the street, the young prostitute, is the daughter of Inanna."[64] Inanna shows what might happen to a wife who is not kept "barefoot and pregnant and in the kitchen." In her search for a real role to play and a secure power-base, She can serve as a fearsome admonition of the dangers of the unencumbered woman.

In her lack of encumbrances, Inanna lives essentially the same existence as young men. Like them, she is called "hero"[65] and "manly."[66] Like them, and even more than they, she loves warfare and seeks lovers. She is a woman in a man's life. This makes her unlike all other women, and places her at the boundary of differences between man and woman. Inanna transcends gender polarities, and is said to turn men into women and women into men. The cult of Inanna exemplifies her role as boundary-melder (and therefore boundary-keeper) of the gender line, for at her festivals men dress as women and women as men, and cultic dancers wear outfits that are men's clothes on the right and women's on the left. In this cultic confusion of genders, and in the hymnic acknowledgment of it, Ishtar serves not only to transcend gender, but ultimately to protect it. As in all rituals and occasions of rebellion, the societally approved, scheduled, and regulated breaking of a norm actually serves to reinforce it.[67] The male-female gender division is not the only polarity that Inanna-Ishtar exemplifies, transcends, mediates, and protects,[68] but it is one that she clearly lives out in her own mythic persona.

Inanna's freedom from domestic encumbrances and the restlessness that it engenders may also account in part for the ferocious energy with which she confronts gods and humans. She represents a woman not occupied with social responsibilities, like a man in many of her wants and capabilities, both threatening and assuring the social order. She is dangerous, fearsome, and threatening because of her freedom, and yet, at the same time, appealing and attractive.[69] In her lack of encumbrances, Inanna is free to be the ultimate femme fatale.

## The Ideology of Gender

Sumerian gender-thinking finds expression through the image of Inanna, but it is hard to know what her image tells us about the nature
of women and men. Is Inanna "alone of all her sex" (a phrase originally
coined of the Virgin Mary to indicate the lack of similarity between her
and mortal women)?[70] Or does Inanna betray a deep suspicion that
without the social constraints placed on women, they would indeed be
very like men? This question is interesting from the point of view of
cultural history. But it is almost irrelevant to the gender role of Inanna
within Sumerian culture. Inanna stands at the boundary of differences
between man and woman. The image of Inanna as a woman in a man's
life-style reinforces social patterns of how men and women were actually expected to behave.

As Mesopotamian culture developed, the distinctive characteristics
of Inanna were understood to constitute a difference between Inanna
and other women. The Agushaya Hymn, an Old Babylonian mythical
hymn about Inanna (by her Semitic name, Ishtar), labels her ferocity
and love of warfare her *zikrutu*, literally, her "manliness." Another literary creation of the Old Babylonian period, the Gilgamesh Epic, also
indicates that in this period the sexes were considered intrinsically different from each other.

In the Gilgamesh story, the superiority of Gilgamesh leads him to
oppress his people. When their outcry reaches the gods, they realize
that Gilgamesh acts this way because he has no peer. They decide upon
the special creation of a new being who will be as an equal to Gilgamesh. In a similar situation, the god of the Bible creates a woman.
But in the Gilgamesh Epic, the mother-goddess takes clay and creates
Enkidu—another male. The true companion for Gilgamesh is not a
woman to occupy his attention, but a male to be his close companion.
The gods' solution to Gilgamesh's arrogance indicates a cultural sense
that the truest bonding possible is between two members of the same
gender. The true equality that leads to great bonding is between male
and male. The closeness of same-sex bonding holds true also for females. In the Agushaya Hymn, Ishtar is undomesticated, fierce, and
wild, quite unlike the other goddesses, and her ferocity had begun to
frighten and dismay the other gods. Their solution is to create a companion who will occupy her, and so the god Enki creates a new goddess, another fierce female, Saltu, and sends her to Ishtar. Once again,
the motivation behind the creation of same-sex companions for Gilgamesh and Ishtar is that there is a difference and distinctiveness be-

tween the genders. To the Babylonians of this period, a man and woman could never be as like each other as a man could be to a man, or a woman to a woman.

Cultural thinking about gender is never static, and in this book we will follow the ideology of gender as it changed drastically in biblical thinking to a metaphysics of gender unity, and later changed even more dramatically in the Hellenistic period to a concept of woman as radically other, a way of thinking about men and women that is now once more going through profound transformation.

# 4

## The Wisdom of Women

### *Goddesses and the Arts of Civilization*

The presence of both gods and goddesses in the ancient Sumerian pantheon provided a divine counterpart for society and meant, moreover, that the cosmos was shared by male and female powers, each of whom had an impact on events and processes. Every aspect of Sumerian religio-philosophical thinking assumed this basic cosmological premise, and culture, nature, and society were all perceived along gender lines. The male/female division of the animal (and human) world was projected onto the cosmic sphere and permeated philosophical reflection. As a result, gender was an immediate and inescapable aspect of Sumerian thought.

When the Sumerians reflected on the events, institutions, and activities that constitute "civilization," they depicted gods and goddesses pursuing the same cultural activities as did the Sumerians, and often believed that the gods had granted the knowledge of these cultural matters to humankind. In this way, both gods and goddesses were patrons of culture; both male and female forces were involved in the creation of civilization. Each craft, each skill, and each field of learning was under the patronage of a deity. The distribution of cultural activities among the deities conformed to societal expectations about the behavior of men and women. Certain activities, such as kingship and lawgiving, were associated with male gods. Other activities, deemed more "womanly" by the culture, had goddesses as their patrons or exemplars.

Goddesses were in charge of the three activities that the Mesopotamians considered basic to a civilized life: the wearing of cloth, the eating of grain, and the drinking of beer. A Sumerian literary composition, "Lahar and Ašnan" ("Ewe and Grain"), relates that the gods gave

32

these essential cultural elements to humans. The Gilgamesh Epic also shows how essential food, beer, and clothing were to the Mesopotamian definition of humanity. In this epic, the wearing of clothes and the drinking of beer were skills that the newly created Enkidu had to master in order to join human society. When he first came to life, he was primitive and uncultured, and identified with animals. The gap between him and civilized humanity is expressed as: "He is garbed like Sumuqan (in skins), he feeds on grass like the gazelles, . . . with the teeming creatures, his heart delights in water."[1] The animal-identified but human Enkidu then protects the animals by filling in the pits and loosening the traps that the hunters set. Because he thereby threatens the livelihood of the people of Sumer, they devise a plan to socialize him. They bring a courtesan before Enkidu, figuring that his sexual attraction for her would bring him into the human world. She bares herself; he, indeed attracted, mates with her for six nights and seven days. Finally sated, he attempts to return to his animals. But three things intervene. The animals run away from him, for now he smells of humans. He attempts to run after them, but (after a week of sexual activity) he can no longer run as fast as before. And third, his eyes have been opened, he understands what has happened, he realizes that he belongs in the human world. He returns to the courtesan, who begins to give him his first lessons in civilization. She gives him some of her clothing, teaches him how to eat, and brings him to the shepherds to learn to drink beer. After that, Enkidu is ready to realize his destiny and the reason for which he was created, and comes to the city to meet Gilgamesh.[2]

Production of these rudiments of civilization is the domain of goddesses. Nisba oversees the growing of grain, which is itself symbolized by the divine grain. Wool, represented by the divine Ewe, is made into cloth by the goddess Uttu, whose image as archetypical wife was discussed in the previous chapter. The brewing of beer is in the hands of Ninkasi, goddess of beer making, "whose brewing vat is of clear lapis lazuli, whose ladle is of mesu silver and gold."[3] Pottery making—less elemental but still basic to civilization— was also in the hands of a goddess, the goddess Ninurra. As the wife of the god Shara, the city-god of Umma, she is known in texts from this period (the Early Dynastic Period) as the "mother of Umma."[4] However, as time went on, Ninurra became a male god and was ultimately absorbed into the figure of Enki-Ea.

In addition to production, the provision of basic goods requires that surplus must be stored and made available. Here, too, the goddesses are in control of the task. The goddess Nisaba, the vegetation goddess closely associated with grain, is also said to arrange the storehouses, and even to *be* the great storage room: "You are his great storage room, you are his seal keeper."[5] The area of the temple called the *giparu*, a food storage area, also served as the private living quarters of the En priest or priestess.[6] The association of goddesses with storage is a reflection of women's social role in the preservation and storage of household goods. Ever since Erikson's (in)famous article on "inner space,"[7] people have been debating whether women's biology predisposes them to "fill up" spaces. Whatever the biological-psychological truths of the matter, sociologically it is clear that women have been entrusted with the storage of foods and valuables. In Sumer, women's role in storage was so thoroughgoing that it has left its mark on the Sumerian language. The word **ama₅**, which means "storehouse," also means the woman's quarters of a house.[8] Clearly, grain and others goods were normally stored in the women's quarters, and women were the managers and guardians of these stored goods. The term **ama₅** is used for the woman's quarters of a goddess as well as for ordinary domestic arrangments. But when the woman was a goddess, her storage quarters were the storage area of the temple and thus the depository for the whole land.[9]

There is a darker side to the containment and storage: the "storage" of people in dungeons and prisons. This also is the job of a goddess, the goddess Nungal, the prison warden[10] of the Ekur temple in Nippur. The role of the prison of Nippur, situated within the temple complex of the reigning god Enlil, the Ekur, is celebrated in the hymn, Nungal in the Ekur. In this poem, Nungal relates the fearsome part that this temple plays in the administration of justice as she describes the great day of judgment and her role in it. On this day, the accused is tried by the river ordeal. He is thrown into the divine river to test whether he is guilty or innocent. If he floats or swims, he passes the test. But even if he fails, he is not allowed to drown. The divine mooring-pole pulls him out of the river and hands him to Nungal, who puts him in her prison, called her "house of life." Nungal describes this dungeon in terms reminiscent of poetic descriptions of hell. Her prison is a place of sighs and groans, in which the distressed pass the day in tears and lamentations. In this place, Nungal keeps the convicted man under guard, until the time that he has appeased "the heart of his god." Then she purifies him and returns him to the "good hand of his god."[11] The goddess Nungal stores and preserves the prisoner, making it possible for him to return to society.

Storage demands retrieval: in order to make goods usable (and pris-
oners redeemable), there has to be a proper system of keeping the books
and organizing consumption. Goddesses were also involved in every
aspect of running the temple complex, and supervising the smooth
functioning of the temple estates. Such management also entails admin-
istering the proper relations among the people on the estate, and thus
requires a sense of social order and social justice. The concern of the
goddess Nanshe in such matters as part of her supervision of the temple
of Lagash is the subject of a long hymn to this goddess.[12]

All these activities are part of the proper running of a household.
It is not hard to understand their attribution to goddesses, for it is a
reflection of human reality. These are the things that women did, and
that Sumerian culture expected them to do. As always, the Sumerian
perception of women determined the literary portrayal of goddesses.
Just as goddesses are the paradigm of women in their familial roles, so,
too, they model women in their economic and cultural contributions.
When we look at the role of women in an ancient household, we find
that it corresponds to a great extent with the picture of the goddess
activities that we have just examined. Like women everywhere, the
women of Sumer were in charge of the production and management of
household goods. The need of mothers to stay near their nursing children required women to stay around the house. But, while at home,
women did not confine their activities to childbearing and child rearing.
On the contrary, their role in the household included the production of
basic goods and the management of household provisions.

Cooking, beer brewing, and the making of cloth and clothes all
share one essential attribute: they are all transformations. Flax and
wool become cloth; indigestible grains are made into bread and beer.
Thus, natural substances not immediately beneficial to humanity are
transformed into cultural product essential to human well-being. This
creation of "civilized" food and clothing out of natural elements is the
basic transformation of "nature" into "culture" and, as such, is the
archetypical female occupation.[13] The change of gender of the goddess/
god Ninurra reflects the early evolution of pot-making, another of these
transformative household jobs, into a full time male profession.

Women were also in charge of household management and administration. This was the job of the adult but not aged woman, typically
the married daughter-in-law. There is a letter from Ludingirra to his
mother[14] which depicts the writer's mother as "managing the house of
her father-in-law on her own."[15] Another Sumerian word, **agrig**, shows
the involvement of goddesses in management. This epithet, meaning

"steward, manager, housekeeper," is applied to the goddesses Nisaba, Ningirim, Nininsinna, Nintinugga, Gula, and Nungal.[16] The use of the term is very illuminating. All the references to a deity refer to goddesses, never to male gods. On the other hand, when the term refers to humans, it is the male rulers of their cities who are called **agrig**. The reason for this disparity is that the **agrig** is not the owner, the "head of the household." On the contrary, the **agrig** is someone who manages and supervises an estate for someone else, the real master of the estate. The kings maintained, provisioned, and administered the temple on behalf of the god who was lord of that temple. Within the divine realm, this was the function of the administrator-goddesses, who are also called **agrig**.

There is an enormous difference between the situation of the ordinary domestic woman managing her own simple household and the portrayal of goddesses managing the large temple and temple estates. But there is a human parallel to the goddess image, for the administrator-goddesses model the behavior of queens. The wives of the rulers of Lagash in the Old Sumerian period were the administrators of the temples and temple estates of the goddess of the city. As such, they engaged in a form of economic diplomacy: a tablet from Lagash contains a detailed list of gifts that the wife of the ruler of Lagash exchanged with the wife of the ruler of Adab.[17] The reality of women's roles within the household conforms exactly to the projection of these roles onto the divine world.

## Goddesses and the Learned Arts

There were also important nonhousehold activities that were considered "womanly" and attributed to goddesses. Many of these grow out of the actions of women in their role as mothers, but extend beyond the household by being performed in public, for people who may not be related to the performer. Chief of these was the singing of laments.[18] Mourning is a manifestation of long lasting love and devotion, and as such is part of, and grows out of, the relational aspect of goddesses/women as mothers, sisters, and wives. Goddesses sing laments over their dead sons, lovers, and brothers. The ancient literary catalogues from ancient Sumer list many laments that the goddess Geshtinanna sang over her brother Dumuzi, who had died and gone to the Nehterworld, as well as laments that Inanna chanted for this same Dumuzi, who had been her spouse. These songs have not yet been recovered by archeologists, but we do have a lament that Inanna sang over the dead King UrNammu, whom she identified with Dumuzi.[19] Sons, too, were mourned, and laments by several goddesses for their dead sons are known.[20]

The role of goddess as mourner extends beyond the family, for the goddesses were the chief singers of public laments in the Sumerian literary tradition, the prime mourners over their destroyed cities. Several literary compositions commemorate historical disasters. One, the Lament over the City of Ur, was written some time after the destruction of the city at the end of the Ur III dynasty. In this poem, Ningal, the goddess of Ur, laments for the city. Significantly, she is shown singing two laments, one before the city had been destroyed, in an attempt to avert the imminent destruction; and then afterwards, when the city had been ravaged, bemoaning the loss of the city and her home. Another such composition, The Eridu Lament, shows the goddess Damgalnunna bewailing the loss of her city, Eridu. The great Lamentation over the Destruction of Sumer and Ur[21] demonstrates that lamenting was the job of the goddess of the city, not of the god. In this composition, the destroyed cities of Sumer are mentioned, one by one. As the god and goddess of each city leave their home, the goddess of the city weeps, "Oh, my destroyed city, my destroyed house." It is the goddess who laments when the goddess is the major deity of the city, like Baba and Ninisinna and Nanshe, and it is also the goddess who weeps when she is merely the minor spouse of the city god (as is Namrat, wife of Numushda in Kazallu).[22] The tradition of the goddess lamenting continued after the Sumerian period, when the Sumerian language continued to be written as a learned language. In this later literature, sometimes called "post-Sumerian," an important genre were congregational laments called **balags**.[23] In these compositions, it is most commonly the goddess Inanna who utters the lament for the destroyed city.

The lamenting of the goddesses was not only a matter of tears and songs. It was an intense performance which entailed dramatic and painful acts. When Ninshubur, Inanna's assistant, set up a cry for Inanna (trapped in the Netherworld), "She clawed at her eyes, she clawed at her nose. She clawed at her inner thigh."[24] So, too, when Damgalnunna cried over Eridu, "She claws at her breast, claws at her eyes, utters a frenzied cry, she holds a dagger and sword in her two hands; they clash together, she tears out her hair like rushes, uttering a bitter lament."[25] And when Ningal cries over Ur, "Her hair she tears out as if it were rushes; on her chest, on the silver fly-ornament, she smites and cries 'woe, my city'; her eyes well with tears, bitteriy she weeps." This self-laceration and frenzy is almost certainly a reflection of mourning behavior on the human scene. As part of a public literary lamentation, it

provided a public expression of grief, and allowed for emotional ca-
tharsis in the performers and listeners of the lament. Judging from our
knowledge of comparative religion, the people of Mesopotamia, hearing the poems, may have entered the occasion, and experienced and
manifested their grief by performing these same dramatic actions.

Despite its passionate character, lament was not primarily a ventila-
tion of emotion. It was a purposeful act, specifically intended to serve
as an intercession. The weeping of Ninshubur in Inanna's Descent to
the Netherworld was goal-oriented: she wept before the gods in order
to prompt them to rescue Inanna, who had been trapped in the Netherworld. So too, in the Lamentation over the Destruction of Ur, Ningal
intended to convince the gods not to destroy Ur. In this case, she was
not successful; but after the destruction, she continued to lament in
order to awaken mercy in the gods. Such intercessory lamentation often
did succeed. The laments of Amageshtinanna were so incessant that the
gods agreed to allow her to take Dumuzi's place in the Netherworld for
part of each year. In the Lamentation over the Destruction of Nippur,[26]
the temple itself laments untill Enlil says that there has been enough
lamenting, that he will be compassionate. In the Lamentation over the
Destruction of Sumer and Ur, Nanna does not accept Enlil's statement
that it is simply time for Ur to be destroyed: he continues mourning
until his father Enlil, relents, promising that the city will be rebuilt. In
the historical laments, the mourning of the goddesses over their destroyed cities were intercessions, for their goal was to get the city rebuilt. All of them should be considered successful intercessions, for the
Lamentations themselves were recited at the time of restoration of the
city and shrine and the return of the gods to their homes, and the compositions often contain mention of the restoration celebrations.[27]

The public cultural contributions of the goddesses also include
dream interpretation, a form of divination. In the Gilgamesh Epic, the
divine mother of Gilgamesh, Ninsun, explains to Gilgamesh the significance of his dream. Half a millennium earlier, in a temple hymn of King
Gudea of Lagash (ca. 2200), the goddess Nanshe is singled out as the
great dream interpreter of the gods, an expert at her specialty, who
interprets Gudea's dream for him.[28] Nanshe is in control of the whole
process of divinatory dreams. In addition to asking her to interpret a
dream that one has had, one can also invoke her for help in "incubating"
a dream, that is, in causing a dream to happen by purposely setting up
a situation which one expects will bring on a dream. This is the role
Nanshe plays in the Song of the Plowing Oxen,[29] in which the farmer

goes to dream with Nanshe and has her stand near him in order to induce the dream.

Lament and dream interpretation are only two of the cultural contributions of goddesses, whose public activities include song, healing, and learning. Several goddesses are mistresses of song. Nanshe and Amageshtinanna are singled out as excellent singers.[30] A different group of goddesses is associated with medical healing, the goddess Gula and those goddesses identified with her: Nintinugga, Ninkarrak, Ninisinna, and Baba.[31] Gula is the one who knows plants, and is the great doctor of the people.[32] In the later Babylonian times, there were two kinds of healing professions, the incantation-healer (*ašipu*) and the medical practitioner (*asu*). Each had its tutelary deities, and the latter type, who healed primarily with nonmagical techniques, was under the tutelage of Gula.[33]

Ultimately, all the cultural arts—and what made them possible, wisdom and writing—were the province of the goddess Nisaba. In the dream of Gudea recorded in his great Temple hymn, Nisaba is the maiden with a stylus of fine silver in her hand who consults a star tablet on her knees.[34] She is often identified with special symbolic writing implements. Nisaba has a lapis lazuli tablet;[35] she is mistress of the writing stylus and of the measuring lines with which she measures off heaven.[36] Nisaba was in charge of writing, accounting, and surveying. At the New Year's review in the temple of Nanshe, which is recorded in the Nanshe Hymn, Nisaba set the precious tablets on her knees, took the golden stylus in hand, and lined up the servants for Nanshe. Nisaba was not a secretary—the actual making of lists in the Nanshe Hymn was done by her husband, Haya. Here, she is the record keeper and advisor of Nanshe; elswhere, she is the scribe of An and the record keeper of Enlil.[37] As a royal hymn of Ishbi-irra states, "in the place she approaches, there is writing."[38]

Nisaba is the paradigmatic wise woman, the "great knowledgeable perceptive one"[39] who knows everything. She is also the great teacher, who gives advice to all the lands[40] and endows kings with wisdom.[41] Nisaba epitomizes both godly wisdom and the gift of learning to humans. In the words of a hymn of King Lipit-Ishter:

> *Nisaba, the woman radiant with joy*
> *faithful woman, scribe, lady who knows everything*
> *guided your fingers on the clay*
> *embellished the writing on the tablets*

*made the hand resplendent with a golden stylus*
*the measuring rod, the gleaming surveyor's line,*
*the cubit ruler which gives wisdom*
*Nisaba lavishly bestowed on you.*[42]

Writing and surveying were essential to the existence of urban civilization, and Nisaba is thereby honored as the one who makes cities possible: "the place which you do not establish, there humankind is not established, cities are not built."[43] Other goddesses were also involved in such learned occupations. Amageshtinanna, who composed laments for her dead brother Dumuzi, was also called "mistress of scribes,"[44] and the goddess Nintu is also called the "great knower who knows everything."[45] But it was primarily Nisaba who filled this role, honored by the scribes who ended their compositions with the short sentence, "Nisaba be praised!"

The scribes praising Nisaba were generally male. Why, then, did they imagine their profession to be under the tutelage of a female? And why did the singers and healers, many of whom were also men, pray to and praise their patron goddesses? The answer lies in the skilled nature of these activities and the contribution of women to their development. The cultural arts are learned occupations which require the accumulation of technological knowledge. They are wise activities and, as such, are attributed to wise women. Part of the reason that women were considered wise is psychological, for women were the chief caretakers of nursing children. This meant that the child developed in the presence of what seemed to her an all-knowing, all-powerful mother of early childhood, the "goddess of the nursery."[46] There is another historical factor that should not be overlooked. Men were engaged in strenuous large-muscle occupations for which their superior upper-arm strength and generally heavier musculature was needed. In early Mesopotamia, they spent their time ploughing with oxen, digging ditches for irrigation, and building city walls for defense. Women, on the other hand, were tending children at home and producing basic goods by cooking, cloth making, and beer brewing. Such activities are technologically sophisticated and complicated and must have appeared particularly intricate in comparison to the activities in which most males were engaged. The skilled nature of women's activities must have reinforced from early childhood the psychological impression of the wise mother. These two factors contribute to an image of the female as accumulating, utilizing, and dispensing expert knowledge.

Indeed, the association of female deities with all these learned arts made sense in human terms. In all the household activities of production, storage, and administration, the relationship of goddesses to the work performed by human women in the households of Sumer is readily apparent. There was a similar congruence of goddesses and women in the learned arts; and from the association of the goddesses with these arts, we can deduce that women were also involved in these occupations. In fact, many of these cultural occupations are a direct extension of women's activities in the house, as a loyal spouse and mother and as producer of household goods. This was clearly the case with lamenting, which grows out of the undying love that mothers and sisters are portrayed as showing their sons and brothers. Even the role of the goddesses as public mourners in the lamentations is an outgrowth of their image as "mothers" of their cities.[47]

Other cultural arts also grew out of the household role of women, particularly mothers. They would have been called upon to explain the world to their children, and to interpret their dreams, just as Gilgamesh's mother explains his to him. Like many of these arts, dream interpretation moved outside the home, and was a specialty of the En priestess of the god Nanna at Ur.[48] Mothers sang lullabies to their children (some of which have been recovered)[49] and were remembered as singers. In the same way, healing as a womanly activity probably also grew out of the household role of women. With their knowledge of plants and their care for dependent members of their households, women were probably the first developers of medicinal practice.

The close association of women with learning in Sumerian thought is intriguing, for until the last hundred years, few women have had the opportunity to become learned. Literature, scholarship, and even the classic languages of learned discourse were all male prerogatives. Given this background, the figure of the goddess Nisaba as the Sumerian divine teacher and patron of writing and learning is particularly striking to modern Western readers. Beyond the psychology of mother-memory and the cultural memory of the more sophisticated technologies of women's productive activity, the constant parallelism between goddesses and women should alert us to the possibility of women's contribution to the development of scholarly learning. There is evidence in Sumerian literature of such female contribution to the earliest literary and wisdom activities of Sumer. In Enmerkar and the Lord of Aratta, a heroic legend about one of the early kings of Sumer, when Enmerkar goes to the city Aratta (which he has besieged in order to get its stones and minerals), his woman sage came to him, in elegant splendor, to advise him and the King of Aratta that they should barter food for precious minerals.⁵⁰ Like all the heroic epics, this text was not written contemporary to the early kings who are their subjects, but there may here be a recollection that in the early times, women did serve as sages. It is a common plot device in Mesopotamian literature that at critical points in the adventures of heroes, they receive advice (solicited or not) from human or divine females, who consistently offer sage counsel.

It may be significant in this regard that the earliest known authored poems were written by a woman—Enheduanna, daughter of Sargon. She was installed by him as En priestess of the god, Nanna, in Ur. In this capacity, she wrote the major poems "Ninmešarra" and "Inninša-gurra," a cycle of hymns to the temples of Sumer, and, perhaps also, "Inanna and Ebih."⁵¹ We are accustomed to thinking of her as an anomaly, a sole woman writing in a domain that belonged to men. But this may be a false scenario. Enheduanna was probably not the first En priestess,⁵² and it may have been part of the duties of this office to compose and write hymns. There is really no reason to assume that anonymous compositions of this period were written by men. Even later, during the Ur III period, the Shusin love lyrics were probably written by his wife, Kubatum, and "UrNammu's Death" may have been written by his widow.⁵³

The earliest impetus to the development of writing was economic, for writing developed from the use of tokens to record transfers of goods, livestock, and services.⁵⁴ Since women were largely in control of the household, and may have engaged in such transfers or a least kept the record of them, we might speculate that it was these women who developed the technique of drawing the transfer tokens on clay, and thus began the art of writing. This would certainly explain why the acts of record keeping and writing, and the wisdom that it enables one to accumulate, are all ascribed to a goddess figure.

Although these cultural contributions of goddesses derive from the actions of women, the relationship between the activity of goddesses and that of women in cultural life is not a direct one-to-one match. At any given moment, the portrayal of goddesses in culture reflects both the actual role of women at the time that the literature was written and cultural memory of the contribution of women to the development of civilization. But despite the inevitable "time lag" between society and image, between role and role-model, shifts in roles between men and women in the ongoing development of culture were ultimately played out on the divine scene. The configuration of the goddesses's cultural involvement was constantly evolving, as is the role of women in culture.

These changes were not random. There is a constant direction to the movement, one in which the areas under goddess control are shrinking, with more and more occupations taken over by male gods.

We have already mentioned one such shift, as Ninurra, goddess of pot making, was transformed into a male god and ultimately absorbed into the figure of Enki. A similar shift occurred in the mantic arts. In the earliest historical period, that of the Abu Salabikh and Fara texts (ca. 2500), there was a very important goddess, Ningirim, who appears prominently in the incantation literature as the exorcist of the gods, the goddess of magical formulae and of water purification.[55] In later Sumerian times, exorcism and incantation are in the hands of Enki and his son, Asarluhi; in still later Mesopotamian literature, their roles are taken by Ea and Marduk.[56] Ningirim never disappears entirely from the magical literature of later Mesopotamia, but she becomes a very minor figure whose role in exorcism and incantation is overshadowed by Enki and Asarluhi and is only a faint echo of her earlier prominence.

In these two instances, goddesses of the earliest period have been diminished or supplanted by the time of the classic Sumerian texts. In other activities, involving goddesses who remain prominent throughout the Sumerian period, male professional practitioners continue to attribute their activities to goddesses. This is a form of culture lag, in which men have taken over the roles that formerly women played, but preserve the cultural memory of women's contribution by projecting their own role onto a goddess figure. In the case of healing, Gula remains the patron goddess, but is found in this role together with Damu. Damu was originally the daughter of Ninisinna and then of Gula, with whom Ninisinna is identified. But at some point, Damu turned into Gula's son and co-worker.[54]

In lament, an interesting development highlights the fact that the culture preserves a memory of women's past contributions. Private laments continued to be performed by women, but the public congregational laments written after the Sumerian period, called **balag**s, were performed by a special kind of male singer known as the **gala**, and not by women. These professional male singers ascribed their activities to goddesses, placing the laments they sang in the mouths of goddesses, particularly Inanna. Moreover, these male singers had a special convention for singing these laments, one also used for recording the speech of goddesses in the mythological texts. They sang these woman-roles in a particular dialect of Sumerian, which they called **eme.sal** ("the thin tongue"). The name of this dialect is an indication that the gala priests sang in a special, thin, probably falsetto voice.[58] This is most probably an indication that these laments were originally sung by female singers. Later, when these lament-singers were replaced by men, their role was taken by special priests who sang in a thin voice to imitate the women that they had replaced.

This diminution of the role of goddesses in cultural affairs is one aspect of a progressively intensifying process in which the goddesses became ever more marginalized. But throughout these changes one factor remained constant. Culture continued to be ascribed to male and female powers, even as the balance between became ever more skewed towards the male. The diminishing role of the goddesses thereby, in itself, served as a paradigm for the recession of women. And since this paradigm of male monopolizing was projected onto the divine sphere, it both modeled and provided sacred warrent for the ongoing cultural displacement of women.

# 5

## In the Body of the Goddess

### *Goddesses and Nature*

As we have seen in the preceding chapters, goddesses are a lot like women, and typify the familial roles and cultural functions that the Sumerians associated with women. But womanness does not entirely define goddesses, for they were not simply celestial women of the imagination. They were deities, with all the powers and characteristics of divinity in the Sumerian pantheon. As gods, they, no less than the male gods, were patrons and overseers of cities and culture, and they were in charge of the cosmos. In the Sumerian view, all the elements of nature—meteorological, geographic, and celestial—were in the hands of the gods. Yet these gods were not simple personifications of nature, and the myths of the gods do not all symbolize natural events, though some stories, of course, do so. Nor do they all express concerns about rain, irrigation, soil, or cataclysm. Because the same gods in control of nature also had political, cultural, and social aspects, the stories about them reflect their complexity. But above and beyond their other roles and characteristics, the gods were immanent in all the forces of nature. They controlled those aspects of nature that most directly affect humankind: its earth, water, weather, and heavens. As deities, goddesses exemplified and controlled various aspects of the natural world. Even in their divinity, goddesses were never far from their feminity. For the most part, the natural elements that the goddesses controlled were as gender-specific as the social relationships that they exemplified. Control over the natural world was not gender-neutral, and there was no free variation between gods and goddesses. All reality and all power are gender-structured.

Not surprisingly, the goddesses did not have power over specific

45

("cosmographic") realms of the physical cosmos. Cosmic geography
was divided along gender lines, and control over geographic realms and
their power elements was not in female hands. The sky was in the hands
of a male god (the god An), as were the air (Enlil) and the waters (Enki).
Meteorological and astronomical phenomena, such as sun, moon, stars,
and storms, were also in the hands of males. Characteristically, Inanna
is the exception that illuminates the rule.[1] She, who did not follow a
woman's life, had a role in the sky, and was notable as the Venus star,
which appears as both the morning and evening star.[2] She also manifests public power to effect the human environment as a rainstorm goddess, along with other, male rainstorm deities such as Ishkur, Ninurta,
and even Enlil.[3]

As with every aspect of the functions of the goddesses, there are
intimations that they had once been more prominent than they are in
the classic Sumerian period. The goddesses may once have had their
cosmic domain in the world below our feet, the productive world
whose activities are largely unseen. The earth was in the hands of a
goddess (Ki, meaning "earth"), who was the partner of An in the original generation of the cosmos. But Ki does not play any further role in
the mythology, and is not responsible for ongoing agricultural fertility.
The events happening on the surface of the earth, the world of humans
and animals, were the domain of the god Enlil. So, too, the seas, particularly the fructifying subterranean seas, may once have belonged to the
goddess Nammu; but, in historical times, Enki is in full control of these
waters. The further down we go into the terrestrial realm, the farther
removed from public activity and the human power structure, the
longer the goddesses could maintain their control. Throughout Sumerian times, the netherworld, from which things grow and to which they
return, where even humans are fashioned before birth and spend their
life after death, was the domain of a goddess, Ereshkigal. But even
here, goddess-control was not quite unassailable and was definitely
passing. One myth has Enki setting sail for the netherworld and being
turned back,[4] another has Inanna seeking to make the netherworld her
domain, and being defeated. The trend towards total marginalization
and privatization of goddesses intensified after Sumerian times and, as
part of the general trend, Ereshkigal was "demoted" to the position of
spouse of Nergal, who became the true ruler of the netherworld.[5]

In this male monopoly of visible power in the kingdoms of the cosmos, the divine world models the absence of women from the power
structure of the ancient Sumerian state, and demonstrates the culture's
expectations that women will not seek such political roles. Part of being

a proper female is to be *not* in control of the sky and the forces of the heavens. Significantly, only the very non-proper Inanna is visible in this realm. The typical goddess's power in nature is, by contrast, the essence of "womanly" power, bodily-based and determined. The males have nature roles not dependent on anatomy; for females, their power in nature is defined by sex. The goddesses are in control of the processes of reproduction, fertility, and sexuality. These are anatomical functions, seen as the quintessence and defining characteristic of "female." Society associates the female, whether human woman or goddess, with sex, reproduction, and fertility. In all these, it is the body, particularly the vagina, that performs the functions that only a female can do. This is not to minimize the importance of the body and its powers, for through their bodies the goddesses had enormous influence over the world of nature, particularly as it effects the survival and quality of life of human beings.

Sexual attraction is in the hands of the goddess Inanna/Ishtar, the nubile young woman, unencumbered by children. She is not preoccupied or distracted by family responsibilities and is therefore restless and interested in relations with men. Pubescent girl, bride, bored young wife, or prostitute, she does not metamorphose into a mother, either psychologically or physically, and remains the object of men's desire. She, for her part, is attracted to males (human, and even animal).[6] Inanna was the very embodiment of sexual attraction and lust, the one on whose presence all sexual desire and copulation depends. The ancient Hymn, The Exaltation of Inanna, written by Enheduanna, the En priestess of Ur, around 2300 B.C.E., makes very clear what the consequence of disobedience to Inanna would be. "Over the city which has not declared, 'the land is yours,'" Inanna departs and "its woman no longer speaks of love with her husband. At night, they no longer have intercourse. She no longer reveals to him her inmost treasures."[7]

Inanna's connection to sexual attraction is expressed most forcefully in The Descent of Ishtar, the Akkadian version of the Descent of Inanna. After Ishtar has been trapped in the Netherworld,

> Bull springs not upon cow, ass impregnates not
>   jenny.
> In the street, a man impregnates not a maiden.
>   Man lies down in his (own) chamber
> Maiden lies down on her side.

Inanna/Ishtar represents the attraction necessary for all sexual copulation, regardless of its social purpose or value. This is sexuality—raw sexual experience and power—unbounded by human conventions, not constrained by marriage. Even the boundaries of human-divine or divine-animal (and thereby human-animal) divisions do not restrain Inanna's sexuality and she is shown as the lover of humans and horses. But Inanna is no outlaw. Unrestrained "free love" is her domain,[8] but so is married, socially-conforming love. Inanna/Ishtar represents and gives patronage to the sexuality of the prostitutes, but as Ishhara, one of her names, she is the patron of marital sexuality, to whom the bed of bride and bridegroom is devoted.[9]

Inanna is the sexual joy (hi-li) of the cosmos, and also the goddess who brings the joy of life to humankind. The power of sex is the power of joy, and Inanna brings happiness to children, brings dances to young women.[10] Inanna is the spirit of play. Her feasts are festivals of games, dances, and music, and she herself is ša-at me-li-ṣi-im, "the one who is joy."[11] Inanna's sexual essence is the source of joy and play for all.

The second great area of goddess body-power is reproduction. Of course, reproduction cannot be solely in the hands of goddesses, for both male and female powers must be involved. The males have two important actions: they copulate and they inseminate. They also initiate sexual activity. In myths such as the Myth of Enki and Ninhursag and the Myth of Enlil and Ninlil, the female may indicate her sexual readiness and availability by coming to the riverbank, but it is the god who comes to her and proposes sex. Moreover, the female was expected to postpone sexual gratification, for Sumerian mores of proper sexual behavior, demonstrated by the Myths of Enlil and Ninlil and of Enki and Ninhursag and the Dumuzi-Inanna poems, required parental permission and marriage ceremony before copulation. The male was expected to formally address the parents of the girl he desired; the female was expected to demur until a formal proposal of marriage has been made. In all these texts, it is the male who proposes; in Sumerian literature, no woman, not even the goddess Inanna, initiates sexual encounters.[12]

The semen of the male brought conception. The role of males in reproduction had been understood at least since the domestication of animals (in the Near East, around 9000 B.C.E.). But the ovum is a very recent discovery, and biology, until early modern times, considered the male sperm to be the sole agent in engendering the child.[13] Sumerian mythology shows the same conception of the power of the sperm. In the Myth of Enki and Ninhursag, the sperm of the god Enki is so powerful that plants grow from it when it is removed from Uttu because of her pains and placed in the ground; when Enki swallowed these plants, he became pregnant. In the same vein, Enki was able to conceive a child without the aid of a female in the Myth of Enki and Ninmah, even though he could not fashion and gestate it properly. When humans reproduced, a man could expect his personal god to help him conceive a child, and this personal god would be "inherited" by the successive males in the family.[14]

Once the semen left a man's body, the stages of childbirth were in the bodies of women and the hands of goddesses. The goddess Gatumdug (the personal goddess of King Gudea of Lagash) was said to cause the semen to enter wombs.[15] After the semen was in the womb, the mother needed to gestate the baby and birth it. Both gestation and birth were under the tutelage of the mother goddess and her assistants. Nisaba enlarged the foetus in the womb;[16] various birth goddesses attended the birth. But above all, the mother goddess was in charge of the development of the baby. The mother goddess was known by several names, Aruru, Ninmah, and—especially—Nintur and Ninhursag.[17] Nintur's symbol which has been described as an "omega" or a "spiral," is a stylized picture of the womb with the fallopian tubes.[18] She was the mother of the gods and the creatress of humankind. She also has a specific role to play in the birth of each human child, for she is the one who shapes the child, fashioning it while it is in the womb.

Nintur brings on the moment of birth,[19] and oversees the entire birth process: cutting the umbilical cord, gathering the placenta, and pronouncing a propitious fate for the baby. As Inanna points out in Enki and the World Order, "To Nintu, the lady of birthing, you have given the birthing brick, the umbilical-cord cutter, and the shiny lapis lazuli pail."[20] But Nintur does not work alone. Her daughters are the healing goddesses, Nungal, Nintinugga, Ninisinna, Gula, Baba, all of them daughters of An and daughters-in-law of Enlil. They serve as her assistant midwives, holding the pail to catch the placenta and the knife for cutting the umbilical cord. In addition, incantation experts like Asarluhi and Enki, and their human counterparts, could be called in to assist ritually at difficult births.

Birth was a frightening time, and the experience of miscarriage and stillbirth was not infrequent. This, too, may have been in the hands of the mother goddess. Nintur, the mother of birth, is also the one who might bring on premature and unsuccessful birth. In a Hymn to Enlil, a series of events that are part of ordinary processes of the world are said to be impossible without Enlil, the overseer of the world. Among them we read, "Nintur could not kill, could not slay. The cow would not lose its calf in its pen, the ewe not bring forth a premature lamb in its sheepfold."[21] The Sumerians did not attribute miscarriage and still-birth to a demonic agent (as did later mythology in Mesopotamia and Europe), but saw them as part of the natural process of birth. Birth and death are not so far apart, and the earth is womb and tomb. Ereshkigal, mistress of the netherworld, is also called "the mother who gives birth."[22] Moreover, Sumerian birth incantations portray the foetus as formed deep in the earth. At the time of birth, the baby sets off from the quay of death and sails down the birth canal to be born. It should therefore not be surprising to find the mother-goddess held responsible for the death of the child whom she, perhaps, did not protect enough. When her son died, the daughter of Ninhursaga, Lisin, cried: "I, to whom should I compare her, my mother who bore me, Ninhursaga, my mother let him die. To whom should I compare her? To the bitch that has no motherly compassion, let me compare her."[23]

The fearsome nature of birth and death is vividly illustrated by an ancient plaque. A female stands with babies at her breast and babies over her shoulder. The birth spiral symbol at the sides of the plaque identify her as the mother goddess. But at each side of the goddess, kneeling on the ground, is a seated demonic figure. This is a death image.[24]

## Agricultural Fertility and the Sacred Marriage

The mother goddess controls human and animal reproduction, but she is not a fertility goddess in the conventional sense, for she has no power over agricultural fecundity. Despite our own use of the word fertility to describe both the ability of humans and animals to reproduce and the ability of the earth to bear fruit, and despite the Bible's linkage of the two capacities, the Sumerians treated the two as analogous but not identical. Neither mother earth nor mother goddess has a control-ling role in ensuring agricultural fertility. Much religious activity was focused on concern for and celebration of he-gál ("abundance"). Many gods were involved in assuring the fertility of the land and the coopera-tion of all the forces of nature was needed for success. But as in human reproduction, the forces of agricultural renewal were set in motion by sexual action. Among the prayers for abundance was one striking rit-ual, the sacred marriage, which has occasioned considerable interest in modern times.[25]

The sacred marriage was an elaborate ritual that can be recon-structed in great detail. There is no single text that describes the whole ritual, but we can reconstruct it painstakingly from the allusions in the sacred marriage songs. As we do so, we begin to get a sense of the importance of this ritual, and of its significance for Sumerian ideas about the interaction of humans, gods, and goddesses. The sacred marriage began with a journey and procession by the king to the *giparu* of Inanna's temple, the site of the marriage, and the preparation of the bride by washing, anointing, and adorning. The procession and meeting of the partners was accompanied by the singing of love songs and other festivities, and finally, a great wedding banquet celebrated the marriage. But the core of the ritual was an act of sexual congress between king and goddess-figure. To the "holy lap" of Inanna, the king went "with lifted head" (proudly), as a desired, awaited partner rather than as a supplicant. He came to the great fertile bed, which had been set up for the ritual, strewn with grasses and covered for Inanna. There, in bed, Inanna gazed at him with her shining countenance, caressed him, and embraced him. This sexual union was intended to promote the fertility of the land.

The sacred marriage was a state occasion, a *royal* ritual, in which the king played the male role, and in which he figures as the god Dumuzi, the spouse of Inanna. The texts do not mention what woman played Inanna. She is called a **nugig**, which has been translated "hierodule" and has given rise to the idea that the female role was played by a sacred prostitute. But, in fact, **nugig** is a term for a woman of high rank.[26] One of the love lyrics addressed to King Shu-Sin of Ur, which may have been recited on the occasion of a sacred marriage, are written by Kubatum, here called a **lukur** (normally, a type of priestess), which would suggest that a priestess played the female role. But the **lukur** Kubatum, who wrote this lyric, was also the wife of King Shusin; it may be her queen-ness rather than priesthood that qualified her to play the role of Inanna in the sacred marriage ceremony. The identity of the woman is not specified because it was not crucial. It was important to the king to participate in this marriage as both god and king, for it bore directly on his kingly role; his female partner was important only as she became the goddess.

The sacred marriage ritual was an ancient rite which dates back to prehistoric times. There is a vase found in Uruk which dates from the end of the fourth millennium B.C.E. that has a sculpted relief whose iconography is close enough to later sacred marriage texts to indicate that the vase illustrates the ritual of the sacred marriage as it was performed in Uruk in the fourth millennium. In Sargonic times, an inscription from the city of Lagash indicates that the sacred marriage was

performed there also, for it records bridal gifts[27] brought by the god
Ningirsu for the goddess Baba. A little later in Lagash, the inscriptions
on statues of King Gudea of Lagash also talk about the bridal gifts
brought by both god and king for the goddess Baba.[28] The Gudea Temple Hymn[29] records the building of a temple to Ningirsu. In this Hymn,
a bed is prepared for Ningirsu, and on that bed Baba and Ningirsu
"made the bed good together."[30] Baba and Ningirsu may have celebrated such a union, and it is possible that various cities of Sumer celebrated sacred marriages between their city deity and his/her spouse.

The actual literary compositions all concern the marriage of Inanna
and Dumuzi. This marriage of the king to Inanna had ancient roots.
The title "beloved spouse of Inanna" had been claimed by the kings of
Sumer since King Eannatum of pre-Sargonic Lagash.[31] The kings of
Mesopotamia may have practiced the sacred marriage rite from earliest
times on. According to the Sumerian Epic tradition (written much later
than events of the epics), the legendary kings of the first dynasty of
Uruk performed this marriage as an integral part of their kingship (see
discussion of these texts in the next chapter). In fact, one of these kings
was King Dumuzi, who is clearly identified with the god Dumuzi, Inanna's spouse.[32]

The sacred marriage of Inanna and Dumuzi is reconstructed from
five compositions. The first datable text is a Shulgi Hymn, Shulgi X,[33]
in which King Shulgi relates how he came by boat to the quay of Uruk-
Kullab with gifts for the Eanna temple. He arrived, put on festal garments and a special wig (hi-li), and came before Inanna. She, struck by
his glory, sang a song in which she recounted her sacred marriage with
Shulgi, and then she blessed him.

The most elaborate sacred marriage composition is a long Hymn
to Inanna by King Iddin-Dagan of Isin (ca. 1900 B.C.E.),[34] in which he
describes her benevolent role as evening star, and her monthly festival.
The culmination of the Hymn deals with the New Year's festival, when
the people of the land prepare the marriage bed. Inanna bathes and
anoints herself, the king approaches her lap proudly, they lie down and
make love, and Inanna pronounces Iddin-Dagan her true beloved. The
third text, The King and Inanna,[35] does not name the king (not, at
least, in the nonbroken sections). This poem tells about the fruitful
bed, and how Inanna desired it. Ninshubur (the divine vizier of Inanna)
brings the king to the lap of Inanna and invokes blessings on the king.
The king then goes proudly to the lap of Inanna.

The next text, Plow my Vulva,[36] is very fragmentary. It begins with
a song by Inanna in which she praises her vulva, how she called Dumuzi

to godship over the land, and then prepared herself by washing and adornment. After a break, the text records the festival, where the **gala** and the singer chanted, and Dumuzi lay by her side. At that point, Inanna exalts him and sings a song about her vulva, the essence of which is "my vulva is a well-watered field—who will plough it?", to which the answer is "Dumuzi will plough it for you." Inanna then pronounces blessings upon Dumuzi.

The last text to refer to an actual ritual is a fragmentary song of Inanna, "Your breast is your field."[37] After a hymn of self-praise by Inanna, the song records how the linen-wearing priests in the Eanna have prepared an altar, and brought water and bread for Dumuzi. They ask Dumuzi to approach Inanna with a chant, which he does, praising the breasts of Inanna as a fertile field and asking to drink from them. In addition to these five texts, there is a whole cycle of songs that refer to the love, courtship, and wedding of Dumuzi and Inanna.[38] Despite the fact that they make no reference to the actual ritual event, we assume that these texts were sung on the occasion of the sacred marriage ceremony.

The encounter between king and goddess was sexual, and the ancient texts describe their embrace.[39] The Iddin-Dagan Hymn is a clear example:

> The king approaches the pure lap with lifted head,
> with lifted head he approaches the lap of Inanna.
> Amausnumgalanna lies down beside her,
> he caresses her pure lap.
> When the lady has stretched out on the bed, in the
>     pure lap,
> when holy Inanna has stretched out on the bed, in
>     the pure lap,
> she makes love to him on her bed,
> she says to Iddin-Dagan, "You are surely my
>     beloved."

This suggestive language leaves open the possibility that the statue of Inanna was to be laid on the bed, and the king lay with this statue. The language of the Shulgi Hymn is more descriptive. Of Inanna, it relates that "by his fair hands my loins were pressed," "he [ruffled] the hair of my lap," "he laid his hands on my pure vulva." Here it is clear that the king is having intercourse with a human partner who represents the goddess.

This sexual union brought fertility to the land.[40] The sexual conjoining of king and goddesses demonstrated the metaphysical connection between human sexuality and the survival and regeneration of the world. When King Gudea of Lagash prepared the bedquarters of the goddess Baba, his goal was to evoke fertility; the temple hymn relates that when Baba entered her room and lay down, she caused green gardens to bear fruit.[41] Fertility is the main focus of The King and Inanna. Inanna's divine steward, Ninshubur, comes to her and urges her first to give the king a firm royal throne, and then

> *May he like a farmer till the fields.*
> *May he like a good shepherd make the folds teem.*
> *May there be vines under him, may there be barley*
> *  under him.*
> *In the river, may there be carp-floods*
> *in the fields, may there be late barley*
> *in the marshes, may fishes and birds chatter*
> *in the canebrake, may dry and fresh reeds grow,*
> *in the high desert, may shrubs grow,*
> *in the forests, may deer and wild goats multiply.*
> *May the watered garden produce honey and wine,*
> *in the vegetable furrows may the lettuce and the*
> *  cress grow high,*
> *in the palace may there be long life.*
>
> *May the Tigris and the Euphrates bring high-riding*
> *  waters*
> *on their banks may the grass grow high, may they*
> *  fill the meadows.*
> *May holy Nisaba pile high the heaps of grain;*
> *  O My lady, mistress of heaven and earth,*
> *  mistress of all heaven and earth*
> *May he spend long days in your [holy] lap!*

Other sacred marriage texts echo this wish. In Plow my Vulva, the very imagery of Inanna as a well-watered field is an agricultural metaphor, as is the image of Inanna's breast in "Your breast is your field":

> *O Lady, your breast is your field,*
> *Inanna, your breast is your field.*
> *Your wide, wide field which pours out plants*
> *Your wide, wide field which pours out grain*

*Water flowing from on high for the lord, bread from*
   *on high*
*. . . I will drink it from you.*

In this prayer, the imagery is directly sexual: it makes explicit the parallel inherent in this ritual between the female body and the earth, between human sexuality and cosmic reproduction.

Agrarian and pastoral fertility were matters of considerable concern to Mesopotamian religion. Many temples are praised for their role in helping produce **he-gál**, the fertility and prosperity of their cities; many gods are invoked for fertility; many kings are lauded for their role in the bringing of fertility. The vegetation goddess Nisaba was, of course, vital to the process, but the great gods Enki and Enlil were also clearly involved with fertility—Enki as the phallic image of the fructifying waters, and Enlil as "the lord who makes the barley sprout forth, the lord who makes the vines sprout forth, the lord who makes yields be, lord of the earth."[42] Enlil's sons Ningizzida and Ninurta were also in part fertility gods, with Ningizzida (Ningishzida) the power in trees and Inurta both rainstorm and—possibly—plough god.[43]

The religious preoccupation with fertility reflects the ecology of Sumer. In Mesopotamia, surplus production resulted from irrigation.[44] This surplus then allowed society to combine technological, demographic, and economic expansion. The early temple, which coordinated irrigation and collected surpluses, was the institution for doing this. Furthermore, religion was the way in which people were motivated to produce this surplus, and ultimately, the king was the figure who enabled the community to control, centralize, and keep a complex balance among scarce resources.[45] Rituals and prayers for fertility decreased anxiety about harvest, motivated people for agricultural labor, and enabled them to express awe and gratification at the existence of a stable agricultural surplus and the benefits that it brought.

The sexual congress of king and goddess-figure in the sacred marriage ritual provides a powerful symbol for the union of forces involved in the creation of fertility. From the prespective of Western culture, this ritual seems alien and bizarre. We are not used to sexual behavior as part of religious ritual, and find such acts alien to our own Judeo-Christian traditions. We also think of sexual intimacy as a consequence of an ongoing relationship, rather than as the sole constituent act of a relationship which has no other expression. Despite the strangeness of the concept, when we look beyond the cultural differences to understand this sacred sex in its own terms, we find a powerful symbolic

drama. The sacred marriage is a multileveled metaphor with powerful
and poetic dimensions of meaning. It is significant that the prime divine
figure in this drama is not a "fertility" or "mother-goddess." Instead,
the ritual involves sexual union with the goddess who represents that
lust which allows for sexual union. This gives sexuality a prominent
place in the cosmic order as an important pathway to fertility. Just as
sexual intercourse leads to human and animal fertility, so too the sexual
congress of the sacred marriage can lead to the agricultural fertility of
the land of Sumer. Human sexuality, familiar for its domestic import,
is seen in this ritual as the known, visible component of the world's
regenerative processes; it is the anatomical analogue or aspect of cosmic
renewal.

Sexuality is such an important force for renewal because sex unites.
The sacred marriage is about *union*, about the coming together of the
many elements that together make a fertile world. Through this act,
renewal and regeneration occur when the male component of fertility
(Dumuzi) combines with the female component (Inanna), thus unifying
the various aspects of the cosmos. Male and Female appear as the inter-
locking pieces which combine to open the riches of the universe. The
union of the two principals in the sacred marriage signifies, expresses,
and effects the meeting of the male-female axis of the world.

To go a step further into the metaphor, the union takes place at the
sacred storehouse, and Inanna, the goddess-partner, is not only the
goddess of sexuality but also deity of the storehouse.[46] Dumuzi, her
divine partner, with whom the king is identified, probably represents
the living spirit within vegetation and animals.[47] Through their union,
civilized endeavor is mated to this natural regenerative ability, and their
combination enables the true surplus abundance upon which urban civilization depends.

In this Sumerian royal ritual, Dumuzi was enacted by the king, who
became the god in the performance of the ritual. The king was the
avatar of Dumuzi, but at the same time, he was also the human king
of the state. Through this act, he received from Inanna the blessings of
a fertile and prosperous reign. In this way, the sacred marriage symbolizes yet another necessary union, for it underscores the important principle that it is through the concerted effort of gods and humans that
the fertility of the world is assured. The gods bring fertility through
their control over rain, air, sun, and soil; humans bring abundance
through their work in fields, canals, and storehouses. The sacred marriage of the king and the goddess is a dramatic expression of this divine-
human partnership.

Yet another layer of symbol lies in the fact that the human/divine partner is the king. The sacred marriage brings together the king and the goddess in the most intimate possible ways, and thereby allows the king access to the world of the gods impossible for other humans to achieve. In this way, goddesses mediate between the world of the gods and the world of the king, a subject that is discussed in the next chapter.

The role of the goddess in the sacred marriage is graphic and immediate: she is the sex-partner. At issue here is not gender, but organic sex. The goddess is important precisely because she is female, because she possesses female sexual organs and can participate in the sexual act. Not surprisingly, it is the goddess of sexuality, the goddess-as-sex-partner, who is the divine partner in the sacred marriage. The graphic language in the sacred marriage hymns is not an indication of sexual prurience or pornographic interest. On the contrary, these hymns are a celebration of Inanna as vulva, of the goddess as "cosmic cunt."

The sexual organ of goddesses provides the way for goddesses to be active in the cosmos, in procreation and agriculture. Even though we know the relationship between copulation and birth, our experience of them is separate and different. And the goddesses are different: it is mother who produces children, and the sex-goddess whose sexual activity brings fertility to earth. But in each case, it is the sex-organ of the goddess that enables her to do her job. It is the producing organ of the mother which gives birth to children, and the interactive organ of the sex-partner through which the universe is regenerated. In ancient Sumer, divine vaginas bring birth and renewal. When, as in the Bible, the divine has no vagina, how can the world be renewed? Clearly, the entire conceptualization of nature has to undergo fundamental change.

# 6

## Bridges to the Gods

### Love, War, and the Goddess Inanna/Ishtar

The sacred marriage expressed a close bond between King and goddess. Through Inanna, their divine partner, the kings of Sumer stepped closer to the world of divinity, reinforcing the king's status and highlighting his superiority. The king, standing above the rest of humanity, was the first step on the staircase to the gods. The next step higher was Inanna. This goddess, unencumbered and fundametally unattached, marginal to the family structure and power hierarchy of the gods, was available and eager to be the intimate of the kings of Sumer. She was the liminal deity, who transcended all boundaries and could bond with the king. She was the divine link to the world of the gods, and when she took the king as a lover, the conjugal pair was a bridge between the people and the gods. The powerful gods who determined the people's survival were much less remote when the king, the people's representative, was intimate with them. Over this bridge to the gods, blessings could flow. The kings received blessings on their reign, success in politics, and victory in war. The people achieved peace-through-triumph, security, and prosperity. The songs of the sacred marriage celebrate the royal power as they sing of the blessings which Inanna bestows on the king after the union, blessings of a long and successful reign.

The key to the ability of the king to reach intimacy with Inanna was erotic attraction. In the sacred marriage, the king was no ordinary mortal worshipper. He came in pride and dignity,[1] for he was the special beloved of Inanna. This infinitely alluring goddess—herself the essence of sexual desire and attractiveness, the **hili** of the whole cosmos, of the earth and its people[2]—looked upon the king who came to her in

58

his splendor as the embodiment to her of sexuality.[3] The king is the object of Inanna's sexual delight, and she actively craves his attentions.

As the goddess's sexual partner, the king had a unique status. He was the counterpart of Dumuzi, celebrated in Sumerian song as the husband of Inanna. The king was ritually transformed into this husband of Inanna, and the sacred marriage texts call him "the king who is the god,"[4] or even simply Amaushumgalanna (a byname of Dumuzi). In this ritual transformation, the king is touched by divinity, and attains suprahuman approval of his powers. The festive ritual procession in which the king was borne publicly to the temple also reinforced the special status of the king. Through his "marriage" to the goddess Inanna, the king achieved intimacy with the divine in a way that was not attainable by other humans. The sacred marriage ritual, performed yearly during the New Year's festival,[5] annually reinforced the divinity and authority of the king.[6]

To be a bridge to the gods, the king had to be superior in his very essence to ordinary people. The early kings were crucial to the development and survival of Sumerian civilization, able as they were to coordinate and motivate the cooperative labor and accumulation of surplus to support a more diversified cultural profile and a greater density of population. They could also expand trade horizons to foreign areas and engage in warfare with other emerging city-states. Kingship was so important in Sumerian thinking that the Sumerian King List records that "kingship came down from heaven."[7] Crucial as they were to state formation, these earliest kings had to find a way to legitimate their power. As they had no weight of historical precedence to buttress the idea of rule, no dynastic principle to assure the rights of a successor, they had to demonstrate that they were greater than the rest of the populace.

The divine world provided the means to elevate the king. Throughout Sumerian history, kings are portrayed as gods, as sons of god and goddess, and as husbands of the goddess Inanna. The divine character of Sumerian kingship starts with the very first kings, who ruled at the dawn of history (the Early Dynastic Period). Writing was just beginning, and there are no original inscriptions from their reigns, but later Sumerian traditions remembered and celebrated the kings of this early heroic age. In these later traditions, the early kings of Sumer were gods and demigods.[8] Even Gilgamesh (son of Ninsun and Lugalbanda), who is portrayed in the Old Babylonian Gilgamesh Epic as "Everyman," the representative of the existential dilemma of humanity, is also considered a god, one of the judges of the netherworld. We do not know what these early kings of Uruk said about themselves, but it is clear that the later Sumerians considered them divine. Did the Sumerians believe that these early heroes achieved divine status because of their greatness? Or was there a legend that at the beginning of time, gods came to rule on earth? In the final analysis, it doesn't really matter. In the eyes of the Sumerians, gods sat on the throne of Uruk in the early days: the kings at the dawn of history were god-men.

This claim of godhood alternates with another divine attribute of the kings, that of "son of god." The kings of the first fully historical period claim in their records that they are the sons of gods.[9] The royal inscriptions of early historical Sumer show us the entire world of the gods attending to, instructing, and bestowing gifts on the newly-born royal scion. There is, moreover, a consistently prominent role for the mother goddess. All the pre-Sargonic kings use a particular epithet in their royal inscriptions, "nourished by the good milk of Ninhursag."[10] By this epithet, the early kings of Sumer indicate that whoever their divine mother may be, Ninhursag, the mother goddess, one of the three prime gods, was their god-mother and nurturer. In this way, the king receives divine authority "with his (divine god) mother's milk."[11]

The next historical period, the Sargonic (Akkadian 2500–2200) period, marked a new stage in state formation: a unified Sumer and Akkad, on a larger geographical scale with a more complex governmental system. The empire was composed of old city-states, each of which still retained its identity, and was ruled by a governor whom the kings of Akkad appointed. The Akkadian kings also instated themselves as the owners of landed property that had previously been under the control of the local temple.[12] It was no longer enough for the king to be "son of god, nursed by god-mother."[13] Instead, the Sargonic kings sounded clearly and explicitly the theme that is implicit in the traditions about the first kings of Uruk: they proclaimed themselves gods.[14] Becoming gods themselves gave them greater warrant for the new suprasegmental powers that they were assuming. As divine beings, they also had a greater warrant for their secularized appropriation of divine property.

The Akkadian period was brought to a close by turmoil and invasion. There was to be no central control in southern Mesopotamia until the next period of national unity, Ur III (2100–2000 B.C.E.). The Ur III kings, faced with the monumental task of bringing a suprastructure to the ancient Sumerian cities, applied every theological concept possible and all the metaphors of divinity by which they could indicate a special status for their kingship. The kings claimed that their authority over all of Sumer had been granted by the divine council under Enlil. They were "sons," of god and goddess,[15] but this relationship, important as it was in bringing them in close relationship to a god, could not differentiate the king from the rest of the populace. All Sumerians claimed divine "parentage."[16] Being son of a god did not make the king special enough, and the kings of Ur III used the title "god,"[17] declaring that they themselves were divine.[18] Many royal hymns were written to and in the name of Shulgi, the second great king of the dynasty. There were offerings and festivals to him and to the sons who succeeded him, and months named after them. There were special places for the worship of Ur III kings. Several chapels have been excavated, and even the Ehursag of Ur, which was built by Shulgi, may have been dedicated to him.[19] Nevertheless, the deification of the kings was limited: they were, after all, human beings who fell sick and died. They were divine, but not actual gods among the gods. Unlike the early legendary hero-kings like Lugalbandanda, and to a lesser extent Gilgamesh, the "divine" kings of Akkad and Ur III were not truly part of the divine world. There are no myths in which these kings act with the gods, no poetry in which the name of a king appears in a row of gods' names. Their iconography is similar to that of the gods, but there are always crucial differences.[20]

The divine status of the Ur III kings, a profound metaphor for their godlike powers and authority, did not erase their obvious humanity. The very human god-kings had to find a way to associate the king closely with the gods, ideologically and psychologically, in their own and the public's eyes. To do this, yet another paradigm of divine human relationships was developed, the metaphor of "spouse," the beloved of the goddess Inanna/Ishtar. This paradigm was developed fairly early. The early king Eannatum of Lagash called himself by the epithet **dam-ki-ága-<sup>d</sup>Innna**, "beloved husband of Inanna," and the early kings of Lagash also entitled themselves "called in the heart of Inanna," another epithet which indicates the love of Inanna for the king. King Naram Sin of Akkad, whose inscriptions are in the Akkadian language, called himself "spouse of Ishtar," and thereafter all the kings of Ur III, Isin, and Larsa used the title "spouse of Inanna." By this metaphor, the king expressed his close relationship to the goddess and stressed his difference from ordinary people. There was no conjugal intimacy with the divine available to nonkings. Through the marital metaphor, the king moved beyond the realm of humanity into the social world of the gods.

The marital metaphor had yet another great advantage over "son-of-godship." The metaphor of "son of god" has the capacity to both elevate and diminish humanity. While on the one hand showing a de-

gree of closeness and intimacy to the deity, at the same time it emphasizes humanity's lesser status to the god, and its dependence on the god's
protection and instruction. The metaphor of "spouse," on the other
hand, expressed the near-equality of the king to the gods. The metaphor of "spouse" and its ritual expression, the sacred marriage,[21] focused on the mutuality of the love between king and goddess. The Neo-
Sumerian sacred marriage songs emphasized that Inanna, well-known
as the goddess of desire, desired the king.[22] It is because *she* loves the
king that she bestows blessings upon him. Desire and sexuality created
the bridge between the king and the goddess, but the result is power.
As close associate of the king, Inanna was with him in all his endeavors.
Warfare was often a way for Inanna/Ishtar to bestow her love-gifts on
the king. The relationship of Inanna to the *power* of kings goes back
to the dawn of history, and was considered a major factor in the rise
and fall of the kings of Uruk and Agade. There is a historical reason
that Inanna can bestow political power: Inanna was the city-goddess
of the important cities of Kish, Uruk (sharing rule there with An), and
(as Ishtar) Akkad. To the Sumerians, control over these cities depended
upon Inanna's will. In this spirit, one of the inscriptions of Eannatum,
an early king of Lagash, records that "Inanna, because she loved him
so, gave him the kinship of Kish in addition to the rulership of Lagash."[23]

The Sumerian epics about Enmerkar, a legendary early king of
Uruk (ca. 2600 B.C.E.), emphasize the importance of the love of Inanna
to the king's power. These stories tell of the relations of Uruk with
Aratta, a non-Sumerian city in the mountains to the far east of Sumer,
and deal with the rivalry and opening of trade between Enmerkar of
Uruk and the Lord of Aratta. In this rivalry, the love of Inanna was the
crucial factor, for both cities worshipped Inanna, and both kings had
a special relationship to her, one which this epic tradition viewed as a
conjugal bond. According to the Epic, Enmerkar and the Lord of Aratta,
the problems of Aratta began because the Lord of Aratta did not please
Inanna as well as did the Lord of Kullab (Enmerkar, who unified the
city of Kullab-Uruk). Enmerkar wanted the stones, precious metals,
and lapis lazuli of Aratta, and upon his asking Inanna to make Aratta
submit to him, Inanna advised Enmerkar to send an envoy. As Aratta's
fortunes rose and fell in the battle of wits that followed, the lord of
Aratta announced his belief that Inanna had not deserted Aratta, that
she had not abandoned the ornate bed, had not delivered it up to the
**girin**-flowered bed, and had not abandoned her lord.[24] Ultimately, Aratta was forced to agree to trade with Uruk. The confrontation between

them proceeded as a battle of wits in which Enmerkar showed himself wise and ingenious, and his very superiority was the clue that Inanna loved him. In another epic about this rivalry, the kings Enmerkar and Ensuhkeshdanna, have made beautiful beds for Inanna, but Inanna prefers Uruk and the fertile bed of the Eanna, and Ensuhkeshdanna capitulates, declaring that "Inanna has called him to her holy lap, he is her beloved."[25] These epics were probably composed during the Ur III dynasty, more than 500 years after the events that they depict, and they show the same philosophy of king-Inanna relations as the sacred marriage texts from this later period. Like most historical epics, they may have had their source in much earlier folk traditions, and may be an indication that this concept of Inanna's love for the king is quite ancient. After all, in the epic, Inanna grants power over Aratta to Enmerkar and Uruk because of her love for king Enmerkar, and in the ancient Old Sumerian inscription of King Eannatum of Lagash, Inanna gave Eannatum the gift of power over Kish because she loved him. Inanna's love for the king grants him expanding power.

The way that Inanna awards power to her beloved is often through victory and conquest. The Epic, Enmerkar and the Lord of Aratta, calls Inanna a warrior, one set for battle. The other two epics about relations with Aratta, the two Lugalbanda epics, relate the battle between the two cities. Inanna accompanied Enmerkar to battle before the walls of Aratta. When the battle did not go well for him, he understood that Inanna had deserted him, that she had returned to Uruk. He interpreted Inanna's departure as an indication that he no longer had his **hili**, his sexual attractiveness and desirability, and that Inanna no longer desired him as her partner.[26] Eventually, Lugalbanda became the next king of Uruk. He also went to war against Aratta, and Inanna came to him to prepare his battle. Yet another historical epic, the Epic of Gilgamesh and Akka, relates the adventures of Lugalbanda's son, Gilgamesh, who continued this close relationship with Inanna. When Akka, king of Kish, threatened Uruk, and the council of Uruk wanted to yield rather than fight, Gilgamesh did not submit, for "he trusted Inanna."[27]

These epics concern the very beginning of Sumerian history. But Mesopotamian tradition also remembered that Inanna, as her Semitic counterpart Ishtar, had a very close relationship with the Sargonic kings of the city of Akkad, who unified Sumer and created the first empire. In the Sumerian Sargon Legend, another Sumerian epic written long after the time of its hero, Inanna is shown protecting Sargon before he became king, while he still worked for King Urzababa: "Inanna was unceasingly at his right side"[28] and acted to protect him. The close relationship (called "love") between Ishtar and Sargon and the rest of his dynasty, is remembered throughout the Mesopotamian historical literature: this dynasty was so closely Ishtar-related that Assyrian chronicles called the much earlier Akkadian period *ina palê Ištar*, "the reign of Ishtar." The Akkadian kings believed themselves the beloved of Ishtar (Inanna), and King Naram-Sin attributed his many victories in battle to her love.[29]

The victory of Akkad had important consequences in the development of Sumerian culture. The Sargonic period (the Akkadian period) witnessed a great flowering of Sumerian religious literature which produced the first major compositions that we can read with any fluency.[30] In compositions of this time, Inanna/Ishtar's prowess as goddess of war was a prominent feature. These works were all written by Enheduanna, the daughter of King Sargon, whom he installed as the En-priestess of the moon-god Nanna at Ur. In this role, she represented the goddess Ningal; in an Akkadian inscription, Naram-Sin's daughter Enmenanna, who held the position after Enheduanna, calls herself "wife of Nanna";[31] she might have taken part in a sacred marriage ceremony there, and is shown otherwise supervising the cult.[32] Enheduanna had a very important theological role in Sumer. She authored two cycles of hymns to the temples of Sumer expressing a theme of cultural unity that was appropriate to the unified Akkadian empire. She also wrote three major hymns to the goddess Inanna, the Hymn Ninmešarra, ("Lady of all the **mes**")[33] the Hymn Inninšagurra ("stout-hearted lady"),[34] and the Hymn Ninmehušša ("Lady of the fierce **mes**," commonly known as the Hymn Inanna and Ebih).[35] In these hymns, Enheduanna portrays Inanna as a strong and ferocious warrior, devastator of the land, one whose rage is not tempered.

The hymns of Enheduanna are, in part, narrative poems. In the Ninmešarra Hymn, Enheduanna relates a rebellion that deposed her from office and Inanna's aid in Enheduanna's restoration to office. In telling this story, she recites a litany "Be it known" that describes Inanna in the most ferocious terms:

> *That you totally destroy rebellious lands—be it*
>   *known!*
> *That you roar at the land—be it known!*
> *That you kill—be it known!*
> *That like a dog you eat the corpses—be it known!*
> *That your glance is terrible—be it known!*
> *That you lift this terrible glance—be it known!*

*That your glance flashes—be it known!*
*at those who do not obey—be it known!*
*That you attain victories—be it known!*[36]

The Hymn, Inanna and Ebih, tells the story of how Inanna devastated the land that would not worship her, a fearsome event that is mentioned in both the Ninmešarra and Inninšagurra hymns as well. Inanna came before An to complain that Ebih was not interested in being obedient to her. He replied that the mountain was very fertile and very awesome, but could not withstand her.[37] As soon (ur₅-gim) as he had spoken, Inanna went to war and totally destroyed Ebih.

In these Enheduanna hymns, the image of Inanna presented is one of force. But Enheduanna's poetry also conveys a message of the cultural unity of all Sumer and Akkad. How does the force of one city-god relate to the polity of the whole nation? And how does the ferocity of one goddess relate to the governance of the gods and the authority of political leadership? Enheduanna's poems emphasize the relationship between the force of Inanna and the authority of An and Enlil.[38] Inanna gets her power directly from An and Enlil. But this is a reflected form of authority. It is not independent power. In the ordering of the pantheon, An and Enlil (particularly Enlil) are the heads of government. Inanna/Ishtar has no position of power among the gods, no political authority over them. She is sheer force, rage, and might, with a physical power, that exists in a somewhat uneasy relationship to the orderly world of the hierarchical pantheon. The nonultimate, noncontrolling nature of Inanna's power manifests itself in the Mesopotamian explanation of the fall of Akkad. Upon the fall of the kingdom of Akkad, the city of Akkad was destroyed and so thoroughly devastated that it was never rebuilt. Historical reality brought a serious question of theodicy: if Inanna/Ishtar so loved the kings of Akkad, how could she let this happen? This question is dealt with in The Curse of Agade, a historiographic tale written during the Ur III dynasty.[39] In this text, Inanna, the patroness of Agade, provisions the city with riches, endows its elders with counsel, gives its maidens dancing grounds, its young men martial might, its children joy. Suddenly, Enlil brings "the matter" of the Ekur (Enlil's temple in Nippur)[40] on a peaceful Agade; no warning is given, no explanation is offered. Inanna grows uneasy and abandons her temple. As she leaves, she, the spirit of battle and fight, takes these qualities out of the city. Later, after King Naramsin commits a sacrilege against Nippur and the Ekur, Enlil brings barbarians to devastate the city, and all the great gods (including Inanna) curse Akkad. The new

tone in this tale is evident from the opening lines: "When Enlil's frown-
ing brow had killed Kish . . . and Enlil then and there had given Sargon
King of Akkad lordship and kingship from south to north." In classic
Sumerian literature, Enlil's decision is conclusive. The kings of Akkad
might have attributed their victory to Inanna/Ishtar, but the religion of
later Sumer clearly envisions a world in which such historical rise and
fall depends on Enlil. The myth reflects historical processes: as Sumer
became a national entity, the individual gods of the old city-states could
no longer decide things on their own. Historical decisions were made
by the council of the gods, with Enlil presiding, and individual gods
had to operate by petitioning this council. Still later, in the latter part of
the second millenium, the state Myth of Enuma Elish signifies another
change in political and historical theology, for in this myth the counsel
is replaced by the kingship of Marduk, who inherits the position of
Enlil and adds to it all the attributes of kingship.

These political power systems do not include Inanna/Ishtar. They
reflect the organization of the state, a male hierarchy. Inanna remains
outside the direct chain of authority. She has no niche in the state political system of the gods, as she has no true niche in the family to occupy
her time. This marginality is, paradoxically, a source of her ongoing
significance. Just as her powers of desire and sexuality—intensified by
their liberation from domestic arrangements—remained a force with
which to reckon, so too her powers of might and war—undefused by
orderly political processes and the constraints of leadership—remain a
constant threat of disruption and disorder. Inanna is **nin-me**, "mistress
of battle," an epithet applied to Inanna in the poem, Inanna and Ebih
(1.23), and later used frequently in the royal inscriptions of Sumerian
kings from the time of Gudea on. In the later empires of Assyria, which
gloried in military conquest, the kings were devoted to Ishtar as the one
who marches before the army and "smites the weapons of the enemy."

Inanna was the very spirit of battle. Warfare, the "festival of manhood," was "Inanna's dance,"[41] a theme that was repeated throughout
Mesopotamian history.[42] Iconographically, she is shown with the bow,
the classic weapon of war and the standard symbol of manliness. In the
words of a first millenium congregational lament, it is in battle that
Inanna holds the spindle and whorl, as she makes the skulls roll.[43] In-
anna/Ishtar is noted for her ferocity, for the strength and devastation
of her rage: the raging heart of Inanna/Ishtar troubles heaven and
earth. Two Old Babylonian compositions stress this rage and ferocity,
and describe how the god Enki acted to make Inanna/Ishtar more con-
trollable. One, in Sumerian,[44] relates that Enki made a special kind of

priest, the **gala,** and gave him songs in order to tame the ferocious rage of Ishtar. The **gala** is a well-known figure in the Mesopotamian cult, the lamentation-priest[45] who recited the great laments; here the creation of this cult-institution is specifically related to the need to assuage Inanna. The other composition, in Akkadian, is the Agushaya Hymn.[46] This text describes Ishtar as a fierce goddess who whirls around in her "manliness," whose feast is battle, who goes out in war. Inanna's ferocity goes to intolerable limits, and in order to control her, Ea creates a new fierce goddess, Ṣaltu, as her counterpart.

How can the goddess of love also be the goddess of ferocity and war? Why should two such apparently disparate emotions be represented by the same figure? It has frequently been suggested that this amalgamation was due to historical factors, that it results from a syncretism of a warlike Semitic Ishtar and a lovable Sumerian Inanna.[47] Other approaches have been anthropological, referring to the Bedouin custom of having a well-adorned daughter of a sheik accompany the warriors to urge them on with ferocious invective,[48] or sociological, attributing the connection of Ishtar with strife to her association with prostitutes.[49] But none of these explanations explain the power and durability of the image of Inanna/Ishtar. This goddess who combines the passions of sex and violence has had a long hold on the human imagination and has been widely manifest throughout human cultures. Even if we were to suppose that Enheduanna had deliberately fused two originally separate goddesses, the readers had to accept this fusion as true. When the last two lines of her poem Ninmešarra respectively consider Inanna as the destroyer of lands and as the embodiment of sexual attraction, this had to make sense within the cognitive framework of the listeners. This fusion of sex and ferocity had to make psychological sense.

The answer to the riddle of Inanna/Ishtar lies partly in the nature of cultural perceptions of sexuality and of women. In the first part, as the bringer of sexual attraction, Ishtar is the bringer of marital harmony. Her absence, therefore, brings on household discord, so that Ishtar becomes the mistress of both conjugal harmony and strife. A clear understanding of this is found in Hittite Hymn to Ishtar, which states, "A man and his wife who love each other and carry their love to fulfillment, that has been decreed by you, Ishtar. But [if] a woman is ha[ted] by her husband [then you, Ishtar] have caused [her] to be hated".[50] She is also the sexual attraction of adulterous liaisons, which by their nature are illicit and liable to lead to social strife. Thus her power is felt both as benevolence and as trouble.

Another part of the answer to the darker nature of Inanna lies in her character as the embodiment of the sexually available woman, the woman undiverted by domestic preoccupations and unencumbered by children. As we have noted, such a woman is free to operate in a man's world. And, in so doing, she embodies female power, and all the anxieties and fears that this engenders.[51] The very notion of a woman not under a man's control awakens the fear of danger to societal harmony. Furthermore, the same sexual interest and availability that makes her so enticing also make her frightening, the classic *vagina dentata* ("vagina with teeth"). The strength of the attractiveness leads to fears about loss of control, about being swept away to one's doom.

There is a biological as well as a psychological factor here. Both sex and violence lead to changes in body metabolism and blood flow. Pulse and respiration change similarly in response to either stimulus; blood flow is modified, genital arousal is experienced. Such responses are inherent in our very concept of lust, and this is true whether the stimulus is sexual lust or blood lust. This similarity of response is one of the factors in the popularity of pornographic violence.

Sex is frequently about control and dominance. Not only is this obvious in such forms of sexual behavior as sadomasochism and dominator/dominatrix slave pairings, it also underlies many of our societal attitudes towards sex. The Greeks clearly perceived that the male exhibited control and dominance over his sexual partner, that in the case of homosexual sex it was the penetrator who exhibited power, while the penetrated exhibited weakness and shameful submission. Societies have long admired such powerful images as Don Giovanni with his thousand and three conquests, while reserving ridicule for the cuckholded husbands. The Mesopotamians shared these concepts: not only does the figure of Inanna/Ishtar exemplify this ideology, but the later Assyrian omen series *šumma ālu*, sometimes called a code of behavior in omen form, also indicates the favorable valuation of the man who exhibits sexual conquest and domination.[52] The goddess who personifies sexual attraction must personify the power of one human to attract another, a power which is inherently threating as long as we perceive of sex as power. Moreover, sex and aggression are both manifestations of our desire to assert ourselves.[53] They are inherently "irrational," causing us to feel that we are not quite in control of our emotions or our actions.

For all of these reasons, Inanna/Ishtar unites erotic attraction with aggression, love with rage, desire with combat. As goddess of might and war, she can bring victory. As goddess of love, not fully involved in family occupations, she reaches across species lines, and particularly desires the king. As a female, she has no real place in the hierarchy of power among the gods, a state hierarchy dominated by males, and thereby seeks her power niche in the upper reaches of human society, in the company of king. Amorous and available, she brings the king into the world of the gods, shrinking the distance between the divine and the human, providing a bridge through which blessings flow.

# 7

## The Marginalization of the Goddesses

The Sumerian pantheon that we have been considering was never uniform or static. During the six hundred years between the time of the Abu Salabikh texts (our earliest religious documents) and the growth of Akkadian literature during the Old Babylonian period, empires came and went, wars were fought, and there were political and economic rivalries between cities. It is hard to imagine that such major changes in life would not cause a constant reordering of the pantheon. With the coming of new peoples to Mesopotamia at the beginning of the second millennium and the establishment thereafter of new city-states and—ultimately—of the Old Babylonian empire (circa 1760 B.C.E.), change continued and intensified.

These changes took place in many aspects of society: in the organization of the state, in the socioeconomic system, in the concept of the nature of kingship and political authority, and in theological conceptions of the world of gods. Among the changes in religion, one trend that becomes very clear is the ongoing eclipse and the marginalization of the goddesses. This process did not suddenly begin in the Old Babylonian period, nor should it be attributed to the influx of new peoples. On the contrary, this process seems already under way as soon as a written record becomes available. Despite the extensive roles of goddesses in Sumerian literature, one gets the impression that things are already in flux and that our documents already reflect a process of supplanting goddesses. An example of this process is the goddess Ningirim. In the earliest historical period, that of the Abu Salabikh and Fara texts, she was an important goddess, who figures prominently in the incantations as the exorcist of the gods, the goddess of magical formulae, and

70

the mistress of purificatory water.[1] In later literature, that of the classic Sumerian period, she is still mentioned occasionally as mistress of incantations, but is a minor figure compared to Enki and his assistant Asalluhi.

Much of the diminution of the goddesses is associated with the god Enki. Enki's mother Nammu was mistress of the watery deeps, the Sumerian prototype of the later Tiamat of the Enuma Elish. However, she is rarely found in god lists or in myths or hymns, and throughout Sumerian literature, it is Enki who is acknowledged lord of the subterranean waters. Another example is the case of Ninurra, who in the third millennium was the god of pot making. She was clearly a goddess, the mother of Umma, for she is named in Early Dynastic texts as the wife of the god Shara of Umma, and is called "the mother who counsels Enki."[2] Later, Ninurra was absorbed (as a male god) into the persona of Enki/Ea.

This diminution of the goddesses continued and intensified in the Old Babylonian periods and later. There are very few stories about females in Akkadian litrature, and those females who do appear are generally in ancillary roles and in the stereotypical figures of mother, advisor, and temptress. Even the major female figures of Sumerian literature have shrunk or disappeared. Gula, the goddess of healing, is still there, but often shares her role with Damu, who was probably originally her daughter,[3] but later becomes her son. Nisaba, patroness of learning, has all but disappeared. The chief figure of wisdom is Enki/Ea, while Nisaba's role as goddess of writing and patron of scribal schools was taken over by Nabu. By the later periods in Mesopotamia, only Ishtar has any real impact and persona. Other goddesses exist primarily as "consorts," mere sexual partners for male deities.

The eclipse of the goddesses can be seen dramatically by the fortunes of mother-figures. The primordial first-mothers disappear early. In the marshy south, the mother of all and the creator of humanity was Nammu, who was then eclipsed by Enki. In another strand of Mesopotamian mythology, the primordial mother was Ki, the earth. According to this theology, the gods resulted from the union of An (heaven) and Ki (earth).[4] But Ki does not appear as a major goddess in any texts. As ruler of the earth she has been supplanted by her first son, Enlil (Lord Air) who is envisioned as the ruler of all that happens on the earth. It is possible that her very name, Ki, is eclipsed by that of Enki.[5]

Ninhursag was the great and active mother-goddess in Sumerian texts. Daughter of An and Ki and sister of Enlil, she was one of the greatest gods of Sumer. Texts from the southern city of Lagash, from the time of Eannatum down to Gudea, recite as the triad of the greatest gods An, Enlil, and Ninhursag.[6] Ninhursag, too, starts to decline in later Sumerian texts. By the time of the Isin and Larsa dynasties (1900-1800 B.C.E.), the supreme divine triad has become An, Enlil, and Enki, with Ninhursag listed as fourth in rank.

Even the role of the mother-goddess in the creation of the first humans is not unchallenged in Sumerian texts. One myth, The Pickaxe, relates the story on Enlil's creation of the pickaxe, the essential agricultural tool. In this story, once Enlil had created the pickaxe, he used it to dig a hole in the earth, and laid into the hole a brick-mold that had the seed of humanity. After he did this, people sprouted up from the ground like grass.[7] In this text, Enlil is clearly the motivating power, and humans are born from the seed that he created. Earth is the womb, but it is an earth devoid of "earth-mother"; it is inanimate and without volition.

Ultimately, it is again Enki who takes over the functions of the mother-goddess. This rivalry between Enki and that of the mother is reflected in two Sumerian myths, that of Enki and Ninmah and that of Enki and Ninhursag, both of which concern birth in some fashion. According to the Myth of Enki and Ninhursag, Enki in primordial times, mated with Ninhursag, the primeval mother, then with Ninnisiga, the daughter of this union; with Ninkurra, the third-generation daughter; then with Ninimma, the fourth-generation daughter; and finally with Uttu, Ninimma's daughter. As we discussed on pp. 22–23, this last union was a domestic arrangement. When Uttu had trouble with pregnancy, Ninhursag came and took Enki's semen out of Uttu's womb, and planted it in the ground, where it grew into plants. Enki ate the plants in order to know (and appropriate) them. However, his semen was so powerful that the plants made Enki pregnant. Since he had no womb, he became sick. Despite her anger over his eating of the plants, Ninhursag came to Enki's aid. Having placed Enki in her vulva, she turned her attention to the parts of the body that were paining Enki, and gave birth to a goddess from each one. There is clearly a rivalry going on between Enki and Ninhursag, but in this myth the two powers seem to have struck a balance: both Enki's semen and Ninhursag's womb are necessary for the creation of goddesses.

The Myth of Enki and Ninmah, which deals with the creation of humans, also reflects this rivalry between the mother-goddess and Enki. The tale begins with a depiction of a situation that existed before the creation of humanity, when the gods were laboring to dig the rivers.

When they came to complain before the dormant Enki, his mother Nammu (called "the primordial creator") urged him to arise to help the suffering gods, suggesting that he fashion a worker to do the work for the gods. Enki agreed, and, for his part, suggested that Nammu make the creature, with Ninmah her helper and the other goddesses assisting. Nammu then created humankind. This is a very difficult text to understand: there are gaps at important lines and the language is sometimes obscure. Nammu was both the originator of the idea of creating humankind and the creator. Enki has some sort of role in this creation, for Nammu does not proceed with her idea until Enki has handed her suggestion back to her. Despite the presence of Enki, it is clearly Nammu who does the actual creation of humankind.[8] But this story is only the first part of the composition, Enki and Ninmah. The myth continues with the feast that Enki then made for Nammu and Ninmah. At this feast, Enki and Ninmah began a boasting-competition, as was often the custom at banquets.[9] In this contest, Ninmah (the mother-goddess who oversees the shaping of the embryo in the womb) declared that the shape of humankind—good or bad—depends solely on her. Enki, for his part, declares that he can mitigate the good or the bad. These two gods go further than mere disputation: Ninmah proceeds to create defective characters: a palsied man, a blind man, a lame man, a moron, barren woman, and a sexless creature.[10] Enki creates societal roles for these imperfect humans: the palsied man, who cannot grasp a weapon, stands at the king's head; the blind man is a musician, the lame man is a smith, the moron (who is no threat) also stands at the head of the king, the barren woman can be a weaver in the queen's household, and the sexless man is a courtier. Enki has proven his point, and Ninmah stops her act of creation. However, Enki then goes a step further, daring Ninmah to find a role for the creature that *he* could create. Enki, who has no womb, asks for a woman to whom he can entrust his semen. But without Ninmah's help, the embryo cannot develop properly, the woman aborts, and Umul is born, probably extremely immature. He cannot eat or lie down, and Ninmah says that she cannot care for him. Enki points out that he was able to find roles for Ninmah's misbegotten creatures, and Ninmah recognizes that she has been defeated. At this point, Enki is gracious and magnanimous. He points out that Umul cannot be helped precisely because he was made without the good services of Ninmah, and he declares that Umul should be a reminder that whenever people praise phallic power (which, he says, they should), they should also remember Ninmah's role. Despite this speech of Enki, Enki has clearly won his challenge, and the balance between the forces has shifted. The poet concludes with the statement that Ninmah did not equal the great lord Enki.

The subsequent accounts of the creation of humankind show the continuing rise of Enki (later called by his Akkadian name, Ea). The Atrahasis Myth was written in Akkadian during the Old Babylonian period, sometime before the main version that we have, a dated three-tablet copy made by a junior scribe during the reign of Ammisaduqa of Babylon (ca. 1500 B.C.E.). This myth is a "primeval history": it begins before the creation of humankind and ends with the re-creation after the flood. The story of the creation is very similar to that of Enki and Ninmah. The gods are laboring, digging the Tigris and Euphrates rivers. Their work is difficult, and finally they decide to strike, and menacingly surround the house of Enlil. Enlil convenes the divine council, and after the striking gods hold fast and refuse to reveal the ringleader of the revolt, Enki suggests that they create a substitute worker to relieve the gods. The council summons the mother-goddess, but she surprisingly replies, "It is not properly mine to do these things, this work belongs to Enki."[11] Enki then conceives a plan and the time to carry it out. He gives her the clay and has the gods slaughter an (otherwise unknown) god who has rationality. Mami ("mommy"), the mother-goddess, mixes the blood with the clay and divides the result into fourteen pieces, reciting an incantation as Enki prompts her. She has fourteen birth-goddesses come to shape the clay and sits counting the nine months, after which she performs the midwifery required. After the gods acclaim her as the creatrix of humanity, the text here interrupts the narrative to inform the hearers that they are to leave the birthing brick in place for a week (or nine days) and give honor to the mother-goddess whenever a baby is born. There is great praise for the mother in this account of creation, but the role of Enki is still quite considerable.

The last stage in the creation of humankind is reached by the Myth of Enuma Elish—the tale of the exaltation of Marduk written in the latter half of the second millennium, a myth that became the great state myth of Babylon. This text relates how the young god Marduk, Ea's son, became the king of all the gods, and proceeded to create the world. As the culminating benefit that this new king bestowed on the gods, he had an artful idea: to create man to be charged with the service of the gods. Ea then conceives a plan and creates humanity from the blood of a slain god:

> . . . Ea, the wise, had created humankind,
> had imposed upon it the service of the gods—

*that work was beyond comprehension;*
*as artfully planned by Marduk, Nudimmud created it.*[12]

In this composition, the clay and the mother who uses it are gone. Ea is the sole creator of humanity, and he is given a special name, Nudimmud, "the man-creator."

These versions of the creation do not replace each other The traditions of the creation of humanity by the mother-goddess do not disappear. Popular ritual commemorates the mother at births, and later scholarly compositions make allusion to "creatures whose clay Aruru took in her fingers."[13] Her role in the bringing of fertility is remembered in the Vassal Treaties of King Esarhaddon of Assyria, which includes among the curses against whoever breaks the covenant the imprecation that Belit-ili should put an end to giving birth in his land.[14] Similarly, the combined role of Enki/Ea and the mother-goddess found in the Atrahasis myth is maintained in this myth itself, for Atrahasis endures throughout Mesopotamian history, and new versions of it are found in the library of Ashurbanipal in Assyria (circa 600 B.C.E.). All the traditions are combined in another scholarly composition, which refers to "Narru (Enlil), king of the gods, who created humankind, and majestic Zulummar (Ea), who dug out their clay, and mistress Mami, who fashioned them."[15] The traditions continue, but each successive layer is a record of an ongoing religious development, of new philosophical sensibilities that view the world in a different light.

This new sensibility that develops in the second millennium clearly sees a world of gods in which all the major figures are male. This viewpoint is encapsulated in the Enuma Elish Myth, from whose account of the creation of humanity the mother goddess is conspicuously absent. There is a mother figure in this myth: Ti'amat, the primordial mother, "she who gave birth to all." Her role in this myth is very revealing, for she represents the ancient order which Marduk must defeat in order to become king of the gods. Ti'amat is not an evil force. When her husband Apsu wanted to fight in order to stem the tide of change in the world of the gods, Ti'amat refused to join him, reacting as a protective mother: "What, should we destroy that we have built? Their ways indeed are most troublesome, but let us be patient."[16] After Apsu has been vanquished, Ti'amat tries to reestablish the old tranquil order, to avenge the death of her husband, and to bring relief to the many gods who want rest. Ti'amat forms an army and appoints a commander-in-chief, frightening the gods of the pantheon, who perceive her might and cannot do battle with her. At this point Marduk, Ea's son, steps forth from the young generation of gods. He is willing to fight her, and does not recognize her might: "what male is it who has pressed his fight against you? . . . Ti'amat, a woman, flies at you with weapons."[17] Marduk defeats Ti'amat in single combat, and becomes king of the gods. From her body, Marduk creates the world and organizes the cosmos as a divine state. We live in the body of the mother, but she has neither activity nor power.

Ultimately, with the establishment of the royal imperial states of Assyria and Babylonia, the Enuma Elish became a royal ritual.[18] The kings began to reenact the part of Marduk in the military and kingly role related by the Enuma Elish. They participated in the right of Marduk to rule and in the proving and bestowal of this right. Thus the later kings took part in a ritual that celebrated stability rather than fertility, order rather than union, monarchy rather than renewal. In such a ritual, women and goddesses could have no role other than as the mother to be deposed.

The royal sacred marriage did not entirely disappear. The myth with which it was associated, the tale of Dumuzi and Inanna, had a very long life. Special songs for Inanna/Ishtar and Dumuzi were still recited in the first millenium, and even the women of Jerusalem were still weeping for Tammuz (Dumuzi) in the times of Ezekiel. But this cult as a whole was no longer state-centered or run, and became a matter for private rather than public worship. A ritual of union between the gods Marduk and Nabu and their spouses was practiced in the temples after the Old Babylonian period, but it was dramatically altered. In these later sacred marriages, a king no longer played the part of the god. Indeed, no humans were involved in the conjugal union. The statues of the gods were brought to a garden (perhaps in procession), hymns were sung, and the statues were left there together overnight.[19] This ritual seems to lack the excitement and the glamour of the Sumerian sacred marriage. More importantly, by the fact that it lacks the human component, it cannot serve to bring people or kings into any particular relationship with the divine. Human sexuality has lost its power to express the congress of the gods except as a vague idea; and the interchange between divine and human is completely lost.

The whole complex of divine kingship, the use of the divine titles, the object of offerings, and even the writing of hymns, all these started to disappear in the Old Babylonian period. The kings of Isin and Larsa (the Early Old Babylonian period) still claimed the special spouse-relationship with Inanna.[20] However, the time of Hammurabi was clearly the dawn of a new sensibility. Not only does Hammurabi not use the divine title "god," even though royal hymns still attribute it to him, but he counts his ancestry from early Amorites rather than from gods. After the Old Babylonian period, even royal hymns disappear.

This change in sensibility may be reflected mythologically in the Gilgamesh Epic. In this tale, written during the Old Babylonian period, Ishtar has become attracted to Gilgamesh, the mighty king of Uruk, and offers to marry him. He however, bluntly refuses and recites an unflattering account of the fate of Ishtar's husbands. In the context of the story, Gilgamesh, who is descended form Lugalbanda and the goddess Ninsun, has rejected the world of the gods. All his actions in the rest of the epic belie his divine origins. He has fantastic adventures, but he remains the representative of every mortal man. His very quest for immortality shows his involvement in the human dilemma. Gilgamesh the king becomes the paradigm of humanity rather than the stepping-stone to the world of the gods. In the broader context of religious history, the rejection of Ishtar may be a reflection of the rejection of the entire philosophy of kingship of the Akkadian and Ur III periods. During the Old Babylonian period, the sacred marriage disappeared, and with it, all the ideas of divinity-in-kingship.

This is not to say that future Mesopotamian kings no longer had any need to differentiate themselves from the people nor to claim special status as warrant for their authority. The Gilgamesh Epic says of Gilgamesh, born of a divine mother and a god-king father, that "his body was the flesh-kin of the gods," and this kinship is also claimed by Tukulti-Ninurta, the king who marks the beginning of Assyrian power.[21] Tukulti-Ninurta is also described as the "image" (ṣalam) of the god Enlil, and this concept of the god's image becomes an attribute of later kings—and only of kings. It is a term of authority, and indicates that the king is god's counterpart on earth.[22] It does not indicate that the king himself belongs to the divine world. As in so many areas of religious thought, the goddesses are no longer prominent in the metaphysics of kingship. They no longer have anything to do with the king's special status, nor are they the king's pathway to the world of the divine.

There is only one goddess who escaped this eclipse: Ishtar (Inanna) not only did not disappear, but continued to grow in importance. Ishtar/Inanna was not easily eradicated. As an unencumbered woman, she could not easily be relegated to the domestic sphere. Her role as representative of sexual attraction could not be taken over by a male god in any way that would be meaningful to the males of ancient Mesopotamia. As goddess of warfare, she maintained and even increased her prominence during the warfare-laden periods of state formation and empire building. This was particularly true in Assyria, whose kings modeled themselves in many ways on the ancient Sargonic kings of Akkadian times. Ishtar, the patron deity of Agade whom Enheduanna had exalted and magnified in ancient Sumerian poetry, was revered in Assyria as "the one who smites the weapons of the enemy." Ishtar was the "manly" goddess, the exception that proved the rule about females. Ultimately, she became a "Great Goddess" to whom was attributed a wide variety of attributes and characteristics, including those of the mother-goddess.

This does not mean that Ishtar was easily loved. On the one hand, she was glorified and exalted as preeminent among gods and men. But she was, to put it mildly, intimidating and frightening. Even her very sexual attractiveness inspired fear, and men expressed their dread that such lust might lead to their doom. Alongside hymns to Ishtar's glory and preeminence, we also find negative portrayals and ultimately a demonization of her image. In the Old Babylonian Gilgamesh Epic, when Gilgamesh refuses Ishtar's propositions he is, in part, renouncing the Sumerian sacred marriage in which kings did become Ishtar's lovers and received through this union blessings and prosperity.[23] Inanna then takes revenge so wantonly destructive that it suggests that this Babylonian epic intends a conscious repudiation and vilification of Ishtar.[24] A similar negative portrayal of Ishtar is found in the Old Babylonian Agushaya Hymn, which portrays Ishtar as so indiscriminately wild and ferocious that the gods cannot control her. Anti-Ishtar feelings persist and focus either on the ferocity of her rage[25] or on the dramatic excesses of her cult in Uruk.[26] Antipathy to Ishtar takes its extreme (though perhaps unconscious) form in the depiction of Lamashtu, the demon who kills newborn children. This demon, daughter of An, shares many characteristics of Ishtar, from her loose hair, to her restlessness, to her association with lions, and may very well be the fearsome side of Ishtar's character split off and demonized into a separate character, an evil doppelganger to the mighty goddess.[27]

Ishtar-bashing is not universal: the Old Babylonian period also produced the beautiful hymn "To the Goddess, Sing,"[28] which talks only about the great grace, beauty, and joy that Ishtar brings. Similarly, later hymns also concentrate on the glory, beauty, and kindness of Ishtar. It is this deep ambivalence towards the powerful sexy female that makes Ishtar such a compelling figure.

By the end of the second millennium, the religious thinkers of Mesopotamia saw the cosmos as controlled and regulated by male gods, with only Ishtar maintaining a position of power. When we see such a pattern of theological change, we must ask whether the religious imagery is leading society, or whether it is following socioeconomic development? Was the supplanting of goddesses in Sumerian religious texts an inner theological development that resulted purely from the tendency to view the world of the gods on the model of an imperial state in which women paid no real political role?[29] Or does it follow in the wake of sociological change, of the development of what might be called "patriarchy"? And if the latter is true, is the change in the world of the gods contemporary to the changes in human society, or does it lag behind it by hundreds of years? To these questions we really have no answer. The general impression that we get from Sumerian texts is that at least some women had a more prominent role than was possible in the succeeding Babylonian and Assyrian periods of Mesopotamian history. But developments within the 600-year period covered by Sumerian literature are more difficult to detect. One slight clue might (very hesitantly) be furnished by a royal document called the Reforms of Uruinimgina." Uruinimgina (whose name is read Urukagina in earlier scholarly literature) was a king of Lagash around 2350 B.C.E. As a nondynastic successor to the throne, he had to justify his power, and wrote a "reform" text in which he related how bad matters were before he became king and described the new reforms that he instituted in order to pursue social justice. Among them we read, "the women of the former days used to take two husbands, but the women of today (if they attempt to do this) are stoned with the stones inscribed with their evil intent." Polyandry (if it ever really existed) has been supplanted by monogamy and occasional polygyny.[30]

In early Sumer, royal women had considerable power. In early Lagash, the wives of the governors managed the large temple estates.[31] The dynasty of Kish was founded by Enmebaragesi, a contemporary of Gilgamesh, who it now appears may have been a woman;[32] later, another woman, Kubaba the tavern lady, became ruler of Kish and founded a dynasty that lasted a hundred years. We do not know how important politically the position of En priestess of Ur was, but it was a high position, occupied by royal women at least from the time of Enheduanna, daughter of Sargon (circa 2300 B.C.E.), and through the time of the sister of Warad-Sin and Rim-Sin of Larsa in the second millennium.[33] The prominence of individual royal women continued throughout the third dynasty of Ur.[34] By contrast, women have very little role to play in the latter half of the second millennium; and in first millennium texts, as in those of the Assyrian period, they are practically invisible.

We do not know all the reasons for this decline. It would be tempting to attribute it to the new ideas brought in by new people with the mass immigration of the West Semites into Mesopotamia at the start of the second millennium. However, this cannot be the true origin. The city of Mari on the Euphrates in Syria around 1800 B.C.E. was a site inhabited to a great extent by West Semites. In the documents from this site, women (again, royal women) played a role in religion and politics that was not less than that played by Sumerian women of the Ur III period (2111–1950 B.C.E.).[35] The causes for the change in women's position is not ethnically based. The dramatic decline of women's visibility does not take place until well into the Old Babylonian period (circa 1600 B.C.E.), and may be function of the change from city-states to larger nation-states and the changes in the social and economic systems that this entailed.

The eclipse of the goddesses was undoubtedly part of the same process that witnessed a decline in the public role of women, with both reflective of fundamental changes in society that we cannot yet specify. The existence and power of a goddess, particularly of Ishtar, is no indication or guarantee of a high status for human women. In Assyria, where Ishtar was so prominent, women were not. The texts rarely mention any individual women, and, according to the Middle Assyrian laws, married women were to be veiled, had no rights to their husband's property (even to movable goods), and could be struck or mutilated by their husbands at will. Ishtar, the female with the fundamental attributes of manhood, does not enable women to transcend their femaleness. In her being and her cult (where she changes men into women and women into men), she provides an outlet for strong feelings about gender, but in the final analysis, she is the supporter and maintainer of the gender order. The world by the end of the second millennium was a male's world, above and below; and the ancient goddesses have all but disappeared.

# PART II

In the Absence
of Goddesses

*Biblical Transformations*

# 8

## Israel and the Master of the Universe

The books of the Bible, written and shaped during a period of a thousand years,[1] witness the formation and development of the social institutions and religious ideas of ancient Israel. Israel grew out of the cultures the ancient Near East. The language and style of biblical poetry continues the traditions of ancient Canaan,[2] the laws are a part of the cuneiform legal tradition,[3] the wisdom literature shares many characteristics with wisdom literature from Egypt and Mesopotamia.[4] Many Israelite ideas about justice, society, and even religion developed from and in counterpoint to Mesopotamian ideas.[5] Ultimately, however, Israel developed a religious system essentially different from any of the great ancient Near Eastern systems, a system which proclaimed the importance of only one God and the irrelevance or nonexistence of all other divine powers. This biblical system, known as monotheism, is the central feature of the Western religions.

There are numerous scholarly disputes about the origin of Israel and of her central ideas. The Bible itself tells a simple "native" view of Israel's sacred history: the Pentateuch relates how God brought Israel out of Egypt, revealed Himself at Mt. Sinai, made a covenant with the people in which they promised to worship God alone, and gave Israel its laws and cultic rituals. The historical books continue: Israel entered the land of Canaan, en masse, bearing this pure monotheist faith. Contact with the pagan nations surrounding Israel brought trouble, for the people were continually tempted into apostasy, worshiped foreign gods, and adopted foreign practices and beliefs to create a "syncretistic" religion.

This picture of the origin of monotheism is undoubtedly skewed. It has been shaped by Israel's desire to understand and justify the fall of Israel in 722 B.C.E. and of Judah in 587 B.C.E., and the accusations of infidelity and apostasy with which these books attack the people is part of their soul-searching and self-blame for the great catastrophe that befell them. Early Israelite poetry shows that in the early stages of biblical religion, Israel believed in other divine beings, none of whom could compare to YHWH. They form the council that declares God's glory in Psalm 29; they are entrusted with the nations of the earth in Deuteronomy 32. These other beings form the divine background and context for the actions of YHWH; they themselves are not comparable to God.[6] They were not to be worshiped independently, for Israel owed allegiance only to YHWH. As time went on, the religious thinkers of Israel developed a more refined monotheism and redefined the cosmos. They emptied the heavens of lesser deities and progressively rid Israel of all elements in their ancient traditions that no longer fit their new religious sensibilities. These they denounced as idolatrous and foreign.[7]

There are several mythological passages in the Bible that present this ascent of YHWH to power and dominance. Those which use the ancient myth of the sea celebrate the kingship of YHWH and his supremacy over the world.[8] To give one example, the brief Psalm 93 alludes to all the major themes that Israel expressed in its cosmogonic story: the kingship of YHWH, YHWH's supremacy over the waters, the establishment of the world, and the presence of the temple.

> The Lord is king: he is robed in grandeur.
> The Lord is robed, he is girded with strength.
> The world stands firm: it cannot be shaken.
>
> Your throne stands firm from of old,
> from eternity you have existed.
>
> The ocean sounds, O Lord,
> the ocean sounds its thunder,
> the ocean sounds its pounding.
>
> Above the thunder of the mighty waters,
> more majestic than the breakers of the sea
> is the Lord, majestic on high.
>
> Your decrees are indeed enduring,
> holiness befits your house, O Lord,
> For all times.

Here YHWH is supreme, occupying the same place in cosmological thinking that Marduk had in Babylon.⁹ But this is only the first stage in the rise of YHWH: the star actor has changed, but the cosmic play remains the same. Israel adds another factor: because of what God has done for Israel, Israel owes God exclusive allegiance. As we will see in the following chapter, this demand for exclusive allegiance ultimately led to the disappearance of all other gods. Psalm 82 is a mythical rendering of the advent of monotheism[10]:

> *God stands in the divine assembly:*
> *among the divine beings He pronounces judgment.*
> *"How long will you judge perversely,*
> *showing favor to the wicked? (For I said),*
> *'Judge the wretched and the orphan,*
> *vindicate the lowly and the poor;*
> *rescue the wretched and the needy,*
> *save them from the hand of the wicked.'*
>
> *They (the gods) neither know nor understand,*
> *they go about in darkness—*
> *all the foundations of the earth totter.*
>
> *I had taken you for gods, sons of the most high, all of*
> *   you.*
> *But you shall die as men do, fall like any prince."*
>
> *Arise O God, judge the earth*
> *for all the nations are your possession.*

This psalm visualizes the moment of the transition to monotheism. At its beginning, God is the leader of a council of gods; at its end, all the gods die and God must reign alone.

The development of monotheism is not simply a form of subtraction. Eliminating other gods and jettisoning old religious practices changes fundamental ideas about the workings of the cosmos. The image of God must expand to include all the functions previously encompassed by an entire pantheon. The religious and philosophical systems must adapt to form a coherent picture of the universe that no longer includes multiple divine powers. The biblical system had to replace both goddesses and gods, and as it did so, it transformed its thinking about nature, culture, gender, and humanity.

In ancient religion, "Nature" reflects an interplay of divine forces and personages. Gods may battle each other, as when the Canaanite goddess Anat defeats Mot, and they may join together, as do the Sumerian Inanna and Dumuzi in the sacred marriage. Gods bring disaster because they envy other gods, as does the Babylonian Irra. Or they cooperate in bestowing blessings on humanity or the king. The relationships between these gods are not static. There is no one polytheism; gods gain and lose their relative status. Pagan religion is characterized by change and flux.[11] On an individual level, the powers and persona of one god can be absorbed by another; functions attributed to one patron may gradually move into the sphere of influence of another. On a macro level, there are clear patterns of development in ancient Near Eastern religion: new gods like Marduk and Nabu took over, fathers were displaced by younger males (the Canaanite El by Ba'al, Anu by Enlil and then by Marduk), male gods took over functions and powers once held by goddesses, the universe was increasingly portrayed as a state headed by a divine king. Nevertheless, despite the fluidity of the individual elements in the apparently ever-changing pagan picture of the universe, the conceptualization of nature does not really change in any fundamental way: as long as powers are shared among the gods, some powers can shift from one to another without changing the overall picture. Throughout the history of polytheism, the universe was always understood as a balance of interactive forces. Nature is an arena of powers and forces in interaction, and the drama "out there" among those various forces determines the condition of the world. Human myths and rituals enable people to operate in this many-directional system, so that they can collaborate with first one god, then another; so that they can help the gods come together and celebrate this union; or so that they can play one god off against another.

No such stratagems could operate in biblical Israel. Israel could not pit one god against another, or ask one god to intercede with another, for the core idea of ancient Israel is the exclusive worship of one God. According to the Bible's understanding, Israel owes all its loyalty and worship to the god who brought the people out of Egypt. Until the eighth or seventh century B.C.E., biblical writers did not categorically deny the existence of other gods. But these deities belonged to other nations: for Israel, there is only YHWH.[12] As we would expect, YHWH, Israel's God, took the supreme position over the pantheon that the young male gods, Ba'al and Marduk, held in polytheism.[13] Moreover, in the monotheist leap, "He" also absorbed all the character and functions of the female goddesses. As a result, the dynamic interactions between the polytheistic gods disappeared into the unity of One. Relations between gods can no longer control the world, and nature, no less than culture and humanity, has to be rethought.

The Bible mandates the exclusive worship of only one God and describes the relationship between Israel and God in terms of a "covenant" between Israel and God. Such covenants were well-known in the diplomacy of the ancient Near East, and Israel utilizes the structure and terminology of these ancient treaties to express its special politicolegal relationship to God.[14] Israel believed that it had been redeemed from Egypt and "saved" by God. As a result, it forever owed God exclusive loyalty. God, moreover, demanded this exclusivity: "You shall have no other gods before me."[15] Israel must not acknowledge or worship other gods: no other god counts, no other god has any claim over Israel, and to serve other gods is to be unfaithful to the all-embracing bond between YHWH and Israel. YHWH alone matters.

There is a promise along with this obligation: in turn for their exclusive loyalty, God will protect and bring blessings upon the people. This bargain is expressed succinctly at the conclusion of the collection of laws known as the Book of the Covenant:

> (When you come to the land) you should not bow down to
> their gods nor worship them nor do as their deeds.
> . . . You shall serve the Lord your God, and He will
> bless your bread and your water.
> And I will remove illness from your midst.
> No woman in your land shall miscarry or be barren,
> and I will give you the full count of your days.
> I will send forth My terror before you,
> and I will throw into panic all the people
> among whom you come,
> and I will make all your enemies
> turn tail before you.[16]

This passage declares that the one God who is to be worshiped can meet all human needs. This is a radically new idea—though worshiping only one god is not in itself new. Within polytheism, crisis situations might impel people temporarily to focus all their energies on one deity. Such a situation prevails in the Atrahasis Epic. As the plague is decimating humanity, Ea declares, "Do not worship your God, do not reverence your goddess. Build a temple to the god Namtar and bring offerings to him, and so induce him to lift the plague."[17] Later, when the drought afflicts humanity, Ea suggests a similar stratagem of worshiping only Adad, God of the rains. In the Atrahasis Epic the intelligent man worships only the one god who has the power to control the situation in which the worshiper finds himself. Worshiping *only* that god induces him to use his power to the benefit of the worshiper. In Atrahasis, the suggestion of exclusive worship of one deity is a temporary response to an emergency situation; in the Bible, it is a permanent demand. The expectation of appropriate reward is nevertheless the same; and Israel cannot commit to worshiping only one God unless that God—all alone—can control the environment so that Israel can thrive in the land. This does not have to imply complete philosophical monotheism,[18] but it leads inexorably to monotheist thinking. The needs of people that used to be met by a whole pantheon of deities still have to be met. If YHWH is the only power that can be addressed, YHWH must be able to provide for all the needs of the people. In this passage from Exodus, God promises to grant the people military victory, agricultural abundance, health, and procreation; in sum, all the requirements for the good life.

God first promises victory. A national god can do no less, and a god without the power to lead a people to victory cannot demand that people's allegiance. In biblical traditions, the victory over Egypt at the dawn of Israel's history established God's credentials as a mighty warrior on the scene of history. Nevertheless, the powers of military might and victory, of kingship and judgeship are not enough: YHWH must be able to control *everything* that YHWH's people might need. The covenant of loyalty must imply the sufficiency of YHWH. The other blessings in Exodus 23 concern the fundamentals of physical well-being: fertility, health, progeny, long life, and victory. All these are God's to grant, to offer as reward for fidelity.

This biblical covenant of loyalty assumes the sufficiency of the one God. To us, who have been taught monotheism for thousands of years, this statement may seem self-evident, and may therefore pass by unnoticed. But in ancient Israel—in the context of the ancient world—it is a radical, even a revolutionary, concept. Gone is the chorus of cosmic powers: all the forces essential to human survival are brought under one umbrella, placed under the control of one will. God is master of nature: all of Israel's well-being depends on one God, and this one God has the power to fulfill all hopes and expectations. When the Bible understands YHWH as mastering not only *most* but *all* of the powers of the universe, the picture of the universe changes dramatically. There is a quantum leap, a fundamental change in paradigm. Interaction among the gods is replaced by solo mastery, and humanity, divinity, and cosmos have to be realigned. The aggregation of these powers leads inexorably to monotheism, to solo mastery and sole presence in the divine order.

In order to serve the purposes and functions of an entire pantheon, the one God of Israel absorbs many types of powers. Each power comes from a different source, and may have had its own unique history in pagan thought. Ultimately, in the Bible, they all end up in the same place, as part of God's bounty. The blessings that God promises in the convenantal statement of Exodus 23:25–26 illustrate the various paths by which YHWH became sole master. Together, these provide the essential blessings of physical well-being: water and food, healing and procreation. Individually, they each have a different polytheistic ancestry. Rain is always considered a male power within Near Eastern polytheism; agricultural fertility is thought to result from the collective activity of male and female deities acting in concert (or consort); healing, once female, becomes associated with male gods during the second millennium, and procreation remains essentially female. AS YHWH appropriates each of these powers, the image of divine mastery emerges, with all its consequences for the conceptualization of nature and humanity.

In Near Eastern polytheism, the young male ruler-gods Ba'al and Marduk were masters of the storm. In the texts known from Ugarit, the Canaanite Ba'al is said to appoint wet and snowy seasons, and to send thunder and lightning.[19] The earliest biblical texts also describe YHWH as rain god.[20] Ba'al is called *rkb 'rpt*, "rider of the clouds," the same phrase used for Yah in Psalm 68. The accounts of God's victory over Israel's foes are often described in imagery befitting a warrior storm-god, for in these mythologically based poems, the storm is the weapon with which the god gains victory. The storm-god, moreover, has a role beyond that of divine warrior, for he is also master of the beneficial rains. Both Ba'al and YHWH are praised for their role as rainmaker, and God's mastery over the rain is one of the fundamental precepts of biblical religion. Poetic passages praise God for the fertilizing rains, and the narratives show that God could bring rain to prove his greatness. As one example, when Samuel delivers his farewell address at Saul's coronation, he invites God to prove God's kingship by producing a thunderstorm during the time of the wheat harvest (in June, after the end of the rainy season). When the people see this rain, they acclaim God as sovereign king.[21] The celebrated contest between Elijah and the priests of Ba'al also revolves around mastery over the rain. In response to Elijah, God sends a thunderbolt to burn up the sacrifice and then brings rain to the drought-filled land.[22]

The emphasis on God's power over rain arises for two reasons. First, Israel cannot ignore a central claim of Canaanite religion, that Ba'al is master of rain and thunderstorm. YHWHism had to match the claims of Ba'alism in order to rival and supplant it. Beyond this, there is a significant ecological reason that *both* Canaan and Israel portray their chief god as master of the fertilizing rains. Unlike the riverine cultures of Mesopotamia and Egypt (with their large irrigation systems), fertility in Israel and Canaan depends directly on rainfall. The hills of Israel cannot be watered from the Jordan river. The people cannot control the bringing of water to the fields and must rely on rainfall. This creates a sense of continual vulnerability, for the Bible believes that God is directly and continually involved in the giving of rainfall. Israel is well aware of its particular environmental situation:

> For the land which you are coming into to possess
> is not like the land of Egypt from which you
>     have come,
> where you planted your seed and watered with your feet
>     like a vegetable garden.
> The land which you are crossing into to occupy
>     is a land of hills and valleys, drinking its water from the rain
>     of the sky.
> This is a land which the Lord your God has to keep an eye on,
> from the beginning to the end of the year.[23]

Israel's vulnerability was intensified by recurrent drought.[24] Even in the Bible's retelling of its protohistory, the ancestor stories of Genesis, drought is a recurrent theme. The confrontation of Elijah and the prophets of Ba'al is carried out during a time of major drought, and YHWH's intervention then ends that drought. The Bible has exquisitely beautiful but painful descriptions of drought:

> The country is ravaged,
> the ground must mourn . . .
> The vine has dried up,
> the fig tree withers.
> Pomegranate, palm, and apple—
> all the trees of the field are sere.

*And joy has dried up among men . . .*
*for food is cut off*
*before our very eyes.*
*And joy and gladness*
*from the House of our Lord. . . .*
*How the beasts groan! . . .*
*the very beasts of the field cry out to you*
*for the watercourses are dried up*
*and fire has consumed the pastures in the wilderness.*[25]

Israel's vulnerability to drought makes it imperative that Israel's God YHWH be in charge of the rain. The attribution of rain to God did not require a revolutionary change in the conceptualization of rain. Dominion over weather and storm belonged first to Enlil and then to Marduk. In Canaan, it belongs to Baal; in Israel, it is claimed by YHWH. The takeover by YHWH is a simple shift of allegiance.

A more significant reorientation accompanies the assertion that YHWH can provide the second blessing of Exodus 23:24–26, the blessing of agricultural abundance (blessing the bread). Agricultural fertility is a matter of vital concern to the peoples of the ancient world, who cannot take fertility for granted and believe that fertility is fragile. Ancient religions provide a way to participate in the creation of fertile abundance and to ensure its continuation. They address a human desire to do everything possible to make the earth fertile and to make the crops grow. In Mesopotamian thinking, labor is divinely ordained and, indeed, the purpose for which humans were created. The gods give humankind the tools of labor and instruct the people on their use.[26] Actual work, however, is only one sphere of activity. The ancient pagan religions also provided a cult of fertility in which people sang, danced, and performed other rituals in order to experience and aid the perpetuation of nature.

It was not ignorance that impelled people to perform these rituals, for they were practiced long after the neolithic revolution, long after the ancients learned that if you put a seed in the ground it will grow, long after people domesticated plants and animals to ensure their food supply. But the ancient farmers were also very aware that sometimes you could put a seed in the ground and it wouldn't grow. The ground might be too saline, or the birds might eat the seed, or locusts might devour the growing plants, the weather conditions might not be right, the earth might have become contaminated. There are so many reasons that a seed might not grow that it is a miracle every time it really does so. Pagan religions celebrated this miracle by offering a ritual life through which one can participate in this miracle. Of course. the fertility ritual does not really "cause" fertility—if it could, rituals would not have to be repeated. But in performing these rituals, the celebrants acknowledge their dependence on fertility and their desire to participate in assuring the continuation of the natural cycle.

Pagan prayers and rituals reflect the idea that fertile abundance is the result of harmonious interaction among various powers in the cosmos. Cultic acts and liturgy may propitiate the various divine powers and facilitate their joining together. In Sumerian cult, this conjoining was achieved sexually in the ritual of the sacred marriage. In later periods, even when sacred marriage was no longer part of the official state cult, it clearly continued in sacred and popular literature. Was there ever a time in which fertility and vegetation were thought to come directly from the womb of the earth mother? This claim, very often assumed in modern recreations of paganism, can only be true (if at all) for the prehistoric period. There may be prehistoric evidence from Old Europe and possibly from Çatal Hüyük that the mother-goddess had this vital function and the all-powerful position that results from it.[27] The historical evidence, from the writings of Sumer and Babylon, indicates that the conceptualization of fertility was much more complex than the simple idea of earth mother and her womb. There are certainly goddesses of vegetation, and the breast of the goddess Nisaba is sometimes considered the source of grain. But more common are the many indications that fertility required many gods, and that no one god was able to insure it. Agricultural abundance depended on an interaction of forces and their divine embodiments, upon the fertility of the earth and its fertilization by water, and upon the joining of the power of life with the exercise of agriculture. This conjoining of forces could be aided by sexual activities on the fertile bed, sexual intercourse into the body of the young nubile goddesses. Even when sexual union is not part of the ritual, this union of forces is the essential metaphysical idea.

Like the other Near Eastern peoples, Israel was concerned with fertility. In order to feel secure on the land, the people must be assured of God's power to ensure fertility. However, the biblical understanding of fertility is radically different from that of ancient Near Eastern polytheism. Israelite prayer and ritual cannot facilitate the union of the forces of the cosmos; only the worship of one God is allowed. Therefore, God alone must unite all the forces that produce fertility. God must be the only power who brings fertility, and God alone must be enough.

To the Bible, God's fertility-bringing power lies in God's power over the rain. The natural state of the earth is fertile: it needs only the rain to activate this natural potential. The creation account in Genesis 1, placed at the opening of the Bible, incorporates this biblical view of the earth's fertility. There, on day one, the creation of light ends the first stage of creation; on the second day as well, one item is created, a firmament that separates the waters. The next stage, on day three, is a condensation, or contraction of the diffuse water that fills the now-bounded universe: the earthly waters, the seas, are gathered together, leaving dry sections, the earth. God marks the end of this phase of creation by pronouncing this new division good, but the creation of dry land and sea does not end the third day. On the very same day that the earth is created, God also creates the plants and the trees. This double creation on the third day emphasizes the significance of the fact that on the very same day that God creates the earth, God makes the earth fertile. There never was, not even for one day, a time that the earth was barren. Furthermore, the vegetation that God creates on this third day is self-propagating, each bearing seed after its own kind. The earth is made fertile in such a way as to insure that it will remain so.

These is a serious religious message in this recitation: there is no need for humans to focus concern on the creation or continuation of this fertility. Just as people do not have to think about helping the sun to rise, because God created it to rise and set, so too they do not have to think about helping the earth to be fertile, for this is the way it was created. Human beings do not have to worry about perpetuating and continuing any of the elements that God creates. As master of creation, God has the power to keep creation going. God's mastery over the physical universe, epitomized in the creative word, is so powerful that we can assume that this universe will continue without our active efforts towards this end.

This view of earthly fertility is not limited to Genesis 1.[28] All the major festivals of Israel, which originally celebrated the barley, wheat, and grape harvests, are transmuted in the Bible to festivals by which the Israelite could celebrate, participate in, and give thanks for the sacred history that began with the Exodus and culminated with the acquisition of the land of Israel. An ancient harvest ritual recorded in Deuteronomy 26[29] prescribes a thanksgiving at harvest time. Every Israelite was to take a basket of first fruits to the priest, and announce, "I acknowledge this day before the Lord your God that I have entered the land which the Lord swore to our fathers to give us. . . ." The priest would then take the basket and set it down in front of the altar of the Lord. At this point, each individual Israelite recited a passage that was apparently expected to be known by all:

> *My father was a wandering Aramean. He went down to*
> *Egypt with meager numbers and sojourned there, but*
> *there he became a great and very populous nation. The*
> *Egyptians dealt harshly with us . . . we cried unto the*
> *Lord the God of our fathers . . . and the Lord heard our*
> *plea and saw our plight. . . . The Lord freed us from Egypt*
> *by a mighty had, by an outstretched arm and awesome*
> *power . . . he brought us to this place and gave us this*
> *land, a land flowing with milk and honey. Wherefore I*
> *now bring the first fruits of the soil which you, O*
> *Lord, have given me.*[30]

In this harvest prayer, Israel offers thanksgiving by reciting how it got to the land. There is a conspicuous absence here: there is no awe, reverence, or gratitude for the fertility of the soil and its bountiful harvest. Indeed, the ability of the earth to grow harvest is assumed rather than celebrated. Awe and thanksgiving are offered for the gift of the land of Israel rather than for its fertility. God's action in history by which God gave Israel the land is recited and commemorated; the fertility of this land is completely taken for granted. In this harvest ritual, as also in the creation account of Genesis 1, that is no need to pray for, ritually work for, or even worry about the ability of the earth to bear, for fertility is its characteristic and natural state.

While biblical texts do not direct human attention to invoking fertility, they do caution that this pristine state of the earth can be disrupted. The world can become polluted, and a contaminated world is less fertile. Three cardinal misdeeds physically pollute the land: murder, improper sexual activity, and idolatry.[31] Such pollution renders the land infertile and makes life on earth (or in the land of Israel) impossible. The dangers of ever-decreasing fertility are dramatically revealed in Israel's presentation of the flood story in the primeval history in Genesis 1–9.[32] As soon as Cain kills Abel, he is told: "When you till the ground it shall no longer yield its strength to you: a wanderer and a vagabond you will be on the earth."[33] By the tenth generation, at the birth of Noah, the barrenness of the ground had become widespread, and Noah was given his name because "this one will comfort us (alternatively "give us rest"[34])from our work and the toil of our hands *because of the ground which God has cursed.*"[35] God, seeing the polluted earth, brings the flood. Afterwards, in order to prevent the earth from becoming so polluted again, God gives humanity its first laws.[36] Unless the earth becomes polluted, there is no reason to be concerned with its fertility. And if the earth does become polluted, there is nothing that anyone can do to avert the consequences. There is no ritual to purify the earth, no way to beg God to ignore or remove the pollution.[37] Instead, the pollution builds up until it reaches a critical mass, when the earth explodes or the land of Israel vomits out its inhabitants.[38] In the absence of such disastrous pollution, the earth is an inherently fertile constant. The variable is the rain. The addition of rain potentiates the inherently fertile nature of the earth and determines whether there is actual fertility. In this way, God's fructifying rain makes God the master of all agricultural abundance.

These two interrelated blessings of water and food add up to God's mastery over the natural environment. The next two blessings of Exodus 23:25–27, healing and procreation, constitute the power of God over the human body. There is nothing startling about YHWH's control over healing. After all, many gods and goddesses in Mesopotamia are involved the healing processes, and human medical practitioners attribute their abilities to the patronage of deities. In early Mesopotamia, the doctors who rely on what we would call "natural" (medicinal) methods of healing call upon the goddesses Gula and Ninsinna. Practitioners of the more "magical" forms of healing rely on the god Ea and his son Asarluhi (later known as Ea and his son Marduk).[39] Other gods are also associated with healing. Often a god "owns" a particular disease which he or she inflicts, and can presumably remove. A number of gods are particularly noted for their healing capacities and called by the epithet *muballiṭ mīti*, literally "who brings life to the dead," an epithet that emphasized their ability to heal the moribund.[40] During the late second to first millennium B.C.E. in Mesopotamia, the magical healing tradition concentrates on the god Marduk. As one litany states:

> To heal the sick. It rests with you, Marduk, to give
>    healing and life.
> to lift up the fallen—it rests with you, Marduk, to give
>    healing and life.
> to take the weak by the hand—it rests with you,
>    Marduk, to give healing and life.[41]

The God of the Bible also assumes control over sickness and health.[42] God can bring illness to punish people or to demonstrate power,[43] prophets can announce whether sick people will die or live, and can intercede and pray for the sick.[44] The sick offer prayers of petition for healing and thanksgiving for this healing.[45] In the Bible (as also in Mesopotamia), illness can an instrument of reward and punishment: because of the sins of their father, the children of King David and King Jeroboam[46] are struck ill and die, and God uses "leprosy"[47] to punish Miriam, Gehazi, and Uzziah.[48] Nevertheless, these instances are rare. People may confess their sins and profess repentance when they ask for help,[49] but on the other hand, Israel does not normally suspect wrong-doing in the case of ordinary illness and does not usually blame sick people for having caused their own sickness.

This reluctance to "blame the victim" is not in evidence when Israel speaks of the state of health of the nation as a whole. In this case, the bringing of illness is part of God's armament with which God directs and punishes. The collective health of Israel depends on its own behavior. As Deuteronomy makes clear, God's mastery over health is both promise and threat[50]: if the people disobey, they will collectively suffer illness and plagues. The most dramatic example of God's ability to bring illness is the story of the Ten Plagues, in which God demonstrated control over nature by bringing natural disasters and illnesses upon Egypt. As the story is told in Exodus, God wants the plagues to demonstrate His mastery, and God's power is an underlying motif in the recitation and commemoration of the plagues:

> "For now I am sending all these plagues upon you and your servants and your people so that you will know that there is none like me in all the earth. . . . Indeed, I have set you up for this purpose, to show you my strength so that my name will be declared in all the earth."[51]

The phrase the "diseases of Egypt" is almost a code word in Deuteronomy and Exodus for God's power over health and God's willingness to use that power as an instrument of control. The little story of "God the Healer" in Exodus 15 also expresses the belief that God can bring the diseases of Egypt upon a disobedient people. Immediately after the triumph at the Red Sea, the people come to Marah. There they find only alkaline water, unsuitable to drink. God instructs Moses to throw a branch into the water and thereby make it potable. When Moses does so, he announces to the people, "If you carefully harken to the voice of the Lord your God and do that which is right in his eyes and listen to his commandments and obey his rules, then I will not bring upon you any of the diseases which I put on Egypt, for I the Lord am your healer."[52] The power to bring health and sickness is God's—the choice of which they will receive is Israel's.

The Bible states without hesitation that God has mastery over health and illness—but it does not state this premise often. By contrast, many more verses declare YHWH's powers over procreation. Similar to health in that it also relates to the workings of the human body, reproduction has a different polytheistic background from healing. Because the art of healing was known as the province of male gods like Enki/Ea and Marduk, it required no major change in philosophy to attribute this power to YHWH. Procreation, however, had remained the domain of the mother goddesses. Despite some rivalry with Ea/Enki and Marduk,[53] the mother-goddess never loses her prominence in creating and assuring childbirth until YHWH asserts control over this area of divine activity. YHWH's prominence in this area is not simply a matter of one (male) god replacing another, and "His" activity in this area must be consciously and explicitly stated and added to the inventory of YHWH's powers. The emphasis that the Bible places on divine control over all aspects of pregnancy and childbirth is an indication of the radical nature of this idea.

Procreation is no light matter to the nation of Israel, which places great value on the birth of children. Unlike Mesopotamia, Israel is never concerned with the danger of overpopulation.[54] Archaeological studies show that Israel had good ecological reason to value reproduction and encourage population growth. The terrain and climatic conditions of Israel demanded a large labor force. Beyond the need to defend boundaries in turbulent times, many people were needed to work the land, build cisterns, and—ultimately—terrace the hills.[55] At the same time, the small size of the houses in ancient Israel indicates that the families were very small.[56] The encouragement of childbirth was vital to Israel's survival, and Israel's philosophy of reproduction corresponds to her survival needs. Israel believes that God's command to "be fruitful and multiply" was given to the first humans and then repeated to Noah in very emphatic language, "and you be fruitful and multiply, swarm over the earth and multiply in it."[57] But despite the obligation that this places on humans to reproduce, pregnancy and birth are not fully in human hands. Pregnancy could be difficult to achieve, miscarriage and perinatal death were common, and death in childbirth was an ever-present danger. The whole enterprise was too doubtful and precarious to take place without divine supervision. Since no other god could be invoked, YHWH had to oversee this vital function. God's powers over procreation are referred to over and over throughout the Bible,[58] and Genesis 49, commonly considered one of the earliest biblical poems, proclaims God's power in this area: "The God of your father who helps you, Shaddai who blesses you, with blessings of heaven above, blessings of the deep that crouches below, blessings of breast and womb."[59]

The ancestor stories of Genesis also underscore the divine nature of reproduction and God's power over it. In these narratives, God can shut and reopen wombs.[60] The power to conceive is not a power possessed by women or by men, and even the family of Abraham, to whom God has promised abundant descendants, has great difficulty in actualizing this promise. First Sarah, then Rebekkah, and then Rachel are all presented as initially barren. It is only when God takes action that the matriarchs, and later Manoah's wife and Hannah, conceive.[61] The great heroes of Israel, Isaac, Jacob, Joseph, Samson, and Samuel, are all born after divine action. This story of the once-barren mother repeatedly conveys the message that God—and God alone—can cause conception.[62] All children are gifts of God: "Sons are the domain of the Lord, the fruit of the women is his reward."[63]

God's role in childbirth extends beyond conception to all functions previously under the supervision of the mother goddesses. God oversees the entire process of gestation and childbirth: God forms and shapes the child in the womb,[64] God takes note of the child in the womb, cares for it there, and may call the child into service there;[65] God is midwife, bringing on the labor and bringing forth the child.[66] There is no more need for a mother goddess, or for divine midwife-assistants and divine labor-attendants. God, the master of all the other elements of the natural world, is master of human reproduction as well.

With God's ability to deliver all the promises of Exodus 23:24–27 to Israel, God is revealed as the master of all the forces of nature. There is no difference between powers that used to be male and those that used to be female; no sense of distinction between power over rain and over food; no gulf between power over the human body and over the natural world. This sense of unity is expressed by the Deuteronomic phrase pĕrî biṭnĕkā ûprî 'admātkā, "the fruit of your womb and the fruit (produce) of your land," both of which are the parallel gifts of God.[67] In this monotheist view, all nature is one unified field. Everything is interrelated and under the control of one deity. In this organic view of the universe, there are no forces in tension and cooperation. All of nature is unified. The rain and the earth, the physical universe and the inner workings of the human body, all are seen as parallel manifestations of the power of one God.

As these essential powers pass into YHWH's hands, the picture of the universe changes dramatically. No more a picture of interacting powers in dynamic interrelationship, the sense of the world is one of God's mastery. God's mastery entails a unified vision of reality, a sense of nature as the creature of God. From the first classical prophets,

Amos and Hosea, to the last, Haggai, Malachi, and Zachariah, all the prophets of Israel declare God's involvement with nature. Hosea emphasizes God's determination of fertility,[68] Amos stresses God's creation of the mountains and stars and God's control over the seas,[69] Deutero-Isaiah sees God's creation and mastery over nature as the foundation of God's ability to create salvation in history.[70] The creation passages in Genesis, the curses and promises of Exodus and Deuteronomy, the depiction of drought in the historical books, the allusions to creation in Biblical poetry and the prophecies of upheaval on the "Day of the Lord"—all assume and declare God's ability to create and to destroy nature, to sustain the earth and to cause it to tremble, to create the world from chaos and return it to chaos again. In these passages, God plays all the roles, for God is creator and sustainer, provider and destroyer. All the jobs previously performed by the pantheon, all the forces exemplified by the many nature deities, now have to be performed by the One God of Israel.

# 9

## But in Ourselves

The Bible's picture of God's sole mastery over the universe creates two major difficulties in understanding the workings of the cosmos. The first problem is theoretical: if God has all the power, and there is no one else in the divine realm, what can impel God to act? Power without motive results in a state of stasis, of equilibrium without movement. And yet it is clear that the universe is not stagnant. *Something* must be the reason and cause of God's actions. The second problem is practical: the idea of God's absolute mastery conflicts with the reality principle. The experience of the people of Israel does not always conform to that which could be expected from such a masterful deity. Despite God's dominance in history, Israel is frequently besieged and overrun in warfare. Despite God's power over rain and fertility, Israel experiences droughts and famine. Despite God's control over health, the people of Israel know plagues and pestilence. And despite God's mastery of procreation, there were still miscarriages and stillbirths in Israel. If God has power over the world, why does not everything go well for Israel? The search for the answers to these questions (what we call theodicy) brings Israel to a new valuation of the role of humankind.

God's good deeds are not always explained. No reason is given in the Bible for God's choosing Abraham or for God's loyalty to David. These two great events in the history of biblical Israel are simply recorded. It is left for later generations to attribute God's choice to Abraham's own prior quest for God[1] or to label this inscrutability of God's action as "prevenient grace." This selection of Abraham and David, and God's promises to them, form the basis for God's later great deeds. It is because God remembers Abraham that God sends Lot out of Sodom before its destruction[2]; it is because of God's covenantal promises to Abraham, Isaac, and Jacob that God acts to rescue Israel from

100

Egypt.[3] It is also because of the memory of God's covenant with Israel that God will bring the people back to their land.[4]

Another operating principle that Israel sees in God's behavior is the desire to become acknowledged throughout the world. In Exodus, as the ten plagues go on, God announces that the pestilence is coming so that "so that you will know that there is none like me in the whole earth."[5] God's concern for God's own reputation is the basis on which Moses convinces God not to destroy the people in the desert.[6] And it is another reason, according to Ezekiel, that God will bring the exiled Israelites back to their land to start again.[7] These two principles—the covenant and promises to Abraham and David, and the importance of God's reputation—are the two arguments by which Israel petitions God for aid in time of trouble. In Psalms 74 and 89, poems of national distress, lament, and petition, the psalmist affirms God's greatness by recounting the mythological days in which God became supreme by smiting the Sea, and reminds God of God's own promises to Abraham and/or David. The Psalmist then describes Israel's present brutal reality, in which the people suffer defeat, and reminds God that the deity's lack of help for Israel will cause others to blaspheme and belittle God because they are able to defeat him. These psalms conclude with a prayer to God to reactivate his well-remembered power and act for the salvation of Israel.[8] Good deeds and salvation are thus understood as resulting from God's need for recognition and as following other acts of grace and the promises that were made then.

But what about the explanation of bad deeds and hard times? The negative inverse of the idea of unwarranted grace is unprovoked harshness. When Nadab and Abihu die as they offer strange fire on the altar, Moses declares this raw power to be proof of God's holiness: "This is what YHWH meant when he said 'through those near to me I show myself holy, and gain glory before all the people.'"[9] Such raw power also smites the people of Beth-Shemesh when they look into the ark of the Lord, and kills Uzzah when he grabs the ark to prevent it from falling.[10] God's use of power may also be explained as "testing," in which God brings danger and horror upon Israel in order to test her loyalty, and perhaps to temper her strength. This is the explicitly stated reason that God tells Abraham to bind Isaac for the sacrifice.[11] It is probably also behind God's attacks on Jacob at the Jabok river[12] and upon Moses on his way to Egypt.[13] The long journey from Egypt to the land of Israel is considered such a test, as are the hunger and thirst in the wilderness.[14] In all these occurrences, there is no warning for the test, and no reason for it. These events represent the darker side of

God, the use of power against people for reasons that the victims cannot discern.

The ideas of "grace" and "test" and "reputation" are philosophies of tragedy in which humanity serves as the pivot around which the world, and God's power, revolve.[15] Israel develops additional explanations of history in which human beings have an even greater role: they are not only the fulcrum of action; they are the initiator of change in the universe. God's absolute power is not arbitrary: it is called into play in reaction to human behavior. Human beings have a direct impact on the environment: ultimately, the well-being of the earth and the people of Israel—or their destruction—is a result of human action. One such philosophy of history revolves around the Biblical concept of the pollution of the earth (or of the land of Israel).[16] Human moral misbehavior pollutes the earth: the primeval consequence was the flood.[17] If the people of Israel pollute the land of Israel, the consequences are inevitable: they will be cast out of the land so that the land can come back to its pristine state. There are historical precedents that can warn Israel of the danger of pollution. In addition to the flood story, there is the more recent historical memory of the takeover of the land of Canaan. Leviticus 18 lists a set of wrong actions, mostly sexual, which the previous inhabitants of the land performed. As a result of these acts, the land became polluted and thereupon vomited out the inhabitants who defiled it. Israel is warned not to commit these acts lest the land vomit them out in the same way.[18] The prophets Hosea, Jeremiah, and Ezekiel declare the land polluted.[19] The implication is clear: the destruction of the nations of first Israel, then Judah, is a catastrophe inevitably resulting from a build-up of pollution into a "critical mass"[20]; the period of exile is seen as a restorative hiatus for the land, until God will purify the people and bring them back to the land to begin again.

Most commonly, the Bible explains disasters in nature and history as God's reaction to human deeds. Sometimes, the reaction is in the form of "chastisement": God acts to "chasten" Israel as a parent chastises a son. The hard times that Israel experiences can remind the people where their true attention should be placed. More often, the Bible portrays God acting as a judge upon Israel's behavior: God's powers over history are the armaments by which God enforces the behavior of the people of Israel. All the blessings which God promises in Exodus 23:24–27 are threat as well as promise. God's control is not rivaled or mitigated by any other divine power: God's actions are dependent upon Israel's fidelity and good behavior.[21]

Nowhere is the threat of divine reward and punishment as explicit as in Israel's thinking about droughts. The droughts to which Israel is prone may be a chastisement to induce Israel to return to God.[22] More commonly, these droughts are seen as God's punishments: "It is your iniquities that have diverted these things, your sins that have withheld the bounty from you."[23] This view of rain and fertility is expressed clearly in the Deuteronomic formulation of the Sinai covenant:

> *If you listen to my commandments which I command you*
>    *today*
> *to love the Lord your god and to worship him*
> *with all your heart and all your soul,*
> *then I will give the rain of your land in its season,*
> *the* yôreh *(first rain) and the* malqôš *(last rain),*
> *and you will gather your grain and your wine and your oil.*
> *And I will give vegetation in your fields to your animals,*
> *and you will eat to contentment.*
> *But watch out that you do not deceive yourselves*
> *and stray and worship other gods*
> *and bow down to them,*
> *and God will become angry with you and stop up the skies*
> *and there will not be rain*
> *and the land will not give its harvest*
> *and you will be quickly lost from this good earth*
> *which God is giving to you.*[24]

Paradoxically, the solo power of God over rain and fertility means that in the final analysis it is *Israel* that determines, by its actions, whether there is rain. God has promised rain if Israel obeys, and God's covenantal faithfulness can be relied upon. The fertile character of the earth is constant, God's ability to bring rain is undoubted, the tie between Israel's behavior and the rain is constant. The only variable is Israel's behavior, which determines, in its fluctuations, the outcome of nature.

In biblical monotheist thought, there are no conflicting powers in the divine world, no harmonizing forces in heaven, no divine-divine interaction. Nevertheless, there is a point-counterpoint interaction in the universe that determines the course of events. This cosmic interplay no longer takes place within the divine world. Instead, the counterbalancing of forces embraces the relationship of human and divine. Divine dominance means divine conditionality, as humankind becomes the reason for—and instigator of—divine action.

The relationship between human action and its results is not mechanistic. In the final analysis, it is God's power over nature that makes this causality of action-reaction possible.[25] God can also interrupt this causality. In response to drought and other indications of God's disfavor, Israel can seek God's favor through prayer. This, indeed, is one of the major functions of the temple, as recorded in Solomon's prayer at the dedication of the Jerusalem temple[26]: and there are psalms specifically recited to pray for rain.[27] But the prophets maintain clearly that prayer and worship are not sufficient. Hosea and Amos acknowledge Israel's ritual diligence. Nevertheless such prayer and supplication, in the absence of proper behavior, cannot move God.[28] Drought or disaster is the time for the people to search out the possible cause and to pray for compassion with a repentant heart. Jeremiah's drought prayer is a moving example of such prayers.[29]

Underlying penitential prayer is an understanding that God does not determine the condition of nature unilaterally. God's control over nature is reactive, and depends ultimately on the action of Israel. Droughts may come, the land becomes cursed, and even the beasts and the birds perish when the inhabitants do evil.[30] In the final analysis, all of nature depends directly upon the actions of humankind, and particularly of Israel. Because of humanity, God returned the world to chaos at the time of the Flood. God can do so again: Isaiah envisions the whole world being destroyed:

> *The earth is breaking, breaking,*
> *the earth is crumbling, crumbling,*
> *the earth is tottering, tottering;*
> *the earth is swaying like a drunkard;*
> *it is rocking to and fro like a hut,*
> *its iniquity shall weigh it down*
> *and it shall fall, to rise no more.*[31]

and Jeremiah depicts the return to chaos:

> *I look at the earth, it is unformed and void;*
> *at the skies, and their light is gone.*
> *I look at the mountains, they are quaking,*
> *and all the hills are rocking.*
> *I look: no human is left, and all the birds of the sky have*
> *    fled.*
> *I look: the far land is desert, and all its towns are in*
> *    ruin—*

*because of the Lord, because of his blazing anger,*
*For thus said the Lord: the whole land shall be desolate,*
  *but*
*I will not make an end of it.*
*For this the earth mourns, and skies are dark above—*
*because I have spoken, I have planned,*
*I will not relent or turn back from it.*[32]

In these passages, the very existence of the cosmos is imperiled because of human misdeeds: not only will Israel be destroyed, but creation itself be reversed and ended.[33] The statement in Genesis that God created humanity to rule the earth has often been taken as a license for human beings to do whatever they want with nature. In the Bible, it clearly does not mean that. On the contrary, all of nature is seen as dependent upon the actions of humankind. Ancient thought sees nature, the animals, humanity, and divinity as lying along a continuum, with the gods, in a sense, mediating between humanity and nature:

HUMANITY————————GODS————————NATURE

In the Bible, the diagram is different:

NATURE————————HUMANITY————————GOD

God's actions towards nature depend on human activity. God cares about nature; after all, the purpose of giving laws immediately after the flood[34] is precisely to prevent nature from being contaminated again. But God's behavior towards nature is reactive. In effect, humans determine what God does, not by prayers and manipulation, but by their behavior. In this way, humanity mediates between God and nature. The ultimate responsibility for what happens to the natural world rests on the behavior of human beings towards nature, towards God, and towards each other.

This monotheist conceptualization of the world is a stark philosophy of action. God's actions are predictable in fixed response to behavior. God's solo mastery would seem to lay stress on Israel's having liturgical and sacrificial interaction with God, to propitiate and manipulate the result. But, at the same time, the prophets announce that such ritual activity will not help. The prophets emphasize that neither Israel's history nor the fertility of her land depended on worship-rituals. Fertility rituals are condemned as faithlessness, and even the officially pre-

scribed sacrificial worship can not ensure peace and fertility. Only non-
ritual activity—fidelity and ethical behavior—bring about the well-
being of the people.[35]

This concept of fertility and natural survival puts enormous responsibility in human hands, for the whole world depends on human behavior. The "monotheist myth" in Psalm 82 relates that it was not always
so: God had a council of divine beings who were charged with uphold-
ing social justice. When they did not do so, the whole world began to
totter. As a result, God made these gods mortal.[36] Since then, God has
reigned alone over all the nations. There are no longer any gods—and
it is up to *humanity* to ensure that the foundations of the earth do not
totter. The way to do this is right behavior and social justice. This is
an enormous task, but the way to accomplish it has been revealed: God
has instructed and continues to instruct the people as to how they are
to behave. The laws and instructions of Israel have a cosmic significance. The people have to listen, to learn, and to observe in order to
fulfill their duty to uphold the universe. Disobeying these instructions
can lead to catastrophe, and as pollution builds up, even repentance
can no longer help.

This theology of God's reactivity locates the fault for disaster in
Israel. Maintaining faith in the constant predictable behavior of God,
it "blames the victim" with ever more exacting faults. After the exile,
when droughts still continued, the prophet Haggai blamed the people
for not having built a new temple, and the prophet Malachi attributed
the droughts to the lack of full tithing. If God has absolute mastery,
and God is always good, then evil and hardships must always be due
to the evil of humanity.[37]

The general problem of theodicy (the justification of God's behavior in the face of adversity) continues to occupy theological thought.
The radical nature of fully developed biblical monotheism, with the
great responsibility that it places on human behavior, has often been
softened by belief in various supernatural powers. After the Babylonian
exile, the skies are once again peopled with celestial beings, the angels.
Still later, forces of evil were believed to be abroad in the world, rivaling
the forces of light. The idea of ultimate human responsibility and divine
reactivity has continued to be misunderstood into our own day. Western culture has assumed that dominion over the world implied a freedom to act at will without concern over negative consequences towards
the earth and its fertility. The modern ecology movement has sometimes sought to find a philosophical-theological rationale for its con-

cern for the earth in the pagan continuum. The biblical theory of God's reactivity is biblical monotheism's way of grounding humanity in its interconnectedness with nature and its ultimate responsibility for nature's well-being and survival.

The absorption by God of all the forces of nature leads humanity onto center stage. Biblical monotheism is essentially anthropocentric, though not in the sense that the world exists to serve humanity. Rather, in the absence of other divine beings, God's audience, partners, foils, and competitors are all human beings, and it is on their interaction with God that the world depends.

# 10

## Homo Sapiens

The central role of humankind in biblical monotheism manifests itself also in the Bible's depiction of the origin of civilization. In ancient Near East myths, the gods provide humanity with all the essentials of human civilization. By contrast, in the Bible, early humans develop their own culture.[1] The human being, a creature created by God, is the initiator and creator of its own culture.

Genesis 1–11, the primeval history placed at the beginning of the Bible, tells the story of the creation and development of humanity, and the relationship between divine and human. In the grand litany of creation that opens the Bible[2], humankind is the earthly counterpart of the divine, created in the form and image of deity and placed in the world as its administrator. Next, Genesis 2–11 traces humanity's development from Adam's beginning as a simple servitor of the land, through the human accumulation of godlike knowledge, to the point at which God acts to reinforce the boundaries between human and divine. Only after humans have been separated from divinity, divided into language-nations and dispersed through the world, does the cycle of stories about the ancestors of Israel begin.[3] These stories show the development of a close relationship between God and one portion of humanity, the family of Abraham and Sarah. In this way, the road that humanity travels in its primeval history leads first to a separation of the divine and human realms and then to the establishment of communication between these separate realms. Along the way, humanity develops from a simple animal-like creature to a complex cultured being who does, indeed, approach the essence of the divine and requires redefinition.

The story of the first people begins in Genesis 2, when God creates Adam, the first human being.[4] The first Adam is a very simple and uncultured being, so simple that in the quest to find Adam a "suitable companion,"⁵ God creates the animals. At this early point in Adam's development, God can entertain the notion that the animals might be fit companions for the lone Adam.⁶ God brings each animal to Adam, and Adam takes notice of each and gives it a name. "But for Adam he didn't find a suitable companion."⁷ God then creates woman.

The nature of humanity changes drastically after the creation of Eve. In response to the serpent's revelation that eating the fruit of the tree of knowledge would make her more godlike, she eats, and by doing so she acquires the knowledge of things—cultural knowledge.⁸ In this way, Eve wrests knowledge from the realm of the divine, takes the first step towards culture, and transforms human existence. The coming of knowledge is stated very simply: "the eyes of both of them were opened and they perceived that they were naked, and they sewed together fig leaves and made themselves loincloths."⁹ Two things have happened: not only have Adam and Eve realized that they are naked, a category they had not perceived in their childlike innocence, but, in addition, they are now able to sew themselves loincloths out of the available fig leaves. Somehow, the knowledge of this skill of sewing, the beginnings of cultural knowledge, has come with the eating of the fruit of the knowledge of all things. The "natural" state of humankind's Edenic beginnings has disappeared: humans become creatures of culture, able to make creations of their own. They leave the garden and embark on their cultural existence.¹⁰

The implications of Eve's act are enormous. In a bite, she has "stolen"¹¹ cultural knowledge, taking it from the sacred realm and bringing it to humankind. Almost immediately, Adam and Eve have to leave the garden of Eden: human beings leave their liminal infancy and enter the world of human reality.¹² God then ratifies this change in their existence, and formally recognizes that they have left the animal world by providing them clothes made out of animal skins.¹³

This story has a long history of interpretation in post-biblical Western tradition, which concentrated on the *sin* of disobeying God.¹⁴ Early post-biblical literature does not focus on this story as an account of the origin of sin, which it derives from the story of the marriage of the angels to human women, a post-Biblical elaboration of Genesis 6: 1–4.¹⁵ From the first century B.C.E. on, the exegetical tradition sees sin originating in the Paradise story,¹⁶ and by the first century C.E. on, Eve is blamed for this fall.¹⁷ Eve is seen as the first yielder to temptation, the one who brought sin and evil into the world.¹⁸

Western writers since Origen have often associated Eve with the Greek myth of Pandora, the first woman, who unleashes misfortune on humankind when she opens the forbidden box.[19] She is, however, better compared to Prometheus, who disobeyed the gods and brought culture (in the form of fire) to humanity.[20] Like Prometheus, Eve acts on her own initiative; like Prometheus, she transforms human existence: and, like Prometheus, she suffers as the result of her gift to humanity.[21] However—unlike Prometheus—Eve, the Bible's first culture bearer, is human. And she is female. This depiction of Eve as culture hero has an inner coherence and logic to it, for Eve's role in this primeval scene is the woman's role in the life of human beings, and that of the goddesses of the ancient Sumerian pantheon.[22] The goddesses are figures of culture and wisdom just as women are the first teachers of cultured existence, the transformers of raw into edible, grass into baskets, fleece and flax into yarn and linen and then into clothes, and babies into social beings. They are the mediators of nature and culture in daily life, and Eve the first woman is the first transformer who begins the change from "natural" simple human beings into cultural humanity.

The ancient Near East tells very different stories about how humans embarked upon culture. The Sumerian dialogue-composition "Lahar and Ašnan" ("Ewe and Grain") describes the early history of humankind:

> *The people of those distant days,*
> *they knew not bread to eat;*
> *they knew not cloth to wear;*
> *They went about with naked limbs in the Land,*
> *And like sheep they ate grass with their mouth,*
> *Drinking water from the ditches.*[23]

The gods fashion the divine ewe, the prototype of sheep, and the divine grain: then Enki and Enlil send them down to humankind, and they bring well-being and wealth wherever they go. By the grace of these gods, humans pass from their primitive animal-like state to the rudiments of culture that define the human being.

In this Sumerian tale, human beings are the recipients of the gift of culture. So, too, in Greek myth. The first element of culture, the gift of fire, was brought to humanity by Prometheus, the Titan who befriended and benefited humanity. In Mesopotamian tradition, the gods are always the benefactors and culture-bringers of humanity. In the Sumerian king list, "Kingship came down from heaven."[24] According to the Myth of Inanna and Enki, first the god Enki and then Inanna

were in charge of the **me**s, a mystical abstract concept of cultural institutions.[25] Mesopotamia also had a myth of the *apkallus*, primeval beings who arose from the sea to give the cultural arts to humanity.[26] In
effect, humanity did not develop any aspect of human culture.[27] In the
Bible, on the contrary, once humans eat the fruit of knowledge, they
become creatures of culture, formidable enough to develop the major
institutions of world civilization without further divine intervention or
instruction.

In the Bible, the unfolding of human civilization is presented as part
of the generations of humanity: as successive generations are born, they
develop the elements of a civilized human existence. Adam and Eve
begin as gatherers in the garden of Eden; forced out of this paradise,
Adam turns to horticulture, laboring on the earth. Of the sons of Adam
and Eve, Cain is a farmer, Abel a shepherd. This is noted in passing:
there is no tale of how humans learned how to farm, how they domesticated animals. The implication is that these things just happened, that
primeval humans discovered them on their own. By contrast, the Sumerians tell a number of tales about how people first learned agriculture,
all of which concentrate on the beneficence of the gods. "How the ce-
reals came to Sumer" begins in a time when people ate only grass, as
do sheep. Then An sent down from the sky cereal, barley, and flax.
Enlil sent them to the mountains. Later, the gods Ninazu and Ninmada
went to the mountains to bring the barley down to Sumer.[28] Other compositions relate how the gods presented humanity with all the implements necessary for agriculture and taught them to grow barley.[29]

In the Bible, Cain the farmer also invents the giving of sacrificial
offerings, again with no divine imperative or instruction. Cain simply
brings an offering, and Abel follows suit. Cain later begins urban civilization as he marries, has a son Enoch, and he (or Enoch) builds a
city.[30] Cain's role in the building of cities is the Bible's implicit recognition that agriculture supports the ancient city;[31] that cities are havens
for people uprooted from their land and kin;[32] and perhaps, that cities
can be places of violent behavior.[33] The genealogy of Cain[34] relates further developments in the history of civilization, for the children of
Cain's descendant Lamech are the ancestors of several important and
interrelated professions:[35] Jabal was the ancestor of pastoralists;[36] Jubal
of those who play the lyre and the pipe; Tubal-Cain of those who work
with metals.[37] The prominence of Cainites as culture-discoverers is
striking: is it simply because these civilized behaviors are part of urban
civilization,[38] because there was a separate historico-mythical tradition

about Cainites related to their connection to smithing,[39] or because the Bible is ambivalent or even negative about urban civilization itself?[40] It is certainly significant that the Biblical culture-heroes are not only human, they also do not come from a particularly heroic lineage. They are not primeval supermen venerated and worshiped for their achievements: they are descendants of Cain and of Lamech, who also committed murder. The significance of this is clear when we compare this genealogy to the "Phoenician History" of Taautos–Sanchuniaton–Philo of Byblos–Eusebius.[41] Philo recounts a tale of the origin of the cosmos that leads into an anthropogeny: the first mortals are born, and they begin to discover civilization. Parts of this tale are decidedly reminiscent of Genesis: the first mortal discovered food obtained from trees, the second generation invented drought-prayers, the third generation discovered fire: later comes animal-skin *ching* (clothing), shipbuilding, hunting, fishing, ironmaking. However, Philo is clearly a euhemerist, who believed (like Euhemerus) that the pagan gods were actually originally humans who were later venerated as gods. The iron-making brothers are Chosur and Hephaistos, the Cainite and Greek gods of metalworking, and Philo relates that they were worshiped as gods after their death. Indeed, most of the culture discoverers listed by Philo can be identified, by their names, with ancient deities, and to the extent to which Philo is relating ancient traditions from Sanchuniaton, he has modified them to accord with the rationalist philosophy of his day.[42] In the ancient world itself, the inventors of culture were always gods.

The descendants of Cain are not the only inventors of human civilization. Enosh, from the line of Seth, first discovered divine worship.[43] Later, after the flood, Noah plants what may be the first vineyard and becomes drunk: still later, Nimrod was the first man of power. The Bible relates no stories of how these achievements came to be. None of these aspects of civilization is said to have been given by God or effected through divine revelation. On the contrary, these achievements of humanity are told in the genealogies, as little addenda to the process of reproduction. There may once have been stories in Israel about the first city, the first music, or the first anything. But the Bible's primeval history simply notes these accomplishments in the genealogies without elaboration, a technique which underscores the fact that the development of human culture is a natural multiplicative process, as inherent a part of human existence as natural reproduction.

Nevertheless. despite the naturalness of this human development of culture, the Bible considers this capacity of humanity for knowledge and culture as somewhat divine. When Adam and Eve eat the fruit of knowledge, God declares. "Now the human has become like one of us, knowing the good and the bad."[44] As humans grow and develop their institutions and their technology, it becomes increasingly likely that they will breach the boundaries to divinity until matters reach a climax with the story of the Tower of Babel in Genesis 11, the last chapter of the primeval history.[45] In this story, people come to Shinar (Sumer), learn how to build with baked brick, and seek to build a great city with an ascending tower (a ziggurat: a meeting place for the divine and human).[46] In reaction, God thinks "If, as one people with one language for all, this is how they have begun to act, then nothing that they may propose to do will be out of their reach."[47] In order to preserve the divine–human distinction, God sets limits on humanity by creating different languages, thus dividing and ultimately scattering humanity. Humanity's knowledge and power have begun to reach the world of the gods, and God acts to prevent this rapprochement. But God never really impedes human progress: after the Tower of Babel, as before it, humanity continues to invent and develop culture. This ability is a defining characteristic of humanity. Neither abject nor passive, humanity is formidable, able to threaten even the gods by its abilities.

In Genesis 1–11, there is a notable exception to the human origin of cultural institutions. Human beings do not develop their own law. Israel was aware that other cultures such as Mesopotamia and the Hittites had highly developed legal systems, for biblical law was part of the same legal tradition as cuneiform law.[48] It does not assume that the laws of the other nations are wrongful or nonexistent. On the contrary, the Bible has a deep reverence for law, and believes that all law is a gift from God. The story of the flood in Genesis 6–9 demonstrates the consequences of a lack of law, the devastation it causes, and God's actions to give law to all humankind.[49] To the Bible, all law is divinely inspired.

God's granting of law to humankind shows us that there is no reason that the Bible could not have imagined God giving other aspects of culture to humanity. There is nothing inherent in Israel's image of God that makes it impossible for God to teach humanity. On the contrary, after the primeval history, God becomes more active in the development of humanity. After humanity separates into nations, Genesis narrows its focus to one couple, Abraham and Sarah, and relates the beginning of a new rapprochement between God and humanity. God reaches across the now secure gap between human and divine and institutes a close relationship with one segment of humanity. The book of Exodus continues the saga of Israel, showing how the people became bonded to God and what this bonding entails. To the Bible, Israel is both God-chosen and God-directed. As soon as God sets up the relationship with Israel, God reveals and *gives* Israel all the cultural institutions that make Israel different from other nations. Israel's Torah, Israel's calendar, with its Sabbaths and festivals, Israel's priesthood, sacrificial system, and temple, Israel's knowledge of its own sacred history, the Davidic monarchy and the institution of prophecy—the Bible considers all these given and decreed by God.

The divine origin of all these cultural institutions of Israel define their "holy" status. Coming from God, they are to remain in a pure holy state that exhibits and protects their divine origin. Maintaining and guarding this holy state is one of the main tasks of the Israelite priesthood, who are to instruct Israel in the details of holiness. These institutions are a part of the sacred, and the people must guard and preserve them. Even the people Israel, the recipient of these special divine gifts, is a holy nation and must take care to maintain both its boundaries and its state of purity.

The origin of the holy institutions of Israel is entirely divine. Human beings, on their own, did not have the capacity to create these holy institutions. God not only calls for a tabernacle and a priesthood, God gives the detailed instructions for their creation. God even provides the special ability that is needed to build these sacred institutions, granting to Bezalel, Oholiab, and the others who worked on the tabernacle with them a "divine spirit of skill, ability, and knowledge in every craft."[50]

The biblical philosophy of culture is very complex. On the one hand, there is ordinary human knowledge, the elements of world civilization. This knowledge is totally in the human realm created by people, who have total control. The Bible prescribes no rituals of observance or thanksgiving for the arts or the sciences. These endeavors are totally secular, humanly conceived and humanly executed. On the other hand, there are the central institutions of Israel. These are "holy"—divinely conceived and granted to Israel, which must guard them as special and sacred, and must demonstrate gratitude for these divine gifts. One cannot profane the holy by treating the holy as secular. One cannot forget God's prerogatives in the treatment of the holy. Such behavior is "trespassing" on God's realm (*ma'al*) and is severely prohibited.[51]

A comparison with the Sumerian portrayal of culture reveals that when we look at the elements of culture that were arranged in Sumer along male-female, god-goddess lines, an interesting pattern emerges. Politics, hierarchy, and law, long the province of the male gods in Mesopotamia, are still treated in the Bible as God's gifts to humanity. The Bible considers the Davidic dynasty, the legal system, the temple and its priesthood—all male preserves—to be divinely granted. These state institutions are considered God's preserve on earth, and they take on aspects of divinity. On the other hand, those elements of culture that were once goddess-linked, such as storage, administration, lamentation, song, and wisdom-writing are entirely within the domain of humankind. They are neither divinely granted nor divinely supervised.

The biblical conception of the temple shows how these ideas about culture were envisioned. The temple, the central religious institution of Israel was holy. The design of the prototype tabernacle was god-granted, the institution of priesthood was divinely revealed, the rules and regulations were divine in origin. Nevertheless, God was not the overseer of the temple, and was not the supervisor of the administration of the household. Nor did God have emissaries, or "angels" as executive directors. The actual running of the temple was the responsibility of the priests. It was their responsibility to manage the temple, to take good care of it, and to keep it pure.[52] In some sense, God lived in the temple; but God was the dweller, not the manager, and took no part in running it. The priests and the people had the duty to make sure that the temple remained a suitable House for God and that it continued to perform the functions for which it had been designed.

In ancient Sumer, the temple also served as a storage repository and redistribution center, with a goddess as supervisor of storage. Storage was no less important in Israel's ecology, for Israel had to cope with the deadly dry seasons and the drought years. Nevertheless, despite its crucial importance to the community, there is no hint of divine involvement in the Israelite storage system, no sense that God oversees the storehouses or protects them from marauders. God's storehouses are celestial, containing hail and other meteorological phenomena. The earthly institution of storage facilities is entirely human. The Bible does not consider even the most massive storage system known to it, Egypt's storage of the grain of seven years of plenty, either God-run or God-invented. When Joseph interprets Pharaoh's dream, he declares that "God has told Pharaoh what He is about to do."[53] God sends the dream to foretell the future: "the matter has been determined by God, and God will soon carry it out."[54] But Joseph never claims that the plan he presents to Pharaoh to build granaries and organize the collection of grain is divinely inspired. He presents the plan as his own, and is placed in command of Egypt to oversee the storage of uncountable quantities of grain.

In the same way, the cultural arts of learning, song, and lamentation, once associated with Sumerian goddesses, are human arts in the Bible. Israel's psalms are written *for* God, but they are written by people. They are "divinely inspired" in the sense that the impulse to write comes from love of deity. But God does not write the psalms, nor does God serve as the muse who enables people to write poetry. The art of poetry, and its related art of music, are earthly human arts which become sacred by their purpose rather than by their origin. So too, the specialized poetic art of lamentation. God may lament, but human laments do not come from God, they come from the ability and knowledge of the poet. Even learning and wisdom are human enterprises. God can grant special "wisdom," like Bezalel's special architectural craftsmanship and Solomon's gift of wisdom. But the enterprise of learning and writing "wisdom" literature, like the writing of poetry, becomes sacred only as it is dedicated to God. It remains, fundamentally a "human" enterprise.[55]

Throughout the Bible, in every aspect of biblical thought, human beings gain in prominence in—and because of—the absence of goddesses. In Israel's philosophy of culture, humans have a greater role in the development and maintenance of the array of powers, functions, occupations and inventions that constitute civilized life than they ever did in ancient Near Eastern myth. Biblical thought urges Israel to devote these powers to God-centered and God-willed activities, to organize the secular world in the direction of the holy. But the Bible recognizes that the origin of this secular world is indeed secular, that humanity has created civilization and continues to develop it.

This is not always a comfortable thought for humankind (then or now). Our knowledge is after all, limited, and was even more limited then than now. As a result, we are sometimes caught between the responsibility that our knowledge offers us and the insufficient nature of our knowledge.[56] There is always a tension between the central importance of humankind, on the one hand, and its insignificance compared to the magnitude of the unknown universe and the immeasurable God. The gap is enormous, and the tension almost demands a mediating figure through which humans can attain the knowledge they require, through which they can avoid the pitfalls of wrong decisions. As we shall see, the centrality of humankind in biblical thought is so threatening that the tension gives rise to nonhuman intermediary figures, literary images such as Lady Wisdom to give us knowledge, holy mothers to lament for us.[57] The very importance of humans in the biblical philosophy of culture creates a flight from the human and a reemergence of females to do some of the work of the ancient goddesses. The reemergence of these figures is a response to the essential insight of monotheism, which is the dialogue between humankind and God, a dialogue which focuses attention and demands on the human partner to be worthy of the interchange.

# 11

## Gender and Its Image

### *Women in the Bible*

In pagan religion, the stories about gods and goddesses exemplify and model the relationships between humans in society. Tales of goddesses illustrate and articulate societal ideas about women, and stories about gods and goddesses provided sacred example and divine warrant for the gendered structure of society. In the Bible, ideas about women and gender are conveyed in stories about human women. Some of these women are well known.[1] There are others who are less familiar,[2] and there are those whose names have never been recorded, who are known only by their relationship to named men,[3] or who are remembered only by the functions they performed or the places in which they performed them.[4] These women are historical figures, legendary characters and fictional inventions. They appear in many different kinds of biblical literature, in poems, historical writings, ancestor-tales, proverbs, and other kinds of learned ("wisdom") literature. Their stories come from different circles and different periods through the millennium of biblical writing, and any investigation must begin with an understanding of each story in context.[5] Nevertheless, despite the diverse origins and nature of these stories, the preexilic biblical texts present a coherent and consistent picture of the nature of women, their goals, and the means by which they attain them.[6]

These narratives present a biblical picture of women's lives, but we must be careful not to confuse this biblical view with the reality of women's lives in ancient Israel. We have no way of knowing what women "really" did in ancient Israel. There are no independent texts, no marriage contracts, bills of sale or court transactions. Ancient Israel

118

did not write on clay tablets, and the more perishable writing materials that they used have not survived. What remains is the Bible's record of the way things were. As a result, the task of extrapolating reality information from the Bible entails several layers of difficulty. First, no one record from any society, even if it intends to describe that society exactly and objectively, can ever be free from the bias of the author: each individual viewpoint presents a partial and partially distorted view of reality. Second, the biblical books are not written with nonobjective description as a goal. The historical narratives are not journals or annals: they are historiographic documents written with the express purpose of interpreting the events of Israel's history and answering the essential concerns of the times in which they were written and rewritten. They are ideological literature,[7] documents with a purpose, and often have specific reasons for concentrating on women.[8] We cannot simply infer social structure from them and ignore their expressed purposes. Similarly, the laws of the Pentateuch are neither fully legislative nor descriptive. The study of comparable legal collections in Mesopotamia has demonstrated that these legal collections are model codes: they are projections, of what the law ought to be in order to truly reflect ideals of justice and equity.[9] As a result, these laws can indicate to us Israel's cultural ideals; in terms of historical reconstruction, they serve to indicate primarily ideology rather than social reality.

Having issued all these caveats, as we look at the position of women in society as expressed in the laws and in the narratives, we see a situation in which women are clearly subordinate to the men in the household.[10] Men exerted the right to control woman's sexuality: a girl was expected to be a virgin when she married and faithful to her husband afterwards. A man could accuse his bride of not being a virgin: if the allegation was "proved" by the lack of blood upon the sheets, she was to be stoned[11]; if, however, the allegation was "disproved," he was not stoned,[12] but simply forfeited the right to divorce her. Similarly, a man could accuse his wife of adultery, thus forcing her to undergo the solemn drinking-oath trial of the waters[13]; if the trial acquitted her, her husband was not punished for false accusation.

The property rights of women were severely limited. Women did not inherit, except in the circumstance when a man died without sons. His daughters could then inherit, but they were obligated to marry an kinsman in order to keep the inheritance within the husband's family. Women's control of property was so circumscribed that the male head of household—father or husband—could annul the vow of a woman if he did so the day that he overheard it.[14] The inferior social position of

women is indicated in economic terms by the fact that women are valued for the payment of vows at thirty shekels, men at fifty.[15]

All this adds up to the classic system of the subordination of women
that we commonly call "patriarchy." This term is increasingly difficult
to define as our ability to analyze gender relations in modern and ancient societies becomes more sophisticated. Research in gender studies
has strongly suggested that the formal structures of male dominance do
not fully indicate the intricate network of power relationships within
any particular culture, and attention has increasingly focused on more
informal relationships of power influence and prestige.[16] "Patriarchy,"
because of its imprecision and its political resonances, is perhaps not
the best term to use to describe gender relationships in the Bible.[17]

The question of the usefulness of the term "patriarchy" is not confined to ancient Israelite society alone. The social system reflected in
the Bible did not originate in Israel, nor is it substantially different in
the Bible than elsewhere in the ancient Near East. Society was structures along gender lines. The public arenas of palace, temple, and law
court were normally male preserves, and women, by and large, oper-
ated in the domestic sphere.[18] The biblical authors accept as given the
various institutions of power and hierarchy, the social cleavages between master-slave, rich-poor, male-female. Biblical laws seek to prevent the abuse of power and privilege and to mitigate the harsh effects
of such cleavage by defining the acceptable parameters of behavior
within these social divisions. But not even the prophets, who castigate
those who exploit the powerless and poor, question the existence of
social cleavage; no one envisions a homogeneous society. In the same
way, the Bible assumes male privilege to be fundamental to human social structure.

The narrative sections of the Bible reinforce the impression of male
privilege conveyed by the laws, even though at the same time they modify our impression of the extent to which women acted as subordinates.
These stories reveal the women of Israel as both victim and actor, and
provide some insight into Israel's conception of gender. They show that
beyond the realities of Israel's social structure, the Bible presents a re-
markably unified vision of humankind, for the stories show women as
having the same inherent characteristics and men. The circumstances
of their lives are different from those of *some* men (those with power),
but there are no innate differences that preclude women from taking
men's roles or men from taking women's roles should the occasion arise
and circumstances warrant it. There is nothing distinctively "female"
about the way that women are portrayed in the Bible.

The picture of biblical women[19] presented by a close study of biblical texts is dramatically different from what we have been led (by our religious and cultural traditions) to believe the Bible says, and from past cultural imperatives that have used the Bible as a basis for support of particular edicts. In fact, there is no real "woman question" in the Bible. The biblical image of women is consistently the same as that of men. In their strengths and weaknesses, in their goals and strategies, the women of the Bible do not differ substantially form the men. This biblical idea that the desires and actions of men and women are similar is tantamount to a radically new concept of gender.

Let us first consider Freud's classic question, "What do women want?" In other words, what are the goals of women, and are these any different from the goals of the culture at large? The women of the Bible are shown primarily within the family, with family-oriented goals. They are shown most often as mothers and as wives, less often as daughters and sisters. The prime figure in the portrayal of women is the mother. Like the mothers in Sumerian mythology, biblical mothers are always beneficent and supporting figures. There are no evil mother-figures in the Bible. On the contrary, mothers are always supportive of their children and loyal to them.

Childbirth itself was not considered an *accomplishment* of women or men, for the woman was considered the eager recipient of the baby, and only God could make women pregnant.[20] The true maternal role of women commenced after birth, when women are shown nurturing children and providing for their future. Biblical women often perform dangerous acts in order to save the life of their child. The mother of Moses disobeyed Pharaoh's command to cast male children into the Nile in order to giver her son Moses a chance. The wife of King Jeroboam traveled disguised to the prophet Ahijah in Shiloh in order to help her sick son Abijah. The wealthy woman of Shunnem went after Elijah to demand that he come back with her to restore her unconscious son.[21] The wise woman of Tekoa relied on Israel's cultural assumption that women implore for their children when she came before King David and told him a story that one of their two sons had killed the other, and the family was demanding the execution of the slayer.[22] This tale was false, and the wise woman was simply using it as a springboard to argue for David to grant leniency to his banished son Absalom, but the background that made the ruse plausible was the cultural expectation that women would plead on behalf of their child's life, and the cultural acceptance and approval of such action.

Women are protectors: when children were at stake, women defied improper commands and were not intimidated by authority. The women who set in motion the events leading to the Exodus were all motivated by their desire to save the lives of little children. The midwives Shifrah and Puah ignored Pharaoh's orders to kill the boy-children: Moses' mother defied Pharaoh's decree to cast the boys into the Nile, Pharaoh's own daughter thwarted his will by rescuing the baby Moses. Much later, this willingness to disobey evil commands is demonstrated again when Jehosheba defied her mother Queen Athaliah's decree to kill the Davidic children, by rescuing and hiding her infant nephew Joash.[23]

Mothers are concerned also with the economic well-being and future security of their children. At the wealthier end of the scale, the ideal "capable wife" of the book of Proverbs "is like a merchant fleet, bringing food from afar," who supplies provisions for her household.[24] At the lower end, Elisha came to the aid of poor widows who were trying to take care of their children economically.[25] The women also acted to secure the child's inheritance. Sarah protected Isaac's right of succession by expelling Hagar, and Rebekkah helped her favored son Jacob receive Isaac's parental blessing over her other son Esau.[26] Much later, Bathsheba convinced the aged King David to grant the throne succession to her own son Solomon.[27] As with the goddess-mothers of Sumer, the devotion of biblical mothers continued even after the child's death. Rizpah (daughter of Aiah), Saul's concubine, spread her sons' bodies on a rock and guarded them from the vultures from the time of the barley harvest, when they were impaled, until the rains came.[28]

The second great societal role of women in the Bible is that of wife. The Bible depicts harmonious relationships between husbands and wives, presenting women as supportive of their husbands. The case of Rachel and Leah is illustrative. Jacob, who had left Canaan, came to live in the house of his kinsman Laban and eventually married Laban's two daughters, Rachel and Leah. When he decided to go back home to Canaan, over Laban's objections, Rachel and Leah sided with their husband over Laban.[29] Similarly, the young David married to Saul's daughter Michal, lived in the household of King Saul. When Saul turned against David, Michal protected David against Saul by helping him escaped from Saul's emissaries and lying to her father.[30] These marriages are explicitly called love relationships,[31] and the cultural expectation of Israel was that marriage involved love, that love formed the woman's allegiance to her husband and made her accept the difficult conditions of marriage. The divine fiat of Genesis 3:16 "your desire shall be for your husband, and he shall rule over you" describes and validates a social reality in which women are subordinate to men. On the other hand, the Bible does not justify this inequality by reference to any putative deficiency or inferiority of women. Genesis recognizes the fact of male dominance, and believes that women are willing to accept the situation because of the love that they feel for their husbands. On the contrary, the stories show them acting to help their husbands, whomever they might have to oppose to do so.[32] This picture of the supportive wife is consistent, so that even the villainess Queen Jezebel acts as a model wife when she steps in to help her husband realize his desire for Naboth's vineyard, defying Israelite limitations on her royal power.

The Bible shows wives wanting children. The beloved Rachel, miserable in her barrenness, says to Jacob, "Give me children, or I shall die." Similarly, Elkanah's wife Hannah weeps despite his protestations: "Why are you so sad? Am I not more devoted to you than ten sons?"[33] Motherhood, according to the Bible, is an essential goal of all women[34]: even the unmarried prostitutes who came before Solomon were anxious to claim a living baby, each claiming that the dead baby belonged to the other woman.[35] This desire for children could set women against each other: Rachel envied her fertile sister Leah. Penina taunted her barren co-wife Hannah. Conversely, for the sake of having children, woman could put aside competition and personal emotions. The barrenness of Sarah and Rachel made them willing to introduce other women into their husband's beds. In order to have a child that would in some way be attributed to her, Sarah offered her handmaiden Hagar to Abraham as surrogate mother, thus giving him another sexual partner. So, too, Rachel offered her handmaiden Bilhah to Jacob (even though he already had children by his other wife Leah), in order that Bilhah could have children to which Rachel had some indirect claim.[36] The rivalry between Rachel and Leah, exacerbated by Leah's fertility and Rachel's barrenness, was put aside when Rachel was willing to trade Jacob's sexual favors for the mandrakes that she believed would bring her fertility.

Women's pursuit of children could even impel them to be sexual aggressors and defy societal norms of propriety and modesty. There are two women—Tamar, daughter-in-law of Judah, and Ruth—who were left as childless widows. Tamar was in a very difficult situation. Tamar's husband Er died young, leaving her a childless widow. By biblical custom, known as the "levirate,"[37] she was still bound to her dead husband's family: a woman whose husband died childless was expected to be mated to his brother so that she would have a child to carry on the lineage of her dead husband. Er's brother Onan should have impregnated her. Not wishing to split the inheritance he would get from his father with a baby who would be considered Er's son, Onan spilled his seed on the ground rather than impregnate her. After this, he too died young, leaving Tamar still a childless widow. The third son, Shelah, was still a boy, and so Judah sent her back to her parental home. She believed that she would be called back when Shelah grew up, but Judah did not do so. When Tamar realizes that she has been abandoned, she disguises herself by putting on a veil[38] and sits in the roadway. A woman in the streets can be propositioned, and Judah offers Tamar a sheep in payment for sexual intercourse. She agrees, but takes his identification (his seal, cord, and staff) as a pledge. Three months later, Judah is told that Tamar is pregnant. Even though he has abandoned her to childless widowhood, she is still bound to his family. In becoming pregnant, she is openly committing a form of adultery, a trespass against Judah's dignity, and he wants to burn her. With his seal, cord, and staff, she proves that the baby is Judah's, and he realizes that Tamar is "more righteous" than he, that she has bested him in their battle of rights and obligations, deception and counter-deception.[39]

Similarly, Ruth, who was a young widow living with her widowed mother-in-law, came in the middle of the night to a kinsman to sleep at his feet and thus induce him to marry her. Tamar and Ruth did not act as proper young women were expected to. And yet, far from being condemned, they were treated as heroines, who acted to have children and maintain the patrilineal line of their marital family. In this, it is doubly significant that they are not originally Israelite women. Tamar, of course, could not be, since she married into the core Israelite family, becoming daughter-in-law to Jacob's son Judah.[40] And Ruth was a Moabite whom Naomi's son married during their sojourn in Moab. It is not that foreign women were more likely to be sexually aggressive,[41] but that they are all the more praiseworthy in being so anxious to maintain the family they married into, even though they were not raised in the system. Their acts were all the more valuable in that the patrilineal line that they acted to preserve turned out to be the ancestry of King David. A more remote ancestor, the daughter of Lot, went to even greater lengths in her pursuit of children. After the destruction of Sodom, they believed that there were no other men left in the world,[42] and acted to repropagate the world, by getting their father drunk so that they could be impregnated by him. In so doing, they committed incest, a major taboo to Israel. The motivation of the author in telling this story is not clear, and it is hard to tell whether the author approves of their resourcefulness, or whether the story is related in order to besmirch the children to whom they gave birth, the ancestors of Ammon and Moab. Despite this uncertainty, the story's portrayal of the way these women act and its ascription of their motivation fits well into the biblical conception of women's actions.

The Bible's portrayal of woman's desire for motherhood may be a true reflection of the real life of women in ancient Israel. Recent writing has questioned the existence of a "maternal instinct" that drives women to have babies, and has focused instead on the patterns of early psychological development and early socialization that create nurturing women and a desire to mother.[43] But there can be no doubt that in a society in which women's role is defined by motherhood and her status depends on it, barren wives can be expected to feel anxious and unsatisfied. Furthermore, in ancient Israel, women did not inherit property. As a result, the well-being of older women depended on their having sons to care for them in their later years. For all these reasons, a wife's desire for a child might be considered a search for self-benefit.[44] However, the Bible did not consider women's search for children to be a selfish or self-preserving act. This goal of producing children was, in fact, a national goal. As a small country surrounded by enemies, Israel was conscious of its vulnerable situation and needed to maintain its population; furthermore the nature of the climate and terrain made it imperative to maximize the labor force.[45] Women's desire for children was thus congruent with the national good, and the Bible encouraged procreation by portraying the pursuit of children as a great goal and celebrating women for striving toward it.

In fact, all the objectives that women are portrayed as following are part of the national ethos of Israel. Women love their husbands, have children, take care of them and protect the land. There is no discernible difference between these considerations and the goals of the people as a whole. The men of Israel want the very things that these women are shown as pursuing. Israel actively supports the monogamous nuclear family structure, encouraging married couples to stay faithful to each other and produce children.

There is, of course, one major difference between women and *some* men: some men were in positions of power with an active role in history. Women were not. This results in a major difference in priorities, for people outside the power structure do not have the same absolute allegiance to it as those within. To those on the bottom of the hierarchy, hierarchy as an absolute has no value, and the women of the Bible sometimes ignore authority in the pursuit of higher goals.[46] In this, the women of Israel were like men who are younger sons in their father's house (Jacob) or resident sons-in-law (Jacob; David in the house of Saul). These men, subject to the control of the patriarch, are sometimes presented as reacting to their powerlessness by pursuing their own aims even when they do not serve the interests of the father. It is no coincidence that Rebekkah's ally is the *younger* son, it is no accident that Michal, Saul's daughter, and Jonathan, Saul's son, are eager to help their beloved David escape from their father. The subordinates are not always as committed to and supportive of the hierarchic arrangement of power in the family as is the head. Biblical law does not expect women to be absolutely obedient to their husbands. The book of Deuteronomy provides a severe penalty for a recalcitrant son. If a son was denounced by his parents for refusing to listen to them (or for terrorizing them after they had grown old), he could be stoned by the congregation. There is no equivalent provision for punishing a woman who does not listen to her husband, even though the Bible assumes that women are to be ruled by their husbands.

The allegiance of daughters to their father may not even have been fully expected. The daughter stories are the most devastating stories in the Bible. Women such as Michal daughter of Saul and the daughter of Pharaoh show a lack of loyalty to their fathers and are willing to disregard their father's wishes. On the other hand (at least in the early periods of Israel's history), the daughters are completely under the control of their fathers, who have powers of life and death over them. The glimpses of patriarchal life in Genesis and Judges show that a father can sacrifice his daughter or his son,[47] that he can give a daughter back to the husband-master from whom she ran away,[48] and that he can hand over his daughters to strangers for sexual abuse.[49] The two times that a girl was molested, the father did nothing to avenge or protect her.[50] The relationship of fathers to children is the flashpoint of patriarchal family structure, and it is no wonder that the children, particularly the daughters, are shown protecting themselves, and advancing their own and their husband's aims, over their father's. It is not any attributed disloyalty of females that causes them to protect themselves, but their extremely vulnerable state within the hierarchy.

Even the evil women of the Bible are not evil for any characteristically female purpose. Queen Jezebel of Israel, the Bible's arch villainess, led a concerted campaign to destroy the native religion of Israel and introduce her own Phoenician religion. Her daughter Athaliah, queen of the southern kingdom of Judah, moved to take over the throne for herself. After her son was killed in battle, she ordered all the babies in the revered Davidic line killed.[51] Jezebel and Athaliah are condemned because their strength has been used in the service of foreign worship and foreign values. It is the magnitude of their crimes that condemns them, not their aggressiveness and decisiveness. Other women are condemned in the Bible for improper worship. The devotion of foreign women to their native deities presented a problem when foreigners entered Israel's households as wives. Israelite women could also be less than devoted to a monistic worship of the Lord of Israel. Maacah, the queen-mother, was deposed by her son after she built an Asherah, a sacred wooden object.[52] The medium at Endor continued her contact with the dead even after King Saul had forbidden such practice as idolatrous,[53] and the women of Jerusalem were castigated by the prophets for weaving veils, weeping for Tammuz, and baking cakes for the queen of heaven. However, this devotion to foreign gods and disapproved cults is not a uniquely feminine act. The men of Israel and some of its kings are also reported to have worshipped the Asherah or the Ba'als, the host of heaven, Moloch, and the Queen of Heaven.[54] These heterodox beliefs and actions were not any more frequent among the women than among the men.

There are no goals of women—good or bad—that are characteristically or distinctively "female." Motifs which express female anger or women's solidarity are conspicuously absent from the biblical stories. The women of the Bible do not kill their husbands, fathers, or sons, or seek any kind of vengeance on them. This is at variance with Greek mythology, which is replete with such tales. The biblical writers do not express a "battle between the sexes," and there is no motif of female rage. Conversely, the biblical stories also do not indicate "sisterly solidarity." Women do not band together to promote women's causes, they do not go out of their way to help each other, and they do not show the consciousness of similar goals or shared experiences that would allow them to understand each other. The co-wives, Rachel and Leah (actual sister) and Penina and Hannah are rivals, and the very word in Hebrew for co-wife ṣārâ means "trouble."[55] So too, in Deborah's victory song,[56] the mothers have no sympathy for other women. The leader Deborah, called "a mother in Israel," seems to mock the mother of the slain Sisera in her pathos as she sits looking out the window for her son to return. Deborah expects the same attitude from her, portraying the mother of Sisera as sitting and counting the women whom her son will despoil. Deborah (and her projection of Sisera's mother) are conscious of the separate identities of Israelites and Canaanites. But neither she nor anyone else in the Bible divides the world into "we, women" and "they, men."

## Strategies in Pursuit of Goals

In the pursuit of their objectives, the women of the Bible came up against the realities of the social order. Biblical Israel believed in a hierarchically ordered world in which everyone had a place. The state had a king, the local villages had elders, the tribes had chiefs, and the household had a male head. With the lines of power clear, the people were expected to conform to the norms and obey the dictates of the leader. Children were to honor their parents, and men had dominion over women. Nevertheless, power was not absolute, and subordination did not imply submission. The rights of the ruler were always to be balanced and contained by abstract standards of justice and right. Naboth was completely within his rights to refuse to sell his land to King Ahab, and there was nothing legally justifiable that the king could do. The prophets, in conformity to their vision of a higher authority, repeatedly committed acts that we might consider high treason. Hierarchy demands allegiance, but there is no value placed on absolute obedience (except, of course, to God).

In the same way, women were not expected to be absolutely subordinate to their men. The authority which a husband had over his wife was different from that of parent over child, and there are no penalties for wifely "insurrection."[57] Moreover the power of husband over wife is not generalized to all men over all females. Both father and mother were to be honored by their children, and even though an elderly widow might be economically dependent upon her son (who had formally inherited the property), she was not expected to be controlled by him.

The superior position of husbands was never justified or explained in the Bible (as it was elsewhere) by claims to innate male superiority or a "natural" female desire to obey. Male dominance was assumed: it was part of the social order of the world that the Bible did not question. The Bible has a new religious vision, but it is not a radical *social* document. Even prophets such as Amos and Isaiah who condemned the increasing pauperization of the poor never questioned the *existence* of "rich" and "poor," only the aggrandizement of the rich at the expense of the poor land exploitation of the poverty of the poor. The Bible mitigates the conditions of slavery, but never considers abolishing the institution of slavery itself. The hierarchical division between men and women was yet another social institution that biblical Israel shared with her neighbors and did not think to question. In the primeval history of Genesis,[58] there is a "historical" explanation of male dominance and hierarchy, a point in mythical time when they came along with culture as a result of the actions of Eve and Adam. The divine declaration to Eve in Genesis 3:16, "your desire is for your husband and he rules you" is part of the divine legitimation of the difficult but unquestioned conditions of human existence: work, pain, hierarchy, and death. This divine warrant validates the status quo. It is a reification of the social order that people already have before them, and is tantamount to saying "it is so because it is so." It places a search for equality on a par with a search for ease and harmony with the animals—as part of a paradise lost, and perhaps of the longing for a return to Eden. At the same time, it does not attribute women's subordination to any innate organic reason, nor does it require that women act in ways that justify, support, or prolong their subordination. The Bible has no expectation that woman will be passive or submissive, no prescription that they should be so. Officially, authority and wealth resided with the men. Within the confines of this system, however, biblical women formulated their own goals and acted to achieve them.

There are arenas in which women have a professional life and make professional decisions independent of family structure. We hear of women singers, musicians, composer/writers, prophets, midwives, lamenters.[59] In the period of the Judges, before the consolidation of the state, women may have had access to direct political power.[60] From the early days of the monarchy, we have the stories of two "Wise Women."[61] The Wise Woman of Abel-Bet-Maacah appeared on the ramparts of her city to talk to David's general Joab as he besieged the city, and Joab approached to talk with this woman.[62] Upon hearing Joab's purpose, the Wise Woman took it upon herself to promise to deliver Sheba ben Bichri, who had taken refuge in the city, declaring "his head shall be thrown over the wall to you." She first committed the town to this action, and only afterwards consulted the people, who cut off Sheba's head and threw it over the wall.

Throughout biblical history. women maintained a sphere of authority within the household. Wealth could bring women a certain freedom of action and the authority to act on their own initiative. Abigail waylaid David on the warpath and persuaded him to abandon his attack. The wealthy woman of Shunnem acted upon her own authority to invite Elisha to dine whenever he passed through Shunnem. She enlisted her husband's cooperation only when she wished to have an addition to the house built for Elisha to lodge in. Later, when her son was ill, she went directly to Elisha for help, neither asking permission of her husband, not even informing him of the reason she was going.[63] Abigail and the Shunnemite are fortunate in their wealth, which allows them great freedom of action. But their actions are not depicted as qualitatively distinct from those of other women, as manly or unfeminine.

Women who did not have the power, economic means, or authority to achieve their goals directly worked indirectly through men in power, convincing and influencing them to do their bidding. Queens petition kings. Bathsheba came to David to convince him to make Solomon king,[64] and later to request Abishag the Shunnemite for Adonijah.[65] Much later Esther went to Ahasuerus, the Persian king, to plead for the people, despite her awareness that she could die for approaching the king uninvited. Ordinary women would also petition the kings, gaining access because of the king's role as highest legal arbiter. Two prostitutes came before King Solomon to lay claim to the living son of one of them.[66] The wise woman of Tekoa pretended to come in petition to ask David's help to rescue her son from execution.[67] The great woman of Shunnem, who had fled to Philistia for seven years because of a great famine, came before the king upon her return to call for the restoration of her land and field.[68]

Women would petition any authority. Abigail came to David to convince him not to slaughter her husband's household;[69] the daughters of Zelophehad came to Moses to request that he modify the laws of inheritance so that they could inherit the property of their father, who had left no sons;[70] Achsah, daughter of Caleb, came to her father to ask for a field.[71] Women would turn to prophets on behalf of their sick children.[72] In all these cases, the power to act resided in the male authority figure, and women were limited in what they could do directly. Petition seemed their only recourse. But this limitation did not make them afraid or unwilling to try to achieve their goals, and (at least in the cases we have cited) they do not seem too cowed by any figure of authority to approach him with their requests. As long as there was a chance that the petition might succeed, they could and would approach to make their demands.

In petition, the petitioner's goal is to use powers of persuasion in order to induce someone with sufficient authority to do what the petitioner requests. This ability to persuade does not depend on one's station in life, or on one's gender. Both men and women can talk, argue, flatter, convince, and persuade. Moreover, there is no "Woman-speech" in the Bible: the form of women's argumentation, the nature of their logic and rhetoric are the same as men's. In the Bible, petition takes a distinct form. Biblical argument—both male and female—begins in a striking way. The opening salvo of a biblical petition is designed to catch the other party off guard. The matriarchs successfully primed their husbands to take action by portraying themselves as wronged or miserable. Sarai (later called Sarah), wanting to take action against the slave-concubine Hagar, attacks Abraham, stating "the wrong done me is your fault! . . . The Lord decide between you and me."[73] Abraham, put sharply in the wrong responds, "Your maid is in your hands. Deal with her as you think right."[74] Similarly, when Rebekkah wants Isaac to send their son Jacob back to Aram-Naharaim to marry a kinswoman, she emphasizes (and perhaps exaggerates) her own mood: "I am disgusted with my life because of the Hittite women. If Jacob marries a Hittite woman like these, from among the native women, what good will life be to me?"[75] A similar dire statement is made by the barren Rachel: "Give me children or I shall die!"[76] Jacob, unable to comply, reacts badly to the rhetoric, responding sharply, "Can I take the place of God, who has denied you fruit of the womb?" But Rachel's next words show him what he can do about it: he can take Rachel's handmaiden Bilhah as consort and surrogate mother.[77]

Such guilt-producing rhetorical tactics are very effective. When Achsah came to her father Caleb to ask for a field, she first puts Caleb in the wrong: "for you have given me away as Negeb land (without a dowry), so give me springs of water."[78] Even prophets were not immune to such manipulation. The widow at Zarephath turned to Elijah, saying, "What harm have I done you, O man of God, that you should come here to recall my sin and cause the death of my son."[79] So, too, when the son of the great woman of Shunnem had a stroke and she went in search of Elisha's help, she began by saying "Did I ask my lord for a son: didn't I say 'don't mislead me?'"[80]

Such guilt-producing tactics remind us of the classic ploys of the exaggeratedly portrayed and much mocked "Jewish mother." Nevertheless, the guilt-provoking introduction is a standard form of Biblical rhetoric, and was not the particular property of women. Moses presents the classic paradigm of such tactics. Distressed with the people, he wants help in leading them, and begins his petition to God on the offensive:

> "Why have you dealt ill with your servant and why have I not enjoyed your favor, that You have laid the burden of all this people upon me. Did I conceive this people, did I bear them, that you should say to me 'carry them in your bosom as a nurse carries and infant . . . ?' I cannot carry all this people by myself, for it is too much for me. If you would deal thus with me, kill me rather, I beg you, and let me see no more of my wretchedness."[81]

God responds by allowing others to experience prophetic communion with God.

In Moses' long summation to the people at the beginning of the book of Deuteronomy, [82] he shows himself a master at inducing guilt. He makes the people of Israel receptive to obedience by first reciting their history as an account of all their previous wrongs.[83] Samuel also uses the rhetoric of guilt. In order to induce the people to abandon wrongdoing and affirm a covenant with God, he accentuates their misdeeds. He prefaces the ceremony of choosing Israel's first king with the statement, "today you have rejected your God who delivered you from all your troubles and calamities."[84] His "farewell address" at the king's inauguration reminds the Israelites of their past guilt for idolatry, of the calamities that God brought and the times God that delivered them, and of their present guilt in choosing a king "though the Lord your God is your king."[85] Samuel's peroration is like that of Moses: both condition the people to obey the Lord.[86] The guilt paves the way for the demand. This technique was so effective that its masters had a reputation in later Israel as its greatest intercessor-debaters: in order to dissuade Jeremiah from argument, God says to Jeremiah, "Even if Moses and Samuel were to stand before me, I would not be won over to that people."[87] Biblical rhetoric revered the offense tactic and showed all its great debaters—male and female—as masters of this technique.

Effective rhetoric demands intelligence and understanding. Three little-remembered women, Abigail, the "Wise Woman of Tekoa" and "The Wise Woman of Abel," show how women could succeed at fair rational argumentation. The story of Abigail is almost a paradigm of the timely intervention of a wise woman, and the ability of her wise speech to influence history.[88] The story is set during the period in which David was on the run from King Saul. He has formed a private outlaw army, which protects the Southern Judaean settlers from marauding Bedouin-type invaders and demands money from the settlers for this protection. Nabal (whose name means "boorish fool") refuses to pay on the grounds that he has not hired David. As soon as David leaves, the servants tell their mistress, the beautiful and intelligent Abigail. She immediately understands the situation and the danger that they are in and takes a large amount of food to David, who has already assembled four hundred troops and is on his way to destroy Nabal's household.

The conversation between Abigail and David casts light on the Bible's conception of the proper relationships between men and women. David did not know her, and could not know her wisdom, yet he paused in the middle of a battle march to have a serious discussion with her. He did not dismiss her as a foolish woman or as a distraction. Abigail did not implore David with tears, nor arouse his pity for the innocent men he might kill. She does not appeal to his sense of morality or justice. Instead, she applies her skill at reasoning and argumentation to convince David by those arguments most likely to succeed.

Abigail's rhetorical strategy is to convince David that she wishes him well, and to present her argument in terms of benefit and detriment to David himself. She begins by prostrating herself before him, thus showing homage to David, who is, after all an outlaw sought by King Saul. Then she makes a curious statement "on me be the iniquity, but let me speak."[89] There is a danger to David's listening to her, for David has just taken a battle oath not to leave a single male alive "who pees against a wall." If David does what Abigail is asking, he runs the risk that his oath against himself might destroy him,[90] and so his fear of this oath could prevent him from desisting from the battle. Abigail sets his fear to rest by deflecting the course onto herself.[91]

Abigail next makes it clear that she has come as one of David's supporters. She insults Nabal, "for he is just what his name says: his name means 'boor' and he is a boor." This certainly does not show honor to her husband, but it shows David that she is on his side. A similar rhetorical ploy was used by the Hebrew midwives, Shifrah and Puah. When they were called to task by Pharaoh for not killing the Hebrew boy-babies, they ingratiated themselves with Pharaoh by insulting the Hebrew women (in a passage generally mistranslated): "because the Hebrew women are not like Egyptian women; they are female animals who give birth before the midwife can come to them."[92] Pharaoh was prepared to think ill of and mock the Hebrew women, and this insult by the midwives was calculated to demonstrate that they shared Pharaoh's distaste for the Hebrews. David and the narrator think of Nabal as a boor, and Abigail's insult shows her to be at one with them. Abigail then shows herself to be a supporter of David even in his great struggle with Saul. She takes a solemn oath against all David's enemies that they should all share the fate of Nabal. She proclaims David to be fighting the Lord's battles, and to be without wrong, and asserts her conviction that the Lord has appointed David to be ruler over Israel.[93]

Having made it utterly clear that she is on David's side, Abigail convinces him by that which is most important to him, his divine right to be king. She explains that bloody vengeance on Nabal would bring the stain of blood guilt upon David, and that this could be a stumbling block on his quest for divinely appointed rule. By this argument, David is completely convinced. He announces that he has heeded her plea; he realizes that she has saved his future. He blesses her for restraining him from seeking redress in blood, and praises the Lord for sending her to meet him.[94] By showing David that his future is at stake, Abigail provides a way in which he could "back down" from his argument with Nabal and ignore his vengeful oath, not because of weakness or cowardice (or even compassion, which might be construed as weakness), but in pursuit of his highest ideals and goals, his quest for divinely approved kingship.

The daughters of Zelophehad also focus on what is most important to the one to whom they come in petition. These five daughters, who had no brother, come before Moses to ask for the right to inherit their father's property. Rather than throw themselves on the mercy of the court, or appeal to vague principles of justice for themselves, they point out that their *father* did not deserve to be punished, for he had not been part of Korah's rebellion. They ask that the law be changed to allow them to inherit his land so that their father's patrimony not be disturbed, so that *his* name not perish: "Let not our father's name be lost to his clan just because he had no son!"[95] The continuation of the patriliny was very important to Israel. Losing it is the subject of several curses, and the worst supernatural sanction envisioned in Israel, $k\bar{a}r\bar{e}t$, seems in fact to have implied the extirpation of this line somewhere in the future.[96] Since Zelophehad did not deserve such dire punishment, the daughters argued, they should be allowed to continue his line for him. The daughters have hit the right note: Moses, the readers, and God all agree, and they are allowed to inherit.

These stories, and the very intricate argument of the wise woman of Tekoa,[97] show how speech could be a major strategy for women to control their destiny and influence events. Of course, its effectiveness as a means of influence depends on the receptivity of the listener as well as on the skill of the speaker. It takes a wise man like David to listen to Abigail and perceive the quality of her arguments. When the party with whom one argues has no discernment, speech has no power. The rape of Tamar[98] is a classic story of the confrontation between a wise girl, arguing rationally, and a strong and privileged male intent on acting badly. Tamar, David's daughter, tries to talk her half-brother Ammon out of raping her with words couched in the language of traditional learning: "Such things should no be done in Israel, so don't do this brutish deed."[99] She appeals to his mercy: "Where shall I go in may shame?"[100] She threatens him with disgrace, "You will be one of the boors in Israel," and promises (rightly or wrongly) that he can have her legitimately: "Speak to the king, for he will not keep me from you."[101] Ammon is in no mood to listen, and "being stronger than she," he rapes her and then kicks her out, leaving her desolate. This story shows us why the Bible preserves so many intelligent speeches by women: they contribute to the glory of Abraham, Jacob, and David, who had an ear receptive to the wise words of the women.

Nagging (persistent verbal manipulation and importuning) is another effective form of persuasive speech. This is talk as a weapon of opportunity, for only someone in close and constant proximity to authority can influence it in this way. As such, nagging is a weapon of lovers and wives. The paradigm story of how a man can be nagged to his doom is the story of Samson.[102] Samson's tale has been transmitted in Western cultural tradition as one of the classic stories of sexual seduction and doom. But this version, a product of later ages, is not in the Hebrew Bible. Neither Samson's first wife nor Delilah used sexual wiles or erotic attraction to seduce him.[103] His women tried to *talk* him into revealing a secret. Both of them implored him persistently and harassed him with tears. The nagging of Samson's women (rather than any sexy wiles) did him in.

The first story of the downfall of Samson is almost trivial. At his wedding, Samson wagers thirty garments that the men of the wedding party can't solve his wedding riddle. The men threaten to set fire to Samson's wife and her household if she doesn't find out the answer. When Samson points out that he has not even told his parents, his wife accuses him of not loving her, "You really hate me, you don't love me." She keeps bringing the matter up, and "continued to harass him with her tears until on the seventh day he told her, because she nagged him so."[104]

Samson, a case of brawn with little brain, was vulnerable to this form of nagging persuasion. He fell victim to this ploy once again, with his beloved Delilah, with whom he lived.[105] Delilah was enticed by an enormous amount of money[106] to join the opponents of Samson and Israel. When Delilah asks Samson what made him so strong, he lies, saying that if he were tied with fresh untied tendons he would be weak. So she binds him with them, and calls, "Samson, the Philistines are upon you." He tears the tendons apart and Delilah accuses him of lying to her. Samson lies again, repeating the story with the variation of new ropes, and then yet again with the weaving of seven locks of hair. At this point, Delilah adopts the tactics of Samson's first wife, saying "How can you say you love me, when you don't confide in me?" Finally, "After she had nagged him and pressed him constantly, he was wearied to death and he confided everything to her."[107] The combination of the guilt-producing accusation that he does not love her and the sheer persistence of its repetition wears away Samson's resistance.

This is a sad tale of the end of one of Israel's heroes. Along with the history lesson, it shows how women's persistent speech can be a weapon of opportunity. The endless repetition of the same argument persuades by its very nuisance value. This type of speech is particularly effective for women, who live in the same household as those they attempt to convince.[108] It is another aspect, along with guilt and wise argumentation, of the Bible's multifaceted picture of discourse as an important power of women. This biblical portrayal of women's talk reflects social reality: most women did not have status or property, and used the strategems and powers at their disposal, which included their wits and their tongue.

Women could also deceive. In this way, they could gain access to areas that would otherwise be closed to them, as when Moses' mother and sister pretended to be strangers to the baby Moses.[109] The story of Rahab is a clear example of how women could lie to save fugitives. Two Israelite spies lodged with the prostitute, Rahab, in Jericho. When the king of Jericho sent orders to Rahab to produce the men, she hid them beneath the flax on her roof, said that the men had left when the gate was about to be closed, and even urged the soldiers to pursue them. Then, after the soldiers left, she let the spies down by a rope over the town wall.[110] In a variation of this theme, Michal, the daughter of King Saul, told her husband David to run for his life lest Saul kill him. She let him down by the window and bought him time to escape by taking a household idol, laying it on the bed, covering its head with goat's-hair, covering it with a blanket, and claiming that David was lying in bed sick.[111] There are also occasions when women lie to protect themselves: Rachel claimed to be menstruating so that she would not have to get up and allow Laban to search her seat for the images that she had taken from him. After Michal, the king's daughter, helped David escape, she claimed that David had threatened to kill her if she didn't help him.[112] In the book of Genesis, in the tales of the ancestors, pretense includes the elaborate tricks of Tamar (see pp. 123–124), and Rebekkah. The aged Isaac sent his favorite and oldest son Esau to hunt and cook game in anticipation of Isaac's death-bed blessing. Since it would have been futile for Rebekkah, Isaac's wife, to try to convince Isaac to choose her favorite, Jacob, she conceived a plan and convinced Jacob to carry it out. She disguised goat meat as game and Jacob as Esau, dressing Jacob in Esau's clothes, and covering his hands and neck

with the skins of the kids. Jacob went in to the blind Isaac pretending
to be Esau and took Esau's blessing for himself. Once given, the blessing could not be retracted, and Esau had to settle for a lesser benedic-
tion.[113]

What are we to make of these stories of deception? Do they tarnish
the image of Rebekkah, a matriarch of Israel, or of Tamar, ancestress
of king David? The Bible shows no hint of condemnation of these
women,[114] The "deceitful" plan of Tamar is not presented as different
from the cunning plan of Naomi, which did not involve deception.
The story of Ruth, Naomi, and Boaz is another story of the ancestry
of David, and is somewhat parallel to the story of Tamar, to which
it explicitly refers. Naomi, a widow whose sons have died, and her
daughter-in-law Ruth, also a childless widow, come back from Moab
to the area in which Naomi's clan lives. Conceiving a plan to ensure
their future, Naomi sends Ruth to glean in the fields of Boaz, a kinsman, so that he can get to know her. Then, after he has been kind to
Ruth and has treated her like one of his household, Naomi sends Ruth
to him again, in the middle of the night, to show her availability and
persuade him to marry her. In this story there is no real "deception,"
since Boaz knows who Ruth is; but there is, in addition to Ruth's bold-
ness, Naomi's crafty planning and cunning manipulation. The actions
of Ruth and Naomi are heroic and laudable in the same way as are the
acts of Rebekkah and Tamar. Rebekkah acted to enable the destiny of
Jacob, announced in her pregnancy oracle, to come to pass. Tamar and
Ruth served society and family by insuring the continuation of the family lineage. Without Rebekkah's trick, Jacob might not have become
the father of all Israel, and without the plots of Tamar and the later
plans of Ruth and Naomi, there would have been no King David! The
cunning and sometimes deceptive women in the Bible serve to effect
God's purpose and actualize God's designs.

The Bible's approval of woman's trickery is not simply a case of the
end justifying the means. These women had no other way to do what
they had to do, what was necessary for them to do in order to achieve
(in Israel's view) God's aims. Trickery and deception have always been
considered characteristics of the underclass. In part, the portrayal of a
tricky underclass reflects fear that its members will somehow dupe
those in power; in large part, it is an accurate description of a reality
in which those without status have nothing to lose and may have something to gain by maneuvering, manipulating, and deceiving. Biblical
women, including heroines of Israel, are portrayed as using tricks and
lies. And so are the men. The great cultural heroes of Israel all lie and

deceive. The patriarch Abram (later called Abraham) instructed Sarai to say that she was his sister when they went down to Egypt so that he might stay alive,[115] a trick he later repeated when they went to Gerar. Although he later mitigates this lie by explaining to Abimelech, king of Gerar, that Sarah was his half-sister, he has neglected to inform the king that she is his wife.[116] This is a thrice-told story,[117] for Isaac also tells the people of Gerar that his wife (Rebekkah) is his sister.[118] In these dangerous situations, Abraham and Isaac save their lives by this ruse, whose three-fold telling reflects a kind of pride in the cunning of Abraham and Isaac. Indeed, there is relish and an entertainment value to these trickster stories. This is particularly evident in the cycle of tales about the patriarch Jacob, which include stories of the trickster and of the trickster tricked. In the first ruse, Rebekkah and Jacob take advantage of the old patriarch's age and blindness.[119] One good trick deserves another, and Jacob gets his comeuppance when Laban substitutes Leah for her sister Rachel at the wedding.[120] Jacob and Laban later have another round of trickmanship, in the involved tale of the speckling of the sheep, by which Jacob becomes very prosperous.[121] The affairs of Jacob and Laban then end in trickery as Rachel tricks Laban. These trickery stories are all told without condemnation.

The Bible also records, without condemnation, the trick by which the Gibeonites made peace with Israel,[122] Moses' deception of Pharaoh about the Israelite plan to go to the desert to worship God at a three-day festival, and David's lies to Ahimelech the priest[123] and to Achish of Gath.[124] In the Hebrew Bible, even God does not have absolute standards of honesty. He fibbed to protect Sarah, claiming that she had laughed because she was old, and not relating that she had said that Abraham was too old.[125] He sent Moses to misinform Pharaoh about the Israelites' plans. Most seriously, the prophet Micaiah has a vision in which God purposely deceives his own prophets.[126] In this vision, God decides to send a "lying spirit" to the prophets of Israel so that they will encourage Ahab to go fight at Ramoth-Gilead. The prophets who promised victory were not false prophets, deceptively telling the king what he wanted to hear. They themselves were deceived by God, who sent a lying spirit into the mouth of the prophets so as to ensure disaster for Ahab.

Not all instances of trickery were admired in Israel. The tricks and lies used by the underdog to escape, survive, or advance are admired, but deception by a superior which involves an abuse of power or contract is clearly considered wrong.[127] The Bible recognizes the power of indirection, and neither the women of the Bible nor the narrators who portray them hold "truth" or "fair play" as absolute values. In this, there is no cultural clash between the storytellers and their female characters, no assumed difference between the women of Israel and the men.[128] On the contrary, the fact that Israel's eponymous ancestor Jacob and great hero-king David are both tricksters should indicate to us that Israel viewed this strategy as a powerful weapon in the hands of the powerless.

We should mention one more strategy that is used by women in the Bible, one that on closer examination turns out to be a strategy of all Israel: the use of food and nurture. Women obviously have close connection with food for sound historical, sociological, and psychological reasons. Men might cook (most often, meat), but women usually cooked the grains and breads that were the dietary staples of most peoples. The close association of women and food finds its way into biblical mythology, for it is the woman Eve who first partakes of the fruit of knowledge and then gives it to Adam. Biblical legend relates how the power of food seduced Israel when it was still in the desert, subsisting on manna. The Moabite women invited them to a sacrificial feast, and when the Israelites ate the food (and thanks were given to the god of the Moabites), they were brought to the great sin of worshiping the god Ba'al-Peor.[129]

The story of Yael and the death of Sisera the Canaanite general[130] is a dramatic illustration of the power of deception and nurture. Yael is a heroine of Israel who made possible the success of Israel in Canaan, and her story is told in both poetry and prose (Judges 4 and 5). Israel defeated the Canaanite forces, But General Sisera escaped and could regroup his troops to fight again. Sisera comes to the tent of Yael, whose husband is in league with Canaanites. She invites him in and assures him that he need not fear. She gives him milk to drink, covers him with a blanket, and offers to stand at the entrance to the tent and misdirect anyone who would pursue him. By this hospitality, she induces in him a sense of well-being and security, and he goes to sleep in confidence. Once he is asleep, she drives a tent pin through his temple.[131] In this story, Sisera has certain expectations: that the private domain will provide sanctuary and that the woman will lie to protect him. Yael uses these expectations to create an opportunity for her to act. Once she has the chance, she acts directly and violently.

Women may be most likely to use food and nurture, for these are the currency of the private domain, the one in which women were most prominent. But particularly in the early pastoral economy, there were also men in the private domain, among them the great culture heroes.

Men, too, had access to food, and they would use it both to offer service and to advance their aims. Once again, Jacob, the ancestor of all Israel, is the male counterpart to woman's use of food. He is described as a "sitter in tents,"i.e., he lived in the domestic world. Therefore, it is not surprising to find him cooking pottage, or to see him use his food to seduce Esau to give away his birthright. Under most circumstances, men were prominent in the public domain and women in the private. When women were in positions of public power, their actions showed no difference from those of men; when men were active in the domestic world (but not as patriarch), they behaved like women. The difference in activity between women and men is circumstantial rather than innate: both use the powers and strategies of the world in which they find themselves.

## The Ideology of Gender

When we survey the biblical record of the goals and strategies of women, a startling fact emerges. There is nothing distinctively "female" about the way that women are portrayed in the Bible, nothing particularly feminine about either their goals or their strategies. The goals of women are the same goals held by the biblical male characters and the authors of the stories. Conversely, those goals which might be considered female-specific, such as female solidarity and rage, are completely absent from the biblical record. Women pursue their goals as actively as men, and use the same techniques and strategies that men in their situation could be expected to use. The Bible does not attribute to women several strategies and powers that became associated with women in Western cultural tradition. Most conspicuously, beauty is never portrayed as a woman's weapon. The beauty of women is a mark of divine favor, as is the beauty of men. Sometimes a woman's beauty can set her up to be a victim, in that men of power might desire and take her. In this way, Sarah was at risk from Pharaoh (as were Sarah and Rebekkah from Abimelech of Gerar in the parallel stories) and Bathsheba was taken by David. In these cases, the women is an object and a victim: she herself is not out to get anything by using her beauty.[132]

The biblical tales of women's persuasion also ignore erotic attraction. There are no stories of sexual enticement, no femmes fatales, no figures like Mata Hari who use sex to seduce and then deceive men. There are women who actively seek sex in the Bible, either for enjoyment (like the "other woman" in Proverbs and Potiphar's wife) or for children (like Tamar and, possibly, Ruth). But in these cases, sex is the woman's goal; it is never a woman's strategy in order to gain power, influence, or information, never a woman's weapon by which she seeks to disarm or weaken men. This ignoring of eros is part of the Bible's homogenization of gender. In stories such as Ammon and Tamar, sexual attraction undoubtedly played a part, but (as with beauty) it sets the woman up as a victim. The Bible never considers eros a tool of women, as something against which men should guard. The Bible does not present beauty and lust—both of which might tend to emphasize the differences between male and female and to codify the woman as "other"—as part of a woman's toolkit at all.

Indeed, there is no woman's toolkit. There are only the strategies that are used along the various axes of power: women-men; men-men of power; Israel-nations. Israel, as a small, beleaguered, and ultimately captured nation had good reason to value the powers of the weak. Intelligence, guilt, trickery, and astuteness are the very attributes that Israel needs to survive. The Bible presents no characteristics of human behavior as "female" or "male," no division of attributes between the poles of "feminine" and "masculine," no hint of distinctions of such polarities as male aggressivity–female receptivity, male innovation-female conservation, male out-thrusting-female containment, male subjecthood-female objecthood, male rationality-female emotionality, male product-female process, male achievement-female bonding, or any of the other polarities by which we are accustomed to think of gender distinctions.[133] As far as the Bible presents humanity, gender is a matter of biology and social roles, it is not a question of basic nature or identity. When the social role of the nation resembles that of a woman in Israelite social structure—then the women symbolize Israel, both in their subordination and in their powers of indirection.[134]

The essential similarity between male and female in biblical thought underlies the story of the creation of Eve. Adam, the primeval human has been created alone, either as male or as androgyne. But Adam is lonely, and God sets out to create a suitable companion for the human. Humanity is at this point so simple, so innocent, that God creates the animals, and brings them before Adam on the chance that Adam will find among them his true companion. Adam names them, establishing a relationship with them, but does not find among them his true companion. God thereupon sets out to make a special creation as this "help-meet" and creates a woman to go with Adam's manhood. These two are so close that they are "flesh of my flesh, bone of my bones" and set the pattern for all future generations in which a man and a woman are to form a close pair-bonding.

The significance of this story for the question of gender is clear, when we see it in the light of two Mesopotamian literary creations, the Epic of Gilgamesh and the Ṣaltu Hymn. In the Gilgamesh story, Gilgamesh is far superior to all the other people in the world (he is, unique among them, part god). As a result of this superiority, he oppresses his people, and their outcry reaches the gods. The gods of Mesopotamia are not simply punitive. They are rational, ethical, and understanding of human nature. They realize that Gilgamesh only acts this way because he has no equal, on one who can meet him on an equal footing. As a result, they decide upon the special creation of a new being who will be as superior as Gilgamesh; the mother-goddess takes clay and creates Enkidu—another male. The true companion for Gilgamesh is not a woman to occupy his attention, but a male to be his close buddy. The truest bonding, the truest similarity possible is between two members of the same gender. Male chauvinism is not the issue, for the gods do not create a male because a female in inherently inferior. But there is a clear sexual distinction: a woman would be different, or other, and could not preoccupy Gilgamesh. The same reasoning applies to Enki's plan for the goddess Ishtar in the Old Babylonian Ṣaltu Hymn. Ishtar is unlike the other goddesses: she is undomesticated, fierce, and wild; her ferocity has begun to frighten and dismay the other gods. Enki does not bring a male to "tame" her; he creates a companion to occupy her time, a new goddess, another fierce female, Ṣaltu, and sends her to Ishtar. The issue is not one of superiority or inferiority; it is a matter of difference, of distinctiveness, of a sense that man and woman can never be as like each other as man to man or woman to woman.

In contrast to such gender-specific thinking, the biblical story of Adam and Eve presents woman and men as the true suitable companions to each other. The same gender ideology also underlies the other biblical tale of the creation of humanity, Genesis 1. Male and female are created at the same time, and they are both created in the image, the likeness of God. The differences between male and female are only a question of genitalia rather than of character. This view of the essential sameness of men and women is most appropriate to monotheism. There are no goddesses to represent "womanhood" or a female principle in the cosmos; there is no conscious sense that there even exists a "feminine." Whenever radical monotheism came to biblical Israel, the consideration of one God influenced and underscored the biblical image of women.

The Bible's gender-free concept of humanity contrasted sharply with Israelite reality. Life in ancient Israel was structured along gender lines. Women were overwhelmingly expected to concern themselves with domestic concerns; some men, at least, were to participate in public life. This gender division was caused in large part by the socioeconomic and physical realities of life: the household was the basic production unit, and women and men had to perform their economic tasks. Women had to have children to ensure the family's survival, in a real as well as a metaphorical sense; for without a labor force, the subsistence chores could not be done. A division of labor within the household was necessary, the particular gender division of tasks had probably been culturally transmitted since the Neolithic development of agriculture and the domestication of animals. The Bible's view of the essential sameness of the sexes does not correspond to this reality, and does not provide the conceptual framework and ideology by which people could understand, appreciate, and find value in the gendered aspect of their lives. The gender-blindness of the biblical view of human nature, appealing as it is to us (who live a much less gender-determined existence than did the people of the ancient world) did not provide the language and tools for a biblical self-understanding of the gendered life of ancient Israel. As a result, this view of a unified humanity was eventually overlaid with new concepts that entered Israel at the end of the biblical period. The stories about women were reinterpreted, and these later reinterpretations, masquerading as the biblical message, were used to support sexist ideology and practice. The stories themselves remained to be rediscovered by an age that could understand and appreciate the biblical metaphysics of gender unity.

# 12

## The Wanton Wife of God

Biblical monotheism's difficult and abstract concept of the importance of humanity and its role as counterpart of God is best understood through metaphor. Israel's gender system, which combines the social inequality of the sexes with an ideological construction of the essential sameness of men and women, makes it possible to imagine the relationship of God and Israel as the marriage of husband and wife. This "marital metaphor" expresses the intense emotionality of the divine–human relationship. In its vision of a relationship between adults, it acknowledges the mature responsibilities of humanity. It thus aptly conveys a sense of the mutuality, intimacy, and turbulence in the relationship between human and divine.

At first glance, it seems very odd to portray God and Israel as a married couple. The partners in this relationship are quite unlike human husbands and wives. The husband is God, masculine in gender, but never conceived as male in sexual terms. The wife is Israel, portrayed as a woman despite the maleness of the prophetic writers and, we assume, of many of their listeners. The marriage between God and Israel is noncorporeal, never portrayed in physical or sexual terms, and the rules of this marriage do not conform to the legal norms of Israelite marriage. Nevertheless, this metaphor, developed primarily in the works of the prophets Hosea, Jeremiah, and Ezekiel, powerfully evokes the intense bonding of Israel and God. The Bible's depiction of women and men as analogous and essentially similar to each other makes it possible to use an image in which the people of Israel are conceptualized collectively as a woman. At the same time, the hierarchical nature of Israelite marriage provides a way to portray a relationship between partners infinitely unequal to each other in power. The marriage that results between these partners is intense and emotional; it also a nightmare of domination in a punitive relationship.

144

The first clear exposition of this theme is found in the first three chapters of Hosea, in which the early prophet Hosea[1] develops and lives out an extended allegory of the relationship between God and Israel as a holy family in which God has a "wife" who is the mother of the children of Israel. Hosea's marriage does not begin auspiciously, for, Hosea relates, he was directed to seek out a "wife of promiscuity."[2] The marriage is scripted for failure, and Hosea's difficult relations with his wife are to be a dramatic parallel to the relations of Israel with God.

The central piece of Hosea's allegory is Chapter 2, a poetic prophetic reflection on the relationship between Israel and God and its impact on fertility. This poem begins with the failed marriage, as God repudiates his wife: "for she is not my wife, and I am not her husband." The reason for this repudiation is infidelity. The wife, Israel, in her anxiety to ensure her well-being, thought:

"I will go after my lovers,[3] who supply my bread and my water, my wool and my linen, my oil and my drink.". . . . And she did not consider this: it was I who bestowed on her the new grain and wine and oil. . . .

As a result, God "will strip her naked as on the day she was born," meaning that he will remove the very fertility she seeks:

I will take back my new grain in its time and my new wine in its season, and I will snatch away my wool and my linen that serve to cover her nakedness. . . . I will lay waste her vines and her fig trees which she thinks are a fee she received from her lovers . . . thus will I punish her for the days of the Baalim on which she brought them offerings when, decked with earrings and jewels, she would go after her lovers, forgetting me.

As a result of this devastation, Israel will come to the realization that God is her only provider. Then the marriage can begin anew:

I will speak coaxingly to her and lead her through the wilderness and speak to her tenderly . . . then she will respond as in the days of her youth, when she came up from the land of Egypt.

The results of this remarriage will be prosperity and fertility:

In that day I will speak, declares the Lord, I will speak to the skies and they will speak to the earth and the earth will speak with new grain and wine and oil, and they shall speak to "Jezreel ["God Sows"]."

This poem encapsulates the classic Israelite view of human action and divine reactivity: the action of Israel determines God's actions in the world. But Hosea's poem, and the metaphor it articulates, captures the drama and pathos of the interaction between God and Israel. Israel is unfaithful, God is angry and jealous, God punishes and then relents. God the husband is agonized by Israel's betrayal, but maintains his steadfast love for his wife. Israel the wife is insecure and wanton, but will return to God after severe punishment. From the point of view of modern society, this is a pathological relationship: God has married a promiscuous wife and Israel has entered a punitive relationship with a dominant husband. Both because of its view of the closeness between Israel and God, and because of its dramatic presentation of the difficulties that this closeness creates, the marital metaphor is a very powerful image.

It is not easy to pinpoint the origin of this metaphor. The book of Psalms contains no trace of it, an indication that it does not grow out of Israelite cultic practice and was not celebrated liturgically. The Pentateuch, however, may hint at such a concept. In general, the tone of the Pentateuch is juridical; its dominant metaphor is the covenant; its concerns are Israel's historical obligation to God, the legal obligations that this creates, and the institutions and laws by which Israel maintains this covenanted relationship to God. Nevertheless, in discussing these covenantal stipulations, the Pentateuch uses metaphorical language such as "love," "jealousy," and "be promiscuous." Three relationships demand absolute fidelity by one partner for the other: the loyalty of vassal to suzerain, the allegiance of wife for husband, and Israel's devotion to God. Love language is used for all three. The ancient Near Eastern political treaties that form the pattern for covenantal formulation, demand the "love" of the vassal for the suzerain.[4] Israel's relationship to God shares this demand for exclusivity: the Ten Commandments begin with the clear and unequivocal demand, "You shall have no other gods before me!" The Torah describes the divine–human bond in the language of these exclusive human relationships. Deuteronomy, which fully develops covenantal language, demands "love" from Israel for God, a "love" which manifests itself by fidelity and obedience to commandments and laws.[5] The Pentateuch also uses marital language to express the breaking of this loyalty-bond and its consequences.[6] Failure to maintain exclusive loyalty to God is called "wantonness" or promiscuity $(znh)$[7] and God's reaction is to this faithfulness is his "jealousy" $(qn^{\circ})$. This legal language[8] has strong emotional impact. The Torah's

use of this imagery may have been influenced by the prophetic development of the marital metaphor. It may also be the source of it.[9]

It seems unlikely that Hosea invented this metaphor because of his
own troubled marriage.[10] After all, the metaphor did not have meaning
only for Hosea; it shared its impact with his listeners and tradents,
those who transmitted his work to later generations. There are elements
in the relationship of God to Israel that make this metaphor odd; nevertheless, it is a natural and powerful image that speaks immediately to
the experience of the people of Israel. First, the metaphor addresses
reality head on: Israel experiences drought and warfare. Israel is suffering, and blames itself. When God is portrayed as betrayed husband
rather than dispassionate judge or insensitive automaton, then God's
own frustrated desires and suffering are brought into focus. The metaphor enables human beings to understand God's emotions by analogy
to those of any cuckolded human husband. Through this imagery, the
people of Israel are enabled to *feel* God's agony. The men know the
worry that their wives will not be loyal, they know about adultery and
the outraged anger that it brings. The women know the honor of fidelity, the shame that a man feels when he has been unable to command
the exclusive loyalty of his wife, the dishonor that a woman feels before
her peers.[11] As a result, the image of God as betrayed husband strikes
deep into the psyche of the people of Israel and enables them to feel the
faithless nature of their actions.

The metaphor undoubtedly rests upon Israelite conceptions of marriage. The love of God and Israel is not the idyllic relationship of the
Song of Songs (when seen as an allegory for God and Israel); it is not
a love affair between equal partners.[12] It is a hierarchical marriage in
which the husband is the dominant partner. Marriage in Israel was certainly not "egalitarian" in the modern sense of the world. At the same
time, it was not the hierarchy of master and servant, but a bond between loving intimates. As such it was an exact paradigm of the biblical
conception of the proper relationship of people and God. The people
are to love and desire God and to accept his governance willingly.
Taken collectively, all together, they stand in relationship to God as a
wife does to her husband. The marital metaphor for the divine–human
relationship helps both the men and women of Israel to understand the
role of loving obedience that is demanded upon them. At the same time,
God-as-husband and Israel-as-wife are bonded as closely as two separate personae can be.

This bond of love and commitment between marital partners provides the positive note in a marriage that might otherwise be called disastrous. The marriage is not a "happily ever after" affair. The wife of Hosea/God is a wanton, and does not give God the steadfast exclusive loyalty that is expected of her. God-as-husband is not forbearing. He is angry, and punishes. Nevertheless, the marriage does not end, for the marital metaphor emphasizes the commitment of God to Israel. The repudiation will only be temporary, and God will come again to woo his bride, and re-espouse her. After the disaster comes the reconciliation; after the destruction, the renewal; after the violence, the love-making.

There is a profoundly disturbing aspect to this marriage, particularly to modern eyes that do not accord punitive rights to husbands. Undoubtedly, this portrait of marriage that seems so abusive to us is intended to declare love for God and God's love for the people, to condemn Israel rather than God, and to offer assurances that God will not abandon the people. Nevertheless, the metaphor rests on the assumption that the husband has the right to punish his wife. Did biblical Israel expect and condone domestic violence? The law collections offer neither knowledge nor approval of such behavior (unlike the Middle Assyrian Laws, which specifically give the husband the right to beat his wife).[13] Nevertheless, even late twentieth-century America, which specifically condemns wife-beating, is finding domestic violence to be far more common than it would like to believe. Furthermore, all the dimorphic metaphors for the relationship of God and Israel are inherently unequal and punitive. A shepherd disciplines the flock, it does not discipline him. A master punishes a slave, and never the slave the master. The king punishes his servants, and not the servants the king. A father disciplines his child, and not the child the parent. And a husband in a hierarchical marriage always has the power (physical, political, and economic), and may be expected to use it to enforce his dominion over his wife.

The question must be asked whether this relationship of God to Israel is intended to serve as the paradigm for Israelite marriage. After all, in polytheism, the relationship between the gods is both mirror of and model for human social relationships. Can this be true in the Bible? Does the metaphor itself give men the right to be jealous of their wives, and to punish them when they do not live up to their husbands' expectations?[14] There are some indications that this was not so. The marriage of God and Israel is conceived as fundamentally unlike human marriage. Israelite norms indicate that a suspicious husband could divorce his wife[15] or could bring her to the temple to be tested by potion to see if she might be guilty.[16] Once he put her away and she married another, however, the husband was prohibited from remarrying his former wife. But God moves beyond these norms and promises to remarry Israel. The seventh-century Judean prophet Jeremiah, who uses and develops Hosea's marital allegory, declares this difference explicitly: even though a human husband who has divorced his wife cannot take her back after she has remarried someone else, God stands ready to take back Israel.[17] There are other deviances from Israelite norms of marriage: God has married (according to Jeremiah) two sisters, Israel and Judah, though Israelite men may not do so.[18] In the future (according to Deutero-Isaiah), both God and the children of Israel will marry the city Zion, whereas in biblical law a man and his son may not both lie with the same women. God's love for Israel is analogous to the love of a husband for his wife, but God's powers are much greater than a human husband's. God's special prerogatives are spelled out explicitly: "for I am God and not a Man."[19] The Israelite listener knew that God was different. After all, biblical law stresses that society cannot punish children for the crimes of their parents; nevertheless, the Ten Commandments declare that God punishes children, grandchildren, and greatgrandchildren for the sins of the parent.[20] The punitive actions of God-as-husband would not have been seen as a model for the behavior of human husbands in ancient Israel. In fact, the descriptions of God's punitive actions would have occasioned no surprise. The people of Israel knew that they were suffering, and accepted that they were being punished. What they seek from this metaphor is reassurance that anger will not displace love, that punishment is not accompanied by permanent rejection. Beyond other metaphors of power and punishment like judge and criminal, king and servant, and like the other family metaphor of father and child, the marital metaphor emphasizes love, pathos, and commitment.

The marital metaphor also draws its power from human worries about sexuality. It portrays Israel's lack of perfect fidelity as sexual license. The free sexuality of the female partner (clearly a source of societal worry in the Bible) becomes the metaphor for religious apostasy. The sexual imagery becomes increasingly graphic as the metaphor is elaborated in Jeremiah and Ezekiel. Jeremiah begins his first address to this Whoring Woman by remembering the bride who followed God into the wilderness,[21] and recounts Israel's past misdeeds as the behavior of a wanton wife and a lascivious lady who reclines as a whore on every high hill and under every verdant tree."[22] Her sexual passion is her undoing; she is like a lustful she-camel running around in heat, parching her throat and wearing out her sandals, unable to stop, saying "I love the strangers and after them I must go." This wife has waited for her lovers on the roadside, lain with them on the heights, defiled the land with whoring and debauchery, refused to be penitent, and stayed convinced that God would always forgive.

For this reason, despite her protestations of innocence—even because of them—she will be punished. Neither Egypt nor Assyria will be able to help her and she will go out with her hand on her head.[23]

Hosea never specifies who the wanton wife is. To him, she is the "mother" of the people of Israel, a personification of the nation as a whole, or, possibly of its capital city and its court. Jeremiah sometimes names her as Jerusalem, and sometimes all of Judah. He draws the parable of two rebel sisters, faithless Israel and faithless Judah.[24] This wife, who is both the city and the nation, is defiled and promiscuous. Jeremiah's language is graphically sexual, perhaps pornographic.[25] Israel's sin is sexual, as she spreads her legs for her lovers, and her punishment will be equally sexual—she will be exposed to the eyes of all: "I will uncover her shame in the very sight of her lovers"; "I in turn will lift your skirts over your face and your shame shall be seen."[26]

The strong sexual tone becomes even more intense in Ezekiel, the prophet of the Babylonian exile.[27] Ezekiel is a Judean deprived of his land, a priest deprived of his temple. He is angry in his exile, and has no love for the city of Jerusalem. Ezekiel speaks of three sinful "sisters": Jerusalem, Samaria, and Sodom. Sodom's sin and its punishment are infamous, but Jerusalem, the bloody city, was even worse. Moreover Jerusalem and Samaria, whom Ezekiel renames Oholah and Oholibah, whored and defiled themselves.[28] Ezekiel devotes a chapter[29] to the story of the Wanton City-woman. This girl was born unwanted to an Amorite mother and a Hittite father, and was exposed at birth, still covered with her birth blood. God found her and saved her. After she grew to womanhood, God espoused her and adorned her. She, however, began to whore with such insatiable lust that she lavished her favors on all comers, and even made phallic images to fornicate with them. She is a lascivious sex-crazed adulteress, running after her lovers, demanding no prostitution fees, and ready even to pay those who will fornicate with her. As her punishment, God will first assemble all the lovers and expose her nakedness in front of them, and will then deliver her into their hands to stone her and strip her.

The explicit sexual imagery used by these prophets to indict the wife has led many to assume that the sin was sexual; that Hosea, in particular, was reacting to sexual rites that his wife and others were

performing. Most probably, there were no sexual religious rites in ancient Israel.[30] Moreover, the prophets Jeremiah and Ezekiel explicitly
name the adulterous deeds of the wife: apostasy (worship of foreign
gods) and political alliances. The worship of other gods is obviously an
offense against God-the-husband. But the courting of foreign political
powers is also understood as promiscuity, for it violates the exclusive
fidelity which the husband claims from his wife. If the wife looks to
others to help her in her distress, it doesn't matter whether these others
are Ba'al or Egypt/Assyria. The approach to another is a breach of
promise to the husband. Nations as well as gods are called "lovers";
when she runs after these, they will fail her: "All your paramours[31] shall
be devoured by the wind and your lovers[32] shall go into captivity."[33]
The intensity of the sexual imagery, both of the misdeed and its punishment, evokes persistent fears of sexually aggressive women and sexually
unsatisfiable adulterous wives.

Does this negative portrayal of Israel-as-wife rise from anti-woman
feelings?[34] Until Ecclesiastes, there are no overt anti-woman statements
in the Hebrew Bible, no respectable misogyny to compare to the classic
comments in the much later apocryphal Testament of Reuben, the New
Testament, or Patristic texts. The depiction of the Wanton City-woman
is the most truly negative portrayal of any female in the Bible. Consciously, the anger of these prophets is directed against the people (or
the city), rather than against its women. Ezekiel even assures us that
the Wanton is unlike wanton women, for she solicits instead of being
solicited, and pays fees instead of being paid.[35] Nevertheless, the intensity of these passages and their sexual fantasies of nymphomania and
revenge seem to be fueled by unconscious fear and rage.[36]

This fear of women's sexual license arises in part from the male's
fear of losing control over his wife. It is not sexuality that is the problem, but the fact that it is not directed towards the husband. The ability
of the marital metaphor to evoke strong unconscious emotions and to
bring these emotions into the arena of the divine–human relationship
adds dramatic impact to the metaphor. The marital image draws on
both marital bonding and conjugal anxiety, and encompasses both the
beauty of the intimacy and mutuality between Israel-as-wife and God-
as-husband and the terror of it. The marital partners, Israel and God,
are *not* equal. There is an enormous power imbalance between the husband and wife, far more than in human marriage. God is not only the
dominant husband: God is God, master of all the powers of the cosmos. When God becomes angry, catastrophe follows. When God repudiates the people, nature languishes and military enemies overrun the

country. The closeness and intensity of the bond can be as terrible as they can be wonderful. The marital metaphor reveals the dramatic inner core of monotheism: the awesome solo mastery of God brings humans into direct unadulterated contact with supreme power. All of humankind's actions stand in sharp relief, and human destiny is irrevocably in human hands; for in this relationship, the people stand directly before and with God. There are no intermediaries, no buffers, no intercessors. There is only us and God.

# 13

## Asherah and Abundance

Sophisticated monotheism is very abstract, for the one God who is worshiped cannot be seen or imaged. The religious thinking of the prophets and Deuteronomy continually made Israel's religion more abstract, eradicating all visual symbols, eliminating the heavenly court, and leaving only human beings and God. Human responsibility was seen as extending to the whole world; human failure could result in the destruction of everything. The very existence of nature, the people of Israel are told, depends on their observance of laws of social behavior which have ostensibly nothing at all to do with the natural order. We can only imagine the bewilderment of farmers who are told that the earth will be fertile so long as farmers remember to treat the poor correctly. Such a theology places the responsibility for fertility on human beings, but it provides no ritual to help assure fertility, no rite by which to celebrate abundance, no way to participate in the mystery of regeneration. It seems impossible that the farmers of Israel could have adhered to a system so abstract, so devoid of symbols for such important matters, so lacking in emotional outlet for their concerns.

The answer is that they did not. Over and over, the prophets assert that the people are "backsliding" or "stiffnecked." The prophets Hosea (eighth century, northern Israel) and Jeremiah (seventh century, Judah) both complain that the people are worshiping "on every lofty hill and under every green tree."[1] Despite the vigorous opposition of the prophets, the people of Israel maintained these rituals and did not find them incompatible with the worship of YHWH. In fact, the complex of altar, tree, hill, and megalith that characterized this worship was an ancient and integral part of Israel's religious life, and the "reforms" of Hezekiah and Josiah that destroyed this complex were a radical innovation rather than a return to some pristine purity.[2] The tenacity of this

153

worship may indicate its importance to the people of Israel; indeed, this nature-oriented worship may have enabled the people of Israel to feel the immanence of God and to continue to worship the abstract and demanding YHWH.

The traditional religion of Israel was in no way aniconographic or abstract. On the contrary, Israel had many religious symbols of God's presence and power. In the settlement period (twelfth to tenth centuries B.C.E.), the portable ark was the visible symbol and manifestation of God's presence. The Jerusalem temple was replete with visual images, and included such architectural features as a large bronze "sea" symbolizing God's dominion over the cosmos. The temple also contained cult objects that represented Israel's sacred history and focused the people's desires. The cherubim and the ark were manifestations of God's presence; the tablets of the law were reminders of the covenant. A sample of the manna (heavenly food) that Israel ate during its desert wanderings was preserved in the temple as a reminder of God's nurturance and provision.[3] The temple also contained a bronze serpent which was said to have been made by Moses at the time of a plague of snakes. Kept in the temple, this icon served as a focus for human desires for health and healing.[4] The sacrificial cult itself was a powerful image of rapprochement with God: the sound, smell, and taste of the animals all served to remind the worshipers of the presence of God in their lives.

The Northern Kingdom (Israel) also had its religious imagery. When the northern tribes seceded from the Davidic monarchy, they were cut off from the Jerusalem temple, its rituals, and its paraphernalia. Jeroboam, the new king of this kingdom realized the pull that all this imagery would exert on the people, and created in their stead statues of bulls in the towns of Bethel and Dan: these were to be symbols of God and seats of the divine presence.[5] The North also had a monument of twelve stones at Gilgal that commemorated Israel's crossing the Jordan into the land of Canaan.[6]

Eventually, the ever-developing radical monotheism of the biblical thinkers led to attacks on these ancient elements of Israelite worship. In the eighth century, the northern prophet Hosea condemns the bulls, and both he and Amos (also a northern prophet) disapprove of the very basis of a sacrificial cult. A century later, in Judah, Jeremiah proclaims that even the temple can be destroyed and declares that those who place their trust in the temple and its cult are practicing a form of idolatry. King Hezekiah of Judah (eighth century) destroyed the bronze serpent and attempted to outlaw the local forms of worship; King Josiah, a century later, contaminated and "eradicated" the local altars. Despite all this, the people continued to practice these forms of worship, which constituted their old religion.

If the Babylonians had not destroyed the temple, would the sacrificial cult eventually have disappeared under the onslaught of radical monotheism? If the ark and the cherubim had not been lost in the Exile, would they some day have been jettisoned as "foreign" or "idolatrous," much as the ancient Israelite bronze serpent was cast out by Hezekiah? Would the one central altar have come to be viewed with the same suspicion as the many local altars? We cannot know the answers to these questions, but we can see and take note of this direction of biblical monotheism. Ancient customs and symbols, long part of Israel's heritage, eventually did not fit the increasingly radical monotheistic sensibility. They were condemned as "foreign" and ultimately eradicated. The bronze serpent is one such symbol, the asherah is another.

The asherah was a cultic installation that appeared at Israel's shrines (bāmôt) together with a cultic stele (maṣṣēbâ) and an altar.[7] The asherah (ašērâ) standing next to the altar was not a statue. The verbs used for its erection show us that it was made out of wood, that it was a stylized tree-image, a pole, or an actual tree.[8] These asherahs (along with the stele and altars) were part of the local worship that was found in Israel "on every lofty hill and under every leafy tree." These local altars and their cult paraphernalia were part of Israel's own native tradition of worship until the eighth century.[9] According to the historian who wrote the Book of Kings (known as the Deuteronomist), the North continued with such worship until its destruction. The Deuteronomist, probably from the time of Josiah, was a radical monotheist; to him this worship was idolatrous, and he considered the continuation of such worship to be the reason that the Assyrians were able to capture the Northern Kingdom.[10] Nevertheless, this worship with asherah, altar, and stele was not a northern aberration. Judah also had a long tradition of asherahs: David's son King Rehoboam planted an asherah in Jerusalem, where it remained until the eighth-century Hezekian reform, when the local shrines were also abolished. Hezekiah got rid of much of the ancient tradition along with the local altars, removing both the bronze serpent and the asherah.[11] The local altars and the asherah reappeared under King Manasseh, who brought the asherah into the temple.[12] By the time of Deuteronomy in the seventh century, the local altars and steles had been labeled "Canaanite" and destroyed,[13] and the Israelites were commanded not to plant an asherah next to an altar or erect a stele.[14] The asherah was finally eradicated during the reform of Josiah.[15]

Asherah is also the name of a Canaanite goddess.[16] As 'Athirat, she was one of the three prominent goddesses of Ugarit, the others being 'Anat and 'Astarte. In the mythological texts discovered in this city, 'Athirat was the consort of El, the head of the Ugaritic pantheon, and was known as the mother of the gods. She was a marine goddess rather than an earth-mother: her title was 'Athirat-yammi, which could mean "Athirat of the Sea" or "she who treads the sea"; her chief servant was the fisherman. 'Athirat was also called Qudshu, "the holy one," a name that connects her with the numerous qudshu figurines known from Israel in the pre-Israelite period.[17] There are no capital letters in Hebrew, and it is often hard to tell whether any given occurrence of the letters 'šrh represents the cultic tree "asherah" or Asherah, the Canaanite goddess.

Asherah has been the subject of much attention since the discovery of Kuntillet Ajrud, a small installation not far from the main highway from Gaza to Eilat on the border of the Sinai.[18] This site, which contained two buildings, was either an Israelite religious center or a lodging for caravans, and was under the control of Northern Israel during the eighth century B.C.E. The smaller building is completely eroded, but the larger building has created a great stir, as it contained numerous inscriptions. Most interesting are the blessings on large storage jars (pithoi); "I bless you  lyhwh šmrn wl'šrth," "by YHWH of Samaria and wl'šrth"; "I bless you by YHWH of Teman wl'šrth." Here is a blessing by the God of Israel (localized as Northern and Southern) and by 'šrh. But how should this be translated: is this YHWH and the Canaanite goddess Asherah? Is this YHWH and an Israelite goddess Asherah, conceived as YHWH's consort ("his Asherah"), or is this the well-known Israelite cult-image ("his/her asherah"), and if so, what does the blessing mean? The question of how to translate wl'šrth has been hotly disputed.[19]

There is one clear mention in the Bible of the foreign goddess Asherah in Israel during the monarchic period. The story of Elijah and the prophets of Ba'al celebrates the victory of Israel's worship over the foreign cult of the Tyrian Ba'al. The Phoenician-born queen Jezebel, married to King Ahab of Israel, tried to import her native Tyrian worship into Israel. She killed all the functionaries of YHWH that she could find and supported 450 prophets of Ba'al and 400 prophets of Asherah. The prophet Elijah challenged all of them to a public contest to demonstrate which god (YHWH or Ba'al) could bring fire from heaven in order to burn the sacrificial offering, and rain to end Israel's three-year drought. The contest was held before the assembled people on Mount Carmel. YHWH demonstrated his superiority, and commanded the people to slaughter the prophets of Ba'al, which they did.[20] The place of Asherah in this story is problematic, and as a result the story cannot show unambiguously that there was a goddess Asherah worshiped in Israel as the consort of Ba'al. In this story, Asherah's prophets do nothing (the contest is purely between Elijah and the prophets of Ba'al) and are not killed with the prophets of Ba'al at the end. Moreover, there is no mention of a goddess Asherah in Tyrian documents, or indeed in any texts anywhere in coastal Phoenicia during the first millennium.[21] Since this second-millennium goddess has no real part in the narrative, could her appearance in this tale be an anachronism or a religious polemic?[22]

Israelite thought did not pursue or condemn the cult-object asherah, or the goddess Asherah, with the same vehemence as it fought the worship of Ba'al. King Ahab built an altar to Ba'al in Samaria as well as making an asherah there. It does not seem to have been in Ba'al's Temple: an asherah stood in the sanctuary at Bethel,[23] and the Samaria asherah probably stood in the sanctuary of YHWH of Samaria. It is noteworthy that when Jehu overthrew Ahab's dynasty, he assembled the worshipers of Ba'al in Ba'al's temple in Samaria and destroyed them and the temple.[24] No mention is made of the asherah, and indeed, an asherah still stood in Samaria until the time of Jehu's son Jehoahaz.[25] It was probably this asherah which is referred to in the Kuntillet Ajrud inscriptions.

The lack of major opposition to the asherah is an indication of the thrust of Israelite polemic. Asherah was not YHWH's rival. There was no great kulturkampf against the goddesses of ancient Canaan: they were largely irrelevant. The early struggle of Israel was against the gods of Canaan—Ba'al and El, who controlled the pantheon and the universe in Canaanite thought. These images of deity were part of Israel's ancient heritage, and the religious thinkers of Israel understood their religion against the backdrop of this Ba'al- and El-centered conceptualization of the universe. Ba'al was the dominant deity of the Canaanite religions contemporary with Israel, and Israel had to confront the issue of the contest between Ba'al and YHWH. Biblical religion did not pit a sole god against "goddess-worship"; on the contrary, its struggle was to win and keep the allegiance of the people for YHWH vis-à-vis the male Canaanite gods. Asherahs next to altars did not pose the same type of threat to the worship of YHWH as did Ba'al.

All the evidence in both the Bible and the inscriptions indicates that "asherah" was associated with the cult of YHWH rather than any cult of Ba'al. Perhaps this "asherah" is to be seen as a native Israelite goddess.[26] In truth, it actually does not matter whether the goddess came from Canaan or not. The question is: once she was ensconced in Samaria, what did she do? If she was a consort, then we would have to say that in the nonpreserved traditions of Israel, YHWH was really male, fully sexed, and modeled appropriate sexual behavior. This we cannot say with any degree of probability, for the Kuntillet Ajrud inscriptions do not indicate this, nor, assuredly, does the biblical record. Even at Kuntillet Ajrud, the asherah does not appear as an active independent figure. The blessing formula is by "YHWH and his/its (Samaria's) asherah," but the asherah doesn't really do anything. A third inscription from Kuntillet Ajrud mentions *lyhwh htmn wl'šrth,* "by YHWH of the South and his/its asherah," but continues with only YHWH as active, "may YHWH give him what his heart desires."[27]

All these scholarly disputes indicate how difficult it is to be sure about any point in ancient religion. What we do know is that the Asherah was real, she existed, and she was tolerated officially until the eighth century. She is not portrayed as doing anything: she simply is. The biblical texts do not speak of Asherah as a consort. The connection of Asherah to trees and groves and her location at altars hint that she represented, in some way, the natural world and its powers of regeneration. The height and majesty of a tree may also be a metaphor for earth-as-it-reaches-towards-heaven. Early Israelite religion could understand Asherah as part of God's divine system. Later, as biblical thinking began to concentrate on human responsibility for natural regeneration, asherah no longer fit. The official cult attacked and destroyed asherah and the altars. Nevertheless, the people persisted in worshiping in this old style, drawing assurance of the divine input in nature even as they were being told to be mindful of the human. In this way, the difficult concepts of covenant and human responsibility were supplemented by the very worship that the monotheistic thinkers condemned.

The most dramatic indication of this fact are the many figurines that have been discovered in Israel from the biblical period (the Iron Age).[28] These are figurines of females; male figurines are practically nonexistent. They are not "Canaanite" figurines: images of upright female figures with divine symbols which were very common in the Late bronze Age (Canaanite occupation) disappear in Israelite times.[29] Even the earliest Israelite figurines, which date from the time of the Judges (the Early Iron Age) are markedly different from those of Canaan. These Israelite figurines are plaques that represent women lying on beds. The style shows considerable continuity with Late Bronze Age styles. But the Israelite difference is clear: the females in the Israelite figurines have no divine headdress or any other symbols of divinity.[30] Even in this early period, the time of the settlement of Canaan, Israel is modifying earlier traditions to eliminate rival deities.

The plaque figurines disappeared from Judah by the time of the monarchy (what archaeologists call Iron Age II, from 1000 B.C.E. on).[31] Only a special type of plaque, the lady holding a round object, continues to be found sporadically in the North.[32] A new type of figurine becomes quite prominent in the eighth century, a solid figure in the round, with a "pillar" base, breasts, and molded head, sometimes with no arms, sometimes with arms holding breasts, and sometimes with arms raised. These figurines are found in two unusual areas that show marked similarities to each other: Jerusalem Cave 1, a manmade cave just outside the walls of the city, which had sixteen of these female figures, and Samaria Locus E 207, perhaps associated with a large, unused sealed tomb. Both of these areas appear cultic in some respect; neither has a sacrificial or incense altar; and both show evidence that food preparation, eating, and drinking took place there. This activity was clearly not part of the official sacrificial cult, but may have been a tolerated nonconformist worship. These pillar figurines are also found in domestic settings—interestingly, from the last years of settlement.[33]

Scholars sometimes call these pillar figurines the *dea nutrix* (the nourishing deity), but they have no overt symbols of any goddess. Since all three major Canaanite goddesses (Asherah, Astarte, and Anat) tended to blend into each other,[34] they have all been presented as candidates for the identification of these figurines, and possibly a merging of all three into one.[35] But these pillars hold no divine insignia, wear no crowns, and carry no symbols of their power. The pillars arise, moreover, long after the Canaanite plaques have disappeared. They are not Canaanite goddess figurines. There is also no reason to suspect that these figurines represent the development of an Israelite goddess. They may not be personalized goddesses at all. Instead, they are a visual metaphor, which show in seeable and touchable form that which is most desired. In other words, they are a kind of tangible prayer for fertility and nourishment.

The shape of these figurines is suggestive. The term "pillar" is a bit misleading, for these pillars have a distinctive shape: the bottom flares out, giving a slightly skirted effect, a little like a bell and a lot like a tree trunk. Could it be possible that the figurine is a kind of tree with breasts? Such a tree of nourishment is known from an Egyptian painting in the tomb of Thutmosis III in which the young king is being suckled from the breast of a large tree.[36] Here the tree is identified with Isis; elsewhere such a tree is an attribute of Hathor. There is an inscribed cult stand discovered in Ta'anach, dated from the late tenth century B.C.E.[37] which has a naked goddess flanked by two lions and, on another register, a tree flanked by two lions. Ruth Hestrin has suggested that these are parallel: the goddess (which she identifies as Asherah) is represented by the sacred tree.[38] If we remember that the word ʾasherah in the Hebrew Bible can refer both to the goddess (associated with Ba'al) and to a wooden tree, stylized tree and/or pole found at the altars of Israel, it seems more than likely that Asherah and/or the asherah is identified as the force of vegetation and nourishment.

It is significant that there are no trappings of divinity on these figurines. Moreover, the same people who had these figurines in their house did not name their children with a name that called for Asherah's blessings or protections.[39] Just as the asherah associated with the stele and altars at the local shrines was not seen by the people to be in conflict with the worship of YHWH, so too it would seem that these figurines were not idolatrous in their eyes. There is no evidence at all to suppose that the people imagined the figurines to represent God's consort. They have no pubic triangle, nothing to suggest erotic attachment, and they appear alone, not as part of a male-female couple. The figurines—and the altar asherah to which they may be analogous—may represent a divine *power*, not fully articulated or personified, not "worshiped" as some sort of a goddess that could rival YHWH.

The dating of these figurines is significant, for they come into being in the eighth century, precisely the period in which the official royal cult has removed the asherah from Samaria. The asherah with its tree-associations had brought the divine and natural worlds closer together. These tree-based breast-figurines may do the same. The breasts, and possibly the tree trunk, address a desire for—and anxiety about—fertility. Through these figurines, the people could be reminded that the divine blessings of fertility are in their midst, that the divine is indeed a beneficent bestower of abundance. A religion that states that fertility depends entirely upon people's behavior creates enormous strain: it places a great responsibility on the people to behave well and, at the same time, requires them to understand the difficult abstract idea that fertility is indeed automatically attendant upon such good behavior.

The asherah-tree at the altars and the tree-based figurines at cult sites and in houses are a way of ensuring and demonstrating the fact that there really is a power of fertility, which can be seen and touched, which guarantees the rewards of right relationship with God. In Israel, where YHWH is the one who grants "the blessings of breast and womb",[40] the force for fertility represented by the figurines may not have been seen as a separate deity.[41] Quite possibly, it was not consciously personalized at all. In this way, the people were able to add a reminder of divinity to their homes, and a visualization of abundance (the lactating tree) while they continued to maintain devotion to the one invisible transcendent God.

# 14

## Our Father and Our Mother

The close interactive relationship between God and Israel needs to be expressed and understood through the use of images drawn from human existence.[1] Traditional metaphors of shepherd and flock, master and servant, king and subject, all express aspects of the divine–human relationship. However, these metaphors serve to emphasize the great gulf in power and wisdom between humans and their divine shepherd-master-king. The metaphor of God-as-parent, like the marital metaphor, emphasizes the emotional aspect of the commitment between the partners.

The metaphor of the Divine Parent expresses God's love for Israel, God's expectations for it, and the responsibility that God feels for instructing Israel in correct behavior.[2] In this metaphor, God redeemed Israel, His first-born son from Egypt,[3] and carried him as a man carries his son.[4] God is also the parent of David and his dynasty. The bond between God and David is portrayed as an adoption, in which God made David God's first-born and David declared "You are my father."[5]

The parental metaphor relies on the human experience of parenthood to provide its connotations of dependable love. From their own experience as parents, the people-as-children know that children cannot possibly fulfill parental expectations, realize that God does not expect them to be perfect, and therefore rely on parental tolerance and forgiveness from God. Nevertheless, God as parent, no matter how loving, has a definite agenda and a mandate to instruct and punish the child, with the result that God's parental love frequently takes the form of strict demanding discipline, what we sometimes today call "tough love." Such discipline is God's parental duty.[6] The parent metaphor thus contains threat as well as promise, as the child can never simply assume forgiveness.[7] This parental metaphor, like the marital metaphor, expresses Israel's ongoing intimate relationship with a far superior power, a relationship that is fraught with danger at each misstep.

God is normally considered male, and God-as-parent is usually portrayed as a father. As the Father, God instructs the child, insists that His instructions be followed, and punishes the disobedient. God's relationship with His children can be stormy, as when children disappoint their parents. The father is clearly the dominant person in a hierarchical family, with great power over the members of his household. As with the marital metaphor, the image of God the Father does not come to teach that God will punish: Biblical writing consistently teaches that Israel's sorrows are its chastisements. It is precisely because Israel recognizes its punishments and acknowledges its culpability that the parental metaphor has its appeal. Parents may punish, but they only repudiate in extreme circumstances.[8] Formal legal relationships almost always demand cancellation in return for nonfulfillment of obligations; parental concern, on the contrary, creates an ongoing sense of continuation. When the Davidic kings do not behave in ideal fashion, when the children of Israel are arrogant and faithless,[9] they can hold fast to the belief that God, their parent, will never abandon them. Even when Israel breaks the terms of its covenant with God, God will not act in strict judicial terms and discard Israel, for God remains bonded to Israel by the strong emotive bonds of parenthood. God loves Israel: "Ever since he was a youth, I have loved him; from Egypt I called him to be my son."[10] The relationship is irrevocable and indissoluble. Instead of abandoning Israel, God chastises it in order to teach a lesson. This chastisement, sometimes harsh, is a source of anguish for God as well as for Israel: "How can I give you up, Ephraim? How can I relinquish you, Israel? My heart is turning over within me, all my tender emotions are stirred."[11] The catastrophes of Israel are its reality: the parental metaphor provides a way to understand them as lessons from God. It offers hope for the people of Israel in the time of their greatest suffering, for it carries with it a sense of anticipatory forgiveness and the end of suffering, the promise of an eternal bond that remains unbroken even through difficult times[12]:

> *Truly, Ephraim is a dear son to me,*
> *a child that is dandled!*
> *Whenever I have turned against him,*
> *my thoughts would dwell on him still.*
> *That is why my heart yearns for him;*
> *I will receive him back in love.*

God the parent is ultimately God the redeemer[13]: the prodigal son is still a son, and the father rejoices when he returns.

Our own concept of parental roles tends to attribute attitudes and behaviors along gender lines. We normally think of the father as punitive and the mother as compassionate, and tend to label those passages in which God expresses compassion as "mother passages," and those in which God pronounces judgment or announces punishment as "father passages." The biblical text itself, however, makes no such division, and God-as-parent transcends our own gendered thinking about parental roles. The same parent is both judgmental and compassionate, punitive and emotional.

During the Babylonian exile, the prophet Deutero-Isaiah uses the parental metaphor with special emphasis and poignancy as he seeks to comfort a people who have lived through the destruction. He seeks images of assurance, of steadfastness and eternal presence, and turns to a clearly maternal image of deity to offer promise of imminent redemption:

> Listen to me, O House of Jacob,
> and all that remain from the house of Israel,
> who have been carried since gestation,
> borne since the womb:
> till you grow old, I will still be the one,
> when you turn gray, I will still be carrying (you).
> I have made, and I will bear,
> I will carry and I will deliver.[14]

The maternal coloration here is clearly biological; God has borne and delivered Israel. Other passages are also unmistakably biologically female. God-as-mother has created Israel: "the rock who gave birth to (or begot) you, the god who birthed you."[15] God-as-mother births the new order in good Lamaze fashion: "Now I will scream like a woman in labor, I will pant and I will gasp."[16] When these biological signifiers are not there, only our culture-bound preconceptions make us identify certain parental functions as maternal rather than parental. Whether *we* consider God's nurturance "maternal" or "paternal,"[17] God is a nurturing parent. The same God who directs also nurtures, the God who judges also has compassion. The Bible does not consider compassion to be a nonfatherly characteristic:

> *As a father has compassion for his children,*
> *so the Lord has compassion for those who fear him.*[18]

But mothers, as we have seen, are particularly noteworthy for their devotion and loyalty:

> *Can a woman forget her baby,*
> *or disown the child of her womb?*
> *Though she might forget,*
> *I never could forget you.*[19]

To view God as parent is to rely upon enduring commitment.

In ancient Mesopotamian religion, every individual had parent gods, personal gods who protected the individual, to whom the individual was accountable, to whom he or she prayed in penitence and called father and mother.[20] These parent gods were not great deities: they were the mediators and intercessors to the realm of the gods. Each individual's personal god would intercede for him or her with the great gods.[21] One of the major roles of a father—both human and divine— was to protect the child from, and intercede for the child with, these higher powers. Intercession and protection are not exclusively female roles. The very term "fatherhood," *abbūtu*, comes to mean protection and intercession.[22]

The situation is different in biblical Israel. God-the-father is also the highest power of the cosmos. In fact, God-the-parent is the entire divine realm. The father-god is also the mother-god; the personal god is also the cosmic power. The national, one, god is at the same time governor of the cosmos. The protector of the nation is also its teacher: the same god loves the nation and acts to render accountable, protect, and redeem Israel and the children of Israel. In Israel, God-the-parent is also the divine warrior who acts in history and the divine king who punishes. This creates enormous problems for the object of God's attention. If the father is the judge, who will speak for the child? When God-the-bridegroom is angry, who will assuage his anger? When God-the-father is disciplining, who will offer unconditional love? Who will be humanity's advocate before God?

The power of God is so awesome, the position so dominant, that intimacy with God is almost impossible to bear without someone to mediate between Israel and God, someone to buffer between humanity and divinity. Such intercession was one of the crucial roles of the prophets.[23] But prophets alone were not enough, and Israel also looked to its ancestral spirit, the eternal holy mother, Rachel. "Mother Rachel" pleads for Israel before God.

Mother Rachel appears in the Bible in Jeremiah's poetic vision of the restoration of Israel with the words:

> *A voice is heard in Ramah—*
> *wailing, bitter weeping—*
> *Rachel, weeping for her children.*
> *She refuses to be comforted*
> *for her children, who are gone.*[24]

The woman's voice is playing a familiar woman's role, weeping and lamenting for her children. But the mourner is not a living woman. She is the long-dead Rachel, wife of the patriarch Jacob, daughter of Labab, younger sister and co-wife of Leah. The story of Rachel in the book of Genesis is short and poignant. Beautiful and beloved, she was married to Jacob after he had been tricked into marrying her elder sister Leah. She stayed barren for a long time, while her sister bore six sons and a daughter and their handmaidens each bore two sons. She finally gave birth to Joseph, the beloved son of Jacob and a great culture-hero.[25] En route to her new home, Rachel died giving birth to her second son, Benjamin, and was buried apart from the rest of the family.

All these events in the life of Rachel happened almost a thousand years before Jeremiah's time. Nevertheless, the Rachel that Jeremiah hears is the matriarch of Genesis, and Jeremiah plants linguistic clues to allude to the Genesis stories.[26] Jeremiah hears the spirit of this ancient Rachel, still alive, still calling and lamenting. Has Jeremiah resurrected Rachel for his poetic vision, or had she already become a figure of Israel's folklore, a once-and-forever personage seen as the mother of Israel?

The son who will be restored to Rachel is Ephraim, son of Rachel's first son, Joseph. Ephraim was the name of the largest tribe in the Northern Kingdom, and the name had been used to personify the Northern Kingdom of Israel at least since the time of Hosea a century earlier.[27] Rachel is a very appropriate figure for Jeremiah's vision, for Rachel and her son are paramount figures of love in the Israelite tradition, both beloved by Jacob.[28] Rachel, moreover, died in childbirth, still young and beloved. It is this eternally young, lovely mother who weeps for her children, and it is Ephraim, son of the beloved Joseph, whom God calls his "dear" son. And it is God's love for Ephraim that is Jeremiah's hope for restoration.

In this vision, Rachel's children are also God's sons. This is a strange metaphor, for Jacob is absent, and God is not Rachel's husband. Instead there is a curious "holy family": The people are personified both by the son Ephraim and by Bat-Yisrael (daughter Israel),[29] and the parents are Rachel and God. "My dear son, Ephraim" has been chastised and has repented, and Bat-Yisrael will come back from her wanderings and henceforth focus her attention only on God.[30] Rachel has no future role after this restoration, for she has achieved her purpose: through her incessant weeping, she has helped bring the restoration of her sons to their land.[31]

As the divine mother, in the tradition of goddess-mothers (and probably human mothers), Rachel laments. Her weeping, like that of the ancient Sumerian goddess-mothers, is unconditional. It does not depend on Ephraim's righteousness, or repentance; it is not based on a claim that Ephraim has been sufficiently punished. It is an expression of love that goes beyond moral valuations. Furthermore, it is perpetual, for Rachel refuses to be comforted.[32] In Jeremiah's vision, Rachel has been weeping for Ephraim for over a hundred years, from the time of the destruction of the Northern Kingdom in 722 B.C.E. until the vision of Jeremiah in the late seventh or early sixth century B.C.E. It is the very steadfastness and repetition of the mourner's weeping that renders it important. In the same way that Geshtinanna's continuing lament finally moved the gods to alleviate Dumuzi's doom, Rachel's very relentless weeping brings the plight of the people continually before God, and finally moves God, in this vision, to remember and restore the people of Israel. This role of advocate in heaven is so important that even Jeremiah, who was punctilious in his radically monotheist desire to divest all religious metaphors of their numinous power,[33] sees Rachel, ancient mother, eternally defending Israel.[34]

# 15

Zion, the Beloved Woman

The prophets Jeremiah and Deutero-Isaiah, uncompromising mono-theists that they were, often portrayed the attachment of God and Israel through the image of Zion, the mystical spirit of the city of Jerusalem. Zion is a multifaceted figure. Mother and beloved, mourned and mourner, abandoned and returned to, daughter and bride. She is bad wife and good mother, mother of Israel and its future bride, spouse of God and future spouse of the people, city abandoned by her exiled people and city-in-exile, accompanying them in Babylon. She shares the mood of the people, lamenting the destruction, fighting for victory, and shouting with joy at the restoration. She is the persona immanent in the city, remaining in the city to lament the people (so Jeremiah and Isaiah), or leaving the city to seek salvation (Micah), or accompanying the people in their exile.[1] She is the mother of the people, and the place of God's presence. She is the beloved of both Israel and God, and brings them closer together in this shared love.

The individual components of this complex image begin to appear early, in the eighth century, at the beginning of the prophetic period. The dominant tone of the prophet Amos is anger at the Northern King-dom of Israel for its lack of social justice. He addresses the people individually, using the second person plural, or collectively, in the masculine singular, as "Joseph" or "pride of Jacob." However, when he changes his tone from castigation to lamentation and begins to intone a dirge over the Kingdom's destruction, then he speaks of Israel as a woman, *bat yiśrā'ēl*, "maid Israel" or "Israel-maid":

*Fallen, not to rise again is Israel-maid;*
*abandoned on her soil with none to lift her up.*[2]

When the prophet imagines the nation as a girl, he can go beyond anger to express love and sorrow. The marital metaphor of God and the Wife enables us to feel deeply the agony of God as God is betrayed by His beloved. Nevertheless, in the visible world, it is the wife who is suffering, the land which is being overrun, the people who are falling prey to foreign powers. The very "woman" upon whom the prophets direct our ire is also ourselves. The image of the young woman as *victim* focuses our attention on the vulnerability and perishability of the nation in God's eyes and allows the prophet and reader to express a sadness that goes beyond questions of justice.

The Wanton Wife and Zion-as-woman express two different aspects of the imagery of God and Israel. It is a bifurcated image, almost the classic "whore" and "virgin." Both represent the difficulty of being God's partner: we are angry at the "whore" when she fails God, we are sorry for the maiden when she is punished. This image of the ruined-maiden victim enables the reader to empathize with the people, to forget the cause of the devastation and join in the sorrow. It is a very important image a hundred and fifty years after Amos, in the literature of the destruction of the Southern Kingdom of Judah. There, "the nation-girl" is Zion, the city of Jerusalem, the capital of Judah, the site of the Davidic monarchy and of the temple. The city-as-woman is, of course, the same city which is the Wanton Wife. Pity and sorrow do not erase the knowledge that she has brought destruction upon herself. Her punishment is a defilement, a sexual embarrassment.[3] But the image of Zion-as-girl goes beyond anger. The name "Zion" is never used in angry passages: it always stands for the beloved. Jeremiah, the great prophet who foresaw and lived to see the destruction, often addresses Jerusalem as the Wanton Wife, venting his anger and frustration at the destructive path Judah is following. At the same time, he expresses his great sorrow at the ruin of his beloved people by the image of the people as a young woman, *bat ʿamî*, "daughter that is my people" or "my people-girl." Jeremiah weeps for Bat Ami, whom he cannot heal.[4] The city also is a young vulnerable victim, *bat-ṣiyyôn*, "daughter who is Zion." She is "lovely and delicate," but the object of destruction and attack. Jeremiah uses the name "Jerusalem" in anger, rebuking her for persistent rebellion, and for conduct deserving of punishment.[5] But he uses the name "Zion" in love, sorrow, and hope rather than in anger.

The names symbolize the differing emotions of the poet. When Jeremiah shifts from addressing the unnamed city to Zion-girl (Bat Zion), we can see clearly the change in mood:

> *and you, who are doomed to ruin,*
> *what do you accomplish by wearing crimson;*
> *by decking yourself in jewels of gold,*
> *by enlarging your eyes with kohl?*
> *you beautify yourself in vain,*
> *lovers despise you,*
> *they seek your life.*
>
> *I hear a voice as of one in travail,*
> *anguish as of a woman bearing her first child.*
> *the voice of Bat-Zion*
> *panting, stretching out her hands:*
> *Alas for me, I faint*
> *before the killers.*[6]

In this passage, Zion the victim is not the passive object of our pity. Object of lamentation, she also becomes the mourning Lamenter, the one who bewails the people of Israel as well as herself. The book of Lamentations, written in response to the destruction of Jerusalem and its temple, portrays the woman-city as a tragic figure for whom the poet (and we) have great sorrow.[7]

This city, once great among nations and now a widow, takes center stage like the city goddesses in the old Sumerian city-laments. The city is the chief actor in the tragedy as she weeps and spreads out her hands, unable to be comforted. The very walls of the city shed tears like a torrent to intercede with God for the life of the infants who faint from hunger, and the city herself rises to recite the great lament over her own destruction, to confess her sins and plead for retribution.[8]

> . . . .
> *For these things I do weep:*
> *my eyes flow with tears.*
> *Far from me is any comforter who might revive my*
> *    spirit.*
> *My children are forlorn,*
> *for the foe has prevailed.*
> . . . .
> *See, O Lord, the distress I am in!*
> *My heart is in anguish*

*my heart has turned over within me,*
*for I disobeyed.*

. . . .

*When they heard how I was sighing, there was none to*
*    comfort me.*
*All my foes heard of my plight and exulted.*

. . . .

*For my sighs are many,*
*and my heart is sick.*

The devastation of Judah cannot pass in silence. Attention must be paid. Someone must weep over the devastation, someone must call out to make humans and God pay heed. Jeremiah calls for mourners. He weeps himself, calls for the women of Zion to set up a lament, and he calls upon the city Zion to take up this role for the people of Judah:

> *"Shear your locks and cast them away,*
> *take up a lament on the heights,*
> *for the Lord has spurned and cast off*
> *the brood that provoked his wrath."*[9]

Jeremiah relates how the city-as-woman came to take on this role as mourner. When the enemy comes arrayed against Bat-Zion, the people come to her in fear, beseeching her to stay inside the city walls and weep for them:

> *Do not go out into the country,*
> *do not walk the fields,*
> *for the sword of the enemy is there,*
> *terror on every side.*
>
> *Oh Bat-Ami*
> *put on sackcloth*
> *and strew dust on yourself*
> *mourn the mourning of an only child*
> *a bitter wailing,*
> *for quickly the destroyer is coming upon us.*[10]

The city then loudly sounds her cries over great distance.[11]

The prophets (and Lamentations)[12] draw on a long literary tradition when they personify the city as a woman. In ancient West-Semitic inscriptions, cities are given titles, such as "lady" or "princess," that indicate that they were personified as females.[13] The image of a city as

female makes good psychological sense, for the city contains the populace within her walls, nurtures it, provides for it, and defends it. Nevertheless, it is not a universal image. Akkadian addresses cities in the
masculine. This Akkadian example shows that the city is not called
"female" out of psychological necessity. There was a literary tradition
in the ancient Near East, in Sumer, and in the Eastern Mediterranean,
that saw cities as female, and Israel was part of this tradition.[14] The
earliest allusion to this image is an Egyptian document, the stele of
Merneptah, which describes Greater Palestine's submission to Egypt by
declaring that it has become a "widow" to Egypt.[15] The city-as-woman
metaphor survived into the Hellenistic period, and Hellenistic coins
show an image of the *tychē Poleōs* of the Hellenistic cities. Similarly,
Roman coins show *Judea Capta*, the conquered kingdom of Judea seen
as a woman.

The biblical prophets portray all the major cities as women figures.
These prophets all work within the monotheist idiom and do not describe victory over foreign nations as a defeat of foreign gods.[16] In the
prophetic vision, there is only one God acting in history. At the same
time, the cities of the world are women-figures, who react to God's
actions in human ways. Micah, speaks of the indwelling "inhabitant"
(*yôšebet*) of Shapir, Zaanan, and Lachish and of how each of these
"women" goes forth naked or hitches steeds to her chariot, and shears
off her hair (in mourning) over her banished children.[17] Later, Jeremiah
also speaks of these foreign cities as women or indwelling women,
perceiving them as females at the instant of their destruction. "The
indweller-inhabitant of Dibon-maid" sits thirsty in the dust and "the
inhabitant of Aroer" stands peering out to the road.[18] Egypt-maid
the indweller (*yôšebet bat miṣrāyim*) must get ready for exile, for there
is no healing for her hero. Indeed, the earth resounds with her screams
and her voice rattles like a snake. Damascus "has grown weak, has
turned around to flee, trembling has seized her, pain and anguish have
taken hold of her like a woman in childbirth." Above all, Babylon will
be shamed and desolate, and all will hiss at her wounds as God requites
Babylon for the wicked things done to Zion. It will be Babylon for
whom one will howl, Babylon for whom one will seek healing balms,
Babylon whose wounds will be incurable.[19] At the time of retribution,
Edom-maid will be exposed and disgraced[20] and Babylon-maid will sit
on the ground, her nakedness uncovered, sitting silent, and retiring into
darkness (Isaiah 47).

The prophet Isaiah applies this image of the female inhabitant in a
powerful image of Yoshevet Zion (*yôšebet ṣiyyôn*): "Oh, shout for joy,

you who lives in Zion! For great in your midst is the Holy One of Israel."[21] Zion is very much the physical city of houses and walls, but Zion is also a *person* who dwells within this physical city. *Yôšebet* is a feminine singular participle. It is not a term for God, who also "lives" (*yôšeb*) in Zion[22] or who "dwells"[23] (*šôkēn*, always with the masculine singular) on Mount Zion. It does not directly refer to the people, to whom Isaiah refers in the plural or, as a mark of God's favor, "my people that lives in Zion," with a masculine singular participle, *yôšeb*.[24] Yoshevet Zion is the essence of the city seen as a female, the immanent presence that lives within the walls. The great all-encompassing love that Isaiah feels for Jerusalem, his confidence that God will always come to the aid of Jerusalem, and his belief that Jerusalem will always be the center of God's activity and attention,[25] combine with this image of Zion-the-dweller to produce a powerful vision of the inner spirit of the city.

The two eighth-century Judean prophets, Isaiah and Micah, both focus their eschatological hopes on the city of Jerusalem and its Temple:

> The mount of the Lord's house will stand firm above the mountains
> . . . and the many peoples shall go and shall say, come, let us go up to
> the Mount of the Lord, to the House of the God of Jacob . . . for instruc-
> tion shall come forth from Zion, the word of the Lord from Jerusalem.[26]

Isaiah, in particular focuses on Jerusalem as a *place*, God's dwelling, which God will (re-) establish and for which God will even lay the bricks. "Then God will reign in Jerusalem"; the whole city and its inhabitants will be holy to God, and God's eternal presence will be over the city with a cloud by day and smoke by night, the same cloud and smoke that once rested on the Tabernacle in the wilderness.[27] After the calamities of history, Zion will stand secure:

> *When you gaze upon Zion, our city of assembly,*
> *your eyes shall behold Jerusalem*
> *as a secure homestead*
> *a tent not to be transported,*
> *whose pegs shall never be pulled up*
> *and none of whose ropes shall break*
> *For there the Lord in his greatness shall be for us*
> *like a region of rivers, of broad streams.*[28]

Micah, Isaiah's younger contemporary, shares Isaiah's passionate commitment to Zion, but does not share his belief that God will rescue it from destruction. He expresses all his intense emotions for the city through woman images. He sees Zion as the suffering victim, whom the nations see exposed and polluted before them. But he also calls upon her to stop crying and take action:

> *Writhe and scream, maiden Zion*
> *as a woman in travail!*
> *For now you will go out of the city*
> *and you will sleep in the fields*
> *till you come to Babylon.*
> *There you will be saved,*
> *there God will redeem you from your enemies.*[29]

In Micah's vision, the woman-Zion can leave the city and go to Babylon. Zion is not simply the stones of the houses, but a mystical person, the essence of the city, who can separate herself from the physical confines of the city walls. This suffering figure goes to seek redemption.[30] She will also participate actively in this redemption:

> *Up and thresh, maiden Zion*
> *for I [God] will give you horns of iron*
> *and provide you with hoofs of bronze*
> *and you will crush the many peoples.*[31]

Micah's picture of Zion as active and able to operate outside the city itself may owe its scope to several Near Eastern images. One is that of the god Aššur, the god of the Assyrians, who destroyed the Northern Kingdom of Israel and almost destroyed Jerusalem. As far as scholarship can tell, the god Aššur was originally a personification of the city of Aššur, and always maintained a close connection with this city, the first capital of the Assyrian empire.[32] Yet the god himself was portrayed as a young warrior god, and was seen as an important source of the overwhelming power of the Assyrian armies. A second major source of this military power was the goddess Ishtar, portrayed in Assyrian official documents as the "breaker of the weapons of the enemies" and envisioned as striding to war before the armies of Assyria. Against this mighty duo, Aššur and Ishtar, Micah sets Zion, the fair maiden who will thresh the enemies with horns of iron and hooves of bronze. When

Assyria sets the siege, Zion gashes herself, either in mourning or as a bloody prebattle preparation[33] and prepares for her role.

The militant tone of Micah's portrayal of Zion is unique to him, and probably represents his own response to the Assyrian threat. It is not picked up in the other prophets. But his image of Zion as a persona that can leave the stone walls of the city, together with Isaiah's picture of Zion as an indweller, expands the inherited metaphor of city-as-woman and gives impetus and expression to the mystique of Jerusalem, beloved woman of God and Israel. Micah transmutes the Judean attachment to Jerusalem to a love for the "spirit" of the city, a movable indwelling presence. Later, when Jeremiah sees the people calling on Bat-Zion to stay, he understands that Bat-Zion takes on the role of intercessor as an act of choice. She could leave the city, but instead stays and weeps. Later, when the exile finally came, Deutero-Isaiah imagines Bat-Zion as a solitary figure, alone among the ruins of the city of Jerusalem, waiting for the people to come back. But Zachariah sees Bat-Zion as the portable city, the spirit of Jerusalem who has accompanied the people into their exile and awaits their return.

The prophets never imagine the destruction of Israel to be the end of the story. It is always a station on the way to future redemption. The redemption brings wholeness, as wanton and victim merge into one: Jerusalem the iniquitous will be healed, and "outcast, Zion, whom no one seeks out" will be restored.[34] The woman figures will be as vocal in the redemption as they were in the destruction. The woman-city will call for revenge:

> Let the violence done me and my kindred be
> upon Babylon
> says Zion-the-indweller,
> let my blood be upon the inhabitants of Chaldea,
> says Jerusalem.[35]

The girl-figures will lead the songs of joy. Jeremiah promises, "O Bat-Yisrael! Again you shall take up your timbrels and go forth to the rhythm of the dancers. Again you shall plant vineyards on the hills of Samaria; men shall plant and live to enjoy them."[36] The prophet Zephaniah (from about 600 B.C.E.), calls,

> Shout for joy, Bat Zion, Cry aloud, O Israel
> Rejoice and be glad with all your heart Bat
>   Jerusalem!

. . . .

*On that day God will say to Jerusalem*
*"Do not fear, Zion, let your arms not be*
*   weak.*
*The Lord your god is in your midst,*
*a warrior who brings victory.*
*He will rejoice over you with happiness*
*He will be silent with his love,*
*He will make merry with glad song."*[37]

The second prophet Isaiah (Deutero-Isaiah), who prophesied during the Babylonian exile, opens his prophecies of restoration and reconciliation with a command to comfort Jerusalem: "Comfort, comfort, my people (says your God)—speak tenderly to Jerusalem and say unto her that her time of service is over. . . . " Zion, who has been mourning her lost children all during the exile can now arise, for the herald comes over the mountains to announce that God is king and the very ruins of the city raise a shout of joy. Zion herself ascends the hills as "Zion the herald of Joy" to announce to the cities of Judah "behold your God."[38]

In the restoration visions of Deutero-Isaiah, yet another aspect of the city-as-woman becomes prominent. Cities are "mothers" of their inhabitants. In the eighth century, the prophet Micah tells Mareshah the indweller to tear out her hair because her children have gone into captivity.[39] Later, at the time of the destruction of Judah, this mother-aspect comes out in the portrait of Zion. The Book of Lamentations sees Jerusalem as a failed mother, whose sons (the "sons of Zion") have become cheap and expendable; her children are hungry, for she can no longer suckle them; they are forlorn; they have gone into captivity.[40] Deutero-Isaiah, speaking in the Babylonian exile, has no punishments to pronounce. He expresses the longing for redemption of the exiled people, and the triumphant confidence of imminent victory. He draws upon all the literary images of the Bible, stressing images of power and those of compassion. He emphasizes the maternity of God, and he stresses the maternity of Zion. In his visions, Zion remains back in the land of Israel, believing herself forsaken, barren and bereaved. and bearing no children. Now, Isaiah carries the message to her children that God has never really divorced their mother, and the children will come back in great numbers, shouting with joy, filling the city in such numbers that there will be no room for them, and they will have to enlarge the city and overfill it. The kings and queens of nations will be their nurses and nannies.[41]

At this restoration, God calls Zion back with vast love. She will nevermore be called "forsaken," but "I delight in her" (*ḥepṣîbâ,* Hephzi-bah ); her land will be called "espoused" (*bĕ'ula,* Beulah); and Zion-girl will be called "sought-out, a city not forsaken." The city can now rouse herself, clothing herself in splendor, for her sons and daughters are coming from afar and she will glow, kings will wait upon her, aliens will rebuild the walls, and the children of those who tormented her will prostrate themselves at her feet, and she will give suck to kings and nations. These triumphalist expectations ran up against the troubled reality of the actual return to Israel. But the prophet keeps speaking for the sake of Zion.[42] He sees the agony of Zion-the-mother as her labor-pains and looks forward to the new birth:

> *"Before she labored, she gave birth,*
> *before her pangs came she delivered a boy"*—
> *who ever heard of such a thing, who ever saw such*
> *     events?*
> *Can a land labor but a single day*
> *can a people be born in an instant?*
> *Zion is laboring—*
> *and she will give birth to her children.*[43]

For God, who causes all births, has brought on this labor and he will see it through for her. Despite the present travail, we who love Jerusalem should be glad for her. She continues to be our mother, and we will yet suck consolation and glory from her breast, will yet be carried on shoulders and dandled upon knees.[44]

Isaiah's vision of Jerusalem as the eternal mother of Israel does not supplant the prophetic vision of the remarriage of God and Israel. God will espouse her "as a bridegroom rejoices over his bride, so will your God rejoice over you."[45] God and Zion will be reunited. But the vision of this espousal goes farther, for the children of Israel also marry Zion: "as a youth espouses a maiden, your sons shall espouse you."[46] Jeru-salem is suckling, nurturing mother: she is also the bride of love. Both God the father and the children of Israel will embrace Jerusalem with love and passion. Clearly, this bond is not like a human family, for father and son do not marry the same woman, Oedipus notwithstand-ing. But Zion goes beyond human family patterns. She is a mystical figure of love for the people of Israel. During the time of their exile, she lamented their loss, an intercessor who kept in mind their plight. During their time of glory, she becomes another kind of mediator be-tween Israel and God. Through their mutual devotion to the city, God and Israel fully join in love together. Through Zion, her children are God's disciples and God can say "you, my people."[47] The love of Zion is the mutual concern of God and Israel. She is the sacred bridge that unites them.

The multifaceted vision of the beloved and loving Zion[48] expresses a sense of the immanent presence of God and of God's concern for Israel. In the increasingly universal perspective of monotheism, in which God, the only deity, is god of all the peoples, Zion expresses the belief in the special position of Israel. Zion herself is not "divine." She does not act in the divine realm. She is the representative of the people, part of the people, and—at the same time—focus of its hopes. The image of Zion is also the image of connectedness, for Zion is a focus for intense passion and longing for the men of Israel. They can express their love directly to this female figure in a way that they cannot have towards the remote, invisible, and masculine God. The fluidity of this image of the woman-city, with all the emotions that it generates, embraces the complex passionate interwoven relationship between the people of Israel, its God, and Jerusalem that characterizes Judaism until this day.

# 16

## Wisdom, the Lover of Man

The post-exilic prophet Isaiah depicts a time of future bliss in which God will rejoice over Zion as a man over his bride, and her sons will marry her as a man marries a bride.[1] In this powerful use of the Zion symbol, God and Israel are united in their joint love of Jerusalem. But this use of the metaphor carries a new element: Israel is not the restored wife of God; but the husband of Zion; Zion is not just mother-Zion, she is also the Bride of Israel. While the interposition of Zion as the connecter-figure between Israel and God has the advantage of mediating and buffering the relationship between Israel and God, the depiction of Zion as bride eliminates the female from Israel's self-image. Mother-Zion's children can be male and female, but Zion-the-bride's husband is male.

The same tendency to conceptualize the "we" as male appears in another post-exilic literary figure, Woman-Wisdom. Like Zion-the-bride, Woman-Wisdom mediates through eros: love of her enables the Israelite to feel connected to God. While Zion-as-bride does this on a national, collective level, Woman-Wisdom offers the individual a strong personal attachment to the divine realm without the mediation of history or polity.

The figure of Woman-Wisdom appears in the first nine chapters of the Book of Proverbs, a separate discourse on Wisdom and the learned life that was probably written in the restoration period (circa 500 B.C.E.). It has often been claimed that Wisdom is a survival of the ancient Near Eastern wisdom goddesses, such as Nisaba in Sumer, Ma'at in Egypt, and even Athena in Greece, and that this wisdom goddess has been tamed in Israel by being acclaimed as first creature rather than creator.[2] But this does not explain what it is about wisdom that made the other cultures of the Near East also exemplify wisdom as a goddess.

179

The answer must lie both in the human psyche and human social structure. The mother, as chief caretaker, is the original figure of wisdom to young children, and teaches that child the first rudiments of culture. Moreover, women continued to be associated with highly important aspects of cultural knowledge, such as medicinal ability and midwifery, and remained the masters of cultural transformations, such as changing raw into cooked, and natural into cultural. In the Bible, women remained figures of wisdom and good sense, possibly because they had very little other access to success. The Book of Proverbs, which opens with the metaphysical Woman-Wisdom, ends with the very prototype of the wise woman, the capable wife ("woman of valor") of Proverbs 31.[3] Wisdom is a protective figure who offers well-being,[4] and rewards her adherents with success and delight.[5] As the instructor tells the young boy:

> Acquire wisdom, acquire discernment;
> do not forget and do not swerve from my words.
> Do not forsake her and she will guard you,
> love her and she will protect you.
> . . . .
> Hug her to you and she will exalt you;
> she will bring you honor if you embrace her.
> she will adorn your head with a graceful wreath;
> crown you with a glorious diadem.[6]

Wisdom also has a cosmic aspect, expressed in her long hymn of self-praise in Chapter 8, in which she presents her story:

> The Lord created me at the beginning of his course
> as the first of his works of old.
> In the distant past I was fashioned,
> at the beginning, at the origin of earth. . .
> He had not yet made earth and fields,
> or the world's first clumps of clay.
> I was there when He set the heavens into place,
> when he fixed the horizon upon the deep . . .
> I was with Him as a ward
> a source of delight every day,
> Rejoicing before Him at all times,
> rejoicing in his inhabited world,
> finding delight with humankind.[7]

This is a very important pedigree: she was brought forth at the very beginning of God's creation.[8] As a creature, she does not rival God or endanger monotheism. However, her presence at the creation means she witnessed and has knowledge of all matters.[9] She is also God's eternal companion. But she is not the mother of humanity. There is nothing maternal about Wisdom. She is not an intercessor. She is not all-forgiving and unconditional in her love, and has no compassion for the transgressor. She is not ever-receptive, and can be vindictive if spurned.[10] Woman-Wisdom is a lover. She is responsive to human love: she loves those who love her, and is available to all who seek her.[11] She also actively seeks men, crying aloud in the public places, the streets, the squares, the gateways, crossroads, and entryways.[12] She even builds a house, prepares a feast, and sends her maids to invite all the simple and senseless to "walk in the way of understanding."[13]

The figure of Wisdom as a woman expresses the profound pull of devotion to scholarship. Desire for learning is a lust: it is a compelling attraction that can absorb a person deeply, that can consume a person's life and desires, and can (in our language) supplant or suppress the libido. The male scholars of antiquity expressed the magnetism of this drive by representing wisdom as a female. But the erotic metaphor is aimed at *men*, as Wisdom states explicitly in Proverbs 8:4: "To you, O men, I call, and my voice is towards the sons of Adam." Here the word for men is *'îšîm*, which emphasizes the maleness of the beloved.[14] It is the erotic-like aspect of this love that made the male scribe follow and show devotion to wisdom as a divine woman.

Wisdom, beloved lover of men, is also the beloved of God: "(I was) a source of delight every day, rejoicing before him at all times, rejoicing in his inhabited world, finding delight with humankind."[15] As the lover of both men and God, she also joins them in her love. Her closeness to God enables her to say, "he who finds me finds life and obtains favor from the Lord" (8:35). In this way, she mediates, in her own way, the gulf between humanity and God. Loving wisdom, the scholar forms an attachment to the cosmic world.

Woman-Wisdom's chief rival is the "other woman," the married adulteress[16] who seeks to seduce. Like Wisdom, the adulteress comes looking for the boy,[17] and relies on her persuasiveness to convince: "the lips of the strange woman drip honey and her palate is smoother than oil."[18] In the morality tale of Proverbs 7, a sage watches from his window as a lad meets this woman, who is bustling about in the street, attired provocatively. She kisses him and invites him home with her, and starts marshalling arguments to persuade him. She tempts him with the delights in store: the meal, the perfumed couch, and the night of lovemaking. She then addresses his major concern—the teaching (emphasized by the sage) that adultery is so dangerous as to be life-threatening, for husbands will take their revenge. She tells him that there will be no consequences, for nobody will know: her husband is off on a long journey. By this, she convinces him: "She sways him with her eloquence, turns him aside with her smooth talk,"[19] and he follows her "like an ox to the slaughter."

To Proverbs 1–9, this woman is the archenemy of life itself,[20] and the archrival of Wisdom, who can save him from her.[21] Woman-Wisdom's ally is the legitimate wife: together they help men avoid another's wife, and the sage urges men to take sexual delight in their wives.[22] The adulteress and Woman-Folly represent unlicensed, unauthorized, and basically antisocial adulterous love. True love of wisdom will teach one that this is folly, that sexuality must serve the purposes of the family. In the Book of Proverbs, Woman-Wisdom buttresses the family structure.

This image of Woman-Wisdom evolved during the Hellenistic period into the powerful image of Sophia, the divine wisdom of the book of Ben Sirach. Men devoted themselves to the service of Sophia, increasingly by abandoning human familial ties.[23] Ultimately, erotic attachment to Sophia became an ascetic enterprise, an exclusive love relationship in which the individual avoided familial attachments in order to stay in direct communion with Sophia.[24] Rabbinic Judaism identified Wisdom with Torah, and made sacred study its form of seeking woman. Judaism made the search for Wisdom a communal affair (of the community of men) and avoided individual celibate devotion. The academy of study and the family became the two pillars of communal life.

Woman-Wisdom arises after the collapse of the Judaean state, when the Jews returned from the Babylonian exile. The old Zion theology of invincibility had long since been disproved, the triumphalist expectations of the imminent Kingdom of God were not realized, the beloved divinely-decreed Davidic monarchy was no more, and the Jews were living as part of an empire, with no king, and even, for a while, no temple. The family increasingly became the major realm of life, and the security of the family a major preoccupation.[25] At the same time, the Jews had been exposed to new gender systems in Babylonia and Assyria, and may have had reason to reflect on the incongruity between the Israelite social life and its ideology. A groundswell of change was beginning, which reflected itself in this new type of symbolism in which the woman, even though desirable and beloved, is clearly outside the community of concern: she is the "other," either good (Wisdom, Zion) or bad (Folly, adulteresses), who tempts and seduces.[26]

Throughout the history of Western religion, the many facets of mother, of the wife-of-god image and the Indweller of Zion result in new powerful female images. The post-biblical legendary writings (the Midrashim) continue the picture of Mother Rachel as the great intercessor, which results in visits, pilgrimages, and petitions at Rachel's tomb.[27] The belief in Mother Rachel and the pilgrimages and petitions to her are similar to, albeit much less extensive than, the theology and cult that have grown up around the figure of Mother Mary.[28] Mothers in heaven, they weep and pray for their children. In the same way, the literary figure Knesset Israel ("the congregation of Israel") became the people's chief advocate in Heaven. The Sabbath became the queen who married God and Israel. The Shekhinah (the "indweller") became the symbol of divine immanence, residing in Jerusalem, among the people, and in humanity. The bride of God became in Christian thought the Church and the individual soul, and the marriage metaphor became the great image of mystical devotion.

These mediating figures did not disappear because they addressed the great existential dilemma of monotheism, the centrality of human-kind, and its sense of inadequacy in the face of divine power. At times, the mediators of the Bible were joined by many layers of intercession and interpositions, angels, archangels, seraphim, cherubim, powers, spirits, demons, as the loneliness of humanity repopulated the heavens to buffer its existence and diffuse the power of the human–divine arena.

These female images are not necessarily bad for woman. Having a literary figure of Woman-Wisdom can reinforce the idea that women are wise; having a beloved Zion teaches that women are lovable. Similarly, the later Jewish images of the sabbath Queen-Bride and the Torah are positive female images that can raise women's prestige and reinforce women's self-esteem. Even the image of the Virgin Mary, which the male culture specifically declared to be unlike other women, has often been experienced as a positive image by Catholic women. Nevertheless, despite the obvious appeal of these images to women, when union with them is described as *marriage*, women are excluded from the symbolic relationship. Both the human community and God become increasingly male, and women are the liminal and marginal figures who buffer the relationship.

# PART III

Sex and Gender

*The Unfinished Agenda*

# 17

## Sex in the Bible

The transformations in thought brought by biblical monotheism did not address sexuality. The Bible focuses on sexual behavior as a form of social behavior, but never really incorporates sexuality into its vision of humanity or its relationship with the divine.[1]

Sexuality is a very complex phenomenon. At once social and physical, "nature" and "culture," it defies categorization. Pagan religions saw sexuality as part of the natural order, part of the same generative force that ultimately resulted in fertility. Erotic attraction had an integral place in the workings of the cosmos. Sexuality could be sacred, part of the continuation of the cosmos, as in the Sumerian sacred marriage ritual. In this ritual, the expression of sexual emotions could be associated with the experience of divinity, and the songs and poems connected with the sacred marriage provided a religious setting for the expression and celebration of sexual desire. Even ordinary sex could be seen as godlike, for the stories of the sexual adventures and misadventures of the gods provided a divine parallel for sexuality. These stories showed that gods also felt these drives and performed these acts. Sexual behavior did not make people *less* like the gods; on the contrary, it reinforced their resemblance to the upper orders of being.[2] The male gods could be models of male virility and sexual potency, their behavior paradigms of proper (and sometimes of improper) sexual activity.

Ancient pagan religion also portrayed the sexual impulse as a goddess of sexual attraction. Male gods, figures of potency, can express sexual activity; they cannot fully express sexual attraction in a predominantly heterosexual, androcentric society. The figure of Inanna/Ishtar provides a way to conceptualize the erotic impulse, a vocabulary to celebrate its presence, and an image with which to comprehend the human experience of sexual desire. Sexual desire comes from the presence of Ishtar. When she is absent,

*The Bull springs not upon the cow,*
*the ass does not inseminate the Jenny.*
*In the street man does not inseminate young woman.*
*The man lies down in his (own) chamber*
*the woman lies down on her side.*[3]

Sexuality was part of the divine realm, most specifically of the female divine. Even when other functions of goddesses were absorbed by male gods, sexuality could not be absorbed into male divinity. Ishtar remained the representative and divine patron of sexual attraction and activity.

All of this religious dimension of sexuality disappears in biblical monotheism. There is no sexual dimension of divine experience. Instead of gods and goddesses interrelating with each other, there is only the one God of Israel. YHWH, moreover, is a predominantly male god, referred to by the masculine pronoun (never by the feminine), and often conceived of in such quintessentially masculine images as warrior and king. In the earliest biblical poem, the Song of the Sea, God is "man of war."[4] God is also king, the prime metaphor of mastery. This, too, has a masculine connotation. But these masculine qualities of God are social male-gender characteristics. The monotheist God is not sexually a male. He is not at all phallic, and does not represent male virility. Biblical anthropomorphic language uses corporeal images of the arm of God, the right hand of God, God's back, and God's tears. God is not imagined below the waist. In Moses' vision at Mount Sinai, God covered Moses with his hand until he had passed by, and Moses saw only his back.[5] In Elijah's vision, there was nothing to be seen, only a "small still voice." In Isaiah's vision (chapter 6), two seraphim hide God's "feet" (normally taken as a euphemism), and in Ezekiel's vision (chapters 1–3), there is only fire below the loins. God is asexual, or transsexual, or metasexual (depending on how we view this phenomenon), but "he" is never sexed.

God does not behave in sexual ways. In the powerful marital metaphor, God is the "husband" of Israel. But this husband–God does not kiss, embrace, fondle, or otherwise express physical affection for Israel, even within the poetic license of the metaphor.[6] Such reticence is not demanded by rhetorical usage, for in the other erotic metaphor, that describing the attachment of men to Lady Wisdom, there is no hesitation to use a physical image, "hug her to you and she will exult you, she will bring you honor if you embrace her."[7] Wisdom is clearly a woman-figure, and can be metaphorically embraced as a woman. But

God is not a sexual male, and therefore even the erotic metaphor of passion reveals a lack of physicality. God is not imaged in erotic terms, and sexuality was simply not part of the divine order.

God is not sexed, God does not model sexuality, and God does not bestow sexual power. God, who is the giver of fertility, procreation, abundance, health, does not explicitly give potency. God does not promise the men of Israel that they will be sexually active or competent. Biblical thought does not see sexuality as a gift of God. To the Bible, the sexual and divine realms have nothing to do with each other. Indeed, the Bible is concerned to maintain their separation, to demarcate the sexual and sacred experiences and to interpose space and time between them. God would not reveal godself or God's purpose on Mount Sinai until Israel abstained from sexual activity for three days.[8] This temporal separation between the sexual and the sacred also underlies the story of David's request for food during his days of fleeing from King Saul. David assured the priest Ahimelech that his men were eligible to eat hallowed bread by asserting that they had been away from women for three days.[9] Sexual activity brings people into a realm of experience which is *unlike* God; conversely, in order to approach God one has to leave the sexual realm.

The impurity provisions of the sacral laws also provide for time to elapse between engaging in sexual activity and coming into the domain of the sacred. Under these regulations, any man who has had a sexual emission, or anybody who has engaged in sexual intercourse, must wash and then remain ritually "impure" until that evening.[10] The overall purpose of Israel's impurity rules was to keep intact the essential divisions of human existence: holy and profane, life and death. Even virtuous and socially necessary acts, like tending the dying and burying the dead, could threaten to cross over and blur these categories. They therefore made the person who performed these acts "impure." "Impure" people were isolated ritually: they could not come to the temple or participate in sacred rites for the duration of their impurity.[11] In this way, the realm of the "holy" was kept separate from matters that were considered not part of divinity, like death and sexuality.[12]

This desacralization of sexuality meant that sexuality was treated as a completely sociological, human phenomenon. Israel discusses sexuality in the language of law; the concerns that it expresses are those of social behavior and social control. In its discussions of sexuality, Israel acts to ensure that sexuality serves the purpose of the polis; that it be a force for the preservation of the social order, and that it be prevented from disturbing social relationships. In the biblical view, sexuality had a prime position in the social realm, for it formed part of the ideal human social pattern, the husband-wife marriage.[13] Israel considered the monogamous nuclear family the first social relationship, established by God at the very beginning of human existence: "therefore a man leaves his father and mother and cleaves to his wife and they become one flesh."[14] Married life is positive and divinely approved: "he who finds a wife, he finds a good thing and gets favor from the Lord."[15] Furthermore, marriage should not be considered a matter of economic convenience or a method of procreation; it is to be a close love-bond. Within this marital structure, sexuality is encouraged. Deuteronomy includes a provision for the exemption of a new bridegroom from campaigns for a year so that he may be free to cause his wife to rejoice.[16] And the proverbial wisdom urges people to enjoy the sexual element in marriage:

> . . . let your fountain be blessed;
> find joy in the wife of our youth—
> a loving doe, a graceful mountain goat.
> Let her breasts satisfy you at all times;
> be infatuated with love of her always.[17]

and the wise man is encouraged to enjoy his marital sexuality.

The priests, guardian of Israel's ongoing contact with the Holy, had to be particularly careful to keep preserve the separation between Israel's priestly functions and attributes and any hint of sexuality.[18] The very wages of a prostitute could not to be given to the temple as a gift.[19] The sons of Eli, the priest, committed an unforgivable wrong by having sexual relations with the women who came to worship; as a result, they lost forever the right of their family to be priests.[20] The priests and their families were to model ideal sexual behavior. The priest's bride had to be a virgin, for he was not allowed to marry a divorcee. His daughters had a particular charge to be chaste while under their father's jurisdiction; should a priest's daughter be sexually active, she was considered to have profaned *her father* and was to be burned.

Sexuality is harnessed to the family; it is confined within the nuclear family and plays, in turn, its part in defining the larger family unit. There are strong incest prohibitions within the family detailed in Leviticus 18, 20 and Deuteronomy 27. One cannot have sex with father and mother, stepmother, paternal uncle[21] and his wife, and both maternal and paternal aunts.[22] In one's own generation, both sister and brother's wife are prohibited.[23] In the next generation, one's daughter-in-law, and, we presume, one's daughter[24] are prohibited, as are one's children's daughters. Furthermore, once one marries, one's wife's lineage is off-limits: mother-in-law, wife's sister (while the wife is alive), wife's daughters and granddaughters.

These complex incest laws declare off-limits all women who are part of the extended family structure. Some (like mothers-in-law) would not live in the same household, even when the extended family might live together (as in some rural situations), and the laws explicitly include father's daughters who are born outside the household. These incest laws define and clarify family lines. The marital bond creates a family even though there are no blood ties,and so father's wife, father's brother's wife, and brother's wife are prohibited because the "nakedness" (the conventional translation for Hebrew *'erwâ*) of the woman is tantamount to the nakedness of her husband. So too, since one's wife is also bonded to him, her bloodline (*šĕ'ēr*) is parallel to his own and thereby prohibited. Sex within the family would blur family lines and relations and cause a collapse of family relations: sex with daughter-in-law is explicitly called *tebel* ("mixing") in Leviticus 20:12.[25]

This bonding of sexuality to family, which gives sexuality an integral place in the social order, raises the issue of the control of sexuality. Care is taken to define the relationships and times in which it is permissible. To a large extent, this means control over female sexuality; the laws delineate who has the right to mate with which females and how should this be done. Men and women were equally bound by the laws, but the laws revolve around the sexual activity of women.[26] For a man to sleep with a woman who belonged to some other household threatened the very definition of "household" and "family"; for a married man to sleep with an unattached woman is not mentioned as an item of concern. The very existence of prostitutes indicates that there were women with whom a man (married or unmarried) could have sexual experiences. However, a married woman could not be approached sexually by anyone but her husband: sexual intercourse with a married woman constituted "adultery" and both the male and female partner were to be killed.[27]

Like sex with a married woman, sexual intercourse with a girl still living in her father's house threatened social order. Unmarried girls were expected to be chaste. The laws of Exodus required a man who seduced an unbetrothed girl to marry her; he had created an obligation that he must not refuse, and he must, moreover, offer the customary bride-price. Her father had the option to refuse her to him, in which case the seducer still had to pay a full virgin's bride-price.[28] The rule of the nonvirgin bride[29] underscores the obligation of a girl to remain chaste while in her father's house. A bride whose new husband finds her not to be a virgin is to be stoned, because "she did a shameful thing in Israel, committing fornication while under her father's authority." There is good reason to suspect that this law was not expected to be followed,[30] but it certainly lays down a theoretical principle very important to Israel: that a girl was expected to be chaste while in her father's house. The choice of stoning reveals the significance of her breach of this obligation. Stoning is a very special penalty, reserved for those offenses which completely upset the hierarchical arrangements of the cosmos. In these cases, the entire community is threatened and endangered, and the entire community serves as the executioner.[31] The girl, by being secretly unchaste, has disrupted the community's expectations of daughterly obligations.

Similarly, if a man has intercourse with a betrothed woman in town, both are stoned; the girl because she did not cry for help (which would have been heard, since they were in town) and the man because he illicitly had sex with his neighbor's wife.[32] This law is not about rape. In the case of actual rape, as when a man grabs the betrothed girl, the offense is capital, but only the man is culpable. Biblical law realizes that forcible rape is a crime of violence and that the girl is a victim: it explicitly compares forcible rape to murder.[33] This law about sex with a betrothed woman assumes that the sex was consensual: even though the word '*nh* is often translated "rape," it rarely corresponds to forcible rape but rather implies the abusive treatment of someone else. In sexual contexts, it means illicit sex; sex with someone with whom one has no right to have sex.[34] Because the girl, although still a virgin, is legally considered married to the man to whom she has been betrothed, both partners are therefore guilty of adultery and are deserving of death. Their offense is even more serious than adultery: in normal instances of adultery, the couple is to be killed, but not stoned. But in this case, the adultery is compounded; the couple has both violated the rights of the future husband and offended against the girl's obligation to her father.

The control of women's sexuality did not stay in the hands of the head of the household. In the laws of Exodus,[35] the father of a seduced girl could decide whether to give her in marriage to her seducer. He himself had the right to determine what would happen to his daughter's sexuality. This *patria potestas* (father-right) was standard procedure in early law. Two biblical tales, Lot's offering his daughters to the men of Sodom,[36] and the man of Gibeah's offering his daughter to the men of Gibeah[37] show what such right can imply. These men were attempting to cope with an emergency situation in which they felt their lives at risk, but the narrative considers them within their rights to offer their daughters. Lot, in particular, is considered the one righteous man in Sodom. The laws of Deuteronomy show a different awareness. At least by the time of Deuteronomy, the father's rights were not all that absolute. In Deuteronomy 22:28–9, if a man takes an unbetrothed girl and they are found, the man is to give the father fifty shekels, and he must marry her without the right to divorce her in the future. Here, there is no mention of the father's right to refuse to give his daughter to this marriage. The laws have superseded his discretion, now requiring what had once been the father's discretionary act. Control over woman's sexuality is also not entirely that of the husband. In the Assyrian laws, a husband has a right to determine the penalty for his adulterous wife, or even to pardon her outright; his freedom is limited only by the fact that whatever he chooses to do to his wife, the same will be done to her adulterous partner. The popular philosophy of the book of Proverbs, in warning the young man against adultery, warns him: "The fury of the husband will be passionate; he will show no pity on his day of vengeance. He will not have regard for any ransom; he will refuse your bribe, however great."[38] This may indicate that there were informal arrangements in which a husband could accept a bribe to let the adulterer go free. In the more formal formulation of the laws, however, the penalty for adultery is clearly death, with no option for leniency. The community's interest in controlling sexuality in the interest of maintaining social order takes precedence over the interest of the head of the household in controlling his family.

Deuteronomy vests some of the control over these matters in the hands of the elders of Israel, who are to uphold the social order and eliminate dangers to it. They try the recalcitrant son; they investigate the question of the bride's virginity; they oversee the release of a levir, (a man obliged to father a child with his dead brother's childless wife); and they perform the decapitated heifer ceremony.[39] But above all, the laws place the locus of control outside the discretion of individuals by prescribing mandatory sentencing for certain offenses and leaving others for divine sanction. In the prohibited relationships of Leviticus 20, adultery, homosexuality, bestiality, and sex with stepmother, mother-in-law, and daughter-in-law are all to be punished by death; sex with a sister, sister-in-law, aunt, uncle's wife, and menstruating women are also prohibited, but they are outside societal sanctions and are to be punished by God.

All of these rules of control are part of the domestication of sexuality, the harnessing of its power in the service of community solidarity. They tacitly acknowledge but do not make explicit the antinomian power of sex. Just as sexual attraction within the marriage can bond the husband and wife, sexual attraction to others is a temptation to break the boundaries and dissolve social categories. Marital ties are endangered by adulterous attractions, and even national boundaries and ethnic distinctions can be forgotten and ultimately destroyed. Israel, determined to preserve its distinct identity and religion, highlights this issue in Genesis 34, a chapter often called the "rape of Dinah," even though it is probably not about a forcible rape, and really is not a story about Dinah at all. It relates how Dinah had "gone out to see the daughters of the land."[40] Shechem saw her and lay with her, thus treating her improperly. He thereby treated her as a "whore,"[41] a woman whose own consent is sufficient because her sexuality is not part of a family structure. Dinah's consent was not enough: the fact that Shechem had not spoken to her parents in advance constituted a serious impropriety, a threat to the integrity of Dinah's family. Dinah's own wishes are almost incidental.[42] Since Shechem loved her, he asked his father Hamor to acquire her for him as his wife. Hamor realized the implication of such a marriage and said to Jacob, "intermarry with us; give your daughters to us and take our daughters for yourselves: you will dwell among us, and the land will be open before you."[43] He further says to his own fellow townsmen, "the men agree with us to dwell among us and be as one kindred," even intermingling their "cattle, substance, and all their beasts." Dinah's mating with Shechem was the great threat to Jacob's family (and endangered all of future Israel, the people who relate the story). Jacob's sons were the first generation of Abraham's line to intermarry with the local inhabitants, but they had to do so under controlled conditions in which they could remain a distinct unit. The free exercise of erotic love by Shechem threatened that type of control and could have resulted (in the eyes of the brothers) with a dissolution of the boundary between them and the native peoples of Canaan.[44]

Sexual attraction might even threaten the categories of being "human." One of the themes of Israel's primeval history[45] is the definition of humanity and the division of humanity from the divine realm, on the one hand, and the animal realm on the other. During the development of humanity, sexual attraction threatened to erase the category of "human" as the lesser divine beings, the *běnê 'Elohim,* mated with them. To preserve the difference between humans and divine, God ensured their separation through a reinforcement of human mortality, a limitation on the human life-span.[46] In practical experience, of course, one did not have to be overly concerned with human–divine matings. No divine beings were observed in the post-flood era seducing human women; presumably women were not successfully attributing unexpected babies to angelic intervention; and there is no record in the Bible of divine females coming to seduce the men of Israel, even in their sleep. The other boundary of humanity, the animal–human boundary, was more problematic. The first humans had much in common with animals, who, according to Genesis 2, were first created as companions to Adam. Once humans took the first steps towards culture, they became less animallike, and God acknowledges this difference by providing them with clothing made of animal skins. The hierarchical boundary between the human and animal world is even more explicit after the flood: humans could kill animals for food (sparing the blood), whereas no animal could kill a human without forfeiting its own life. The boundary between human and animal is uncrossable and part of the very definition of human being. However, in experiential reality, this uncrossable boundary of human existence could be crossed by mating with animals. Such human–animal matings are widespread in folklore and probably have a basis in the behavior of rural humans. The blurring of the human–animal border would be a return to chaos.[47] Every legal collection strongly forbids bestiality;[48] Leviticus 18:23 further explains that bestiality is *tebel* "(improper) mixing." The maintaining of categories is particularly important in the priestly writings, for one of the essential priestly functions was the maintenance of the categories of existence (pure and impure, holy and profane, permissible and impermissible foods, family lines, sacred time, sacred space). But preoccupation with neatness is not limited to Leviticus, for Deuteronomy also manifests this concern, prohibiting even the wearing of linsey-woolsey cloth, which combines wool, from animals, and linen, from plants.[49] The Bible's extreme aversion to homosexuality is part of this concern not to let sexual activity destroy the categories of orderly existence. Leviticus proscribes male homosexuality under penalty of death.[50] Homosexual activity, as known in the ancient world, exists outside the pair-bond structure, which is the social locus of permissible sexuality. Furthermore, it blurs the distinction between male and female, and this cannot be tolerated in the biblical system. Anything that smacks of homosexual blurring is similarly prohibited, such as cross-dressing.[51] It has long been noted that lesbianism is not mentioned. This is not because these Levitical laws concern only male behavior: bestiality is explicitly specified to include both male and female interaction with beasts. But lesbianism was probably considered a trivial matter: it involved only women, with no risk of pregnancy; and, most important, did not result in true physical "union" (by the male entering the female).

Forbidden sexuality, like adultery, incest, homosexuality, and bestiality goes beyond the private affairs of families, and becomes a national concern. Such sexual behavior is a threat to social order, as is murder, and, again like murder, it is said to pollute the land and thereby endanger the very survival of Israel. Leviticus 18 relates that the pre-Israel inhabitants of the land indulged in the incestuous relations listed there, in bestiality, homosexuality, and molech-worship, and that—as a result—the land became defiled and vomited out its inhabitants. It warns Israel not to do these same abominations, "Let not the land spew you out for defiling it, as it spewed out the nation that came before you."[52] Israel's right of occupation is contingent upon its care not to do these things, for murder, illicit sex and idolatry will pollute the land, and a polluted land will not sustain them. The pollution vocabulary with which Israel thinks about such matters means that everything connected to murder is dangerous. The people must not only refrain from murder, they must not pollute the land by letting murderers go free or allowing accidental murderers to leave the city of refuge[53] or by leaving the corpses of the executed unburied.[54] The same is true of sexual abominations. Illicit sex such as adultery and incest poses a threat to society. Even technical aspects of the issue pose this danger: if a man remarries his divorced and since remarried wife, this too will pollute the land.[55]

The danger to the nation that ensues from murder and adultery explains the mandatory death sentence; it also clarifies two very odd Biblical rituals. In the ceremony of the decapitated heifer, a corpse is found but none can identify the murderer. The elders of the city nearest the corpse go to a *wadi* (dry riverbed) and decapitate a heifer, declaring their lack of culpability and seeking to avert the blood-pollution of the land.[54] The second ritual is the trial of the suspected adulteress,[57] which provides that whenever a husband suspects his wife, he is to bring her to the temple, where upon presentation of a flour offering, she is to drink a potion made from holy water, dust from the floor of the sanctuary, and the dissolved words of Numbers 5:11–31, while answering "amen" to a priestly adjuration that should she be guilty the water will enter into her and cause her "belly to swell and her thigh to drop" (probably a prolapsed uterus). After this oath, she returns to her husband. This ritual allowed a husband to resume marital relations after he suspected adultery. Otherwise, intercourse with a wife who had slept with another man could be expected to pollute the land in the same way as remarriage to a divorced wife who had been married in the interim.

Ostensibly, the Bible considers human sexual behavior to be part of human society rather than the natural God-created order. These laws channel this behavior into its proper family structure, providing the proper outlet for the force of sexual attraction. But these very laws reveal that sexual attraction had the capacity to destroy society. It could blur the lines of family and rip families apart; it could lead to the assimilation into the nations of Israel, which was concerned to keep itself distinct. Sexual attraction could lead to behavior that could pollute the land and imperil Israel's right to occupy it. Sexual activity could even blur the categories of human existence, and could cause the collapse of civilized order into cosmos.[58] Wrongful sexual activity can bring disaster to the world.

The Bible treats sexuality as a question of social control and behavior: who with whom and when. But matters are not so easily controlled. The stories of the Pharaoh and Sarah, David and Bathsheba, and Amnon and Tamar show a sense that erotic attraction can cause men to abuse their superior position and strength.[59] The capacity of free uncontrolled sexual behavior to destroy all of civilization implies that there is more to sexuality than human mores. The force of sexual attraction goes beyond human invention. But the Bible does not explicitly discuss this dimension of sexuality. The one exception is the Song of Songs, which presents an idyll of romantic love unconstrained by societal considerations, and recognizes the great force of love: "For love is fierce as death, passion is mighty as Sheol, its darts are darts of fire, a blazing flame. Vast floods cannot quench love, nor rivers drown it."[60]

The biblical discussion of the force of sexual attraction (as opposed to sexual behavior) is inchoate and essentially inarticulate. There is no vocabulary in the Bible in which to discuss such matters, no divine image or symbolic system by which to mediate it. YHWH cannot model sex. Moreover, YHWH is not the patron of sexual behavior, and is not even recorded as the guarantor of potency; and there is no other divine figure who can serve to control or mediate this volatile, creative, and potentially chaotic force. The power of love and attraction serves as the basis for the powerful metaphor of Israel and God as wife and husband. But the Bible's lack of discussion of the dynamics and implications of sex creates a tension within the biblical system. There is a vacuum in an essential area of human concern. This vacuum was ultimately filled (in Hellenistic times) by the complex of antiwoman, anticarnal ideas that had such a large impact on the development of Western religion and civilization.

# 18

## Sex and the People

### The Myth of Orgy

The lack of emphasis on eros in biblical thought creates a vacuum that has been filled by some modern biblical scholars, who describe a "sex cult"[1] that the people practiced in Hosea's time. According to these scholars, Israel knew a "sexual orgiasticism,"[2] which included sacred prostitutes, festive orgies, and a peculiar initiation rite in which every young girl offered herself to the divinity by having sex with a stranger inside the holy area, in return for which she expected fertility. Scholars have claimed that this was a Canaanite rite, that Canaanite religion was basically orgiastic, that the Israelites were being seduced by this foreign sexual worship into a syncretistic religion, and that syncretism was the cause of the prophetic denunciation. According to many scholars, this sexual activity was a result of goddess worship. Often, scholars seem either to condemn Israel for this cult or praise it for its closeness with nature.[3] Recently, certain fundamental questions have begun to be asked: Did Canaan have any religiosexual rites? Is there any evidence for initiation rites or any nonprofessional sexual activity? Is there any evidence for professional sexual activity such as cultic prostitution? Is there evidence for any type of sexual service?

When these questions are asked, it becomes clear that the whole idea of a sex cult—in Israel or in Canaan—is a chimera, the product of ancient and modern sexual fantasies.[4] Ever since the beginnings of modern biblical scholarship, it has been assumed that Semitic religion was very sexy, that the temples "thronged with sacred prostitutes,"[5] and that there was a widespread worship of a great mother-goddess in which sexual union at the sanctuary ensured fruitfulness.[6] No real evidence for this has been unearthed, but most contemporary scholars simply assume the existence of sexual licentiousness, referring in foot-notes to each other and to William Albright, Gerhard von Rad, and Hans Walter Wolff.[7] Even scholars who have reviewed the data and acknowledged the lack of evidence have still assumed that there must be some basis to such a widespread opinion.[8]

There is no native evidence for sexual religious cult activity. The charge that the women of Canaan and Israel had a sexual initiation with a stranger derives ultimately from classical allegations, in particu-lar Herodotus' "description" of the practices at the Mylitta (Ishtar) tem-ple in Babylon:

> The foulest Babylonian custom is that which compels every woman of the land once in her life to sit in the temple of Aphrodite and have inter-course with some stranger. . . . When a woman has once taken her place there she goes not away to her home before some stranger has cast money into her lap and had intercourse with her outside the temple, but while he casts the money, he must say "I demand thee in the name of Mylitta (that is the Assyrian name for Aphrodite)." It matters not what be the sum of money, the woman will never refuse. . . . After their intercourse she has made herself holy in the goddess' sight and goes away to her home; and thereafter there is no bribe however great that will get her. So then the women that are fair and tall are soon free to depart, but the uncomely have long to wait. . . . [9]

Herodotus is talking about Babylon, not Syria or Israel. Further-more, this does not seem to be an accurate description of Babylonian practice. No cuneiform text supports the idea that the women of Assyria or Babylon did this. Herodotus' observations about Babylon are gener-ally not as accurate as those about Egypt,[10] and even his observations about Egypt are not that trustworthy.[11] Herodotus, like all Greeks, wrote about "barbarians" with the intention of proving the superiority of Greeks, and allegations of cannibalism and sexual licentiousness abound. In his descriptions of barbarian sexual mores, he may also have been trying to show the horrible results that could follow if proper women were not kept as guarded and secluded as they were in Greece.[12] All the later Roman and Christian allegations of sexual initiation ulti-mately derive from this one passage in Herodotus.[13] There is no reason to believe that the people of ancient Israel—or even of Canaan—had reli-gious cultic activities which involved or celebrated sexual activity.

The same conclusion is inescapable when we examine the question of professional cultic prostitution. All the evidence for the existence of cultic prostitutes in Israel rests on the translation *qedeshah (qĕdēšâ)*,[14] literally "holy woman" or "tabooed woman." This word has long been translated "sacred prostitute." The *qedeshot* (feminine plural) have been explained as female prostitutes, and the *qedeshim* (masculine plural) as male prostitutes, i.e., catamites. *Qedeshim* and *qedeshot* were clearly prohibited in the biblical tradition. As Deuteronomy states, "let there be no *qedeshah* from among the Israelite women and let there be no *qadesh* from among the Israelite men."[15] Successive reforms by Israelite kings periodically got rid of the *qedeshim*.[16] The *qedeshim* are often mentioned together with the local shrines, pillars, altars, and asherahs and seem to have been part of the folk worship identified as foreign and improper by the emerging biblical monotheist tradition.[17]

The term *qadesh* is known from the Ugaritic texts, where he was a type of priest. The *qadesh* could be married, and could be raised to the rank of nobleman.[18] In lists of cultic functionaries from Ugarit, the *qedeshim* are ranked right behind the *kohanim* (major priests).[19] They are not mentioned in sexual contexts, and don't seem to have had anything to do with sex. The earliest translations of the Bible do not understand the term to mean a male prostitute.[20] Moreover, if the *qadesh* was not a male prostitute, why should we assume that the *qedeshah* was a female prostitute?[21] Even the Babylonian *qadištu* priestess cannot be called a sacred prostitute, for the texts have no hint of sexual activity.[22] There is one case where the same woman is called a *zônâ* (harlot) and a *qedeshah*: in the story of Tamar, who disguised herself as a harlot so that Judah would sleep with her. When his emissary went looking for on the road way where Judah had found her, he asked "Where is the *qedeshah?*" and was told that no such a one had been there. The *zonah* and the *qedeshah* clearly shared one important attribute: they were women outside the family structure, with no male to protect them. As such, the *qedeshah* was vulnerable to sexual approach, and, for all we know, may have been permitted sexual freedom, as was the harlot. But why believe that this sexual activity was the essential part of her role? Clearly, the *qadesh* and the *qedeshah* were involved in some form of worship, either Canaanite or native in origin, that was discarded by the evolving tradition of Israel. But the only real depiction of what the *qedeshot* did is that they were weaving garments for Asherah.[23] They could have been vestal-type virgins who spent their days weaving garments for the goddess!

The Mesopotamian temples contained all kinds of women functionaries, long translated "priestesses" or "hierodules." Once again, serious study of the documents relating to these women shows that there is no evidence that any of them performed sexual acts as part of their sacred duties.[24] The only form of sexual service that we do not have to doubt was the sacred marriage of Sumerian times. There we have unequivocal statements that the king slept with the "goddess."[25] But even this one sexual ritual disappeared after Sumerian times as the sacred marriage underwent a radical transformation: instead of being played out by human beings, it was represented by placing statues of the god and goddess in a garden for the night. This is hardly what might be considered orgiastic religion. The whole tradition of considering ancient pagan religion sexy and its women cultic functionaries as sex partners is a myth. It speaks more about its adherents than it does about the ancients. It is born of conflicted attitudes towards sexual activity in Western civilization, of the inability to think of roles for women priestesses in any arena other than sexual. Nevertheless, it points out the absence of biblical discourse on sexuality. It is hard to imagine that ancient Israel did not have more to say about sexuality than the Bible offers. The Bible recognizes the power of eros; there must have been writings and ideas in Israel about sexuality. In the absence of a biblical record, the imagination and fantasies of early modern scholars created a sex cult in ancient Israel.

Not talking about sex does not make it go away, and the lack of discourse about sexuality is not a stable situation. Sex has a way of reminding people about itself. Biblical law's concern with regulating sexual behavior indicates that Israel was as aware as we are of the power of human attraction. In the Song of Songs, this awareness finds expression in the phrase "for love is stronger than death." This awareness also underlies all the uses of the erotic metaphor, for they rely on our experience of the sexual bond as a bond of connectedness. The Bible is aware of the strength of sexual attraction and the sensations of communion, but it offers no vision to help understand and integrate this experience of human sexuality. Biblical monotheism's lack of a clear and compelling vision on sex and gender was tantamount to an unfinished revolution. But no culture can exist without some ideas about an experience as compelling as sexuality. When powerful emotions cannot be integrated into our vision of humanity, society, and divinity, then they are feared. This fear of eros can lead to a desire to avoid the occasions of temptation, thus rigidly reinforcing gender lines and making society ever more conscious of gender divisions. This weakness in the fabric of biblical monotheism begins to emerge in the stresses of the destruction of Jerusalem, the Babylonian exile, and the difficult restoration period. Then, when Israel becomes exposed to Greek ideas in the Hellenistic period, Greek concepts of sex and gender fill the vacuum in decidedly antiwoman, anticarnal ways that have long influenced the Western religious tradition.

# 19

## Gifts of the Greeks

Israel's ideas about sex and gender changed after the conquest of Judea by Alexander the Great in 333 B.C.E. Jewish thinking[1] about these matters was inherently unstable and was already undergoing modification, but the direction was firmly established by the confrontation with Greek civilization, which considered itself greatly superior to the East and actively promoted the spread of Greek culture. Jewish tradition has long held that there were two factions of Jews, the "Hellenizers," who adopted Greek modes of dress and behavior, and the pious, who did not.[2] However, even the most loyal and pious were influenced by Greek ideas,[3] and Hellenistic Judaism develops in dialogue with Greco-Roman civilization.

The Greeks had a distinctive complex of ideas and institutions relating to women and sex,[4] paralleled by a social system which, at least in Athens, was very gender-segregated.[5] Greek philosophy portrayed females as inherently and essentially different from men, and fundamentally less valued. The male–female distinction was one of the great polarities of the Greek dualistic system. The earliest Greek literature, the works of Hesiod, portrays the genesis of the gods as a battle and alternation between males and females, which is finally brought to an end only when Zeus usurps the female power of procreation and creates nonsexual females who serve rather than threaten male dominance.[6] The Pythagorean philosophical system divided the world into dualistic category pairs, with male and female an essential division of the universe. The Greeks considered females to be inherently so different from males that they spoke of a *genes gynaikon,* a "race of women," as if women were an entirely different species from men.[7] In all such divisions in Greece, women were considered "natural" and untamed, even animal-like;[8] the males represented civilized humanity.

Greek myths portray the relationship between men and women in terms of a battle of the sexes. The Athenians glorify and portray their early victory over the Amazons, who are confronted and defeated by both Heracles and Theseus.[9] Stories such as those of Clytemnestra, Medea, the Danaids, and the Lemnian women show women murdering their husbands and children out of anger and revenge. Rituals and myths such as those in the worship of Dionysus portray and channel female anger.[10] Even a less toxic story like Lysistrata shows a "we against them" mentality in which women unite against men. Does this battleground correspond to reality? It may be that women living under such a system would have felt great rage and would have taken this anger out on their children, particularly their male children.[11] On the other hand, these myths of female revenge may have less to do with actual female behavior than with the projection of male feelings about the woman (mother) who loomed so powerful in their early days and then had to be abandoned.[12]

The battle in these myths is deadly serious, for the Greeks considered this victory of males over females, whether in Hesiod's *Theogony* or in the Amazonomachy, the foundation for civilized existence. To the Greek mind, the "Female" was wild and beastly, and needed to be controlled and dominated by the civilized male. This philosophy of female subordination also underlies the great tragic cycle of Aeschylus, the *Oresteia*.[13] Here, Clytemnestra is enraged at Agamemnon's sacrifice of their daughter and kills Agamemnon. In turn, Orestes' their son, kills her, whom he perceives as hostile to him as well as to his father. Nor does the story end there, for Orestes is now attacked by the avenging Furies. At this point, civilization intervenes, as Orestes is brought to trial for matricide. His defense completely denies that attention has to be paid to women, even to mothers, claiming that mothers are not real parents:

> The mother is no parent of that which is called her child, but only nurse of the new-planted seed that grows. The parent is he who mounts. A stranger, she preserves a stranger's seed, if no god interfere.[14]

In this total denial of mother-right, Orestes is granted victory by Athena, the goddess of Athens, sexlessly virginal and detoxified. She is the very symbol of male dominance, created entirely by Zeus after he had swallowed Metis.[15] Athena declares "I am always for the male with all my heart, and strongly on my father's side."[16] Mother-right and the power of the Furies who protect it have been conquered; the Furies are domesticated and placed at the service of the justice system of the nonfamily civilized state.

Greek literature has a strong streak of misogyny that begins with Hesiod and continues unabated in Roman times. This misogyny is embedded in Hesiod's story of Pandora, the first woman, who was given to men in anger as the price they had to pay for getting fire. She was the *Kallon Kakon,* the beautiful evil, the lovely curse, and "from her has sprung the race of womankind, the deadly race and tribes of womankind, great pain to mortal men with whom they live . . . so women are a curse to mortal men."[17] This sense of woman as totally other is also found in Semonides of Amorgos (seventh century B.C.E.), who wrote a diatribe on women in which he calls them "the worst plague Zeus has made."[18] Misogyny remained an important Greek literary motif, and antiwoman themes and comments are prevalent in Greek literature. The Greek philosophical tradition proceeds from a presupposition of both the otherness and inferiority of women. Plato codifies this clear hierarchical ranking.[19] Aristotle "proves" women inferior and defective, bringing scientific language to popular conceptions.[20] Even Greek tragedy, which is not always misogynist, is preoccupied with the relationships between the sexes.[21]

In such a system, erotic desire is clearly a problem. As is well-known, there is a strong glorification of pederastic homophilia in Greek writing, a result and a reinforcement of the separation of the sexes and the limitation of public life to males. But the possibility of erotic attraction to women was not denied. Greek speculation focused on the lover more than the beloved, on the effects of eros upon him, and on his proper response to it.[22] The Greeks clearly felt that eros was an overwhelming force, that even the wisest of men could be made fools and swept away by sexual desire. Prodicus (fifth century) defined eros as "desire doubled"—and eros doubled is madness.[23] The great fear was that erotic desire was an absolutely uncontrollable force, and that the mere sight of a beautiful male or female could arouse great erotic desire. Much Greek discussion of sexuality centers on the need to control it, to master one's passions, to impose discipline, refinement, and civilization on this unruly emotion.[24]

The coming of this tradition to Israel had an enormous impact on Israelite (and later religious) thinking. In the book of Ecclesiastes, clearly written in the early Hellenistic period,[25] the first openly misogynistic statement in the Bible appears:

> Now I find woman more bitter than death; she is all traps, her hands are fetters and her heart is snares. He who is pleasing to God escapes

her, and he who is displeasing is caught by her. . . . I found only one
human being in a thousand, and I never found a woman among so many.

The Wisdom of Ben Sira, which was written in reaction to Hellenistic
ideas,[26] is decidedly misogynistic[27]: "Better is the wickedness of a man
than the goodness of a woman,"[28] and may contain the condemnation of
women so well known from the New Testament and later literature:
"from a woman did sin originate, and because of her we all must die."[29]
Ben Sira combines his derogatory view of women with a fear that a
man could be overwhelmed by erotic attraction to them. Looking on
beauty is a great danger.[30] This conception of beauty overwhelming the
senses is common in Greek literature. It is also known from the Epic
of Gilgamesh,[31] in which the courtesan is able to attract Enkidu simply
by baring her private parts.

    The Bible, on the other hand, does not consider beauty a power or
strategy of women.[32] The beauty of Sarah and Bathsheba make them
objects of attention, victims of the superior male. Sarah and Bathsheba
do not consciously use their beauty to attract: their beauty is their vulnerability rather than their power. Beauty as weapon first appears in
the Apocrypha, in the story of Judith, by form a typically Greek no-
vella[33] probably written in Pharisaic times.[34] In this story, the city of
Bethulia (perhaps Jerusalem) is besieged by the "Assyrian" (Greek) general Holofernes, who gives the city a few days to capitulate. Judith, a
virtuous widow, decides to save her city. She takes off her widow's
garments, dresses herself sumptuously, and dresses her hair in a
"tower," (today we call it a "beehive"), with the result that her beauty
is so stunning that heads turn when she passes. Judith leaves the town
and heads for the camp of Holofernes, who invites her to dinner. She,
being a virtuous Israelite woman, goes to the dinner bearing her little
bag of parched corn (kosher food) and sits with Holofernes at the banquet. He "was so delighted with her that he drank a great deal of wine,
much more than he had ever drunk on a single day since he was born"[35]
and fell down drunk at her feet, whereupon Judith cut off his head with
his own sword and returned to her city, whose townspeople rejoiced
both at their deliverance and at the fact that Judith was victorious before she could be violated.

    This is not a misogynist work. Judith is a great savior and heroine,
and the story emphasizes her virtue and her piety. But the story is noteworthy for its depiction and emphasis of Judith's conscious use of her
beauty to attract Holofernes, and of the magnetic attraction of this
beauty. Other Apocryphal works, written in the Hellenistic period, also

show worry about the power of erotic attraction. The biblical story of the mating of the divine beings with human women[36] is elaborated into the story of the "watchers." In the book of Enoch, the watchers came and raped the women.[37] The later Testament of Reuben, part of the Testaments of the Twelve Patriarchs, states that women consciously allured the "watcher," drawing the lesson, "For evil are women, my children, and since they have no power or strength over man, they use wiles by outward attractions . . . by a harlot's bearing she beguiles him."[38]

The natural result of this fear that women might sweep men away with their attractiveness is to keep them away and separate. Both Ben Sira[39] and the Testaments of the Twelve Patriarchs call for segregation from women.[40] This desire for separation and the fear of attraction is expressed in the Mishnah, in the law of *yihûd* ("union"), a provision that forbids a man and a woman to be alone together. The Mishnah further elaborates this prohibition by forbidding two women and a man from being alone together.[41] It does allow two men to be alone with a woman (since they would control each other[42]). The assumption underlying this rule is that the mere presence of women would tempt men into sexual immorality. The Mishnah does not explicitly state this reason, for the Mishnah does not generally justify its provisions.[43] Justifications are usually provided by the Gemara, the record of study, deliberation, and decision—written between the second and sixth centuries—that forms the bulk of the Babylonian Talmud. The Talmud on the Mishnah that prescribes *yihûd* states the overwhelming nature of sexual attraction, "even in the time of his mourning, his desire overwhelms him." The Talmud then tells cautionary tales that are intended to demonstrate the overwhelming nature of this attraction and the need to keep women separate. These tales are told, not about average insignificant people, but about the great spiritual leaders of the day. Even these great leaders could succumb to sexual attraction. Such a one was Rabbi Meir:

> Rabbi Meir used to mock those who transgressed. One day, Satan appeared to him in the guise of a woman on the opposite bank of the river. There was no ferry, so he seized the [ferry] rope and proceeded [to climb hand over hand] across. When he had reached halfway along the rope, he [Satan] let go, saying "had they not proclaimed in Heaven, 'take heed of R. Meir and his learning' your life would have been worth two cents."

This story is followed immediately by a similar story about Rabbi xnAkiba, the greatest sage of the second century C.E:

Rabbi Akiba used to mock those who transgressed. One day, Satan appeared to him in the guise of a woman on the top of a palm tree. He grabbed hold of the tree and proceeded to climb up. When he reached half-way up the tree, he [Satan] let him go, saying, "Had they not proclaimed in heaven, 'take heed of R. Akiba and his learning,' your life would have been worth two cents."[44]

In these Talmudic stories the very sight of a woman is enough to beguile, tempt, and doom even the greatest of all men.[45] As the Talmud says elsewhere, "even the most pious of the pious cannot be guardians against unchastity."[46]

The message is that men—even the most learned and pious—are vulnerable to this kind of erotic madness and need to guard against it. This is underscored by a dialogue between Rav and Rab Judah, again, great figures of their generation.

Rav and Rab Judah were walking on a road, and a woman was walking in front of them. Said Rav to Rab Judah, "lift your feet from hell." "But you yourself said that in the case of respectable people we don't have to worry" (Rab Judah) protested. "Who says that 'respectable people' means such as you and I?'" retorted (Rav). "Then such as who?" (said Rabbi Judah). "Such as Hanina b. Pappi."[47]

We know the story of R. Hanina b. Pappi. A matron tried to seduce him, and he pronounced a magic formula that caused his skin to break out in boils and scabs. She, however, did something to heal him, and he thereupon fled. He hid in a bathhouse so dangerous that two men together in daylight would not be safe. But he stayed overnight, and when he emerged he told the rabbis that two imperial guards had guarded him all night. The rabbis immediately understood that he must have been tempted with immortality and successfully resisted, for they had a dictum, "He who is tempted with immorality and successfully resists, a miracle is performed for him."[48]

Rabbi Amram also managed to resist in the nick of time. He was tempted by seeing women lodged in an upper chamber of his house through the skylights and was so overtaken with temptation that he seized a ladder that ten men could not raise, set it up, and proceeded to ascend all by himself. When he had gone halfway he managed to stop by shouting "A fire at Rabbi Amram's!" so that the other rabbis came running.[49] Another rabbi was saved when the fringes of his prayer shawl slapped him in the face,[50] but Rabbi Hiyya was not so fortunate.

He often prayed that God would save him from the evil inclination (sexual desire), and even refrained from having sexual relations with his wife. She disguised herself as a wanton and pretended to be a recently returned harlot. As her fee, she asked for the pomegranate atop the nearby tree, and he leaped to the uppermost bough. Afterwards he was so overcome with remorse that he climbed into the stove, even though his wife told him that he had not really committed immorality.[51]

These stories caution that even great men may not be able to resist sexual desire,[52] and trying to resist temptation was an act of heroism in the face of an almost irresistible force. Under the influence of sexual desire (in what we would call a stupendous adrenaline rush), men could perform superhuman feats. Scholars could climb hand over hand across ferry ropes; they could shimmy up palm trees; they could leap to the top of a pomegranate tree in a single bound; they could carry ladders so heavy that ten men were required to lift them. It is because of the extraordinary nature of this resistance that the Torah cantillation (singing phrases) to the Joseph story has a special note (a "shalshelet") under the words "and he refused." This very prolonged and noticeable note is used only four times in the whole Torah, and highlights, extols, and expresses amazement at Joseph's refusal of Potiphar's wife.

Biblical stories were retold and eroticized in both Hellenistic and rabbinic writings. In the Bible, Yael lulled Sisera to sleep by giving him warm milk, covering him with a blanket, and offering to stand guard over him. In the Talmud, the verse, "Between her feet he sank, he fell, he lay; at her feet he sank, he fell; where he sank, there he fell down dead"[53] is interpreted to mean that Yael slept with Sisera seven times.[54] In the Bible, Delilah nags Samson to death, but in the Talmud we read that the means by which she influenced him was that "at the time of the consummation she detached herself from him."[55] Abigail stands out in the Bible as an intelligent, persuasive woman who—by her wise arguments—convinced David not to slaughter Nabal's family; but in the Talmud we read, "the passage teaches that she bared her thigh and he went three parasangs [a unit of distance] by the light of it": the wise woman of the Bible has become a Talmudic vamp.[56]

Many of the biblical heroines were remembered as objects of lust: "Rahab inspired lust by her name, Yael by her voice, Abigail by her memory, Michal daughter of Saul by her appearance."[57] But the most famous eroticization of a biblical story is that of Adam and Eve. In Genesis, the noble serpent convinces Eve that eating of the fruit of knowledge would make her more godlike, and it is this thirst for knowledge and for divinity that makes her listen. In the literature of the

Apocrypha and pseudepigrapha, the serpent (originally a chameleon[58]) becomes a snake, the snake becomes a phallus of Satan, and Eve is seduced sexually so that lust enters the world.[59] Such a tradition is also known in the Talmud: "Rabbi Yohanan said, 'when the serpent entered Eve he brought lust.'" This version of the Adam and Eve story entered Christian literature, but disappeared from later Jewish sources.

In Judaic tradition, this misogyny and phobia are not taken to their two logical extremes, the phallicism of the Athenian Greeks, or the asceticism of the Hellenistic era.[60] The rabbis explicitly rejected asceticism, declaring that men should marry as early as possible, and should enjoy good conjugal relations with their wives. But this fear of the power of the *yēṣer hārāʿ* ("the evil impulse," the rabbinic term for desire), and the "need" to protect oneself from occasions that might awaken it as the ideological component, have practical effects. Ultimately, women began to be separated and secluded from men, and were totally excluded from public life. Laws of *yiḥûd* and the refusal to teach women kept women from the academy; they were further rendered invisible by the "modesty" laws that swathed them with coverings and basically secluded them in their homes. The source of these modesty regulations is clearly sexual phobia: since women's voice could be a sexual temptation,[61] it must be silenced; so, too, women's hair and limbs must be covered. Women were separated during prayer, and ultimately discouraged from participation in communal prayer. They were also urged to stay home, as "the glory of the queen is inward,"[62] for there was a fear that a woman who ventured outside would succumb to temptation.[63]

This rabbinic system is not a description of reality in the days in which the rabbis composed the Mishnah. There is good evidence that in the early Roman period, at least some women held public office in the synagogues.[64] Early rabbinic law is a legal–conceptual system expressed in terms of laws, and was not immediately binding, particularly in nonrabbinic circles. This literary–legal rabbinic treatment of women prescribes isolation.[65]

By the Greco-Roman period, woman has become indisputably "other." Philo uses "male" and "female" as philosophical opposites, and portrays a marked symbolic misogyny[66]; the rabbinic system is characterized by a sense that women are different from men.[67] The prescribed isolation and separation of women, their confinement to the noncommunal sphere of activities, is sometimes justified both by reference to the overwhelming nature of sexual desire and to the inferior nature of women.

It is hard to pinpoint the exact reasons for such a change. In part, this is an exacerbation of the change in gender ideology that is already seen in postexilic concepts of Zion-the-bride and wisdom literature. It is intensified by the influence of Greek popular and intellectual traditions, ideas that Israel identified with a superior world culture. In part, Israel may have been influenced by the Imperial Roman buttressing of the patriarchal family and the paterfamilias. The stress of conquest and the destruction of the Temple may also have led the men of Israel to react by asserting dominance over their women.[68] The cosmopolitanism, commercialism, and centralization of the Greco-Roman period may also have acted to create the socioeconomic conditions for an increased domination over women. And there is a possibility that the stress of the Roman period in Israel may indeed have resulted in a collapse of traditional sexual mores. Talmud Sotah records that the traditional trial of suspected adulteresses was canceled during the time of Rabbi Yochanan ben Zakkai. It may be that this trial, which would have been held at the Temple by Temple priests, was abrogated when the Temple was destroyed, much as the sacrificial system was. This, however, is not the reason given by the Talmud, which reports instead that the trial was canceled because the number of adulterers had become too numerous to be deterred by the threat of such trial.[69]

The rabbinic system represents a dramatic change from the Bible in the conceptualization of women and of sex. In place of the Bible's portrayal of women and men as fundamentally similar, the rabbis express a gender-polarized view of humanity. In place of the Bible's silence about sexual attraction, the rabbis portray sexual attraction as a mighty, at times dangerous and irresistible, force. The Church, heir to both the Bible and Hellenism, went further than the rabbis; to the Church Fathers, sexuality was the very antithesis of holiness, a demonic power, and woman was the embodiment of this power.[70] This gender-polarized and negative view of women at least had the advantage of explaining why women did not have the same access to public life that men did. A metaphysics of gender unity could not become meaningful until social and economic forces could support a society in which anatomy does not have to be destiny. The understanding of humanity inherent in biblical monotheism could not be understood until human experience could make it relevant.

The unfinished agenda of biblical monotheism is sexuality. Sex is important in people's lives. People do not always experience sexual desire as part of a neat marital system which harnesses desire to harmony. On the contrary, they frequently experience sexual desire as a force of nature, disorderly, counterproductive, sometimes destructive. Somehow, this seemingly chaotic force must be integrated into our view of the universe. In the pagan Near East, the goddess Ishtar brought divine order through chaos, as the upholder of gender and the bringer of sexual desire, the delightful charmer and the ferocious fighter. Biblical monotheism did not replace her with an alternate vision of the power of sexuality. The negative vision of the Greeks that filled this vacuum has now lost its appeal in most Christian and Jewish circles. Finding a vision of sexuality commensurate with the significance of sex in people's lives remains monotheism's unfinished agenda.

# Epilogue

## Religion in the Wake of the Goddesses

The monotheist transformation of biblical religion created profound changes in the way people looked at God, the universe, humanity, and nature. Some of these changes permanently transformed the consciousness of those people involved in the religions that ultimately developed from the Bible. Other biblical ideas, however, proved less enduring and have been modified repeatedly since biblical times. Often, the Bible simply demanded more of its worshippers than people were capable of giving. In some areas, the Bible does not offer extensive discussion of matters that people need to consider. This is true most often in areas that had once been understood through the images of goddesses; in their wake, the Bible offers an alternative system that does not fully answer human needs. In these areas, the transformative insights of biblical monotheism were insufficient, and the biblical system was vulnerable to the major transformation of ideas that came with the Hellenistic period.

A serious vacuum in biblical religion is caused by its denying or ignoring two important aspects of human experience, gender and sex. There is little gender talk in the Bible, and no sense of gender differences. It presents an ideology at variance with the social reality of people living in a world organized along gender lines. And the Bible offers little discussion of erotic attraction and sexual expression—again an example of disharmony with a world in which sexual attraction was obvious and the legal system sought to contain it. After the exile, as Israel encountered other cultural traditions, the vacuum became more noticeable; it was ultimately filled by the introduction of Hellenistic misogyny and sexual phobia into the biblical tradition. The influence

213

of these ideas on the newly emerging Christianity was very powerful. Christianity inherited Hellenistic and Judeo-Hellenistic ideas about women, particularly those expressed in the books of the Apocrypha, which were preserved by the Church as sacred scripture, and in the writings of Philo, who was (wrongly) considered an early Christian philosopher. These ideas were emphasized and magnified by two disparate sources: the philosophic tradition of Plato and neoplatonism with its distinctly anticarnal bias, and the politico-sociological example of imperial Rome with its conscious promotion of the patriarchal household and the power of the paterfamilias. As the Church became more Greek, it became more patriarchal; as it became Roman, the process intensified. Emerging Christianity incorporated these misogynistic and antierotic themes and made them central to its ideas about human existence.

The Hellenic complex of ideas about women and sex also had a major impact on Judaism, one somewhat different from its impact on Christianity. These ideas entered Rabbinic Judaism in its formative years and influenced the development of a legal system which codified the newly perceived gender differences into a strict complementarity of roles, and reinforced this system with a host of restrictions aimed at segregating the sexes and restricting the possibilities of private, potentially sexual, contact between them. The wave of sexual phobia and outright misogyny disappeared rather early and was replaced by a positive valuation of sexuality in marriage (beyond its importance to procreation) and an honoring of domesticated women as value-keepers, family preservers, and queens of the home. Thereafter, throughout Jewish history, the ideas about women fluctuated, occasionally resulting in misogynist statements, but more often seeing women and sexual expression as part of the divine order. But even though the Hellenistic outlook on gender and sex was transitory, the laws of segregation and "modesty" to which it gave rise became embedded in the legal system and did not disappear when their explicit rationale went out of fashion.

The biblical system also proved vulnerable to another element of Hellenic thought, its view of nature. The Bible doesn't really speak of "nature," but rather of *tēbēl* (the inhabitable world) and *hā'āreṣ* ("the earth," and especially "the land"). In Genesis, humanity is given dominion over this world, but the rest of the Bible shows that this power entails enormous responsibility in that human behavior can destroy the land and the world. The Greeks had a different concept of nature, as an unruly female, the very antithesis of civilization. It was humanity's role to impose its will on nature, to mold the natural world to conform to civilization's needs and requirements. Even when tamed, nature remained a potentially chaotic force.[1] This idea determined Western ideas toward nature, supplanting the biblical notion which it claimed to represent.

In this case the Greek idea of the relationship between nature and humanity supplanted the biblical in the area of fertility, to which the Bible had devoted a great deal of attention. The Bible offered a statement of human responsibility and causation instead of a sense of participation in and celebration of fertility. But in Israel in the Greco-Roman period, Jewish thinking on fertility turned to focus on rainmaking, with a whole mythology about celebrated rainmakers and the rainbringing powers of the virtuous, a system of public fasts for the removal of drought, and the selection of the rain promise-and-threat of Deuteronomy 11 as the central part of the basic twice-daily prayer, the Shmaʿ. Perhaps in the commercial urbanized world of the Hellenistic period, the land component of fertility could more easily be taken for granted. And perhaps the amount of attention paid to rain is an indication of a drought-stricken period, one in which attention would necessarily have focused upon ensuring the rain.

But the rain fasts point to another problem with the biblical view of nature that paved the way for the Greek system. In the Deuteronomic system, humans themselves mediate between God and nature, determining the state of the world. The Greco-Roman fasts emphasized God's ability to bring the rain. Human responsibility is acknowledged only in the sense of repentance, by which humans interpose God's volitional action as a judge between themselves and nature. Repentance, along with petition and fasting, attempts to ameliorate human responsibility for the world. If God's bringing of a drought can be influenced by prayer and sacrifice, then God rather than humanity ultimately controls nature and has final responsibility for it.[2] This shifting of the weight of responsibility may have been a reaction to the turbulent times, a reluctance to keep blaming oneself for the continuing progression of disasters. In times of stress, it is very difficult to maintain belief in the importance and responsibility of humanity. The Greco-Roman period was a time of enormous stress, both because of the cultural ambiguities that accompanied an explosion of knowledge with competing cultural systems, and because of the devastating historical events that resulted in the loss of Israelite autonomy, the destruction of Jerusalem, the end of the Temple, and the ultimate loss of the Jewish national polity. This period witnessed a great retreat from the stark role of humanity under biblical monotheism and the great responsibility it entailed. In texts from this period we find a great emphasis on repentance and fasting, on supplication and petition, and a desire to rely on the grace of "God the father." At this time of felt weakness, the idea of power was attractive, and Greek ideas of conquest and dominance over nature took root.

In the contemporary world, these issues are once again undergoing reevaluation, and some branches of Judaism and Christianity are witnessing a dismantling of the Greek heritage in all these areas. Many churches have been redefining their historic attitudes towards sexuality, the liberal branches of Judaism have been removing the restrictive and segregating laws from women, and all Western society has been reexamining its fundamental suppositions about the role of gender and about the human relationship with nature. At the same time, more "fundamentalist" branches of these religions are reiterating and reinforcing traditional views on all these matters. It is a tremendous irony that these conservative groups, who hold to the literal authenticity of biblical statements, view these statements through the prism of later interpretation and are in fact reinforcing Hellenistic rather than (Hebrew) biblical ideas.

The reexamination of these ideas is the result of the great changes brought in the human situation in modern times. The economic and technological revolutions of the past few hundred years have created, in the West, the material preconditions for a far less gender-ordered universe, and the successive waves of feminism have given us a vision of such a universe. The explosion of human technological ability has given us a sense of human power so enormous that it forces us to confront it. One reaction is to retreat from this sense of power into the currently popular fundamentalism. The other is to embrace power as part of our self-definition and thereby assume our own responsibility for it. By the 1940s, humanity had achieved the destructive power to slaughter twelve million people in death camps and to kill in an instant hundreds of thousands at Hiroshima and Nagasaki. By the 1980s, even this power had been dwarfed by the megaton capacities of our missiles and warheads. As destroyers, humans could be second to none, for we could create a worldwide devastation no less thorough than that of the Great Flood. Humankind has attained knowledge and power to rival the destructive power of God. At the same time, the enormous horror of the Holocaust has indicated to many that God will not intervene to prevent or redirect our use of power. This power, and its ability to destroy civilization and nature, is our responsibility.

In a different way, the flight of Sputnik and the moon-landing, have also demonstrated that humanity is now on its own in its development and application of knowledge. The mythological significance of the space events of this century have supplanted the lesson of the tower of Babel. When God did not kill Adam and Eve, God allowed a process to begin in which human beings would eventually amass great amounts of knowledge and power. God retarded the process at the tower of Babel as they were scattered and diversified. But in our day, God has not intervened to stop us. As we probe the mysteries of space and as we amass the knowledge to make ourselves masters of our own biology, we now believe that God will not act to stop or direct us. We may come to amass sufficient knowledge and technological ability to become full partners to the one God, even in the restructuring of humanity.

The capability to tamper with human genetics and to create life is profoundly disturbing, and frightens us with the realization that we must find the means and the direction to control this power. Our anxiety is heightened by our knowledge that we have also achieved the capacity to wreak havoc on ourselves and the universe even when we are not aiming at destruction. Without really wanting to, we are changing the environment, destroying the rainforests, eradicating species, damaging the ozone, polluting the groundwater, and contaminating the earth. Perhaps more than the ability to destroy consciously, these inadvertent results of even our most well-intended actions demonstrate our power and transform the way we look upon the world and upon each other.

In this time of changing consciousness, we are forced to reevaluate our religious heritage vis à vis all these issues. And in every instance, the Bible speaks more directly to us on these matters than do the intervening Greek-influenced religious traditions. The biblical concept of an essential unity of males and females makes sense in our more egalitarian world; the biblical lack of discussion of sexuality and physicality is at least more palatable than the negative sentiments of postbiblical religion. And the radical monotheism of the Bible seems more within our power to achieve. In a real sense, the world is being transformed so that it more truly resembles biblical ideas of it. Our consciousness of this transformation makes it possible for us to better understand and answer the biblical challenge.

Radical monotheism has never been truly tried. Later religions have concentrated on supplication and petition, both of which diminish direct human responsibility. In addition, they have peopled the heavens with a multiplicity of divine beings. The cast of characters who accompany YHWH shifts and changes, but has never disappeared for very long. In early biblical times, Israel believed in a council of gods and the Host of Heaven. Later, these were excluded from Israel's worship. Jeremiah denied the efficacy of any other gods, and Deutero-Isaiah even their existence. Nevertheless, YHWH is not left alone in heaven. The gods have disappeared, but the angels come to the court of God. In the Persian period and in the Hellenistic period, the heavens teemed with angels. The Greco-Roman period witnessed belief systems with angels, archangels, demons, princes, Sophia, and a whole plethora of sons of light and darkness. This peopling of the heavens remained in Christianity—with the Christian mystification of monotheism into the Trinity, with its attendant heavenly host, its saints, angels, and devils. In the various traditions of Judaism, demons and angels have come and gone. Periodically, all these lesser spiritual beings have passed out of favor as more radically monotheistic impulses have taken over, but they have not permanently succeeded in leaving God as the sole inhabitant of the invisible world.

The persistence of all these beings highlights the stark and overwhelming nature of a monotheist belief which leaves humanity the sole partner and counterpart to a force infinitely larger and more powerful. The partnership is so uneven, the human position so precarious and the human task so enormous, that there is an almost irresistible attraction to posit intermediary figures, beings lesser than God, but other than human. Sometimes, these may be envisioned as mediator figures, who intercede for humanity before a God who stands in judgment upon it. Sometimes, they may be seen as protectors, who are entrusted with guarding us from pitfalls. Sometimes, they are negative images, demons and devils upon whom we can unload some of the responsibility for our actions. And even when they are none of these, the thought of more beings in the world is comforting, for it indicates that the power in the universe is not solely concentrated in one awesome God. The divine power may radiate from the one God, but it is diffused through all these divine beings; and through this diffusion, the divine power seems less stark and more accessible. These semi-divine images lessen the loneliness of monotheist humanity, which seeks partnership with a God before whom we nevertheless feel small and childlike and before whom we seek to justify ourselves.

But if monotheism is so stark and difficult, we could well ask why we should bother with it at all. For some, of course, this is not a question: monotheism must be wrestled with because it is there, because the call of God is felt so strongly that it is not open to existential doubt. Further, for many people, monotheism is so rooted in their sense of personal identity—in their present community and in a past history that gives them their grounding—that for them to question the value of monotheism is either deeply threatening or almost meaningless. This is a strange and dangerous question, because it is very hard for a proponent and believer of religious pluralism actually to say that one form of religious belief is superior to another in any aspect. To say anything like this seems enormous hubris in the face of all the possible answers that different individuals might find in their quest for ultimate values. Moreover, it is also practically impossible to answer this question objectively, because anybody formulating it already has an emotional stance—whether of distance or of commitment—that has come about for reasons other than any rational advantages this belief system might have.

Despite these difficulties, the question must be asked because it *is* being asked. Much of our society has been secular for a long time, no longer finding its answers in the traditional religions. But contemporary society is witnessing a renewed interest in religious matters, with increasingly widespread interest in nonmonotheist religions, in Eastern mysticisms, in occult beliefs, in mediums and channels, in neopaganism and goddess worship. Goddess worshipers have claimed that the goddesses can give women a sense of self-validation and, at the same time, lead to a more harmonious relationship with nature. Advocates of many of these spiritual quests declare that they can put humanity in better touch with its own nature and its unity with the world. In the face of the many alternatives, it is valid and imperative to ask whether there is an advantage in pursuing the almost impossible goal of radical monotheism, whether monotheism offers something to the human spirit that these other religious experiences do not.

Like secular humanism, radical monotheism places the burden of the world in human hands. This burden is frightening. It is the reason many flee from radical monotheism into quasi monotheisms with their helpers and intercessors. But this burden is also advantageous, for monotheism does not (or should not) allow us to hide behind any other powers, including those of God. Fully integrated and understood, radical monotheism is religious humanism. At the same time, monotheism shares with other forms of religion its ability to direct people beyond themselves, to enable them to experience the trans-personal: the verticality of being part of a long tradition of human quest for meaning, the horizontality of joining others in a contemporary community of search and experience, and the sense of ultimate reality beyond the boundaries of individual and even collective humanity. And monotheism adds to this general benefit of religion its sense that ultimate reality is a unity, neither a multiplicity of counterbalancing forces that compete for our attention and allegiance, nor a complementarity of "male" and "female" yin and yang. Beyond the categories that human culture might impose on the way we see the world, there is a singleness that can inform our consciousness. Such a concept of unity may also be reached in the high traditions of the great Eastern polytheisms in which the "one" may lie behind the "many." In radical monotheism, this unity is much more immediate and accessible: it is not only revealed in mystic visions after a spiritual quest, it is the primary compelling message as well as the profound essence of its religious teaching.

This does not mean that the biblical system is perfect. The Bible faced an enormous task in its initial attempts to conceive and develop a new way to deal with issues once mediated by the presence of many gods and goddesses, and did not fully succeed in filling the gaps left in the wake of the goddesses. Some of those gaps have been filled by our own development and the transformation of the world. It is now our task to weave the rest of the Bible's religious fabric by filling in the remaining areas, in particular those that deal with the incorporation of all aspects of physicality into our religious view of the universe. After a long detour, we are now ready to return to the path upon which the Bible sets out and to try to take further steps along this journey.

# Appendix

## The Goddesses of Sumer

Additional studies of the pantheon can be found in A. Falkenstein, *Die Inschriften Gudeas von Lagas,* Analecta Orientalia 30 (1966); D. O. Edzard, "Mesopotamien" in *Worterbuch der Mythologie,* in H. Haussig, ed., vol. 1 *Gotter und Mythen im Vorderen Orient* (Stuttgart: 1965); W. Römer, "Religion of Ancient Mesopotamia," *Historia religionum,* vol. 1, Religions of the Past, Bleeker and Wildengren, eds. (Leiden: 1969), 115–194; J. J. van Dijk, "Sumerische Religion" in *Handbuch der Religionsgeschichte,* vol. 1, Jes Asmussen et al., eds. (Gottingen: 1971), 431–496; Th. Jacobsen, *Treasures of Darkness* (New Haven: Yale University Press, 1977), 93–145; and Th. Jacobsen, "Mesopotamian Religions: An Overview," *The Encyclopedia of Religion* (New York: Macmillan, 1987), 447–469. Studies of individual gods can be found in the RlA which has now reached the letter M.

BABA (Ba'u) is best known in records from Lagash, a major city in southern Mesopotamia. She has been brought into harmony with the other goddesses in two distinct ways. Inanna is sometimes called Baba in the context of the sacred marriage hymns, an indication that, like Inanna, Baba was a young goddess whose copulation with her mate (who might have been ritually associated with the ruler of Lagash, see chapter 6) was essential to the fertility and well-being of the city. But as daughter of An and wife of Ningirsu, Enlil's son, Baba occupied the same position in the pantheon as Gula, Nintinugga, and Ninisinna, and, like them, was considered a goddess of healing (see p. 39). Baba also has a relationship to Enki, being called the daughter-in-law of Eridu.

INANNA[1] is the most fascinating of the goddesses, both to the ancients and to modern writers. As daughter of the god Nanna (the moon god), she is in a junior generation, fourth in the genealogical line of An–Enlil–Nanna–Inanna, and she maintains her persona as an ever-young woman. Despite this, she early becomes the chief goddess of the city of Uruk, sharing this role, and the temple Eanna, with An (occasionally considered her spouse) and ultimately displacing him there in importance. Inanna has many facets, being a goddess of rainstorms (a minor aspect), of the evening and morning star, and of the storehouse, in addition to her major roles as goddess of sexuality and of warfare (for which see discussions in Chapters 5 and 6). One myth, the myth of Inanna and Enki, relates how she came into possession of the great **mes**, the divine attributes of civilization, many of which are clearly associated with her own activities. In her "infinite variety" Inanna was also a very important political goddess, for she was the divine overseer of the separate and often rival early cities of Uruk, Kish, Zabalam, Badtibira, and Akkad (as Ištar, her Semitic counterpart, with whom Inanna was early and thoroughly identified), and a factor in their rise to power. She was also considered the divine overseer of the non-Sumerian city of Aratta, and it was her choice of Uruk over Aratta that enabled the Sumerian city to subdue the distant land (for discussion, see pp. 62–63).

KI: the first generation of gods is the couple of An, the heavens, and Ki, the earth. An remains titular head of the pantheon, although the real power of chief executive belongs to Enlil, and An's power as city god of Uruk is shared early by the goddess, Inanna. Ki (also called Urash) is known as an active deity only for the first, primeval act, the union of sky and earth that started the pantheon. She is never shown active in any other role.

NAMMU, another shadowy proto-goddess, belongs more to the pantheon of the marshy south. She, too, is another primeval mother, possibly the water depths or the mother mud. She appears in only one myth, that of Enki and Ninmah, in which she is shown creating humankind (see p. 73). Nammu is known primarily as the mother of Enki, who becomes the lord of the watery subterranean ocean.

NANŠE (NANSHE) was the daughter of the god Enki, and was the goddess of fish and fowl. She is also the sister of Ningirsu, who is normally considered the son of Enlil, but is associated with Enki through Nanše and Baba. Nanše is known primarily in the city of Lagash. She figures there in two literary creations, the Temple Hymn of Gudea, in which she serves as the divine dream interpreter (see discussion, pp. 38–39), and from the Nanše Hymn, in which she is seen as the administrator of the temple and the arbiter of social justice.

NINHURSAG-NINTUR[2]: Ninhursag, the "mountain lady," was the great mother-goddess of Sumer, produced from the union of An and Ki that also produced Enlil and Enki. Ninhursag has many names in Mesopotamian mythology. She was identified very early (in prehistoric times) with Nintur. The two names are used interchangeably for the birth goddess. The other names of this mother-goddess are Ninmah ("great lady"), Aruru, Ninmenna ("lady of the turban"), and Belit-Ili ("mistress of the gods"), in Akkadian texts. Ninhursag is frequently associated with Enki, either as wife or rival. Ninhursag is discussed on pp. 14–19.

NINISINNA[3] was the city goddess of Isin, and is not heard of until the Ur III period. She becomes most prominent, of course, with the rise of Isin to prominence during the Ur III dynasty and the Isin dynasty that follows. Ninisinna is primarily a goddess of healing (see p. 39) and is associated with the other goddesses of healing—Gula, Baba, and Nintinugga. As the chief goddess of her city, moreover, she is the divine partner of King Iddindagan in the sacred marriage (see pp. 50–59). She thereby also shows characteristics of the goddess Inanna.

NINLIL is the wife of Enlil, and is the subject of two myths, the myth of Enlil and Sud, and the myth of Enlil and Ninlil, which tell how she became his wife. Ninlil is a mother figure. The myth, Enlil and Ninlil, relates the birth from Ninlil of several of the major gods of Sumer. Another myth, the myth of Lugal-e, recounts the exploits of her son Ninurta, such as building the foothill mountains to control flooding and then giving them to her. In this text, Ninlil is originally called Ninmah. Once Ninurta renames her Ninhursag when he gives her the foothills, Ninlil is completely identified in this text as a great mother-goddess.[4]

NINSUN: A bovine goddess, Ninsun is prominent because she is the tutelary goddess of the kings of Uruk and of Ur, who claim descent from her. She is the wife of Lugalbanda, a legendary god-king of Uruk, and appears as the divine mother of Gilgamesh, another legendary king of Uruk, in the Gilgamesh Epic. Ninsun is thus an important link between the worlds of gods and kings (see discussion, pp. 60–61).

NISABA[5] was in part a grain goddess, for the sign with which her name is written is an ear of corn with blades, and the Hymn, Great Matriarch, states "your growth is surely the furrow, your form is surely cereal, your figure is surely its grain."[6] But she is more commonly presented as the great goddess of wisdom, learning, and surveying (see discussion, pp. 39–41). Nisaba is related to the national pantheon as the daughter of An and sister of Enlil. She is also mother of Ninlil (in which role she is sometimes called Nunbaršegunu), and is thus the mother-in-law of the god Enlil and the great matriarch of Sumer. She is clearly an ancient goddess. Her genealogy is somewhat confused, however, for in the Lagash pantheon, she was considered the sister of Ningirsu, and thus the daughter of Enlil. Nisaba is also associated with the mother-goddess; Nisaba is described as "born of Urash" (Earth) and "Aruru of the Nation".[7]

# Abbreviations

GENERAL AND MISCELLANEOUS

| | |
|---|---|
| A | Museum siglum, National Museum, Copenhagen |
| AdRNA | Avot de Rabbi Nathan, Version A. Cited from Judah Goldin, ed., *The Fathers According to Rabbi Nathan*. Yale Judaica Series 10 (New Haven: Yale University Press, 1955). |
| BM | Museum siglum, British Museum (London) |
| BT | Babylonian Talmud |
| cyl | cylinder |
| K | Museum siglum, Kuyunjik Collection, British Museum (London) |
| OB | Old Babylonian |
| rev | reverse |
| SBL | Society of Biblical Literature |
| YT | Yerushalmi Talmud |

JOURNALS

| | |
|---|---|
| *AfO* | *Archiv für Orientforschung* |
| *AJSReview* | *Association for Jewish Studies Review* |
| *BAss* | *Beiträge zur Assyriologie und vergleichenden semitischen Sprachwissenschaft* (1890–1913) |
| *BA* | *Biblical Archeologist* (1938) |
| *BAR* | *Biblical Archeology Review* |
| *BASOR* | *Bulletin of the American Schools of Oriental Research* |
| *Belleten* | *Belleten Türk Tarih Kurumu* |
| *CBQ* | *Catholic Biblical Quarterly* |
| *ET* | *Evangelische Theologie* |
| *HAR* | *Hebrew Annual Review* |
| *HTR* | *Harvard Theological Review* |
| *IEJ* | *Israel Exploration Journal* |
| *JAAR* | *Journal of the American Academy of Religion* |
| *JANES* | *Journal of the Ancient Near Eastern Society (of Columbia University)* |
| *JAOS* | *Journal of the American Oriental Society* |
| *JBL* | *Journal of Biblical Literature* |
| *JCS* | *Journal of Cuneiform Studies* |
| *JESHO* | *Journal of the Economic and Social History of the Orient* |
| *JHS* | *Journal of Historical Studies* |
| *JNES* | *Journal of Near Eastern Studies* |
| *JQR* | *Jewish Quarterly Review* |
| *JSOT* | *Journal for the Study of the Old Testament* |

| | |
|---|---|
| *Or.* | *Orientalia* |
| *OTS* | *Oudtestamentische Studiën* |
| *PAPS* | *Proceedings of the American Philosophical Society* |
| *RA* | *Revue d'assyriologie et d'archéologie orientale* |
| *RB* | *Revue biblique* |
| *RES* | *Revue des études sémitiques* |
| *RSO* | *Rivista degli studi orientali* |
| *VT* | *Vetus Testamentum* |
| *WO* | *Die Welt des Orients* |
| *ZA* | *Zeitschrift für Assyriologie und vorderasiatische Archäologie* |
| *ZAW* | *Zeitschrift für die alttestamentliche Wissenschaft* |

## SERIES

| | |
|---|---|
| AfO Beiheft | *Archiv für Orientforschung* |
| AOAT | Alter Orient und Altes Testament (Kevelaer/Neukirchen-Vluyn: Verlag Butzon und Bercker/Neukirchener Verlag) |
| AOS | American Oriental Society |
| AS | Assyriological Studies (Chicago: The Oriental Institute, University of Chicago) |
| BE | The Babylonian Expedition of the University of Pennsylvania, Series A: Cuneiform Texts |
| BibOr | Biblica et Orientalia (Rome: Pontifical Biblical Institute) |
| BZAW | Beihefte zur *Zeitschrift für die alttestamentliche Wissenschaft* (Berlin: de Gruyter) |
| CRRA | Compte rendu de la . . . Rencontre Assyriologique Internationale |
| CT | Cuneiform Texts from Babylonian Tablets in the British Museum |
| HSM | Harvard Semitic Monographs |
| HSS | Harvard Semitic Series |
| JSOTSupp | *Journal for the Study of the Old Testament.* Supplement Series (Sheffield) |
| OECT | Oxford Editions of Cuneiform Texts |
| PBS | Publications of the Babylonian Section (Philadelphia: University Museum, University of Pennsylvania) |
| SBLDS | Society of Biblical Literature Dissertation Series (Missoula/Chico/Atlanta: Scholars Press) |
| TAPS | Transactions of the American Philosophical Society (Philadelphia) |
| TCS | Texts from Cuneiform Sources (Locust Valley, N.Y.: J. J. Augustin) |
| TCL | Textes cunéiformes. Departement des Antiquités orientales, Musée du Louvre |
| UET | Ur Excavation Texts |
| VTS | Supplements to *Vetus Testamentum* (Leiden) |
| YNER | Yale Near Eastern Researches (New Haven) |

## BOOKS

| | |
|---|---|
| ANET | James B. Pritchard, ed., *Ancient Near Eastern Texts Relating to the Old Testament,* 3d ed. (Princeton University Press, 1969) |
| BRM | *Babylonian Records in the Library of J. Pierpont Morgan* (New Haven) |
| BWL | W. G. Lambert, *Babylonian Wisdom Literature* (Oxford: Clarendon, 1960) |
| CAD | I. J. Gelb, A. L. Oppenheim, E. Reiner, et al., eds., *The Assyrian Dictionary of the Oriental Institute of the University of Chicago* (Glückstadt/Locust Valley, N.Y.: J. J. Augustin, 1956–) |
| CTA | A. Herdner, *Corpus des tablettes en cunéiforme alphabétiques,* Mission de Ras Shamra 10. (Paris: Imprimerie Nationale/Paul Geuthner, 1963). |

| | |
|---|---|
| *EncRel* | Mircea Eliade et al., eds., *Encyclopedia of Religion* (New York: Macmillan, 1987). |
| *Harps* | Thorkild Jacobsen, *The Harps That Once . . . Sumerian Poetry in Translation* (New Haven: Yale University Press, 1987). |
| REC | F. Thureau-Dangin, *Recherches sur l'origine de l'écriture cunéiforme* (Paris: E. Leroux, 1898). |
| RlA | Erich Ebeling, Ernst Weidner, Dietz Otto Edzard, et al., eds., *Reallexikon der Assyriologie und vorderasiastischen Archäologie* (Berlin: Walter de Gruyter, 1932–) |
| SGL | Adam Falkenstein and J. van Dijk. 1959–1960. *Sumerische Götterlieder.* Abhandlungen der Heidelberger Akademie der Wissenschaften. Philosophisch-historische Klasse 1959/1, 1960/1. |
| SKIZ | W. H. Ph. Römer, *Sumerische "Königshymnen der Isin-Zeit.* (Leiden: Brill, 1965). |
| SLTNi | S. N. Kramer, *Sumerian Literary Texts from Nippur in the Museum of the Ancient Orient at Istanbul,* vol. 1, Annual of the American Schools of Oriental Research 33 (New Haven: ASOR, 1944). S. N. Kramer and I. Bernhardt, vol. 2. (Berlin, 1961). |
| SM | S. N. Kramer. *Sumerian Mythology,* 2d ed. (New York: Harper and Row, 1961) (originally published, 1944). |
| SRT | Edward Chiera, *Sumerian Religious Texts* (Upland, Pa.: 1924). |
| STVC | Edward Chiera, *Sumerian Texts of Varied Contents,* Oriental Institute Publications 16. (Chicago: 1934) |
| *Šurpu* | Erica Reiner, ed., *Šurpu: A Collection of Sumerian and Akkadian Incantations.* Archiv für Orientforschung Beiheft 11 (Graz: 1958) |
| *Tammuz* | Thorkild Jacobsen, *Toward the Image of Tammuz and Other Essays on Mesopotamian History and Culture,* W. L. Moran., ed., HSS 21 (Cambridge: Harvard University Press, 1970) |
| *Treasures* | Thorkild Jacobsen, *The Treasures of Darkness: A History of Mesopotamian Religion* (New Haven: Yale University Press, 1976) |
| WbMyth. | H. W. Haussig, ed., *Wörterbuch der Mythologie,* 1 Abteilung. Die alten Kulturvölker. 1. Götter und Mythen im vorderen Orient. (Stuttgart: Klett, 1965) |

# Notes

CHAPTER 1   Introduction: On the Nature of Monotheism

1. Writing on cuneiform tablets continued into the first century C.E. (the non-Christocentric way of writing A.D.). However, these are learned scientific texts. After the fifth century, more and more documents were in Aramaic and were written on parchment. The historical record, therefore, becomes more scanty.

CHAPTER 2   The Pantheon

1. For example, the personal deities of the royal house of Ur in Ur III were Ninsun and Lugalbanda.
2. See Hans J. Nissen, "'Sumerian' vs. 'Akkadian' Art: Art and Politics in Babylonia of the Midthird Millennium B.C.," *Insight through Images. Studies in Honor of Edith Porada*, Marilyn Kelly–Buccellati, ed. (Malibu, Calif.: Undena, 1985),   188–196, interesting ecological explanation for this tension between centrality and locality.
3. See J. J. M. Roberts, *The Earliest Semitic Pantheon* (Baltimore: Johns Hopkins University Press, 1972), esp. 152ff.
4. On this issue, see, initially Jerrold Cooper, "Sumerians and Akkadians in Sumer and Akkad," *Or.* 42 (1973): 239–246; Benjamin Foster, "Ethnicity and Onomasticon in Sargonic Mesopotamia," *Or.* 51 (1982): 297–354; and D. O. Edzart, "Literatur," *RlA* 7:39.
5. See Pietro Mandler, *Il Pantheon di Abu-Salabikh* (Naples: 1986).
6. The edition has been promised by W. G. Lambert. In the meantime, some studies of the pantheon have been assembled in *Études sur le panthéon systématique et les panthéons locaux*, CRRA 21, 1976, *Or.* 45 (1976): 1–226.

CHAPTER 3   "Godwomen"

1. J. van Dijk, *Lugal ud melám-bi nir-gál* (Leiden: Brill, 1983); English translation by Thorkild Jacobsen, *The Harps that Once: Sumerian Poetry in Translation* (New Haven: Yale University Press), 1987, 253–272 (cited hereafter as *Harps*).
2. Lugal-e, line 368.
3. There are several oddities in this episode. In terms of Sumerian pantheons, the story may originally have concerned the god Ningirsu of Lagash, the son of Ninhursag and Enlil. By the time the epic was composed, Ningirsu had become thoroughly identified with Ninurta, the son of Enlil and Ninlil of Nippur. The text clearly considers Ninlil and Ninhursag to be the same goddess. We should also note that Ninhursag is a very early name for the mother-goddess, a name in use before this epic was written (probably in the period of Gudea, ca 2200 B.C.E.).
4. Miguel Civil, "The Message of Lú.Dingir.ra to His Mother and a Group of Akkado-

229

Hittite Proverbs," JNES 23 (1964): 1–11, lines 22–25. See also S. N. Kramer and M. Çig., "The Ideal Mother: A Sumerian Portrait," *Belleten* 40 (1976): 403–421; and Nougayrol, "Signalement Lyrique, R. S. 25:421," *Ugaritica* 5: 310–319.

5. Dumuzi-Inanna H. See Sefati, *Love Songs,* 209–217. English translation by Jacobsen as "The Wiles of Women," *Harps,* 10–12.

6. Or, just possibly, *not* to do so. As do so many other ancient Near Eastern languages, Sumerian presents us with a strange peculiarity of grammar, in that a very strong asseverative, "You must indeed do this," takes the same form as the negative "Do not do this." This peculiarity adds a joyful note of ambiguity to our attempts to understand crucial passages. In the present case, Hermann Behrens, in his text edition, *Enlil and Ninlil* (Rome: 1978), understands Nunbarshegunu to be advising Ninlil as to how she might attract Enlil. Jerrold Cooper, in his review, *JCS* 32 (1980), argued that the mother was telling the girl not to go, an interpretation also adopted by Thorkild Jacobsen in his English translation, *Harps,* 167–180.

7. Enuma Elish, lines 45–46. See the translation by Stephanie Dalley, *Myths from Mesopotamia* (Oxford, 1989), 233–277.

8. See discussion, chapter 7.

9. The examples are cited in S. N. Kramer, "Lisin: The Weeping Goddess: A New Sumerian Lament," *Zikir Šumim: Assyriological Studies Presented to F. R. Kraus,* G. Van Driel, Th. J. H. Keispijn, M. Stol, and K. R. Veenhof, eds. (Leiden: Brill, 1982), 133–144; Kramer, "BM 98396: A Sumerian Prototype of the Mater Dolorosa," in *Eretz-Israel 16: Harry Orlinsky AV,* B. Levine and A. Malamat, eds. (Jerusalem: Israel Exploration Society and Hebrew Union College, 1982): 141–146; and Kramer, "The Weeping Goddess: Sumerian Prototypes of the Mater Dolorosa," *BA* 46 (1983): 69–80.

10. For Enki and Ninhursag, see the translations by Jacobsen, *Harps,* 181–234; and S. N. Kramer and John Maier, *Myths of Enki, the Crafty God* (New York and Oxford: Oxford University Press, 1989), hereafter, Kramer, *Enki.*

11. For Enki and Ninmah, see the translations in Jacobsen, *Harps,* 151–166; and Kramer, *Enki,* 31–37.

12. See the Nanše Hymn, edited by W. Heimpel, "The Nanše Hymn," *JCS* 33 (1891): 65–139, with additional translation by Jacobsen, *Harps,* 125–142.

13. See note 10.

14. For the text edition and translation, see van Dijk, *Lugal ud,* 1983. Of course, the way for this association was paved by the fact that, just as Ninlil was the mother of Ninurta, so Ninhursag was the mother of Ningirsu, with whom Ninurta was identified. For translation, see Jacobsen, *Harps,* 233–272.

15. Marriage of Sud, line 152.

16. For the most recent treatment of this text, see Miguel Civil, "Enlil and Ninlil: The Marriage of Sud," *JAOS* 103.1 (1983): 43–64, with comments by W. G. Lambert, ibid., 64–66.

17. For discussion of the word **ú-zuh**, see Behrens, *Enlil and Ninlil,* 150–159, and *Musukku,* CAD, M 2:239. The banishment may not be a legal so much as a ritual measure: himself impure, he must leave to avoid spreading the contamination.

18. Jacobsen points out that before the Ur III period, only Ninlil is written with the lil sign. He interprets Ninlil's name as Nin-lil$_x$ (REC 425), a personification of the full-grown barley plant, whereas Enlil is written with the líl that means spirit or wind (REC 423). See "The lil$_2$ of $^d$En-lil$_2$," in *Duma É.dub.ba.a: Studies in Honor of Åke W. Sjöberg,* Hermann Behrens, Darlene Loding, and Martha Roth, eds. Occasional publications of the Samuel Noah Kramer Fund vol. 11 (Philadelphia, 1989), 267–276. However, from the Ur III period on, the names are not distinguishable.

19. See, e.g., **egi-zalzalag,** OECT 5 text 8, line 73.

20. Temple Hymn 3, TCS 3 19:43.

21. See Claus Wilcke, "Sumerische literarische Texte in Manchester und Liverpool," *AfO* 24:7, lines 1–2.

22. **Enlil sù(d)-rá-šè,** lines 161–164, SGL 1:5–80, English translation as "Hymn to Enlil," *Harps,* 101–111.

23. **Mas-su,** OECT 5:8, 73; **igi-gál,** OECT 5:9, 73; **ga-al-ga-sù,** Šulgi H BE 31: 4, lines 1, 3.

24. SGL 1: 19, line 158; SRT 11:31, also in *ZA* 53 (1959): 107, line 31.

25. See W. W. Hallo, "Women of Sumer," in *The Legacy of Sumer,* Denise Schmandt-Besserat, ed. (Malibu, Calif: Undena, 1976), 23–40; P. Michalowski, "Royal Women of the Ur III Period," *JCS* 31 (1979): 171–176; P. Steinkeller, "More on the Ur III Royal Wives," *Acta Sumerologica* 3 (1981): 77–92.

26. Jacobsen's translation of line 208, "was stabbing at her underbelly, began hitting her parts," indicates brutal sex. The term háš . . . $gi_4$-$gi_4$ is not clearly understood, however, and it is probably best not to read too much into the phrase as to the Mesopotamian image of marital sex.

27. Exodus 1:19.

28. Enki and the World Order, lines 381–386. For English translation, see Kramer, "Enki and Inanna," in Enki, 38–56.

29. As we shall see later, this notion that culture has come from the gods is basic to Sumerian culture. Israel evolved a very different view of the coming of culture to humanity. See the discussion in chapter 10, pp. 108–117.

30. Lahar and Ashnan, lines 3–25, 96, edited by Bendt Alster and Herman Vanstiphout, "Lahar and Ashnan," Acta Sumerologica 9 (1987), 1–43.

31. Lahar and Ashnan 17, line 96.

32. Šurpu, V–VI, lines 144–16. See Erica Reiner, Šurpu, AfO 11 (1958).

33. For munus dím.ma, see Šurpu, tablets V–VI, 148; for munus-zi, see "Enki and the World Order," line 381. Munus-zi is not specific to Uttu; it is applied to numerous goddesses. There is no counterpart "faithful man" applied to the male gods.

34. See Harry Hoffner, "Symbols for Masculinity and Femininity: Their Use in Ancient Near Eastern Sympathetic Magic Rituals," JBL 85 (1964): pp. 326–334.

35. These poems have been collected and edited by Yizhak Sefati, Love Songs in Sumerian Literature: A Critical Edition of the Dumuzi-Inanna Songs, Ph.D. diss., Bar-Ilan University, 1965, with complete bibliography, translation, and philological commentary in Hebrew. The most recent translation into English is by T. Jacobsen, Harps, 1987.

36. Dumuzi-Inanna I. Sefati, Love Songs, 218–229. Jacobsen's translation as "the new house," Harps, 3–7, is accepted here over that of Wilcke AS 20(1976): 293–315, and of Sefati.

37. Dumuzi-Inanna D. Sefati, Love Songs, 115–124. The English translation by Jacobsen is called "The Sister's Message," Harps, 8–9.

38. Dumuzi-Inanna H. Sefati, Love Songs, 209–217. English translation by Jacobsen as "The Wiles of Women," Harps, 10–12.

39. S. N. Kramer, "BM 23631: Bread for Enlil, Sex for Inanna," Or. 54 (1985): 117–130, lines 138–140.

40. Dumuzi-Inanna C. Sefati, Love Songs, 146–170. Note that Jacobsen understands the text quite differently, as a dialogue between Inanna and Utu ("Let Him Come," Harps, 16–18). In Dumuzi-Inanna $C_1$, Dumuzi approaches his wedding carrying food gifts. (Sefati, Love Songs, 323–339; translated into English by Jacobsen, "Dumuzi's Wedding," Harps, 19–23).

41. Bendt Alster, "Sumerian Literary Texts in the National Museum, Copenhagen," Acta Sumerologica 10 (1988): 2, text A10096, line 15.

42. Dumuzi-Inanna A. Sefati, Love Songs, 115–124. Translated by Jacobsen as "The Bridal Sheets," Harps, 13–15.

43. Dumuzi-Inanna $C_1$. Sefati, Love Songs, 323–339, col iv, lines 5, 14–18. Translated into English by Jacobsen, "Dumuzi's Wedding," Harps, 19–23.

44. Dumuzi-Inanna $C_1$, col iv, lines 6–13.

45. ibid.

46. There may be some resolution of these two differing perspectives on the role of Inanna, but the text is badly damaged at this point. For Inanna and war, see chapter 6, "Bridges to the Gods: Love, War and the Goddess Inanna–Ishtar."

47. See, for example, Inanna F, Römer, "Eine sumerische Hymne mit selbstlob Inannas," Or. 38 (1969): 97f.

48. The mes have usually been considered the great principles of culture, but more recently attention has been paid to this other aspect of them. For discussions, see the text editions by Farber-Flügge, Enki and Inanna; A Cavigneaux, "L'Essence divine," JCS 30 (1978): 177–185; and G. Glassner, "Inanna et les mes," paper presented at the Rencontre Assyriologique (1988).

49. Dumuzi-Inanna O. Sefati, Love Songs, 234f. di-da-mu-dè di-da-mu-dè gu-$i_7$-nun-na $dib_5$-ba-mu-dè gú $i_7$ -buranun-na šu-nigín-na-mu-dè.

50. B. Alster, "Sumerian Literary Texts in the National Museum, Copenhagen," Acta Sumerologica 10 (1988): p. 2, text A10096, lines 18–23.

51. In Inanna and Ebih, ki-nigín-na-mu-dè, and Inanna and Sukalletuda an-ki mu-un-nigín-na-ta; Alster Acta Sumerologica 10: è-a-mu-dè.

52. E. Reiner, "A Sumero-Akkadian Hymn of Nanâ, JNES (1974) 33:224. mu[t-tal-lu]m sa-hir-tú mu-ter-ri-bat É.MEŠ.

53. Laws of Hammurabi 143; cf. 141. The Old Babylonian lexical list Proto-Diri includes as one of the Akkadian equivalents of **kar-kid,** "prostitute," *waṣitum,* "one who goes out" (CAD H: *harimtu,* lexical section). There is a danger in commenting on Sumerian-language literary texts with the aid of Old-Babylonian Akkadian evidence. However, we should also remember that most of the Sumerian texts that we have come from Old Babylonian copies, so that the portrayal of Inanna as one who goes about was being read and copied (and sometimes composed) by people who also read and copied the Akkadian-language texts. The expectation that proper women don't gad about survives in the use of Aramaic *nafqa*—literally, "she who goes out"—as the colloquial Aramaic and, later, Yiddish term for prostitute. The rabbinic authors of midrashim also find nuances of this concept in the fact that Gen. 34:1 says that Dinah "went out."

54. Edition forthcoming by Hermann Behrens, who was kind enough to let me see his manuscript.

55. Inanna-Ninegalla, lines 199–200: [é-é]-a in-ku₄-ku₄-dè-en [e-sír]-e-sír-ra gú mu-un-gíd-gíd-dè-en, with thanks to Hermann Behrens for showing me the text.

56. Neo-Babylonian Balag composition, BRM 4, 9, line 404. The phrase also occurs in the instructions of Shuruppak (B. Alster, *The Instructions of Šuruppak* [Copenhagen: Akademisk Forlag, (1974)], 230–233, where it is said of a **munus.gù-mur-ak,** and in Lugalbanda-Hurrum in a difficult context.

57. Lamaštu, like Inanna, has a close association with lions, wears her hair loose, and is the daughter of An. She is quite possibly the feared side of Inanna. For Lamaštu and Inanna, see Wolfgang Fauth, "Ištar als Löwengöttin und die löwenköpfige Lamaštu," WO 72 (1981): 21–36.

58. SLTNi 131 II 4, cited by B. Alster, *The Instructions of Šuruppak.* 116 gi₄-inu₃-mu-un gam ga-ša-an gam sila-a úr zé-zé ("the slave girl—because of her master's death, because of her mistress' death, she had to roam about the streets").

59. See the discussion by J. J. Finkelstein, "Sex Offenses in Sumerian Laws," *JAOS* 86 (1966): 255–372.

60. Miguel Civil, "Enlil and Ninlil: The Marriage of Sud," *JAOS* 103 (1983): 43–63.

61. E. Reiner, "A Sumero-Akkadian Hymn of Nanâ, *JNES* 33 (1974): 224, line 3.

62. CAD *aštammu,* lexical section.

63. The Ninegalla Hymn. The connection between Inanna and prostitutes has been noted by J. Bottero "La femme, l'amour et la guerre en Mesopotamie ancienne" in *Poikilia: Études offertes à J. P. Vernant* (Paris: Éditions de l'École dês hautes études en sciences sociales, 1987, 172f. However, Bottero claims that Inanna is basically a prostitute, and derives most of her characteristics from the societal image of prostitutes. His claim that she is never a wife seems clearly contradicted by the Dumuzi-Inanna tales, and her role as goddess of love (see discussion above, pp. 26–28, 50–51) is frequently related to marital relations rather than amour libre.

64. ki-sikil sag₉-ga sila-a gub-ba ki-sikil kar-kid dumu ᵈInanna. See Civil, *JAOS* 103 (1983): 61.

65. For **ur-sag,** see Römer, "Eine sumerische Hymne" and Castellino *RSO 36.*

66. See especially The Agushaya Hymn, *RA* 75 (1981): 107–134.

67. For a discussion of this concept of rituals of rebellion, see Anthony Wallace, *Religion: An Anthropological View* (New York: Random House, 1966).

68. For discussion of Inanna-Ištar and boundaries, see Rivkah Harris, "Ishtar," paper presented at the Rencontre Assyriologique, Philadelphia 1987.

69. In his pioneering essay, "Adoration: A Divine Model of the Liberated Woman", in *From the Poetry of Sumer: Creation, Glorification, Adoration* (Berkeley: University of California Press, 1979), 71–98, S. N. Kramer concentrates on the strengths of Inanna, but pays very little attention to the bitchiness she is portrayed as having and the negative feelings she often engenders. See also Frymer-Kensky, "Inanna: The Quintessential Femme Fatale," *BAR* 10 (1984): 62–64.

70. This phrase, coined by Caelius Sedalius, was taken by Marina Warner as the title of her book on Mary, *Alone of All Her Sex: The Myth and the Cult of the Virgin Mary* (New York: Random House, 1976).

CHAPTER 4   The Wisdom of Women: Goddesses and the Arts of Civilization

1. Gilgamesh, tablet I, lines 37–41; for translation, see Dalley, *Myths from Mesopotamia* (Oxford: Oxford University Press 1989), 39–135.

2. OB Gilgamesh, tablet III, lines 1–20. For translation, see Dalley, *Myths from Mesopotamia,* 136–153.

3. Lugalbanda and Anzu, lines 17–18. See the translation by Jacobsen, *Harps,* 322. See

also M. Civil, "A Hymn to the Beer-goddess and a Drinking Song," *Studies Presented to A. Leo Oppenheim, June 7, 1964* (Chicago: Oriental Institute Press, 1964), 67–89.

4. *Or.* 28 (1959) 338–339.

5. Daniel Riesman, "A Royal hymn of Išbi-Erra to the Goddess Nisaba," AOAT 25: 360–361, lines 47, 57, 62–66.

6. TCL 16:136; see CAD *giparu*. The two meanings for *giparu*, in fact, may be related. The sacred marriage between the goddess Inanna and the king as representative of the god Dumuzi (a ritual discussed on pp. 50–57) took place at the *giparu*. One very important meaning attached to this ritual is that the sacred marriage is the mating between Dumuzi as the essence of life itself and Ianna as the power within and symbol of the communal storehouse. The iconographic symbol that represents Inanna is most probably a schematic depiction of a gatepost with rolled-up mat. According to Thorkild Jacobsen, *Treasures,* p. 36, this was the gatepost of the storehouse.

7. "Womanhood and the Inner Space," *Daedalus* 93, 2 (Spring 1964): 210–220.

8. The Sumerian dictionary (as yet unpublished) suggests that this double meaning may have arisen by an original writing ÉxSAL for women's quarters and GÁxSAL for storehouse. There is no evidence for an original distinction, and the disparate meanings are more probably connected sociosemantically.

9. In this context, we should note the depiction of the quarters of Sud in the Myth of Enlil and Sud and of the sanctuary of Agade as Inanna's domaine in the Curse of Agade.

10. *Šabbutitu, Šurpu* 3: 77, see K.5218 (BA 10/1, no. 15:93, and OECT 5: text 9, rev. line 5. ᵈMa-nun-gal nin-é-kur-ra-ke₄.:ᵈMin be-li-it ṣi-bit-ti.

11. See Åke Sjöberg, "Nungal in the Ekur," AFO 24 (1974): 19–46, and Tikva Frymer, "The Nungal-Hymn and the Ekur-Prison," *JESHO* 20 (1977): 78–89.

12. Wolfgang Heimpel, "The Nanshe Hymn," *JCS* 33 (1981): 65–139; see differing translation in Jacobsen, *Harps,* 125–142.

13. For an anthropological analysis, see Sherry Ortner "Is Female to Male as Nature Is to Culture?" in M. Rosaldo and R. Lamphere, eds., *Women in Culture and Society* (Stanford: Stanford University Press, 1974), 67–88. For a psychological analysis of this connection of women to transformations, see Erich Neumann, *The Great Mother* (Princeton: Princeton University Press, 1970).

14. M. Civil, *JNES* 23 (1964), and S. N. Kramer and M. Çig, "The Ideal Mother: A Sumerian Portrait," *Belleten* 40 (1976): 403–421.

15. Line 14. There is some question as to whether the "mother" of this text is the actual mother of the writer or his divine "mother", for she is described with great hyperbole and called "a fair goddess"; but current opinion is that this is a florid tribute to mothers. At any rate, the statement of line 14 is clearly meant to be understandable in terms of human household arrangements.

16. Ningirim (**agrig-mah-dingir-re-ne**) Lugalzagesi 1. i. 34–35, Nisaba (**agrig-zi-an-na** in Nisaba and É-gal-la, **agrig-zi hé-me-en** in Ninmulangim), Nininsinna (**agrig-arali nin agrig-zi-ᵈEn-líl-lá-ka.** Nintinugga: (Inannaka to Nintinugga) **agrig-ᵈEn-líl-la** Nungal: **agrig-zi-ᵈEn-líla.** Gula: agrig-šu-dim₄-ma-ke₄ VAS 17 33: 35, Or. 44:57, line 49. References cited according to the *Sumerian Dictionary* (Philadelphia: University of Pennsylvania Museum).

17. See W. W. Hallo, "Women of Sumer," in *The Legacy of Sumer,* Denise Schmandt-Besserat, ed., Bibliotheca Mesopotamica 4 (Malibu, Calif.: Undena, 1976), 23–40; and J. M. Asher-Grève, *Frauen in Altsumerisher Zeit,* Bibliotheca Mesopotamica 18 (Malibu, Calif.: Undena, 1985).

18. The importance of laments as a role for women continues in ancient Israel; see pp. 166–167 for Rachel and pp. 170–172 for Zion.

19. See Claus Wilcke, "Eine Schicksalsentscheidung für den toten Urnammu," CRRA 17 (1970):81–92.

20. See the references in S. N. Kramer, "Lisin: The Weeping Mother Goddess: A New Sumerian Lament," in *Zikir Šumim: Assyriological Studies Presented to F. R. Kraus* (Leiden: Brill, 1982), 133–144; S. N. Kramer, "BM 98396:A Sumerian Prototype of the Mater Dolorosa," in *Eretz-Israel I6:Harry Orlinsky AV,* B. Levine and A. Malamat, eds. (Jerusalem: Israel Exploration Society and Hebrew Union College, 1982), 141–146; and S. N. Kramer, "The Weeping Goddess: Sumerian Prototypes of the Mater Dolorosa, *Biblical Archaeologist* 46 (1983): 69–80.

21. See Piotr Michalowski, *The Lamentation over the Destruction of Sumer and Ur* (Winona Lake, Ind.: Eisenbrauns, 1988).

22. In this lamentation, there is one exception to the rule that the female laments. This is the capital city of Ur, where it is Nanna—the chief god of the city—non Ninlil, who approaches Enlil. But this exception only indicates more clearly the family paradigm and relational character

of lamenting, for Nanna is the first son of Enlil and approaches him as a son to his father. Moreover, he comes not only to lament, but to demand an explanation for the destruction, to which Enlil replies that it is simply Ur's turn to give up the kingship.

23. Mark E. Cohen, ed., *The Canonical Lamentations of Ancient Mesopotamia* (Potomac, Md.: Capital Decisions Limited, 1988).

24. Inanna's Descent to the Netherworld," lines 179–180.

25. Quoted according to Margaret Green, "The Eridu Lament," *JCS* 30 (1978): 127–167.

26. See S. N. Kramer, "Lamentation over the Destruction of Nippur," *Eretz-Israel* 9 (1969): 89–93.

27. For the timing of the Lamentations, see Margaret Green, *Eridu in Sumerian Literature,* Ph.D. diss., University of Chicago, 1975, 277–325.

28. Gudea Cyl A ii 1–3, iv 12.

29. M. Civil, "The Song of the Plowing Oxen," in *Kramer Anniversary Volume,* ed. Barry Eichler, AOAT 25 (1976): 83–95.

30. Nanshe is praised in the Gudea cylinders as one who can intone holy incantations, one who knows the sacred songs (Cyl B iv 5–6). Amageshtinanna is the "singer expert in song" in S. N. Kramer, "The Jolly Brother: A Sumerian Dumuzi Tale," *JANES* 5(1973): 243–251, quoted from line 29.

31. See D. Edzard, "Mesopotamie," WbMyth., l, 1: 77ff; Römer, "Religion of Ancient Mesopotamia," in *Historia Religionum,* 1, C. J. Bleeker and G. Widengren, eds. (Leiden: Brill, 1969), 115–194; Frankena, "Gula," RlA 3 (1957–71): 694–697; and Römer, "Einige Beobachtungen zur Göttin Nini(n)sina auf Grund von Quellen der Ur III-Zeit und der altbabylonischen Periode," *Lišan mithurti: Festschrift Woltram Freiherr von Soden,* M. Dietrich and W. Rollig, eds., AOAT, 1 (1969), 279–305.

32. For example, in Temple Hymn 21. Sjöbert, TCS 3 1969 line 268, and references cited there, p. 105.

33. Edith K. Ritter, "Magical Expert ( = Ašipu) and Physician ( = Asu): Notes on Two Complementary Professions in Babylonian Medicine," *Studies in Honor of Benno Landsberger,* Hans Güterbock and Thorkild Jacobsen, eds., *Assyriological Studies* 16 (1965): 299–322.

34. Gudea Cyl A col v–vi.

35. In the Hymn Buršumagal, W. W. Hallo, "The Cultic Setting of Sumerian Poetry," CRRA 17: 116–134, and Temple Hymn 42, TCS 3, line 338.

36. Enki and the World Order, line 44; and Temple Hymn, line 541.

37. Buršumagal; W. W. Hallo, "The Cultic Setting," line 12.

38. Daniel Riesman, "A 'Royal' Hymn of Išbi-Erra to the Goddess Nisaba," in *Kramer Anniversary Volume,* Barry Eichler, ed., AOAT (25): 357–365, lines 2, 7–8.

39. Hallo, "The Cultic Setting," line 13.

40. Temple Hymn, line 539.

41. Literally, "opens her house of understanding" in Gudea Cyl A xvii 15–16, and "Enmerkar and the Lord of Aratta," 320–322; see Šulgi B 18–19; Sin-Iddinam Hymn, UET 6/1, 99; rev v, 25–27.

42. H. L. J. Vanstiphout, "Lipit-Eshtar's Praise in the Edubba," *JCS* 30 (1978): 33–61, line 18f.

43. D. Riesman, "A 'Royal' Hymn," 359, lines 23–24.

44. S. N. Kramer, "The Jolly Brother: A Sumerian Dumuzi Tale," *JANES* 5 (1973): 243–251.

45. Šulgi C, STVC 50.

46. For this term and a discussion of the mother of early childhood, see Dorothy Dinnerstein, *The Mermaid and the Minotaur: Sexual Arrangements and Human Malaise,* (New York: Harper, 1976).

47. Mourning continued to be closely associated with women throughout the history of the ancient Near East. In Israel, Jeremiah sent for women dirge-singers and wise women to start a wailing for the city that could cause them all to cry (Jer. 9:16–20), and portrayed mother Rachel as weeping for her children (Jer 31:11–21). Later, the Arab poet(ess) Al-Khansa (710–720) wrote a famous lament for her brothers who were tribal leaders. And in fact, in the early Arabic tradition, when women wrote, they wrote laments (according to a personal communication from James Bellamy). Still later, Maimonides urged everyone to set aside funds to have two women mourners at their funerals.

48. W. W. Hallo, "Women of Sumer," in *The Legacy of Sumer,* Denise Schmandt-Besserat,

ed., Bibliotecha Mesopotamica 4 (Malibu, Calif.: Undena, 1976) 23–40, quoting YNER 3 (1968) 59f.

49. See W. Farber, *Schlaf, Kindchen Schlaf* (Winona Lake, Ind.: Eisenbrauns, 1988).

50. Enmerkar and the Lord of Arratta, lines 589–630.

51. See A. Falkenstein, "Enheduana, die Tochter Sargons von Akkade," *RA* 52(1958): 129f; W. W. Hallo and J. J. van Dijk, *The Exaltation of Inanna*, YNER 3 (1968); and Irene Winter, "Women in Public: The Disk of Enheduanna, The Beginning of the Office of En-priestess and the Weight of Visual Evidence," in *La Femme dans le proche orient antique* (Paris: Editions Recherche sur les Civilizations, 1987), 189–201: and Joan Goodnik Westenholz, "Enheduanna, En-Priestess, Hen of Nanna, Spouse of Nanna," in *Dumu.é.dub.ba.a: Studies presented to Ake Sjöberg*, Hermann Behrens, Darlene Loding, and Martha Roth, eds. (Philadelphia: University of Pennsylvania Museum 1989): 539–556.

52. As Winter has argued on the basis of continuity between the scene on the disk of Enheduanna and the earlier Ur plaque. It would seem logical that Sargon, in his effort to unify Sumerian culture, would have installed his daughter in a traditional position.

53. See C. Wilcke, "Eine Schicksalentscheidung für den toten Urnammu," CRRA 17 (1970):81–92.

54. See the works of Denise Schmandt-Besserat; among them, "From Tokens to Tablets: A Reevaluation of the So-called 'Numerical Tablets'," *Visible Language* 15 (1981): 321–344, and "The Origins of Writing," *Written Communication* 3 (1986): 31–45; for another view, see Stephen Lieberman, "Of Clay Pebbles, Hollow Clay Balls and Writing: a Sumerian View," *American Journal of Archaeology* 84 (1980): 339–358.

55. See Manfred Krebernik, *Die Beschwörungen aus Fara und Ebla* (Hildesheim and New York: Olms Verlag, 1984), 233–263.

56. Ea is the name for Enki in Akkadian language texts, and Marduk, originally separate from Asarluhi, was associated with him even before the rise of Babylon. The difference between the pairs Enki–Asarluhi and Ea–Marduk is that Enki is much more important than the rather obscure Asarluhi in the pantheon, whereas Marduk is dominant god, the king of the pantheon.

57. See T. Jacobsen, "Mesopotamian Religion," *Enc Rel, M*, 447–469.

58. This dialect, recognizable because it is written syllabically, used to be called **eme.mí**, "woman's tongue." The reading is **eme.sal, sal**, "thin," being written with the same sign as **munus/mí**, "woman."

CHAPTER 5   In the Body of the Goddess

1. In the Isin period, there is evidence that Nininsinna acquired many of the characteristics of Inanna, including her astral significance, but this is a secondary development resulting from the exaltation of the Lady of Isin in the Isin period.

2. It has been suggested—for example, by J. J. Roberts, *The Earliest Semitic Pantheon: A Study of the Semitic Deities Attested in Mesopotamia Before Ur III* (Baltimore: Johns Hopkins University, 1972)—that originally Inanna was the evening star, and Ishtar, with whom she was so early identified, was the morning star; but such a separate origin would have been long before historic times and has left no trace in recorded texts.

3. For Inanna as rainstorm, see T. Jacobsen, *Treasures*, 137–138.

4. See "Gilgamesh, Enkidu and the Netherworld"; English translation in S. N. Kramer and John Maier, *Myths of Enki the Crafty God* (New York and Oxford: Oxford University Press, 1989).

5. The Akkadian-language myth Nergal and Ereshkigal was written to account for this takeover.

6. As she was to Šulgi in one of the Šulgi Hymns (discussed below) and to Gilgamesh in the Akkadian Gilgamesh Epic.

7. Translation and edition by W. W. Hallo and J. J. van Dijk, *The Exaltation of Inanna*, YNER (1968), lines 55–57.

8. Bottero has argued, in "La femme, l'amour et la guerre en Mesopotamie ancienne," in *Poikilia. Études offertes à J. P. Vernant* (Paris: Éditions de l'École des hautes études en sciences sociales, 1987), 172f, that Inanna typifies only free love.

9. The Atrahasis Epic I, 299–304; see also the Gilgamesh Epic II ii 35–50, where the bed is laid for Ishhara.

10. See The Curse of Agade, lines 31, 33.

11. From an old Babylonian Hymn to Ishtar in favor of King Ammiditana, *RA* 22 (1928): 170f, line 5.

12. In the Old Babylonian period and later, Ishtar does proposition a male, Gilgamesh, who immediately rejects her.

13. This idea was so firmly entrenched in Western science that the first people to look at sperm through an early microscope believed that they "saw" the little man (homunculus) in the sperm.

14. For the idea of a personal god, see discussion, chapter 7 and Jacobsen, *Treasures,* 147–164.

15. See Gudea A iii 8–9.

16. Reisman, AOAT 25 360 lines 50–51.

17. T. Jacobsen, in "Notes on Nintur," *Or.* 42 (1973): 274–298, equates the name with **tùr** ("the birthhut"), a word which can be used metaphorically for the womb.

18. H. Frankfort, "A Note on the Lady of Birth," *JNES* 3 (1944): 198f., first identified this symbol as a uterus. He assumed it was the uterus of a cow, but I can see no reason not to read it as the uterus of a woman.

19. See the examples in Jacobsen, "Notes on Nintur."

20. Enki and the World Order, lines 395–403.

21. "Enlil Sudrashe," SGL 1, 19 (1959): 125–126.

22. Inanna's Descent, line 227.

23. Lisin lament, UET 6, line 144. Passage quoted by Jacobsen in "Notes on Nintur." According to Jacobsen, Ninhursag is invoked here because as the mistress of the foothills, she has the power both to give birth to, and to starve, wildlife. According to Kramer, Lisin is probably to be identified not only as an animal but as the ruler of their city, Adab-Kesh.

24. See Edith Porada, "An Emaciated Male Figure of Bronze in the Cincinnati Museum," in *Studies presented to Leo A. Oppenheim, June 7, 1964* (Chicago: Oriental Institute Press, 1964), 159–166.

25. See the studies in Karl Oberhuber, "Zum Problem der 'Heiligen Hochzeit' im Bereich des Alten Orients," in *Studien zur Sprachwissenschaft und Kulturkunde: Gedenkschrift fur Wilhelm Brandenstein,* Innsbrucker Beiträge zur Kulturwissenschaft 14 (Innsbruck: 1968) 269f; J. Renger, "Heilige Hochzeit," RlA 4 (1975): 251–259; J. S. Cooper "Heilige Hochzeit: Archäologische," RlA 4 (1975): 259–269; W. H. Ph. Römer, "Einige Überlegungen zur heiligen Hochzeit' nach altorientalischen Texten," in *Von Kanaan bis Kerala, Festschrift . . . van der Ploeg,* Delsman et al., eds., AOAT 211 *Neukirchen-Vluyn,* (1982): 411–427; Mary Wakeman, "The Sacred Marriage," *JSOT* (22) (1982); 21–31; Urs Winter, *Frau und Göttin: Exegetische und ikonographische Studien zum Weiblichen Göttesbild im Alten Testament und in desen Umwelt,* Orbis Biblicus et Orientalis (Freiburg: Universitätsverlag Gottingen, 1983); Kramer, *The Sacred Marriage Rite;* Jacobsen, *Treasures,* 25–73; Yitschak Sefati, *Love Songs in Sumerian Literature—Critical Edition of the Dumuzi-Inanna Songs,* Ph.D. diss., Bar-Ilan University, 1985, 15–35 (in Hebrew).

26. See J. Renger, *ZA* 58:183, note 514.

27. **nì-mi-ús-sa** or **nì-munus-ús-sa.**

28. In statue E (v 1–vii 21), the gifts were brought by the god Ningirsu for Baba at the festival of Baba on the New Year, when Ningirsu and Baba rejoice (see also statue G). In statue D(ii 1), King Gudea brought the gifts, possibly an indication that Gudea took part in this festival.

29. Cylinders A and B.

30. Cyl B ix 6–17; B xvi 19.

31. King Mesannepada of Ur, even earlier, uses the title, "spouse of the hierodule." The Akkadian equivalent, "spouse of Ištar-Anunnitum," was used in Old Akkadian texts by Naram-Sin. This title continued to be used by Sumerian kings throughout the Ur III, Isin, and Larsa dynasties.

32. The god Dumuzi, who has no role in Mesopotamian mythology other than his role as Inanna's spouse and as personification of fertility, may originally have been a divinized king, for which see Renger, "Heilige Hochzeit," and Kramer, *Sacred Marriage Rite.* The use of the phrase, "beloved spouse of Inanna," in Old Lagash inscriptions indicates that the rite was not confined to Uruk (the major cult-site of Inanna). We can surmise that the kings of later Uruk may also have practiced this rite, and Ur Nammu, the first king of the dynasty or Ur, who was the son of Utuhegal of Uruk, continued this practice. For Ur Nammu and the sacred marriage, see Ur Nammu B, in R. Castellino, "Ur Nammu: Three Religious Texts," *ZA* 53 (1959):120, "In the Gipar I put on a linen garment (and on the) splendid bed I lay down"; for the lament of Inanna

for her dead spouse, UrNammu, see Claus Wilcke, "Eine Schicksalentscheidung für den toten Urnammu," CRRA 17 (1970):81–92.

33. Jacob Klein, ed., *Three Šulgi Hymns* (Tel Aviv: Bar-Ilan Univ., 1982), 124f.

34. W. H. Ph. Römer, SKIZ, 129f., Daniel Reisman, "Iddin-Dagan's Sacred Marriage Hymn," *JCS* 25(1973): 185–202; Jacobsen, *Harps,* 112–124.

35. CT 42/4, for which see S. N. Kramer, *PAPS* 107 (1963): 501–503; Sefati Dumuzi-Inanna $D_1$, 340–352. Translation by Kramer in Pritchard, ANET (1969): 640–641.

36. Editions by Kramer, *PAPS* 107 (1963): 505–507; Sefati, Dumuzi-Inanna P, in *Love Songs,* 243–261.

37. Inanna G, Kramer, ed. *PAPS* 107 (1963): 503–505.

38. Collected and edited by Sefati, *Love Songs.*

39. In addition to the five texts described, the Ishmedagan Hymn, Išmedagan and the Chariot of Enlil, uses similar language. There, the author requests from Enlil (lines 93–96), "give him your great daughter Inanna as a wife, forever may they embrace ($u_4$ ul-še gu-da ha-mu-ri-in-la, forever may they embrace sexiness (**hi-li**), sweetness (**nì-ku₇-ku₇**), and the holy lap; may they lengthen days in a surpassing life."

40. There were other purposes to this union: The kings achieved a special relationship with the goddess which was to assure them a long and rewarding reign. For this reason, J. Renger has suggested that rite was a coronation ritual for the new king. However, the Iddin-Dagan Hymn indicates an annual festival, and the Šulgi Hymn (which has no mention of the New Year) has been shown by J. Klein to be a journey to Inanna in which she remembers the sacred marriage, rather than an actual performance of the ceremony. In addition, this special relationship reinforced a particular importance to the very institution of kinship, enabling the kings to transcend the boundaries between gods and humans (see discussion, next chapter).

41. Gudea Cyl B v.

42. Enlil and Ninlil, lines 147–149.

43. See Jacobsen, *Treasures,* 127–135.

44. Nissen has pointed out that there was a climatic change during the fourth millennium B.C.E. which caused the amount of water available for irrigation to decrease, and that therefore from the ED I period on, it became necessary to irrigate by canal. See Hans Nissen, "Sumerian vs. 'Akkadian' Art: Art and Politics in Babylonia of the Mid-third Millennium B.C.E.," in *Insight through Images: Studies in Honor of Edith Porada,* ed. Marilyn Kelly-Buccellati (Malibu, Calif.: Undena, 1985), 170.

45. See Lamberg Karlovsky, "The Economic World of Sumer," in *The Legacy of Sumer,* Denise Schmandt-Besserat, ed., Bibliotheca Mesopotamica 4 (Malibu, Calif.: Undena, 1976), 59–68.

46. Jacobsen has pointed out that the symbol of Inanna represents the doorway of the store-house. For this interpretation of Dumuzi and Inanna, see T. Jacobsen, *Treasures,* 23–74.

47. For this interpretation of Dumuzi, see Jacobsen, ibid., and Jacobsen, *Towards the Image of Tammuz* (Cambridge: Harvard University Press, 1970), 73–103.


CHAPTER 6    Bridges to the Gods: Love, War, and the Goddess Inanna-Ishtar

1. **sag..íl**, "with raised head."

2. For this sense of **hili** as desire, see CAD *kuzbu* and the sacred-marriage passages. For Inanna as **hili**, in addition to the Šulgi and Iddin Dagan hymns discussed in the preceding chapter, see Šulgi A 82.

3. A Hymn of King Šulgi of Ur, Šulgi X, recounts how the king comes to Uruk and puts on his festal garments, and then caps his adornment with "**hili** as a crown." The **hili** in this song is a wig (as it is in votive inscriptions); the wig, in turn, symbolizes this sexual allure, and Inanna is smitten with his appearance. Šulgi is also called Inanna's **hili** elsewhere (Šulgi A 15), as are later kings. See, for example, Lipit-Ištar B, "for holy Inanna in the region of Uruk, you are her heart's delight," JCS 30

4. **lugal dingir-àm.**

5. The close association of the sacred marriage and blessings on the kingship has led to the suggestion that the ritual was performed only once in the king's reign, as a type of coronation rite. However, the texts also mention New Year's, and the sacred marriage also had a fertility dimension. It is more likely that the ritual was performed often, probably annually.

6. W. W. Hallo has suggested that the sacred marriage was connected to the divine status of kings in an even more tangible way: that the divine descent of kings is an indication that the kings were themselves born from a sacred marriage (Hallo, "The Birth of Kings," *Love and Death in the Ancient Near East: Essays in Honor of Marvin H. Pope,* John H. Marks and Robert M. Good, eds., [Guilford, Conn.: Four Quarters Publishing, 1987], 45–52.) For this, there is no direct evidence; moreover, if there was a sacred marriage for the engendering of Ur III kings, it would more likely have been a ceremony involving Ninsun, the divine mother of these kings, than the nonmaternal Inanna. There is one intriguing economic text involving sacrifices in various cities for the lustrations of Ninsun on the eve of the New Year: this may be an indication that such a marriage was celebrated for Ninsun. It is not, however, referred to explicitly in our texts. There is also no hint that the kings were born of ritually achieved pregnancies. On the other hand, we should note that the king achieves a divine or quasi-divine status in the sacred marriage ritual, and therefore all future sexual acts of the king might have an aura of sacrality. In this sense, then, all the sons of the king were children of sacred marriage.

7. In historical fact, kingship probably developed gradually from earlier forms of government. T. Jacobsen has suggested that at one point the chief ruler of a town was defined by his or her religious function, as the **en** of the god or goddess: if the city god was male, the **en** would be female; if the city god was female, the **en** would be a male. In times of warfare, the male **en** of a city whose god was female would be awarded military-civilian powers; in those cities in which the **en** was female, a parallel office would spring up, that of king ("Early Political Developments in Mesopotamia," *ZA* 52 (1957): 91–140). This explanation has been generally accepted, but we should note that it is predicated on the assumption that only a male **en** would have grasped the reins of political and military power. This may in fact have been the case, but it pays to ask at what point it became inconceivable for females to be military rulers.

8. The Sumerian king list records that the first two kings of Uruk—Meškiaggašir and Enmerkar—were descended from the sun-god Utu. In the epic literature written about the kings of this dynasty, Enmerkar is remembered as the son of Utu. Enmerkar's successor, Lugalbanda, appears purely human in the epics. But in the religious literature, which includes sacrificial offering lists, he is remembered as a god, the spouse of the goddess Ninsun. Lugalbanda's son Dumuzi, an early king of Uruk, also shows this confusion between human and divine. In the king list, Dumuzi is listed as one of the early kings of Uruk. In the literature concerning the sacred marriage, Dumuzi is divine, the spouse of Inanna. Dumuzi is a limited god, whose only role among the gods is as Inanna's consort, but he is explicitly divine in the sacred marriage texts. Dumuzi is so thoroughly divine that one of the major scholars of this literature, Thorkild Jacobsen, has explained Dumuzi as the *élan vital,* the divine power immanent in nature. Thorkild Jacobsen, *Towards the Image of Tammuz* (Cambridge: Harvard University Press, (1970), 73–103. Another major scholar of this literature, Samuel Noah Kramer, believes that Dumuzi's true original identity was as human king. According to Kramer, the third-millenium theologians, probably within King Dumuzi's lifetime, conceived "the cheering and reassuring notion of having the king of his city become the lover and husband of the goddess (Inanna of Uruk) and thus share her invaluable fertility, power and potency and to some extent even her immortality." (S. N. Kramer "The Dumuzi Sacred Marriage Rite:Origin, Development, Character," CRRA 17:135f.

9. For the question of divine descent, see W. W. Hallo, "The Birth of Kings," 45–52; and Åke Sjöberg, "Die göttliche Abstammung der sumerisch-babylonischen Herrscher," *Orientalia Suecana* 21 (1973): 87–89. A very early inscription from Mesilim of Kish announces his descent from Ninhursag. One hundred years later, King Eannatum of Lagash claimed descent from both Ninhursag and Ningirsu. After him, all kings claimed divine descent.

10. See ga-zi-kú-a- ᵈNin-hur-ság-gá in the Eannatum Stele rev iv, lines 47–48, the Entemena vase, lines 7–8, and elsewhere in these early inscriptions.

11. Ninhursag's role in the birth of kings is remembered in classical Sumerian literature. In the temple hymn to the temple of Ninhursag (TCS 3, line 46f.), Nintu is both the one who gives birth to, and the one who places the crown on the head of, the king and the en. In the words of "Enki and the World Order," Nintu was the "one in charge of giving birth to en, giving birth to king." Because of her close association with the creation of kings, Ninhursag-Nintu is also called Ninmenna, "Lady of the Crown." T. Jacobsen, "Notes on Nintur," *Or.* 42 (1973):p. 294, holds that the reason that Ninhursag-Ninmenna, "Lady of the Headdress," is related to kings is that it was hard to fit midwife into the new royal metaphors, so that the headdress with which the midwife traditionally covered her hair became reinterpreted as an emblem of priestly and royal crowns. In the light of the strong relationship of mother-goddess to kings, it may be more correct

to understand the word "men" as the crown, and suggest that midwives wore turbans (if they did) in honor of the mother-goddess.

12. Hans J. Nissen, "Sumerian" vs. "Akkadian" Art: Art and Politics in Babylonia of the Mid-third Millenium B.C.E.," *Insight through Images: Studies in Honor of Edith Porada* (Malibu, Calif.: Undena, 1988): 189–196. Nissen also suggests that this was the dreadful sin of Naram-Sin punished in the Curse of Agade.

13. The earlier pre-Sargonic epithet, "nourished with the good milk of Ninhursag" disappeared, and is not used in the royal inscriptions of the later Sumerian kings.

14. The very first king of Akkad, Sargon, did not claim the title of "god" in his own inscriptions. Nevertheless, the personal name found on the Manishtushu Obelisk, *Šarru-kin-ili,* "Sargon is my god," certainly indicates that he was considered divine soon after his death, if not during his life. Two later kings of this dynasty, Naram-sin and Šar-kali-Šarri, applied the appelation "god" to themselves. In addition, Naram-sin is pictured on his stele wearing the horned crown, the iconographic symbol of divinity, and his officers called him "god of Akkad."

15. Cf. W. W. Hallo, *Early Mesopotamian Titles,* AOS 43 (New Haven: AOS, 1957), 134–135.

16. On the personal gods of Mesopotamia, see A. Leo Oppenheim, *Ancient Mesopotamia: Portrait of a Dead Civilization* (Chicago: University of Chicago Press, 1977), 198–205; and Thorkild Jacobsen, *Treasures,* 147–154. Everybody had divine parents, a divine mother and father who encouraged and protected him or her. The divine parents of king and citizen were not exactly the same, of course. The divine parents of an anonymous citizen were very minor deities, whose names have generally not come down to us; the divine parents of a king were the major gods of the pantheon. But the god of the king differed only in degree of importance and power, not in kind.

17. As with the Akkadian dynasty, the deification is more pronounced with the successors of the founder of the dynasty than with the first monarch himself. The first king of the Ur III dynasty, Ur-Nammu, did not claim the title of "god" in his royal inscriptions, but is described as divine in a royal hymn, and was fully deified after his death. His son, Šulgi, called himself "god."

18. For divine kingship, see M-th. Barrelet, "La figure du roi," in *Le Palai et la royauté,* CRRA 19 (1971): 27–138; Jacob Klein, *Three Šulgi Hymns,* (Ramat Gan: Bar-Ilan Univ., 1982), 29–36; E. D. van Buren, "Homage to a Deified King," *ZA* 50 (1952): 92–120; Joan Westenholz, review of Brian Lewis, *The Sargon Legend,* in *JNES* 43 (1984): 73–79; Wilcke, "Zum Königtum in der Ur III Zeit," in *Le Palai et la royauté,* P. Garelli, ed., CRRA 19 (1971): 177–232; Irene Winter, "The King and the Cup," in *Insight through Images* (Paris: Geuthner, 1974), 253–268.

19. By the last king of Ur III, Ibbisin, we no longer hear of chapels and festivals, but the title of "god" continues to be used by all the kings of Isin and some of Larsa. Even Hammurabi, who never used the title in his own inscriptions, is called god in one of the royal hymns. After this, however, the concept of divine king totally disappears.

20. A clear example is in the "presentation scene," one of the major topics of Ur III seal impressions. In this scene, an individual, often accompanied by a goddess, stands before a seated god, identified by the horned headdress of divinity and a flounced garment, who sits on a throne that looks like a temple facade. This is not really a "worship" scene, for the individual does not come bearing gifts or other signs of supplication. Rather, the individual represented in the seal has come before the god to experience and share the god's presence, and to draw authority from it. In one variation on this theme, the individual comes before a seated figure who wears a round cap and sits holding a cup. This is the king, who stands in a godlike relationship to his servant, but is distinguished from the great gods by his lack of the horned crown. He generally wears a fringed rather than flounced garment, and he almost always sits on a stool rather than a temple-facade throne. These cylinder seals are tokens of legitimacy and authority within the state system. The represention of the bearer of the seal before the king shows that the bearer partakes of the king's authority and thereby really does have legitimate status. (See I. J. Winter, "The King and the Cup," 253–268).

21. To Frankfort, *Kingship and the Gods: A Study of Ancient Near Eastern Religion as the Integration of Society & Nature* (Chicago: University of Chicago Press, 1948), 247, the participation in the sacred marriage was the key to the deification. This may be overstating the case.

22. At the very beginning of Ur III, King Ur Nammu is called the (**hili**) of Inanna. He is her beloved, and she laments after his death, "to my sanctuary Eanna they will not let him come from the mountain (of death), my shepherd in his sexiness (**hili**) cannot enter there, I can (no longer) enter there." His successors continue to emphasize their desirability to the goddess; see Claus

Wilcke, "Eine Schicksalentscheidung für den toten Urnammu," CRRA 17 (1970): 81–92. We have not yet recovered an Urnammu sacred marriage text but it seems that he already was Inanna's delight. J. Renger, RlA, suggested that Šulgi was the first to perform the sacred marriage as a royal ritual, but we should not hurry to reach this conclusion.

23. Inscription La 3.5 in Jerrold Cooper, *Sumerian and Akkadian Royal Inscriptions,* AOS Translation Ser., vol. 1 (New Haven: American Oriental Society, 1986).

24. "Enmerkar and the Lord of Aratta," 563–564; see the edition by Sol Cohen, *Enmerkar and the Lord of Aratta,* Ph.D. diss., University of Pennsylvania, 1973.

25. Enmerkar and Ensuhkušdanna, lines 275–276. See Adele Berlin, ed., *Enmerkar and Ensuhkešdanna: a Sumerian Narrative Poem,* Occasional Publications of the Babylonian Fund, 2 (Philadelphia: University of Pennsylvania Museum, 1979).

26. Lugalbanda Epic, 306–320. Another hero, Lugalbanda, makes the dangerous journey back to Uruk, whereupon Inanna "looked at him as if he were her husband Amaušumgalanna and spoke to him as if he were her son Šara," Lugalbanda, 350–353. Lines quoted according to C. Wilcke, *das Lugalbandaepos* (Wiesbaden: Harrasowitz, 1969). For this interpretation, see J. Cooper and W. Heimpel, "The Sumerian Sargon Legend," *JAOS* 103.1 (1983): 79.

27. Gilgamesh and Akka, 10–17.

28. "The Sumerian Sargon Legend," *JAOS* line 39.

29. See Joan Goodnick Westenholz, review of Lewis, *The Sargon Legend,* in *JNES* 43 (1984); 78–79; and the Naram-Sin inscription cited there.

30. There are literary texts from Abu Salabikh and Ebla, but they are very difficult.

31. UET VIII 12. W. W. Hallo refers to a statue of a later En priestess at Ur, Enannatumma, daughter of King Iddin-Dagan of Isin, a statue which has six copper nails in the head showing that an ornament, probably the horned crown, had adorned the statue. Since this horned crown is the symbol of divinity, the statue might have represented Enannatuma-as Ningal. Hallo, "Women at Sumer," in Denise Schmandt-Besserat, ed., *The Legacy of Sumer,* Bibliotheca Mesopotamica 4 (1987): 32–33, and fig. 16. See also Joan Goodnick Westenholz, "Enheduanna, En-Priestess, Hen of Nanna, Spouse of Nanna," in Hermann Behrens, Darlene Loding, and Martha Roth, eds., *Dumu é.dub.ba.a,: Studies in Honor of Åke Sjöberg* (Philadelphia: University of Pennsylvania Museum, 1989), 539–556.

32. See the picture and study of the disk of Enheduanna published by Irene Winter, "Women in Public: The Disk of Enheduanna, the Beginning of the Office of En-priestess and the Weight of the Visual Evidence" in *La Femme dans le proche orient antique,* Jean-Marie Durand, ed., CRRA 33 (Paris: Editions Recherche sur les Civilisations, 1987), 189–201.

33. Edited by W. W. Hallo and J. van Dik, *The Exaltation of Inanna,* YNER 3, 1968.

34. Åke Sjöberg, ed., *ZA* 65 (1975).

35. The text is as yet unedited and untranslated, and has been promised by Barry Eichler.

36. Ninmešarra 125–132.

37. There is an important question as to whether Inanna acted against or in accord with An's wishes in Inanna and Ebih. The question hinges on the lines 129–130, hur-ság-gá-bi huš-a ki-sikil ᵈInanna sag nu-mu-un-dè-gá-gá, ("the great mountain, its aura is fierce. Maiden Inanna, they cannot withstand you."). Did he encourage her by saying they could not withstand her, and she went according to his word; or had she gone against him?

38. In Inanna and Ebih, Inanna comes to An to express her desire for Ebih; whether she listens to his answer is a matter of ambiguous translation. The Myth of Inanna and Ebih emphasizes Inanna's close relations with the gods of power. Inanna says to An, "You are the one who made my word unrivalled in heaven and earth" (line 57), and declares, "my father Enlil placed the fear of me in all the lands" (line 168). So, too, the Hymn "Ninmešarra" declares, "You are at the service of the decrees of An" (line 19). The Hymn, Inninšagurra, also deals with this issue: Enheduanna declares that Inanna rivals the great An (line 1), that the gods crawl before her words and An dares not proceed against her command (lines 5–6), and that without Inanna the great An has not made a decision, Enlil has not determined destiny (line 14). Enheduanna portrays Inanna ascendant, sitting on the seat of An and Enlil (line 97), and explains how she achieved this position: because of his fear of Inanna, An let Inanna take her seat in his dwelling place, and handed to her his great ordinances (line 106). In the vision of this text, when Inanna makes a decree, An and Enlil back it up (lines 197–207). See also Sjöberg, "A Hymn to Inanna and Her Self-Praise," *JCS* 40 (1988): 165–186.

39. See J. Cooper, *The Curse of Agade* (Baltimore: The Johns Hopkins University Press, 1973).

40. What this matter was has been the subject of some dispute, and we do not know whether it was a mysterious anti-Agade pronouncement (so, J. Cooper) or permission denied to rebuild Ekur (so T. Jacobsen *Harps*), or Enlil's pronouncement that she could not have a real temple suitable to accommodate all the rich offerings (so, J. M. Durand, see J. M. Durand report in *Annuaire de l'école pratique des hautes études,* ive section, 1974/5).

41. Lugal-e, line 137.

42. See the examples cited in CAD, M vol. 2, under 2 *melultu, melulu.*

43. See "Utuamirabi," in Mark E. Cohen ed. and trans., *The Canonical Lamentations of Ancient Mesopotamia* (Potomac, Md.: Capital Decisions, 1988).

44. S. N. Kramer, "BM 29616, The Fashioning of the Gala," *Acta Sumerologica* 3 (1981): 1–11.

45. See CAD, *Kalu.*

46. See most recently, B. Groneberg, "Philologische Bearbeitung des Agušayahymnus" RA 75 (1981) 107–134; also see Benjamin Foster "Ea and Saltu," in *Essays on the Ancient Near East in Memory of Jacob Joel Finkelstein,* M. Ellis, ed., Memoirs of the Connecticut Academy of Arts and Sciences XIX, Hamden, Conn.: Archon Books, (1977), 79–86.

47. This theory gains plausibility from the fact that the first real mention of a military Inanna is in the compositions of Enheduanna; of course, we cannot really read any earlier literary texts. Van Dijk has suggested that the fierce Inanna of Enheduanna's hymns is really an image of the Sargonic Ishtar, and that, furthermore, this image of Ishtar is really a projection of the victorious city of Akkad. (J. van Dijk "Les contact ethniques dans la Mesopotamie et les syncretismes de la religion sumerienne" in *Syncretism,* Sven Hartman, ed., (Stockhold: Almgvist & Wiksell, 1969), esp 194–203). J. J. Roberts has argued that early Ishtar is a composite figure, a combination of the military morning star, found in West Semitic texts as the male god Attar, and the loving evening star, originally Inanna: M. Roberts, *The Earliest Semitic Pantheon,* Baltimore: The Johns Hopkins University Press, 1972).

48. Bottero, "La femme, l'amour et la guerre en Mesopotamie ancienne," *Poikilia: Études offertes à J. P. Vernant* (Paris: Editions de l'École des houtes études 1987), 172f, citing A. J. Jaussen, *Coutoumes des Arabes au pays de Moab* (Paris: J. Gabalda et cie, 1908, 1948), 174ff.

49. According to Bottéro, "La femme . . . ," the prostitute had all the men of society at her mercy, and was not submissive to anyone. Outside the margins of society, she pursued her own ends. This was inherently divisive in society, and therefore the prostitute, and Inanna who represented her, were considered the personifications of discord. To my mind, Bottéro's image of prostitutes is highly romanticized, and it is dubious whether they were actually women with any power at all other than power-over-oneself, which in most economic conditions is the power to suffer.

50. Hans Güterbock, "A Hurro-Hittite Hymn to Ištar," *JAOS* 103.1 (1983): 155–164; translation by Guterbock.

51. For this fear of female power, see Dorothy Dinnerstein, *The Mermaid and the Minotaur* (New York: Harper, 1966).

52. Ann Guinan has been preparing a study of the behavioral omens of *šumma alu* as her Ph.D. dissertation, and I thank her for sharing her observations on *šumma alu* with me.

53. For this concept, see Rollo May, *Love and Will* (New York: Dell, 1974). May calls sex and aggression "daimonic."

CHAPTER 7    The Marginalization of the Goddesses

1. See M. Krebernik, *Die Beschwörungen aus Fara and Ebla,* (Hildesheim and New York: Olms Verlag, 1985), 233–263.

2. *Or.* 28 (1959): 338, lines 9–10.

3. See J. J. van Dijk, "Le motif cosmique dans la pensée sumérienne," *Acta Orientalia* 29, 196. So T. Jacobsen, *Enc Rel,* vol. 9, M, 447–469.

4. See S. N. Kramer, "Poets and Psalmists: Goddesses and Theologians," in *The Legacy of Sumer,* Denise Schmandt-Besserat, ed. (Malibu, Calif.: Undena, 1976): 3–22.

5. Enki may be read as En for "lord" and Ki for "earth": "Lord of the Earth."

6. See A. Poebel, PBS 4: 24–31. Jacobsen has suggested that the economic prominence of calving and milk in the cowherder's world might have accounted for the early prominence of Ninhursag ("Notes on Nintur," *Or.* 42), but there are many reasons to expect a mother-goddess to be prominent in early religion.

7. The text, as yet unedited, has been published (in cuneiform) in TCL 16 n. 72 and UET VI/2. For these lines, see J. J. van Dijk, *Acta Orientalia* 28. Van Dijk lists this as an example of creation "by emersio," but in fact, people did not sprout until after Enlil planted the mold.

8. Jacobsen's translation, *Harps*, 157, "[without] the sperm of a ma[le] she gave [birth] to off[spring], to the [em]bryo of mankind" certainly brings out this point. However, this is a very daring translation in the light of all the lacuna, particularly since the word for "sperm" in Sumerian is simply *a*, which (since the rest of the line is missing) could also be a grammatical particle or a part of another noun. Nevertheless, the sense of the passage does indicate that—in the final analysis—Nammu acted alone.

9. See M. Glassner, "Mahlzeit," RlA 7 (1988): 263–264. The idea of disputations and boasting competitions is well rooted in Sumerian culture, and a whole genre of literature, the "disputation texts," is based on the idea of dialogues that proclaim the merits of the disputing partners.

10. There is one more, the **lu-a-sur-sur**, who may be "incontinent" (so Jacobsen, in *Harps*) or may be "promiscuous" or "unable to hold his semen." The social role is equally obscure.

11. Atrahasis I 200–201. For text, edition, and translation, see W. Lambert and R. Millard, *The Atrahasis Epic: The Babylonian Story of the Flood* (Oxford University Press, 1969) and Stephanie Dalley, *Myths from Mesopotamia: Creation, the Flood, Gilgamesh and Others* (Oxford and New York, Oxford University Press, 1989), 1–38.

12. Enuma Elish VI 35–38. For translation, see Dalley, *Myths,* 228–277.

13. *Ludlul bel nemeqi* IV 31; cf. W. G. Lambert, BWL, 59.

14. See ANET, 538.

15. From the ancient text, "The Babylonian Theodicy," Lambert, BWL, 89 lines 276–278.

16. Enuma Elish I 45–6.

17. Enuma Elish II 110–111.

18. We do not have any information about what rituals the kings of the latter half of the second millennium performed. Evidence is only available for the first millennium.

19. For this later ritual, see Bottero, "Le Hierogamie après l'époque 'sumérienne,'" in S. N. Kramer, *Le Mariage sacrée: à sumer et à Babylone,* translated and adapted by Jean Bottero (Paris: Berg International, 1983), 175–215; Eiko Matsushima, "Les Rituels du Mariage Divin dans les Documents Accadiens," *Acta Sumerologica* 10 (1988): 95–128; Eiko Matsushima, "Le Rituel Hierogamique de Nabu," *Acta Sumerologica* 9 (1987): 131–171.

20. Note Enlilbani (A. Kapp, ZA 51 (1961): 76f.), 151–158: "Inanna . . . brings you greatly to her holy bed and spends the night there (with you)."

21. Tukulti-Ninurta is also "poured through the channel of the womb of the gods"; see P. Machinist, "Literature as Politics: The Tukulti-Ninurta Epic and the Bible," *CBQ* 38 (1976): 455–482. In line with the discussion in chapter 8, we might note the absence of the mother-goddess, previously so important to kingship. It is by the decree of Nudimmud (Ea) that the king is poured through the channel of the womb, and it is not even the womb of the mother-goddess, but that of "the gods."

22. Discussion by J. Tigay, "The Image of God and the Flood: Some New Developments," in A. Shapiro and B. Cohen, eds., *Studies in Jewish Education* (1984), 169–182.

23. D. O. Edzard, WbMyth., 81–89; cf. CRRA 2 (1951): 21ff.

24. Jeffrey Tigay alludes to the fact that the Old Babylonian version of the Gilgamesh Epic refers to the Eanna as the abode of the god An, even though this temple had long been shared by Inanna-Ishtar. Tigay considers this a deliberate omission, *The Evolution of the Gilgamesh Epic* (Philadelphia: University of Pennsylvania Press, 1982), 68.

25. As in the first millennium version of the Congregational Lament Uruamirabi, Mark Cohen, *The Canonical Lamentations of Ancient Mesopotamia* (Potomac, Md.: Capital Decisions, 1988), which has an episode in which Ishtar takes harsh vengeance against a slave girl who has slept with her master.

26. The Erra Epic tablet IV 52–58.

27. For the similarities between Ištar and Lamaštu, see Wolfgang Fauth, "Ištar als Löwengöttin and die löwenköpfige Lamaštu," WO 12 (1981): 21–36.

28. Royal Hymn to Ištar in favor of King Ammiditana, for which, see RA 22 (1928): 170ff.

29. So T. Jacobsen, "Notes on Nintur," Or. 42: 294ff, who argues that the use of royal metaphors made it hard to fit a mother into the royal system.

30. See S. N. Kramer, "Poets and Psalmists: Goddesses and Theologians" in *The Legacy of Sumer,* 3–22.

31. See J. M. Asher-Grève, *Frauen in altsumerischer Zeit,* Bibliotheca Mesopotamica 18 (Malibu, Calif.: Undena, 1985).

32. So Aaron Shaffer, "Gilgamesh, the Cedar Forest and Mesopotamian History," *JAOS* 103 (1983) 310–313, who comes to this conclusion from Gilgamesh's speech to Huwawa, "I promise to bring my elder sister Enmebaragesi into the land for you as a wife."

33. Cf. Dominque Charpin, *Le clergé d'Ur au siècle d'Hammurabi (xix–xvii siècles AV. J.C.)* Geneva: Librairie Droz, 1986.

34. W. W. Hallo, "Women of Sumer," in *The Legacy of Sumer,* 23–40; P. Michalowski, "Royal Women of the Ur III Period," *JCS* 31 (1979): 171–176; P. Steinkeller, "More on the Ur III Royal Wives," *Acta Sumerologica* 3 (1981): 77–92.

35. See Bernard Batto, *Studies on Women at Mari* (Baltimore: Johns Hopkins University Press, 1974).

## CHAPTER 8   Israel and the Master of the Universe

1. The earliest poems contained in the Bible were written in the early days of Israel, around 1200–1000 B.C.E. The latest books come from the beginning of the Hellenistic period, after the conquest of Israel by Alexander the Great. The books that constitute the Hebrew Bible (the "canon") had been mostly selected by the time of the conquest of Alexander the Great, and Israel developed a tradition that prophecy stopped at the end of the Persian period. A few books written later joined the Biblical canon, mostly because they are "pseudepigraphic," attributed to ancient authors. These include the book of Ecclesiastes, and possibly the Song of Songs.

2. For biblical poetry see Michael Patrick O'Connor, *Hebrew Verse Structure* (Winona Lake, Ind.: Eisenbrauns, 1980), and James L. Kugel, *Parallelism and Its History* (New Haven and London: Yale University Press, 1981) and the literature cited there.

3. The literature dealing with biblical law and its ancient Near Eastern counterparts is vast. See, initially, Shalom Paul, *Studies in the Book of the Covenant in the Light of Cuneiform and Biblical Law,* VTS 18 (Leiden: E. J. Brill, 1970), with earlier bibliography cited; Paul "Biblical Analogues to Middle Assyrian Law," in *Religion and Law: Biblical-Judaic and Islamic Perspectives,* Firmage, Weiss, and Welch, eds. (Winona Lake, Ind.: Eisenbrauns, 1990): 334–350; Moshe Greenberg, "Some Postulates of Biblical Criminal Law," in *Yehezkel Kaufman Jubilee Volume* M. Harran, ed. Jerusalem: 1960; Dale Patrick, *Old Testament Law* (Atlanta: John Knox, 1985); Raymond Westbrook, *Studies in Biblical and Near Eastern Law,* (Paris: Gabalda, 1988); and Moshe Weinfeld, *mišpat u ṣedaqa . . . (Equity and Freedom in Ancient Israel in Light of Social Justice in the Ancient Near East)* Jerusalem: (Hebrew University-Magnes Press, 1985 in Hebrew).

4. For an introduction to the wisdom literature, see Crenshaw, *Old Testament Wisdom: An Introduction,* (Atlanta, John Knox, 1981); and the articles in *The Sage in Israel and the Ancient Near East,* James Gammie and Leo Purdue, eds., (Winona Lake, Ind.: Eisenbrauns, 1990).

5. During the last decades scholarly opinion has rejected the idea that Israel is always unique. See, on this topic, A. Gamper, *Gott als Richter in Mesopotamien und im Alten Testament: zum Verständnis einer Gebetsbitt* (Innsbruck: Universitätsverlag Wagner, 1966); B. Albrektson, *History and the Gods: An essay of the Idea of Historical Events as Divine Manifestations in the Ancient Near East and in Israel* (Lund: Gleerup, 1967); J. L. Crenshaw, *Prophetic Conflict: Its Effect Upon Israelite Religion* BZAW 124 (Berlin: de Gruyter, 1971); W. G. Lambert, "Destiny and Divine Intervention in Babylon and Israel," *OTS* 17(1972): 65–72; H. W. F. Saggs, *The Encounter with the Divine in Israel and Babylon* (London: Athlone, 1978).

6. For this idea, see C. J. Labuschagne, *The Incomparability of Yahweh in the Old Testament* (Leiden: E. J. Brill, 1966).

7. For a discussion of this process, see Baruch Halpern, "Brisker Pipes than Poetry: The Development of Israelite Monotheism," in *Judaic Perspectives on the Bible* Jacob Nensner, Baruch A. Levine, and Ernest S. Frerichs, eds., (Philadelphia: Fortress, 1987), 77–115.

8. See B. W. Anderson, *Creation versus Chaos: The Reinterpretation of Mythical Symbolism in the Bible* (New York: Association Press, 1967); Mary Wakeman, *God's Battle with the Monster* (Leiden: E. J. Brill, 1973); and John Day, *God's Conflict with the Dragon and the Sea: Echoes of a Canaanite Myth in the Old Testament* (Cambridge: Cambridge University Press, 1985), with extensive bibliography. Some of these poems may have been "enthronement psalms," liturgical evocations and celebrations of YHWH's kingship. They may have been recited at an

annual cultic commemoration of the "Enthronement of YHWH," for which, see S. Mowinckel, *The Psalms in Israel's Worship* (Oxford: Blackwell, 1962).

9. It has long been noted that YHWH unites both the functions of Canaanite El as creator and Baal as king. But the Babylonian Marduk also unites these two powers. In this, as in many other ways, Babylonian mythology seems closer to Biblical thought than Ugaritic. We should be careful not to assume Babylonian influence on the Bible. The Enuma Elish is written long after the West Semitic infiltration of Mesopotamia, and the myth of the sea seems more at home on the Mediterranean coast than the Persian. We can be dealing with very ancient West Semitic mythology told by the ancestors of the Hebrews and their migrating branches.

10. For studies of this psalm, see Jon Levenson, *Sinai and Zion: An Entry into the Jewish Bible* (Minneapolis: Winston Press, 1985), 61–62 and the earlier literature cited there.

11. One could argue that all religion is characterized by change, for without the ability to transform themselves and adapt to new human situations, religions stagnate and eventually disappear.

12. In fact, despite the impression that the prophets give us, Israel was overwhelmingly monotheist. As Jeffrey Tigay has shown, Israelites did not give their children names in which the theophoric (divine) element was the name of another god, an indication that they were not praying to other gods for the well-being of their children. See the discussion in Jeffrey Tigay, *You Shall Have No Other Gods: Israelite Religion in the Light of Hebrew Inscriptions* Harvard Semitic Series 3 (Atlanta: Scholars Press, 1987).

13. In Babylonia, the Enuma Elish records how the young god Marduk, son of Ea, became the king of the gods and was granted dominion over them by the senior gods. In Ugarit, the Baal Epic relates how Baal became king of the Canaanite pantheon. Ever since S. Mowinckel, *Psalmenstudien II. Das Thronbesteigungsfest Jahwas und der Ursprung der Eschatologie* (Kristiana: J. Dybwad, 1922) scholars have noted psalms—such as Psalm 93—that celebrate the kingship of YHWH, and the association of kingship with divine victory and with creation. On this, see B. W. Anderson, *Creation versus Chaos;* Mary Wakeman, *God's Battle;* John Day, *God's Conflict.*

14. The covenant literature is very large. A convenient and thorough history of the question and bibliography is Ernest Nicholson, *God and His People: Covenant and Theology in the Old Testament* (Oxford: Clarendon, 1986). Of particular importance are G. E. Mendenhall, "Covenant Forms in Israelite Tradition," *BA* 17 (1954): 50–76; William Moran, "The Ancient Near Eastern Background of the Love of God in Deuteronomy," *CBQ* 24 (1963): 77–87; D. J. McCarthy, "Notes on the Love of God in Deuteronomy and the Father-Son Relationship between Yahweh and Israel," *CBQ* 27 (1965) 144–147. D. J. McCarthy, *Treaty and Covenant,* enlarged, revised ed., Analecta Biblica 21A, Rome 1978; Moshe Weinfeld, "Covenant," *Encyclopedia Judaica,* vol. 5, cols. 1012–22 (Jerusalem, 1971); Moshe Weinfeld, "Brith," in *Theological Dictionary of the Old Testament,* G. Johaness Botterweck and Helner Ringgren, eds., John T. Willis, trans., 2: (Grand Rapids: Erdmans, 1977); 253–279 and Jon Levenson, *Sinai and Zion.* For a study of changing attitudes towards the antiquity of covenant, see Robert A. Oden, Jr., "The Place of Covenant in the Religion of Israel," in *Ancient Israelite Religion* Patrick Miller, P. Hanson, and D. McBride, eds. (Minneapolis: Fortress, 1987), 429–447.

15. Exod. 20:3;

16. Exod. 23:25–27. As is often the case in the Pentateuch, we cannot pinpoint the exact date of this verse, but this core covenantal idea is expressed throughout the Bible, in writings from various periods in Israel's history. This passage has sometimes been attributed to several sources. A. Noth, *Exodus: A Commentary,* (Philadelphia: Westminster, 1962), holds that 25b–31a are from an older source, while 23–25a and 31–33 come from a Deuteronomic addition. B. Childs, *Exodus: The Book of a Critical Theological Commentary,* (Philadelphia: Westminster, 1974); believes that the whole passage served a homilectical purpose in Deuteronomistic circles. There is no reason to believe that the idea of exclusive worship and God's rewarding it comes late to Israel. The covenantal idea is developed and expanded in Deuteronomy, which also emphasizes the other half of the proposition, that apostasy and disobedience result in God's cursing the nation and the land. The curses of Deuteronomy and their Near Eastern milieu have been the subject of considerable study, most completely by D. R. Hillers, *Treaty-curse and the Old Testament Prophets, Biblica et Orientalia* 16 (1964), and see also M. Weinfeld, *Deuteronomy and the Deuteronomic School* (Oxford: Clarendon, 1972).

17. Atrahasis Epic, 1:377–413

18. Sometimes also called radical monotheism, in which even the existence of all other gods is denied. For the development of monotheism in Israel, see Baruch Halpern, "Brisker Pipes than

Poetry: The Development of Israelite Monotheism," *Judaic Perspectives on Ancient Israel* (Philadelphia: Fortress, 1987), 77–115.

19. CTA, 4:5, lines 668–670.

20. See David Noel Freedman, "Who Is Like Thee Among the Gods: The Religion of Early Israel," in *Ancient Israelite Religion,* P. Miller et al, eds., 315–335; and Frank Cross, *Canaanite Myth and Hebrew Epic: Essays in the History of the Religion of Israel* (Cambridge: Harvard University Press, 1973), 147–184.

21. 1 Sam. 12:16–19.

22. 1 Kings 18.

23. Deut. 11:8–12. Watering with the feet is a method of simple irrigation. In order to maneuver the water within its canals, one can make or open a little dam with one's feet.

24. The rainfall in Israel is erratic: three out of ten years have less than normal rainfall, and these arid years tend to cluster together. See David C. Hopkins, "Life on the Land: The Subsistence Struggles of Early Israel," *BA* 50 (1987): 179–191.

25. Selected from Joel 1:10–20.

26. The gods themselves, says the Akkadian-language Atrahasis Epic, had once worked to grow their own food. Tiring of this, they created human beings who could do the work for them. In order to make sure that they would receive good food, says the Sumerian-language composition Lahar and Ashnan, the gods created and gave to humankind the divine Grain and the divine Ewe. Agriculture and pastorage, both vital to human survival, are given sacred warrant by these stories, and the practical pursuit of abundance is given another layer of significance. For more on the development of agriculture, see chapter 10.

27. For ancient Europe, see Maria Gimbutas, *Goddesses and Gods of Old Europe, 7000–3500 B.C.* (Berkeley: University of California Press, 1982); Gimbutas, *The Language of the Goddess* (San Francisco: Harper & Row, 1989). For Çatal Huyuk, see James Melaart, *Çatal Huyuk: a Neolithic Town in Anatolia* (New York: McGraw-Hill, 1967).

28. The solemn, possibly liturgical, recitation of Genesis 1 encapsulates much of the visions of the priestly traditions in Israel.

29. Most scholars, following von Rad, believe this passage to be a very early text, reflecting a ritual performed in the time of the Judges, in the first phase of the settlement of the land. For a summary of the arguments about the age of this passage, see J. I. Durham, "Credo," *The Interpreter's Dictionary of the Bible,* supplementary vol. (Nashville: Abingdon, 1976), 197–199.

30. Deut. 26:1–10. This central recitation of the harvest season was such a strong tradition in Israel, so intimately connected to the harvest festival, that later, when the Passover liturgy (the Haggadah) was written, it did not recite the story of the exodus by reading the book of Exodus, but rather by reading an explication (*midrash*) of this passage in which almost every phrase of this recitation is related to the Exodus story.

31. Murder: Gen. 4:10–12, Num. 35:31–34; sexual impropriety: Lev. 18, Lev. 19:29, Jer. 3:9, Ezek. 23:17, Deut. 24:1–4; idolatry: Ezek. 36:18.

32. See Tikva Frymer-Kensky, "The Atrahasis Epic and Its Significance for Our Understanding of Genesis 1–9," *BA* 40/4 (1977): 147–155.

33. Gen. 4:10–12

34. The Hebrew verb, *yĕnahămēnū,* ("he will comfort us"), seems rather to be an explanation of the name Nahum than Noah. The Septuagint reads, "he will give us rest," in Hebrew, *yanīh-e-mēnū* (with enclitic *mem*), which would be a good explanation for Noah.

35. Gen. 5:29; emphasis added.

36. Gen. 6:12; 8:21.

37. There is one ritual to prevent contamination in the case of an unsolved homicide. This is the ritual of the decapitated heifer, Deut. 21:1–9, in which the elders of the town closest to which a corpse was found performed the ritual, declared their innocence, and petitioned God not to allow their land to become polluted. See Ziony Zevit, "The Ègla Ritual of Deuteronomy 21:1–9," *JBL* 95 (1976): 377–390; and Raphael Patai, "The ʿegla ʿArufa or the Expiation of the Polluted Land," 30:59–69.

38. The prophets Hosea, Jeremiah, and Ezekiel attribute the ultimate destruction of Israel to the fact that the land has become polluted by these deeds. In this paradigm of historical thinking, the destruction is not seen as legal punishment for Israel's crimes, but as the inevitable catastrophe resulting from a buildup of pollution into a "critical mass." The exile is seen as a restorative hiatus for the land before God will purify the people and bring them back to try again. For this theory of catastrophe as exemplified in Rabbinic Judaism, see Tikva Frymer-Kensky, "The Theol-

ogy of Catastrophe" (in Hebrew) in *Beersheba,* vol. 3, Memorial Volume for Moshe Held: Studies by the Department of Bikle and Near East, Mordechai Cogan, ed. (Jerusalem: Magnes, 1988), 121–124. For more on pollution, see Tikva Frymer-Kensky "Pollution, Purification and Purgation in Biblical Israel," in *The Word of the Lord Shall Go forth: Essays in Honor of David Noel Freedman,* Carol Meyers and Michael O'Connor, eds. (Winona Lake, Ind.: Eisenbrauns, 1983), 399–414.

39. Typically, these healing-practitioners recited a "Marduk-Ea" incantation in which Marduk described the disease to Ea, and Ea prescribed a healing ritual (which was then performed). See Edith K. Ritter, "Magical Expert ( = *ašipu*) and Physician ( = *asû*): Notes on Two Complementary Professions in Babylonian Medicine," in *Studies in Honor of Benno Landsberger on His Seventy-Fifth Birthday, April 21, 1965,* Hans Güterbock and Thorkild Jacobsen, eds., AS 16 (Chicago: University of Chicago Press, 1965): 209–322.

40. See Hans Hirsch, "Den Toten zu Beleben," *AfO* 22 (1968/9): 39–58.

41. Šurpu IV 16–18. See Erica Reiner, *Šurpu–a Collection of Sumerian and Akkadian Incantations. AfO* Beiheft 11, Graz, 1956.

42. See Norbert Lohfink, "Ich bin Jahwe, dein Arzt (Ex. 15:26)," in *Ich will euer Gott werden: Beispiele biblischen Redens von Gott,* Helmut Merklein and Erich Zenger, eds., Stuttgarter Bibelstudien 100 (Stuttgart: Verlag Katholisches Bibelwerk, 1981), 11–74.

43. 2 Sam. 12:15–23; 1 Kings 13:6; 1 Kings 14:1–18.

44. Announcements: 1 Kings 14:1–18, 2 Kings 20:2f; intercessions: 1 Kings 13:6, 1 Kings 17:19–21, 2 Kings 4:33–35

45. Petition: Ps. 6:2–8, Ps. 41; thanksgiving: Ps. 107:19–20.

46. 2 Sam. 12:15; 1 Kings 14:1.

47. *Ṣāraʿat,* normally translated "leprosy," is probably a severe form of dermatitis rather than Hansen's disease. For a discussion of this issue, and of other matters pertaining to medicine and the Bible, see the unpublished paper by Gail Beitman, "Medicine in the Bible," 1989. Paper is available through Beitman, Reconstructionist Rabbinical College, Church Rd. and Greenwood Ave., Wyncote, PA 19095.

48. Num. 12:10–15; 2 Kings 5:27; 2 Chron. 26:19–21.

49. As in Ps. 41:5.

50. Deut. 28:27,35,60

51. Exod. 9:14,16; similar passages throughout the narrative.

52. Ex. 15:26.

53. There had been considerable rivalry between Enki/Ea and the mother-goddess as to who created the first humans, and Ea eventually became considered Nudimmud, the "man-creator." Enki/Ea was also called upon to assist in difficult childbirths.

54. Mesopotamia, which had a riverine ecology, worried about such dangers. In the Mesopotamian version of the primeval flood story, the flood was the result of the unstoppable growth of human population. See Anne Kilmer, "The Mesopotamian Concept of Overpopulation and Its Solution as Represented in the Mythology," *Or.* 41 (1972): 160–177; and Tikva Frymer-Kensky, "The Atrahasis Epic."

55. For the conditions in Israel in the settlement period, see David C. Hopkins, "Life on the Land." Carol Meyers has pointed out that the Bible's many stories about the massive casualties that early Israel experienced through war, pestilence, and other natural disasters imply that Israel sensed its own underpopulation. Carol Meyers, "The Roots of Restriction: Women in Early Israel," *BA* 41 (1978): 91:103.

56. See Larry Stager, "The Archaeology of the Family in Ancient Israel," *BASOR* 260 (1985): 1–35. Hopkins reports that the birth rate in the eastern Mediterranean at this period was not great; it has been calculated at 4.1 pregnancies per woman, with only 1.9 live births (not all of whom survived childhood). See J. L Angel, "Ecology and Population in the Eastern Mediterranean," *World Archaeology* 4 (1972): 88–105.

57. Gen. 1:8, 9:1, 9:7.

58. See the passages cited in notes 64–66.

59. Gen. 49:25. For the early dating, see D. N. Freedman, "Who Is Like Thee Among the Gods." Freedman assumes that the words "blessing of breast and womb" must refer to a mother-goddess and imply that God had a consort. However, the verse specifically states that God provides these blessings, an indication that God has already coopted the powers of the mother-goddess by the time of this poem.

60. As God did in Abimelech's household (Gen. 20:18–18).

61. Gen. 21:1, 25:21, 32:22; Judges 13:2, 1 Sam. 1:5,6.

62. Mary Callaway suggests that this pattern is characteristic of J, the first literary source of the Pentateuch, probably composed in the tenth century B.C.E. Callaway suggests that this is part of the monotheizing theology, which wants to stress dependence on divine grace. Mary Callaway, *Sing, O Barren One: A Study in Comparative Midrash,* SBL Dissertation Series 91, (Decatur, Ga.: Scholars Press, 1986) 29–33. There is certainly no reason to assume that the idea of God's dominance over reproduction is any later than J.

63. Ps. 127:3.

64. Isa. 44:2,24, 49:5; Jer. 1:5, Ps. 139:13–16; Job 10:8–11, 31:13–15.

65. Is. 46:3–4, 49:1, Ps. 22:10–11, 71:5, 139:13–16.

66. Is. 66: 9; Job 10:18. For a discussion of childbirth, see Phyllis Trible, *God and the Rhetoric of Sexuality* (Philadelphia: Fortress, 1978), 34–38; and Charles Fontinoy, "La Naissance de l'enfant chez les Israelites de l'ancien Testament," in *L'enfant dans les civilizations orientales, Acta Orientalia Belgica* 2, A. Theodorides, P. Naster, and J. Ries, eds. (Leuven: Pecters, 1980), 103–118, and the early literature cited there. See also Marten Stol, *Zwangerschap en geboorte bij de Babyloniërs en in de Bijbel* (Leiden: Ex Oriente Lux, 1983).

67. This was not necessarily so in Mesopotamia. In Sumer, different gods oversaw the different dimensions of fertility. Human and animal reproduction were in the hands (or womb) of the mother-goddess, whereas agricultural fertility came from the sacred marriage between a male god and a goddess who was not the mother-goddess (most often, the goddess Inanna, the nubile young sexual goddess). But there is no division of powers in the Bible, and all manifestations of fertility are parallel.

68. Hos. 2.

69. Amos 4:13, 5:8.

70. It is sometimes claimed that Israel began to consider God a "creating" divinity very late in its history, perhaps even in the Babylonian exile. The only way to maintain such a view is to consider all passages in earlier books (such as Amos) to be later interpolations. There is no reason to suspect this and no evidence to support it.

## CHAPTER 9   But in Ourselves

1. The Midrashim (collections of rabbinic writings on biblical passages) contain legends of Abraham discovering God through his own intellectual and pious faculties. For the story, see Louis Ginzberg, *Legends of the Jews,* vol. 1 (Philadelphia: Jewish Publication society, 1913), 189. For the references, see ibid., vol. 5, p. 210, n. 16.

2. Gen. 19:29 states specifically that it was because of Abraham that God saved Lot: after all, God had not promised to save the innocent from the destruction, but rather to cancel the destruction if there were sufficient innocent.

3. Ex. 2:24, 6:5.

4. Ezek. 17:60.

5. Ex. 9:14.

6. Num. 14:13–16; cf. Ezek. 20:21–22.

7. Ezek. 36:20–21.

8. See the analysis of Psalm 74 in Jon Levenson, *Creation and the Persistence of Evil: The Jewish Drama of Divine Omnipotence* (San Francisco: Harper and Row, 1988).

9. Lev. 10:3.

10. Beth Shemesh: 1 Sam. 6:17; Uzzah: 2 Sam 6:6–7.

11. Gen. 22:1.

12. Gen. 33: 24–30.

13. Exod. 4:24–26.

14. For a discussion on testing, with bibliography, see Norbert Lohfink, "Ich bin Jahwe, dein Arzt (Ex. 15,16): Gott, Gesellschaft und menschliche Gesundheit in der Theologie einer nachexilischen Pentateuchbearbeitung (Ex. 15,25b–26)," in *"Ich will euer Gott werden": Beispiele biblischen Redens von Gott* Helmut Merklein and Erich Zenge, eds., Stuttgarter Bibelstudien 100 (Stuttgart: Verlag Katholosches Bibelwerk, 1981), 11–74, esp. 58–69.

15. In this biblical reconceptualization of the natural universe, God's sole mastery, while absolute, is not arbitrary, and humankind becomes the fulcrum around which the give and take of nature turns.

16. Tikva Frymer-Kensky, "Pollution, Purification and Purgation in Biblical Israel," in *The Word of the Lord Shall Go Forth: Essays in Honor of David Noel Freedman,* Carol Meyers and Michael O'Connor, eds. (Winona Lake, Ind.: Eisenbrauns, 1983), 399–414.

17. In addition to the above article, see Tikva Frymer-Kensky, "Atrahasis and the Meaning of Gen. 1–9," *BA* 40/4 (1977): 147–155.

18. Lev. 18:24–28.

19. Hos. 6:10; Jer. 2:7; Ezek. 36:18.

20. For this theory of catastrophe as exemplified in Rabbinic Judaism, see Tikva Frymer-Kensky, "The Theology of Catastrophe" (in Hebrew), in *Beersheba,* vol. 3, Memorial Volume for Moshe Held (Jerusalem: Magnes, 1988), 121–124.

21. This idea of reward and punishment comes to full expression in Deuteronomy, and is presented in Deuteronomy as part of the covenantal stipulations between Israel and God (Deut. 6:3, 7:13–14, 28:4,11,18, and 30:9). However, it is not limited to the Deuteronomic strand of the Bible or to the classical prophets.

22. In these passages, droughts are a method of instruction, a way of calling Israel to attention. Thus Amos: "I therefore withheld the rain from you three months before harvest time: I would make it rain on one town and not on another. One field would be rained upon while another on which it did not rain would wither. . . . Yet you did not turn back to me" (Amos 4:6–8). See also Jer. 2:3.

23. Jer. 5:25.

24. Deut. 11:13–17. See, also, Deut. 8:12–13, If then, you obey these norms and observe them faithfully, the Lord your God will keep with you the gracious covenant that He made on oath with your fathers, He will love you and bless you and multiply you, He will bless the issue of your womb and the produce of your soil, your new grain and wine and oil, the calving of your herd and the lambing of your flock, in the land that He swore to your fathers to give you. The priestly record of the Sinai covenant also stresses the impact of Israel's observance of the covenant on the rain (Lev. 25:9–10; 26:3–5, 14, 19–20), as do the prophets. All the major voices in the biblical tradition speak very clearly on this issue with a uniform voice, if Israel is good, God gives rain; and if Israel is not good, God will not give rain—with the result that the earth will not be able to be fruitful.

25. The notion that there is ever a mental image of an external judge standing outside the causality and determining to punish or reward has been questioned by Klaus Koch, "Gibt es ein Vergeltungsdogma in alten Testament?" *Zeitschrift für Theologie und Kirche* 52 (1955): 1–42, most of which has been translated as "Is There a Doctrine of Retribution in the Old Testament?" in *Theodicy in the Old Testament,* James L. Crenshaw, ed., Issues in Religion and Theology, Vol. 4 (Philadelphia: Fortress Press, 1983). Koch builds on K. Fahlgren's *Sedaka, nahestehende und entgegengesetzte Begriffe im Alten Testament* (Uppsala: Almquist & Wiksell, 1932), in which Fahlgren identified Hebrew roots which mean both actions and their consequences. In my own study of Akkadian legal terminology, I found that the Akkadian words for misdeed, *arnu, šertu, hittu,* and *sartu* refer both to the deed itself and to its legal and legal/religious penalty (Tikva Frymer-Kensky, "Babylonian Words for Sin and Penalty," unpublished Yale University thesis, 1966). See also K. van der Toorn, *Sin and Sanction in Israel and Mesopotamia: A Comparative Study,* Studia Semitica Neerlandica. Van Gorcum, the Netherlands, 1985.

26. 1 Kings 8:34–35: "Should the heavens be shut up and there be no rain, because they have sinned against you, and then they pray toward this place and acknowledge your name and repent of their sins, when you answer them, O hear in heaven and pardon the sin of your servants, our people Israel, after you have shown them the proper way in which they are to walk; and send down rain upon the land which You gave to Your people as their heritage.

27. Psalms 4, 65, 67, 84, and 85 contain prayers for rain. Psalms 65 and 67 mention rain explicitly. The other psalms are prayers for God's "good" or "bounty" (*ṭôb*). Mitchell Dahood has argued persuasively that this was a term for rain (Psalms I, Anchor, Doubleday, 1971, 25f, and *Biblica* 45 [1964]: 411). The context in Ps. 85:13, "for his part God will give the 'good' and our land will yield its produce" certainly indicates rain.

28. In Amos, rains have not come because the people continue to defraud the poor and needy (Amos 4). The reasons given for God's displeasure may vary: to Hosea, it is "because there is no honesty and no goodness and no obedience to God in the land . . . crime follows upon crime" (Hosea 4:1–2); to Jeremiah, "waywardness" (Jer. 3), or rites to other gods (Jer. 7:20); to the postexilic prophet Haggai, the desultoriness towards rebuilding the temple (Hag. 1:10–11), and to Malachi, negligence towards the tithes (Mal. 3:8).

29. From Jeremiah 14:

> *Because of the ground there is dismay*
> *for there has been no rain on the earth.*
> *Though our iniquities testify against us,*
> *act, O lord, for the sake of your name*
> *though our rebellions are many.*
> *and we have sinned against you.*
> . . . .
>
> *We acknowledge our wickedness, O Lord—*
> *the iniquity of our fathers—*
> *for we have sinned against you.*
> *for your name's sake, do not disown us;*
> *do not dishonor your glorious throne.*
> *Remember, do not annul your covenant with us.*
> *Can any of the false gods of the nations give us rain?*
> *Can the skies of themselves give showers?*
> *Only you can, O Lord our God!*
> *So we hope in you,*
> *for only You made all these things.*

30. Jer. 12:4, cf. Hos. 4:3
31. Is. 24:19–23.
32. Jer. 4:23–28.
33. This idea of the reversal of creation is also found in Zephaniah 1:2–3:

> *I will utterly sweep away everything from the face of the earth.*
> *I will sweep away human and beast;*
> *I will sweep away the birds of the air and the fish of the sea. . . .*
> *I will cut off humankind from the face of the earth.*

On this passage, see Michael De Roche, "Zephaniah 1:2–3: The 'sweeping' of Creation," *VT* 30 (1980): 104–109.

34. Gen. 9.
35. It is not surprising that the people of ancient Israel persevered in their search for fertility insurance despite vociferous opposition from the prophets. See discussion, pp. 155–161.
36. Ps. 82:7 "therefore like Adam you will die." For this interpretation of this Psalm, see J. Levenson, *Sinai and Zion: An Entry into the Jewish Bible* (Minneapolis: Winston Press, 1985) 61–62, with earlier literature cited there.
37. The theology of "testing" is sometimes appealing precisely because it does not assume the guilt of the sufferer. Job is right in declaring that he doesn't deserve his sufferings; the readers (ancient and modern) know (from the introduction to the book) that the whole thing is a test of Job's faithfulness. Both Job and Ecclesiastes call the very notion of human causality into doubt.

## CHAPTER 10   *Homo Sapiens*

1. See, on this point, Umberto Cassuto, *From Adam to Noah: A Commentary on Genesis 1-6:8,* English version, (Jerusalem: Magnes 1961) 188–189, (original in Hebrew, 1944); and Yizhak Avishur and Yaakov Klein, in Menahem Haran et al., eds., *Olam Hatanakh:Bereshit,* (Tel-Aviv: Revivim, 1982), 42–43.

2. Gen. 1–2:4
3. Gen. 12.
4. The name Adam is clearly a sound play on "Adamah," earth. Phyllis Trible suggests translating Adam as "earth creature" ("from the earth"). See P. Trible, *God and the Rhetoric of Sexuality* (Philadelphia: Fortress Press, 1978), 77. In oral communications, Trible also suggests "human from the humus," or "soul from the soil" to capture the flavor of the original. Similar translations are suggested by Carol Meyers, "earthling of clods from the earth" or "human from clods of the humus." Meyers points out that the English "human" is itself derived from a theoret-

ical Indo-European root *ghum* "earth, ground," from which comes the Latin, *humus* (earth) and the Old English, *guma* (man). Meyers suggests that this wordplay reveals that essence of human life is its organic connection to the earth, see C. Meyers, *Discovering Eve: Ancient Israelite Women in Context,* (New York: Oxford University Press, 1988), 81–82. Plöger emphasizes that the earth here is *ādāmâ,* the humus that can be cultivated and support life, see J. G. Plöger, "adhamah" *Theological Dictionary of the Old Testament,* vol. 1 (Grand Rapids, Mich. Eerdmans, 1974), 88–98. Westermann suggests that the wordplay comes from the basic relationship between soil and person that characterizes agricultural life, see Claus Westermann, *Genesis 1–11: A Commentary,* John Scullion S. J., trans., (Minneapolis: Augsburg Publishing House, 1984), 199.

5. For the translation of *ʿezer kĕnegdô* as "companion corresponding to it," see Trible, *God and the Rhetoric of Sexuality,* 88–90. Since Trible's original article, "Depatriarchalizing in Biblical Interpretation," *JAAR* 41 (1973): 30–48, most modern commentators have accepted Trible's interpretation of this text. See, for example, Mieke Bal, "Sexuality, Sin and Sorrow: The Emergence of Female Character [A Reading of Genesis 2–3]" in *The Female Body in Western Culture* Susan Rubin Suleiman, ed. (Cambridge: Harvard University Press, 1986), 317–338. Susan Lanser raises the objection from a speech-act perspective that the text must be relying on the reader to supply cultural assumptions; see Susan Lanser, "(Feminist) Criticism in the Garden: Inferring Genesis 2–3," in *Speech Act Theory and Biblical Criticism,* Hugh C. White, ed., *Semeia* 41, SBL (1988): 67–134. However, Lanser seems to assume that the biblical reader is expected to bring to the text the same androcentric assumptions as Western readers do. Despite the Bible's undoubted androcentrism, the attitude in the Bible to gender relations is quite different (see chapter 11). Most recently, David Clines has argued that the act of helping always implies subordination to another's plan rather than being an equal of a companion. Clines goes back to the Augustinian idea that Eve is to be a helper in procreation, see David Clines: "What Does Eve Do to Help? and Other Readerly Questions to the Old Testament," *JSOT* suppl. ser. 94 (1990) 25–48. However, Clines's remarks are unconvincing, and seem to be mainly for the purpose of expressing a willingness to jettison biblical ideas when they no longer seem palatable.

6. J. Heimpel, "Apoxysmata: Vorarbeiten auf einer Religionsgeschichte und Theologie des Alten Testaments," BZAW 81 (1961): 198–229, expresses doubt that God could really have intended for the animals to be true companions, but as Westermann points out, the text suggests this expectation.

7. Gen. 2:20.

8. For a recapitulation of the many arguments about "knowledge of good and evil," see C. Westermann, *Genesis 1–11,* 241–248. Modern consensus is that the sense is holistic: "knowledge of good and bad (things)" = knowledge of all. See the detailed discussion in Howard N. Wallace, *The Eden Narrative,* HSM 32, (Atlanta: Scholars Press, 1985): 115–132.

9. Gen. 3:7.

10. As noted by Susan Niditch, *Chaos to Cosmos: Studies in Biblical Patterns of Creation* (Chico, Calif.: Scholars Press, 1985) the world as created in Genesis 2 is, in terms of human social structure, a sort of pre-reality. The Garden story is a tale of emergence which relates how humans reached their present state, how reality came about (Niditch, *Chaos to Cosmos,* 25–37). The Tower of Babel, which ends this cycle, is also such a tale of emergence. It is worth noting that the apocryphal Book of Enoch, Chapter 1, relates the Adam and Eve story as a tale of the acquisition of civilization: evil first comes in the elaboration of the "watcher" tale of the angels marrying human women (Book of Enoch, chapter 6f). Philip R. Davies also notes that the tale is about an acquisition of a divine quality of knowledge, see Philip R. Davies, "Sons of Cain," in *A Word in Season: Essays in Honor of William McKane.* James D. Martin and Philip R. Davies, eds., JSOT suppl. ser. 42, (1986), 35–36.

11. Chaim Luzzato, one of the traditional Jewish commentators, makes the suggestion that humankind was "set up" by God; that God knew that they would disobey and start the ball rolling. This would make the story similar to the tale of "beans in the nose," in which the mother warns her children not to put beans up their nose. Though this is not something they would have thought of themselves, the prohibition irresistibly tempts them. In this reading of the text, God intended for humans to become civilized, but wished them to take their own initiative. In either case, humans act to acquire culture, and take responsibility for it.It is worth noting that this changed, as did so much else, in the Hellenistic period. Ben Sira specifically states that God gave humans knowledge of good and evil (17:7). The book of Enoch attributes the arts of civilization to the watchers (section 6f). For further on the Hellenistic transformation of biblical traditions, see chapter 19.

12. Human reality is far from Edenic in many respects, and God spells out the implications of this transformation, the differences between the human world they are entering and the life of the animals. These are the "curses" of Genesis 3: a depiction of human life as we and ancient Israel knew it. Humans have to work hard; they labor in the production of food and they labor in the production of children. Humans leave the garden, they enter stratified society (with the husband dominant over the wife), and they enter the world of work. For an understanding of these curses as descriptive rather than prescriptive, see Carol Meyers, *Discovering Eve: Ancient Israelite Women in Context* (New York: Oxford University Press, 1988), 86–121. Meyers associates these oracles with the particular condition of premonarchic Israel, with its need for intensive agricultural labor and a population of large families to do it. Meyers, however, makes a distinction between God's statements (in poetry) and the prose context that they are in, and believes that the prose narrative is seeing these as punishment. I believe that the prose narrative, which deals with the evolution of human life, also provides a description of reality rather than a divine judgment.

13. Isaac Kikawada and Arthur Quinn explain the garment of skins as God exchanging the clothes of tillers (fig leaves) for the clothes of herders; they see leaving the garden as an abandonment of agricultural life for nomadism. See I. Kikawada and A. Quinn, *Before Abraham Was: The Unity of Genesis 1–11* (Nashville, Tenn.: Abingdon, 1985), 68. However, God's speech to Adam does not tell him to abandon horticulture: on the contrary, it describes the difficult agricultural life with which the settlers were familiar.

14. The literature on "original sin" is vast. For a preliminary bibliography on modern biblicists' discussion of this sin, see Westermann, *Genesis 1–11*, 256.

15. The Book of Enoch, for example, spends almost no time on Genesis 2–3 and goes directly to its elaboration of Genesis 6:1–4 (the "watcher" story) which it presents as the origin of evil (En. 6:1–5, 7:1–6, 15:2–16:1). The book of Jubilees also treats sin as a result of these "angel marriages." (Jub. 5:1–6; 10:1,5–9; 11: ). See Bruce J. Malina, "Some Observations on the Origin of Sin in Judaism and St. Paul," *CBQ* 31 (1969): 18–34; and Bernard Prusak, "Woman: Seductive Siren and Source of Sin? Pseudepigraphical Myth and Christian Origins," in *Religion and Sexism: Images of woman in the Jewish and Christian Traditions,* Rosemary Radford Reuther, ed. (New York: Simon and Schuster, 1974), 89–116.

16. In this period, the emphasis is on the transgression of Adam (2 Bar 54:15–19, 56:6, 17:3, 2 Esdras (4 Ezra)4:30, 17:116–21, Midrash Bamidbar Rabbah 13; 2 Baruch 17:2–3).

17. Books of Adam and Eve, 3:1–3, 5:3; 1 Tim. 2:11–15; Targum Pseudo-Jonathan Gen 3:19. For details see Malina, "Some observations . . ."

18. The earliest attribution of sin to Eve is commonly held to be The Wisdom of Ben Sira 25:24, "in a woman was sin's beginning: on her account we all die," Patrick Skehan, trans., *Anchor Bible* (New York: Doubleday, 1987), 39. Recently, Jack Levison has argued that Ben Sira does not read Genesis 3 as a story of the "fall" and that this verse refers to wives and husbands; see J. Levison, "Is Eve to Blame? A Contextual Analysis of Sirach 25:24" *CBQ* 47 (1985): 617–623. His view is rejected by Alexander Dillela, *The Wisdom of Ben Sirach, Anchor Bible,* 34, who admits that the context is one of wives, but sees an allusion to the Genesis story in v. 26, "cut her away from your flesh." See also Warren Trenchard, *Ben Sira's View of Women: A Literary Analysis,* Brown Judaic Studies 38, (Chico, Calif.: Scholars Press, 1982), 81–92, where Trenchard claims that Ben Sirach deliberately associates the bad wife with Eve as the origin of Evil. In the time of Ben Sira, sin was more commonly believed to come from the fallen angels and their progeny (see note 10). For the later theological approach to Eve as temptress, see Jean M. Higgins, "The Myth of Eve: The Temptress," *JAAR* 44 (1976): 639–647. More recently, this view of Eve has begun to change. Mary Daley pointed out that this very story is patriarchy's own fall, "the primordial lie" in which women have been the scapegoats. See Mary Daley, "Exorcising Evil from Eve: The Fall into Freedom," in Daley, *Beyond God the Father: Towards a Philosophy of Women's Liberation* (Boston: Beacon Press, 1973) 44–68. Daley assumes that the Eve-temptress-sin interpretation of the text is the original meaning, though she sees "intimations (not consciously intended) of a dreaded future in which women search for knowledge and then share it." Phyllis Trible's careful analysis of the biblical text shows that the woman is never cursed, never singled out for blame more than the man, and both are held to have disobeyed. See Phyllis Trible, *God and the Rhetoric of Sexuality* (Minneapolis: Fortress 1978), 105–143. It is becoming increasingly clear that the traditional Western interpretation of this story is not reflective of the sense of the Hebrew text, that it became prevalent early in the common era, and that it should be seen as reflective of the ideology of that time and not of biblical ideas.

19. For Origen, see *Contra Celsum IV.* The myth of Pandora is best known from the version

presented by Hesiod, *Works and Days,* 57–101 and *Theogony,* 570–590. The uses of the myth in Western literature and art have been traced by Dora and Erwin Panofsky, *Pandora's Box: The Changing Aspects of a Mythical Symbol* (New York: Harper Torchbook, 1965). For the adventures of Eve and Eve-Pandora in Western literature, see J. A. Phillips, *Eve: The History of An Idea* (New York: Harper and Row, 1984; Elaine Pagels, *Adam and Eve and the Serpent* (New York: Random House, 1988), and Margaret R. Miles, *Carnal Knowing: Female Nakedness and Religious Meaning in the Christian West* (Boston: Beacon Press, 1989), 85–116. For Rabbinic use of this motif, see Samuel Lachs, "The Pandora-Eve Motif in Rabbinic Literature," *Harvard Theological Review* 67(1974): 341–345.

20. For the myth of Prometheus, see Hesiod, *Works and Days,* 42f., and the Prometheus trilogy by Aeschylus. Jean-Paul Audet also sees the Prometheus story, particularly in Aeschylus, as a tale of the origin of culture and notes some similarity of function to Genesis. He, however, concentrates on the introduction of smithing under Tubalcain and remarks on the fact that the Bible does not seem to believe in "secrets of nature." He does not note the similarity to the Eve story, when the first spark of cultural knowledge was indeed stolen. See Jean-Paul Audet, "La revanche de prométhée ou le drame de la religion et de la culture," *RB* 63 (1966): 5–29.

21. Prometheus suffers in Aeschylus' version, *Prometheus Bound.* See the translation by Herbert Weirsmyth, *Aeschylus,* Loeb Classics (Cambridge: Harvard University Press, 1922), vol. 1, 214–315. See esp. Prometheus' speech, 224–27, lines 88–112.

22. See discussion, chapter 4. This is somewhat foreign to us in the West, because (as discussed in chapter 19) the Greeks attributed culture to the male, assigning nature to the female.

23. Lines 20–25. The text has been edited by Bendt Alster and Herman Vanstiphout, "Lahar and Ashnan: Presentation and Analysis of a Sumerian Disputation," *Acta Sumerologica* 9 (1987): 1–44.

24. Thorkild Jacobsen, *The Sumerian King List* (Chicago: University of Chicago Press, 1939).

25. For a discussion of the me's, see Gertrude Farber-Flügge, *Der Mythos "Inanna und Enki" unter besonderer Berücksichtigung der Liste der 'me',* Studia Pohl 10 (Rome: Biblical Institute Press, 1973).

26. See Erica Reiner, "The Etiological Myth of the 'Seven Sages,'" *Or.* 30 (1961): 1–11; and Benjamin Foster, "Wisdom and the Gods in Ancient Mesopotamia," *Or.* 43 (1974): 344–354.

27. See G. Castellino, "Les origines de la civilisation selon les textes bibliques et les textes cuneiforms," *Congress Volume 1956, VTS* 4 (Leiden: Brill, 1957), 116–137, and W. G. Lambert, "Destiny and Divine Intervention in Babylon and Israel," *OTS* 17 (1972): 65–72.

28. Text published by S. N. Kramer and I. Bernhardt, *Sumerische literarische Texte aus Nippur,* 5; translated by Kramer in Jean Bottero and Samuel Noah Kramer, *Lorsque les dieux faisaient l'homme: mythologie mesopotamienne* (Paris: Gallinard, 1989), 515–517.

29. The Creation of the Pickaxe (SM, 51–53), translation by Kramer and Bottero, *Lorsque les dieux,* 508–510; text BM 23103, published by E. Sollberger, "The Rulers of Lagash," *JCS* 21 (1969): 279–291. Commentary and translation by Kramer and Bottero, *Lorsque les dieux,* 520–525.

30. There is a line of exegesis starting with K. Budde, *Die Biblische Urgeschichte,* 1883, which holds that Cain's son Enoch, rather than Cain, built the first city (pp. 120f; see also V. Cassuto, *From Adam to Noah,* 229, who stresses the similarity in form between v. 2 and v. 7). This suggestion is accepted by William W. Hallo, "Antediluvian Cities," *JCS* 23 (1970): 57–67, who adds that—in this case—Enoch would have named it after his son, Irad. This would make the city's name reminiscent of Eridu, one of the earliest cities in Sumerian tradition. Robert Wilson, *Genealogy and History in the Biblical World* (New Haven: Yale University Press, 1977), 13–58, points out that the city builder could be expected to be the second on a genealogical list, and to name his city after his son. The assumption of these scholars is that the final Enoch ("and he named it after his son Enoch") is a later error by someone who no longer knew the conventions of Biblical genealogies. Isaac Kikawada and Arthur Quinn make a somewhat different suggestion. Accepting the thesis that the original genealogy had Enoch building the city, they suggest that the biblical author purposely manipulated genealogical conventions in order to have the murderer Cain be the founder of the city. See I. Kikawada and A. Quinn, *Before Abraham Was: The Unity of Genesis 1–11* (Nashville, Tenn.: Abingdon, 1985), 55–56.

31. As C. Westermann points out (*Genesis 1–11,* 327), the attribution of the founding of a

city to Cain means that cities were considered part of sedentary civilization, the basis of which was agriculture, and that Israel believed that this happened long before the rise of Israel.

32. See, in particular, Gerhard Wallis, "Die Stadt in den Überlieferungen der Genesis," *ZAW* 78 (1966): 133–139. A somewhat different emphasis is given by Gevaryahu in response to Wallis' paper—Gevaryahu holds that the issue here is a small fortified city and that the building of the city was an amelioration of Cain's wandering punishment. See Hayyim Gevaryahu, "The Punishment of Cain and the City that He Built," *Beth Mikra* 13/32 (1968), 27–36 (in Hebrew).

33. The negative valuation of cities is particularly stressed by Kikawada and Quinn, *Before Abraham Was,* who see an antiurban bias in Genesis.

34. Genesis 4:17–26.

35. Music, smithing, and pastoralism are often related. As C. Westerman points out (*Genesis 1–11,* 324), instrumental music and metallurgy are part of the life of a nomad. Westermann distinguishes between the children of Ada, who were cattle breeders and musicians, and the Children of Zillah, who were smiths, workers of metal, singers. N. Sarna, *JPS Torah: Genesis* (Philadelphia: Jewish Publication Society, 1989), 35–37, points to the rock tomb of Khnumhotep at Ben Hasan (160 miles south of Cairo), ca. 1900 B.C.E.: the relief shows a caravan of Asiatics, among whose baggage is livestock, lyre, and bellows.

36. Abel already tended sheep, but Jabal is the father of *yôšēb ôhel ûmiqneh.* The word *miqneh* means "livestock," and Jabal is the ancestor of those who trade in livestock. Opinion is divided as to whether these are primarily wandering dealers (so J. F. A. Sawyer, "Cain and Hephaestus," *Abr-Nahrain* 24 (1986): 155–166), or those who settle in the outskirts of a city and take care of the city's herds (so Wallis, "Die Stadt").

37. The term used is *ltš kl ḥrš nḥšt wbrzl.* Sawyer points out that the word *ltš* means "to sharpen, or burnish." Tubal-Cain is either the inventor of the new technique of sharpening (iron) or of the making of sharp instruments like weapons of war. The rest of the phrase extends Tubal-Cain's activity to all metalworking. It is worth noting that both parts of this compound name mean "smith."

38. So C. Westerman, *Genesis 1–11,* 333, who remarks that progress in technology, like metallurgy, facilitates life in community. On the other hand, J. Maxwell Miller is struck by the discontinuity between Cain the farmer and Cain the ancestor of civilized arts, and suggests that there were originally two Cain stories, with these later geneological notes belonging to an eponymous hero of the Kenite metal workers. See J. Maxwell Miller, "The Descendants of Cain: Notes on Genesis 4," *ZAW* 86 (1974): 164–173.

39. The most extensive presentation of the metallurgical side to the Cain story is by John F. A. Sawyer, "Cain and Hephaestus: Possible Relics of Metalworking Traditions in Genesis 4," *Abr-Nahrain* 24 (1986): 155–166. Sawyer remarks on the special position of metalworkers in ancient societies, who were often the objects of envy and fear, and had to be specially protected. Both because of the violence of the activity of smithing and the violence of the warfare that it facilitates, smiths are often the subject of violent emotions. Often of foreign stock, they are held to have brought violence into the world. Sawyer further points to the Edomite connections of the names Ada and Sillah, and to the historical fact that coppermining in the Arabah, which had begun in the fourth millennium, came to an end at the end of the Late Bronze Age. He believes that there were Edomite traditions about Cain and his descendants that related the story of smithing, its antagonisms, and the forced wandering when the copper mines closed. Ultimately, these were incorporated into the Bible.

40. The strongest modern proponents of the anti-urban theory are I. Kikawada and A. Quinn, *Before Abraham Was.* Early postbiblical and rabbinic interpretation also depicted these inventions as negatives, and the culture heros are regarded as having used their tools in violent fashion. Fraade points out that this conforms to the "cultural primitivism" of that time, found also in Greek and Latin authors, who held that inventions encourage greed, hubris, and violence and turn men away from a life of natural harmony. See discussion in Steven D. Fraade, *Enosh and His Generation: Pre-Israelite Hero and History in Postbiblical Interpretation* (Chico, Calif.: Scholars Press, 1984), 195–227, with extensive documentation.

41. These names are used interchangeably in scholarly literature, often to confusing effect. The church father Eusebius, in his *Preparation for the Gospel,* records fragments of ancient authors. Most prominent is Philo of Byblos, a Hellenistic author. Philo himself claims that he is merely translating a "Phoenician History" written in Phoenician by an ancient writer, Sanchunya-

ton. Sanchunyaton in turn relates that he derives his history from documents that he found which were written by Tauutos, the inventor of writing. Correspondences of Sanchunyaton with known Canaanite literature indicates that Philo may indeed have had a Phoenician source. It is equally clear that the work was shaped by Philo and reflects many Hellenistic ideas. For details see Albert I. Baumgarten, *The Phoenician History of Philo of Byblos: A Commentary* (Leiden: Brill, 1981), and Howard W. Attridge and Robert A. Oden, Jr., *Philo of Byblos: The Phoenician History: Introduction, Critical Text, Translation, Notes.* CBQ monograph ser. 9 (Catholic Biblical Association, 1981).

42. For discussion, see A. I. Baumgarten, *The Phoenician History of Philo of Byblos,* 140–179.

43. Later religious traditions have disagreed as to whether Enosh invented true religious worship or idolatry. See the discussion of these issues in S. D. Fraade, *Enosh and His Generation.*

44. Gen. 3:22.

45. For discussion of this chapter see C. Westermann, *Genesis 1–11,* 531–557, with copious bibliography listed there; and Nahum Sarna, *Understanding Genesis* (New York: Schocken Books, 1970), 63–77.

46. For the tower as ziggurat, see A. Parrot, "Ziggurats et Tour de Babel," *RB* 57 (1950): 449–454; and Sarna, *Understanding Genesis.*

47. Gen. 11:6.

48. On biblical and Near Eastern legal connections, see note 3 in chapter 8.

49. See Tikva Frymer-Kensky, "The Atrahasis Epic and Its Significance for our Understanding of Genesis 1–9," *BA,* 40 (1977): 147–154.

50. Ex. 31:2–4. See also Ex. 35:30–31,34; 36:1,4,8; and, similarly, for Aaron's garments, Exod. 28:3.

51. The punishment is *kārēt,* a divine sanction in which God acts to extirpate the offender's heritage. See Tikva Frymer-Kensky, "Pollution, Purification and Purgation in Biblical Israel" in *The Word of the Lord Shall Go Forth: Essays in Honor of David Noel Freedman in Celebration of his Sixtieth Birthday,* Carol Meyers and Michael O'Connor, eds. (Winona Lake, Ind.: Eisenbrauns, 1983), 399–414, and Donald Wold, "The Kareth Penalty in P: Rationale and Cases," *Society of Biblical Literature 1979 Seminar Papers,* 1, (Missoula, Mont.: Scholars Press, 1979), 1–46. There is a further type of knowledge which belongs wholly to the divine realm and should be left alone. The Bible prohibits gaining esoteric knowledge by consulting mediums or birds and by engaging in other mantic practices. The Bible does not deny that divination *works.* Instead, it prohibits Israel from using such means. Cosmic knowledge is the provenience of the divine. God reveals it only at God's will, and only through the channels that God reveals and controls: throwing lots, (as in the division of the land and the choosing of Saul); the *'ûrîm wětûmmîm,* Israel's priestly divinatory mechanism; and approved Prophecy.

52. Occasionally, kings would assert their right to supervise the temple, and would claim that the priests misspent the money they collected. But even this was not presented as the assertion of God's direction.

53. Gen. 41:25.

54. Gen. 41:32.

55. For more on learning see John Gammie and Leo Purdue, eds., *The Sage in Ancient Israel and the Ancient Near East* (Winona Lake, Ind.: Eisenbrauns, 1990).

56. The book of Job makes a particular point of the fact that humans do not really know what goes on in the universe that they cannot see (Job 11:7–8; 15:7–8; 28:12–21; and ch. 38–39). There are things people cannot see and do not know, and this makes their cultural knowledge puny.

57. See discussions in chapters 14 and 16.

CHAPTER 11    Gender and Its Image: Women in the Bible

1. These include the matriarchs Sarah, Rebekkah, Rachel, Leah, the prophetesses Miriam and Deborah, the villainesses Delilah and Jezebel, and Hannah, Bathsheba, Ruth, Naomi, and Esther.

2. It is an honor and a responsibility to continue to mention those whose names have come down to us, and I remember Hagar, Bilhah, Zilpah, Dinah, Tamar—the daughter-in-law of Judah,

Shifrah, Puah, Zipporah, Achsah, Jael, Penina, Michal, Merab, Abigail, Rizpah, Tamar—the daughter of David, Abishag, Maacah, Athaliah, Jehosheba, Huldah, Noiada, Vashti, and Zeresh.

3. By the names of their fathers: the daughter of Jephthah, the daughters of Lot, the daughter of Pharaoh, the daughters of Zelophehad, the daughter-in-law of Eli. By the name of their husbands: the wife of Lot, the wife of Potiphar, the wife of Manoah, the wife of Samson, the wife of Jeroboam. By the names of their sons: the mother of Moses in Exodus 2 (elsewhere, she is identified as Jachebed), the mother of Sisera, the mother of Micah, the nursemaid of Mephibosheth.

4. Such are the concubine in Gibeah, the wife of the man of Bahurim, the necromancer of Endor, the wise women of Abel and Tekoa, the queen of Sheba, the prostitutes before Solomon, the great woman of Shunem, the widow of a prophetic disciple, the widow at Zarephath. Possibly in this category are the capable wife ("Woman of Valor") and the "other" woman of the Book of Proverbs and the bride in the Song of Songs. These three, however, are more likely symbolic prototypes than actual people.

5. Uncovering biblical thought is always a multi-layered process. Biblical ideas are not laid out systematically, and often not explicitly. The reader who wishes to abstract order from these texts is engaged in a kind of "search and combine" mission to identify and unite elements of biblical theology and world view. The first step has to be an understanding of ideas in context. Each individual biblical text must be studied and analyzed by itself, using all available tools of philological and literary analysis. Only afterwards can the text be "deconstructed" so that units and ideas can be combined with ideas from other texts. Without the first close reading of the biblical texts, we run the risk of misunderstanding biblical ideas and of building—without control—structures to suit our own imagination.

6. Before one can compare stories of such diverse origin, several preliminary studies must be taken. The first involves taking each story individually, and analyzing it for the information it contains, for its historicity, and for its literary nature and form. Next, this sizable corpus of material needs to be read by time of composition and by genre, for it is possible that different people, schools, or periods during the millennium in which the Bible was written had different ideas about what women were like. This is not the place to present the analytical charts that result from such preliminary studies, but the analysis clearly reveals that one is justified in talking about a common pre-exilic sense of gender. For post-exilic changes, see Chapters 16 and 19.

7. See, on this question, Meir Sternberg, *The Poetics of Biblical Narrative: Ideological Literature and the Drama of Reading,* (Bloomington: Indiana University Press, 1985).

8. Sometimes these narratives concentrate on women because of their symbolic value as representatives of Israel or as vulnerable or marginal figures through whose treatment one can detect the state of the nation as a whole. See D. L. Christensen, "Huldah and the Men of Anathoth," *Society of Biblical Literature 1984 Seminar Papers* (Chico, Calif: Scholars Press, 1984), 399–404; Michael O'Connor, "The Women in the Book of Judges," *HAR* 10: 277–293; and M. O'Connor, "The Necromancer's Dinner," forthcoming. According to Esther Fuchs, these stories are part of a "sexual politics" in which the culture, purposely and deceptively, portrays women in a certain light in order to perpetuate their subordination; (E. Fuchs, "Who Is Hiding the Truth? Deceptive Women and Biblical Androcentrism," in *Feminist Perspectives on Biblical Scholarship.* SBL centennial publications, Adela Collins, ed. (Chico, Calif.: Scholars Press, 1985) 137–144. I am not convinced that the authors of the tales could stand outside their own culture and distinguish their own perception of women from the ideas that they wanted to convey. For more general studies of how narratives about women are expressions of male ideas, see Kate Millet, *Sexual Politics* (New York: Avon, 1971), 3–30; Simone de Beauvoir, *The Second Sex* (New York: Bantam, 1961), 224–300; H. R. Hays, *The Dangerous Sex: The Myth of Feminine Evil* (New York: Putnam, 1964).

9. See T. Frymer, *The Judicial Ordeal in the Ancient Near East* (Malibu, Calif.: Undena Publications, forthcoming); and Raymond Westbrook, "Biblical and Cuneiform Law Codes," *RB* 93 (1986): 52–69.

10. For a short summary of the laws relating to women see Phyllis Trible, "Woman in the O.T.," *Interpreter's Dictionary of the Bible,* suppl. vol. (Nashville: Abingdon, 1976), 961–966; and Tikva Frymer-Kensky, "Women," *Harper's Bible Dictionary* (New York: Harper, 1985) 1138–1141.

11. Dent. 11:28–29.

12. In cases of false accusation, we might normally expect the accuser to be punished with the same penalty that the accused would have accrued if convicted.

13. Num. 5:11–31. See Frymer-Kensky, "The Strange Case of the Suspected Sotah," *VT* 34 (1984): 11–26.

14. Num. 30:5–18.

15. Lev. 27:3–4.

16. See Michelle Zimbalist Rosaldo, "Women, Culture and Society: A Theoretical Overview," in *Women, Culture and Society,* Michelle Rosaldo and Louise Lamphere, eds. (Stanford: Stanford University Press, 1974) 17–42; Sherry Ortner and Harriet Whitehead, eds., *Sexual Meanings: The Cultural Construction of Gender and Sexuality,* (Cambridge: Cambridge University Press, 1981), esp. 1–29; Jill Dubisch, introduction to Jill Dubisch, ed., *Gender and Power in Rural Greece,* (Princeton: Princeton University Press, 1986) 3–41; and Linda J. Nicholson, *Gender and History: The Limits of Social Theory in the Age of the Family,* (New York: Columbia University Press, 1986), 69–104, 216–220.

17. See Carol Meyers, *Discovering Eve: Ancient Israelite Women in Context,* (New York: Oxford University Press, 1988), 24–46. For an opposing view of the usefulness of the term "patriarchy," see Judith M. Bennett, "Feminism and History," *Gender and History* 1 (1989): 251–272.

18. In the early days in Israel, in the period of settlement, social units were smaller, and there was less distinction between public and private. It is quite likely that in this early setting, gender divisions were not as important as they became later. On this, see Carol Meyers, *Discovering Eve.*

19. This is a portrait of biblical, not ancient Israelite, women. It would be interesting to know what the women of ancient Israel were like, but there is not enough information to determine this. It is awkward to keep saying "woman are portrayed as" or "women were believed to be" but some such sentiment should always be understood, for all our evidence is literary and demonstrates historical social reality only as it was understood and interpreted by the ancient authors.

20. See discussion, pp. 97–98.

21. 1 Kings 14:1–18; 2 Kings 4:8. Both women had husbands, yet in both cases, it is the woman who undertook the journey. Jeroboam sent his wife to Ahijah, but the Shunnemite did not even tell her husband the nature of her mission, saying only "shalom" ("it's okay") when he asked her why she was going to Elijah.

22. 2 Sam. 14.

23. 1 Kings 11:1–13. This story shows how the role of protector may impel women onto the arena of history. Similarly, when the danger to their household comes from external enemies, women negotiate with these enemies or fight against them. Abigail ran to dissuade David from destroying her household (1 Sam. 25); Deborah rallied the troops of Israel against the Canaanites and Jael killed the retreating Canaanite general (Judg. 4–5); a woman of Thebez saved her town by dropping a millstone on the besieging Abimelech's head (Judg. 9); and the Wise Woman of Abel-Maacah appeared on the ramparts of her city to implore Joab to lift his siege, describing herself as "one of those who seek the welfare of the faithful in Israel" (1 Sam. 20:15–22).

24. Prov. 31:14–15.

25. 1 Kings 17:8–24; 2 Kings 4:1–7.

26. Gen. 22. For a portrayal of the role of mothers, see J. Cheryl Exum, "'Mother in Israel': A Familiar Figure Reconsidered," in *Feminist Interpretation of the Bible,* Letty Russell, ed. (Philadelphia: Westminster, 1985), 73–85. See also Esther Fuchs, "The Literary Characterization of Mothers and Sexual Politics in the Hebrew Bible," in *Feminist Perspectives on Biblical Scholarship,* Adela Yarbro Collins, ed., SBL centennial publications (1985), 117–136.

27. 1 Kings 11–31.

28. 2 Sam. 21:7–14. It is possible that the reason that they were impaled or spread out was to placate God into ending the drought. Even if this were so, the drought could not be expected to end until the following rainy season six months later, and there was no compelling reason, other than devotion, for Rizpah to remain with them.

29. Gen. 31:14–16.

30. 1 Sam. 19:11–17.

31. Gen. 29:18; 1 Sam. 18.

32. In order to save Moses, Zipporah was prepared to stand up even to God (Exod. 4:24–26).

33. Gen. 30:1; 1 Sam. 1:8.

34. According to Fuchs, the stories of Barren Wives are purposely included in order to promote the institution of motherhood. See Esther Fuchs, "The Literary Characterization of Mothers and Sexual Politics in the Hebrew Bible," in *Feminist Perspectives,* 117–36. Fuchs holds that moth-

erhood in Israel is purely a patriarchal institution and that only wives are portrayed as wanting children. However, the story of the prostitutes indicates that the Bible considered children a strong motivating force for all women.

35. 1 Kings 3:16–28.

36. For the custom of surrogate motherhood in the ancient Near East, see Tikva Frymer-Kensky, "Near Eastern Law and the Patriarchal Family," BA 44 (1981): 209–214.

37. The Levirate is known also from the Middle Assyrian Laws, law A30.

38. It has been suggested that the veil was the mark of a prostitute. This doesn't conform to what we know of Near Eastern custom. In fact, the Assyrian laws specifically forbade prostitutes from wearing a veil, which respectable married women did wear. In the Bible, Rebekkah, who was certainly not a prostitute, veiled herself as she came within sight of Isaac (whom she was coming to marry), and Jacob's bride must have been similarly veiled, for otherwise how could he not know that he was marrying Leah and not Rachel? The purpose of the veil in the Tamar story was not to identify her as a prostitute, but to hide her identity so that Judah would not recognize her.

39. On this story see J. A. Emerton, "Judah and Tamar," VT 29 (1979): 403–415; J. Emerton, "Some Problems in Genesis 38," VT 25 (1975): 338–361; J. Emerton, "An Examination of a Recent Structuralist Interpretation of Genesis 38," VT 26 (1966): 79–98; Eryl W. Davies, "Inheritance Rights and the Hebrew Levirate Marriage," VT 31 (1981): 138–144, 257–268; Susan Niditch, "The Wronged Woman Righted: An Analysis of Genesis 38, HTR 72 (1979): 143–148; Johanna Bos, "Out of the Shadows: Genesis 38; Judges 4:17–22, Ruth 3," Semeia 42 (1988): 37–67; Phyllis Bird, "The Harlot as Heroine: Narrative Art and Social Presupposition in Three Old Testament Texts," Semeia 46 (1989): 119–139.

40. After the split with Laban, Jacob, in effect, has struck out on his own, and has no more clan. He himself married a girl from his father's kin, as did his father before him, but his own sons seek local women.

41. The sexually aggressive adulteress of the book of Proverbs is called a "foreign" woman. Most scholars today do not believe that the term here refers to a non-Israelite, but rather to one outside the family structure of the young man being cautioned against her. See P. Humbert, "La femme étrangère du livre des proverbes," RES 27 (1937): 49f; and P. Humbert, "Les adjectifs zar et nokri et la femme étrangerè des Proverbes bibliques," Mélanges syriens offerts à R. Dussaud, 1 (Paris: Geuthner, 1939), 259f.

42. Gen. 19:20–38.

43. Much of the discussion started with Nancy Chodorow, The Reproduction of Mothering: Psychoanalysis and the Sociology of Gender (Berkeley: University of California Press, 1978). See the discussion and bibliography in Heather Jon Maroney, "Embracing Motherhood: New Feminist Theory," Canadian Journal of Political and Social Theory 9 (1985): 40–63; and Hester Eisenstein, Contemporary Feminist Thought (London: Unwin, 1984), 69–95.

44. It may be significant that the one childless woman who does not seem to be anxious is the wealthy woman of Shunem. When Elisha asks her what she desires, she asks for nothing, saying "I live among my own people." Not she, but Elisha's servant, Gehazi, informs the prophet that "she has no son and her husband is old" (2 Kings 4:8–16). This woman who is both wealthy and secure among her own kin is less driven to motherhood than the woman whose position is more precarious.

45. See Tikva Frymer-Kensky, "The Atrahasis Epic and its Significance for Our Understanding of Genesis 1–9," BA 40, (1977), 147–165; Carol Meyers, "The Roots of Restriction: Women in Early Israel," BA 41 (1978): 91–103; Carol Meyers, "Procreation, Production and Protection: Male-Female Balance in Early Israel," JAAR 51 (1984), 569–593; and David C. Hopkins, "Life on the Land: The Subsistence Struggles of Early Israel," BA 50 (1987): 179–191; and Carol Meyers, Discovering Eve. See also discussion, pp. 89–91, 97–99.

46. In this way, Abigail acted against her husband's decision not to pay David as well as without her husband's knowledge; the woman of Shunem also acted without her husband's permission. For these stories, see pp. 129–134.

47. Son: binding of Isaac, Gen. 22; daughter: daughter of Jephthah, Judg. 11.

48. The concubine in Gibeah, Judg. 19.

49. Lot and his daughters, Gen. 19; the man in Gibeah, Judg. 19.

50. The affair of Dinah, Gen. 34; the rape of Tamar, daughter of David, 2 Sam. 13.

51. 1 Kings 11:1–13.

52. 1 Kings 15:9–15. See the discussion on the Asherah, chapter 13.

53. 1 Sam. 28.

54. The worship of the queen of heaven is often understood as a women's ritual, for women baked cakes in her image and offered libations and incense to her (Jer. 7:18; 44:15,19). For this interpretation, see Susan Ackerman, "'And the Women Knead Dough': the Worship of the Queen of Heaven in Sixth-Century Judah," in *Gender and Difference in Ancient Israel,* Peggy L. Day, ed. (Philadelphia: Fortress, 1989), 109–124, who characterizes this queen as a syncretism of West Semitic Astarte and East Semitic Ištar. However, there is no reason to assume that this cult attracted mostly women. Jeremiah 7: 18 indicts the whole family: "the children gather wood, the fathers kindle fire and the women knead dough to make cakes for the queen of heaven." Nor was this simply domestic peasant religion, for, according to Jeremiah 44:17 and 21, the kings and princes of Judah also worshiped her.

55. The only case of women banding together is the story of Naomi and her daughter-in-law, Ruth. In part, the book of Ruth is a moral tale of the good that can result when people are kinder to each other than society and convention expect (behavior known as *hesed* ). See Edward Campbell, Jr., *Ruth,* Anchor (New York: Doubleday, 1975).

56. Judg. 5.

57. As we can see from the contrast with the penalties for a recalcitrant son in Deut. 21:18–21. See p. 126.

58. Gen. 1–11.

59. For professions of women see S. D. Goitein, "Women as Inventors of Biblical Genres," *Prooftexts* 8 (1988): 1–33 (orig., in Hebrew, *Iyyunim bamiqra,* 1957); Phyllis Bird, "The Place of Women in the Israelite Cultus," in *Ancient Israelite Religion: Essays in Honor of Frank M. Cross,* Paul D. Hanson, Patrick D. Miller, and S. Dean McBride, eds. (Philadelphia: Fortress, 1987), 397–419. Deborah, the prophet, was also remembered as the poet who wrote the victory song of Deborah, Judg. 5, and Miriam may have written the song of Miriam. According to Harold Bloom, *The Book of J* (New York: Grove Weidenfeld, 1990), the author of J, the earliest Pentateuchal strand, was also a woman, an idea suggested by Richard Friedman, *Who Wrote the Bible?* (Englewood Cliffs, N.J.: Prentice Hall, 1987).

60. For women in Judges, see Joann Hackett, "In the Days of Yael: Reclaiming the History of Women in Ancient Israel," in *Immaculate and Powerful: The Female in Sacred Image and Social Reality,* Clarissa W. Atkinson, Constance Buchanan, and Margaret Miles, eds. (Boston: Beacon, 1985), 15–38; and Michael O'Connor, "Women in the Book of Judges," *HAR* 10 (1987): 277–293.

61. 2 Sam. 20:15–22. There has been some discussion as to whether the two women called "wise" were private women who happened to be clever, or whether there actually was an office of *wise woman* in this early period. A solid discussion of this question can be found in Claudia Camp, "The Wise Women of 2 Samuel: A Role Model for Women in Early Israel," *CBQ* 43 (1981): 14–29. I have not repeated her cogent reasons for concluding, as I do, that this was at least a semi-official office, but have confined myself to mentioning some arguments that she did not present.

62. Joab himself recalled how Abimelech had died when a woman dropped a millstone on his head (2 Sam. 11:8; for the original story, Judg. 9:53). His willingness to parlay despite this knowledge is an indication that the "wise woman" was not simply a clever woman, but that she had come to negotiate as the official representative of the city. The fact that she describes herself as follows, "I am one of those who seek the welfare of the faithful in Israel" (2 Sam. 20:19), is also an indication that "wise woman" refers to official status rather than personal characteristics, for otherwise, her statement is ludicrously immodest.

63. 2 Kings 4.

64. 1 Kings 11–28. In this, she acted like a whole line of mothers of kings' younger sons who maneuvered their sons into kingship. See Zafrira Ben-Barak, "The Queen Consort and the Struggle for Succession to the Throne," in *La Femme dans le Proche-Orient Antique,* Jean-Marie Durand, ed., CRRA 33, Paris 1986 (Paris: Editions Recherche sur les Civilisations, 1987), 33–40.

65. In this latter quest, she was unsuccessful, for Solomon took the request as an indication that Adonijah still had ambitions to the throne and had him killed (1 Kings 2:13–25). David Noel Freedman suggests in a private communication that Bathsheba was very "successful," that she was not a docile or stupid woman and must have known how Solomon would react to Adonijah's request.

66. 2 Kings 3:16–28.

67. 2 Sam. 14.

68. 2 Kings 8:1–6. There is another tale of a woman petitioning. During that same horrible famine, an anonymous woman came before the king to ask for help because another woman had helped her eat her son and would not now give up her own (2 Kings 6:24–30). The king does not even try to settle the dispute. He rends his clothes in mourning, and nothing is said of the fate of the woman. In fact, this is probably not a real occurrence, but the idea of women eating their children is a well-known literary motif used to indicate the extreme deprivation caused by famine in ancient Near Eastern literature. It is told as a story of horror, and as a coming true of the treaty curse that parents would eat their children. The very ghastliness of a woman acting so contrary to the child-devotion expected of women shows the extremely cursed situation of Israel at this time.

69. 1 Sam. 25.

70. Num. 27:1–11.

71. Josh. 15:16–19; Judg. 1:12–15

72. The wife of Jeroboam went to Shiloh to see Ahijah (1 Kings 14:1–19); the great woman of Shunem went to Mount Carmel in search of Elisha and refused to leave until he came in aid of her son (2 Kings 4:18–37). The widow at Zarephath turned to Elijah when her son fell sick (1 Kings 17:8–24); the widow of a disciple asked Elisha's help because a creditor was coming to take her children as slaves (2 Kings 4:1–5).

73. Gen. 16:5.

74. Gen. 16:6.

75. Gen. 27:46.

76. Gen. 30:1.

77. Gen. 30:1–6. Rachel's initial angst-producing plea was just a "softening-up" introduction to her real request. Jacob already had four sons, and did not seem actively to be seeking more: it was Rachel who wanted Bilhah to have a son so that Rachel could experience a form of motherhood. After the baby was born, Rachel showed her eagerness for Bilhah's child: "God has vindicated me; indeed, he has heeded my plea and given me a son."

78. Caleb, the son of Jephunneh, had given his daughter Achsah in marriage to Othniel, the Kenizzite, as a reward for conquering Kiryath-sefer. The ploy worked, and Caleb gave Achsah upper and lower Gulloth ("springs"). See Josh. 15:16–19 and Judg. 1:12–15.

79. 1 Kings 17:8.

80. 2 Kings 4:17–37.

81. Num. 10:11–15.

82. Deut. 1–3. This is not to imply that these are Moses' own words. On the contrary, the tradition presents the argument of male and female characters in the same way.

83. He even lays the guilt for his own failing on them: "because of you the Lord was incensed with me too, and He said: you shall not enter it either" (Deut. 1:37). This, of course, is not the reason we are given in Numbers, where Moses is said to have incensed God by his own action in striking the rock at Meribah (Num. 20:7–13).

84. 1 Sam. 10:19.

85. 1 Sam. 12:9–12.

86. 1 Sam. 12:14,24.

87. Jer. 15:1.

88. For an analysis of this passage as fable, see Jon Levenson, "1 Samuel 25 as Literature and as History," *CBQ* 40 (1978): 11–28.

89. Similar statements are made by other women seeking to persuade men to a course of action. When Rebekkah sought to convince a reluctant Jacob to fool Isaac into giving his blessing to Jacob, he feared that the plan would boomerang: "If my father touches me, I shall appear to him as a trickster and bring upon myself a curse, not a blessing." In response, Rebekkah transferred this risk from Jacob to herself, stating, "your curse, my son, be upon me!" This relieved Jacob's anxieties and persuaded him to act (Gen. 27:34). Similarly, the wise woman of Tekoa told David "may the guilt be upon me and on my ancestral house: your majesty and his throne are guiltless," thereby removing him of the burden of bloodguilt that might fall on him for allowing a murderer to go free (2 Sam. 14:9) Rebekkah and the wise woman are asking the men to do something that might have supernatural repercussions: Isaac might curse Jacob, David might incur bloodguilt. Curse and blood are palpable powers. They cannot simply be annulled, and the women offer themselves as magnets to deflect these powers into themselves.

90. The Masoretic text has, "May God do thus and more to the enemies of David" to avoid

the imprecation of David against himself; the Septuagint does not have this phrase. In the light of what we know of curses that begin "may God do thus and more," it would seem that the Septuagint version is authentic, and that the addition of the phrase "to the enemies of David" was a later attempt to understand how it was that David was not destroyed by the oath that he swore and then did not fulfill.

91. There is, of course, narrative license here, for even though the oath is taken just before Abigail speaks, in reality she would not have been in a position to know about the oath. There is also another kind of poetic language here. The Bible contains no instances of God allowing the curse intended for one person to devolve upon another, and this self-deflection of Abigail, the wise woman of Tekoa, and Rebekkah would probably not have been understood literally. Just as wearing an amulet can be said to deflect the evil eye back to its sender, and the uttering of counter-formulas can return black magic to its pronouncer, so, too, the women's gracious interposing of themselves in the path of the curse could have been taken seriously, even if not fully literally.

92. Exod. 1:19. The word "female animals" is usually translated as an adjective "lively, vigorous." It is hardly likely that the midwives would have defended themselves to Pharaoh by insulting Egyptian women for not being vigorous.

93. A similar validation by a woman is given by the widow of Zarephath, who told Elijah, "Now I know that you are a man of God and that the word of the Lord is truly in your mouth" (1 Kings 17:24).

94. 1 Sam. 25.

95. Num. 27:1–4.

96. See Donald Wold, "The *kareth* Penalty in P: Rationale and Cases," in *Society of Biblical Literature 1979 Seminar Papers,* P. J. Achtemeir, ed. (Missoula, Mont.: Scholars Press, 1979), 1:1–46.

97. For this scene, see J. Hoftijzer, "David and the Tekoite Woman," *VT* 20 (1970): 419–444, with the literature cited there; Claudia Camp, "The Wise Woman of 2 Samuel: A Role Model for Women in Early Israel," *CBQ* 43 (1981): 14–29; and Tikva Frymer-Kensky, "The Wise Woman of Tekoa and the Biblical Art of Persuasion," forthcoming.

98. 2 Sam. 13.

99. 2 Sam. 13:12.

100. She is the only woman to argue her case by appealing to the mercy of the petitioned. It is not a powerful tactic, and is not successful. An appeal for mercy only works with God, the merciful one.

101. 2 Sam. 13:13.

102. Judg. 14,16.

103. The word used to describe the actions of these women, *pattî,* which is sometimes translated "entice," has no sexual connotations. On the contrary, *pattî* is the word used to describe the action of Abner towards King David when he came to "learn your comings and going and find out all that you are planning" (2 Sam. 3:25). It is etymologically related to the word for "fool," and occurs often with words for "speech." The basic sense of the verb is "to persuade," though often with a negative connotation of "to con," somewhat in the sense of "to fast-talk someone," "to talk someone into something." According to Psalm 78:36, Israel conned (*pattî*) God with their speech, while in reality their hearts were inconstant. In Micaiah's vision in 1 Kings 22:20–23, God sent a lying spirit to Ahab to talk him into (*pattî*) going to battle. Such deception by God is also anticipated in Ezekiel 14:9. God's persuasiveness is often expressed by the verb *pattî.* It does not usually involve deception, but it always indicates the art of verbal convincing. Jeremiah complained that God has talked him into being a prophet, and he (Jeremiah) is reviled for it (Jer. 20:7). And Hosea envisions God promising to talk Israel into returning to the desert so that he can re-espouse her there (Hos. 2:16).

104. Judg. 14:17.

105. Delilah is often assumed to have been a Philistine. This assumption makes her a "foreign woman," like Potiphar's wife, the Moabite women in Numbers, and the "other woman" in Proverbs 1–9; and these stories are then read as cautionary tales against the attractions of foreign women. However, the text never tells us that Delilah was a foreigner. The valley of Sorek is only thirteen miles west-southwest of Jerusalem, guarded by Beth Shemesh. This was Danite territory, and was still occupied by Israelites. It was a border area that may not even have been under Philistine control. Even if it had been, the population had not been displaced or deported. Since the text does not mention that Delilah was a Philistine, there is no reason to assume it. Similarly, the "other woman" in Proverbs 1–9 is a woman married to another household rather than one

coming from another people, and the Moabite Ruth is certainly not a dangerous figure. As far as we can tell, there was no blanket condemnation or fear of foreign women until the time of Ezra, and it is a mistake to read these stories with a later generation's eyes.

106. She was offered 5500 shekels of silver, 1100 shekels from each of the five Philistine lords. The shekel is a measure of the weight of silver. Its value remains relatively constant. When we consider that Judas was enticed by only thirty shekels, the enormity of the Philistine offer is clear.

107. Judg. 16:1–17.

108. The book of Proverbs contains statements about women's persistent talk: "The nagging of a wife is like the endless dripping of water" (Prov. 19:13); "An endless dripping on a rainy day and a contentious wife are alike; as soon repress her as repress the wind or declare one's right hand to be oil" (Prov. 27:15–16); and "Dwelling in a corner of a roof is better than a nagging wife in a spacious house" (Prov. 21:9, 25:24); or "It is better to live in the desert than with a contentious, vexatious wife" (Prov. 21:19).

109. The essence of a parable involves a deception—giving the listener the impression that the story he is hearing is true, and only later, after the listener has reacted, informing him that it was, in fact, made up for a purpose. In this way, the prophet Nathan also deceives David. But the woman of Tekoa goes a step further: she not only tells a story about a widow, she dresses and acts out the part. Like all the pretenses of women, it has a parallel in a story about a man, for the anonymous prophet who confronted Ahab did the same (1 Kings 21:38–42).

110. Josh. 2. For further analysis of this story, see Phyllis Bird, "The Harlot as Heroine: Narrative Art and Social Presupposition in Three Old Testament Texts," *Semeia* 46 (1989): 119–139. A similar story is told of the wife of a man in Bahurim, who hid Jonathan and Ahimaaz in a well and told Absalom's servants, who were looking for them, that they had gone on (2 Sam. 17:15–20).

111. 1 Sam. 19:11–17.

112. 1 Sam. 19:11–17.

113. Gen. 27.

114. Esther Fuchs, "Who Is Hiding the Truth? Deceptive Women and Biblical Androcentrism," in *Feminist Perspectives on Biblical Scholarship,* Adela Yarbro Collins, ed., SBL centennial publications (Chico, Calif.: Scholars Press, 1985), 137–144, has a very negative view of these deception stories. She notes that "Woman's deception is acceptable and even recommended when her motives are selfless and when she attempts to promote the cause of man. Yet the ascription of deceptiveness even to the most exalted female role models tarnishes their luminousness." But her claim that the stories about women point to their inherent moral inferiority is based on her negative apperception of deception, and her belief that the Bible presented tales of women's deceitfulness in order to dishonor them.

115. Gen. 12.

116. Gen. 20.

117. Needless to say, source criticism alerts us that there may have been different versions of the same story preserved by different authors. In the compilation of Genesis, however, all three are consciously preserved, thus presenting a thrice-told tale.

118. Gen. 26.

119. The scene between Isaac and Jacob in Genesis 27 is artfully told. Full of righteous indignation as *we* may be (it is hard to tell about the original listeners), we cannot help but note the burlesque qualities of this tragicomic scene as Isaac feels the goat skins and is convinced that they are the hairy hands of Esau.

120. Gen. 29. In case the reader misses the retributive nature of this trick, Laban explains that he substituted Leah because the older had the right to be married before the younger. The one who took his elder brother's place in Isaac's blessing has been tricked into marrying the one who took her younger sister's place at the wedding.

121. Gen. 31. Jacob asks for the spotted and speckled animals as wages for the years that he spent working in Laban's household. Although Laban agrees, he attempts to deceive Jacob by first removing all the speckled and spotted animals from the herd. But Jacob out-tricks Laban: he gets the flock to produce spotted and speckled young by showing them shoots off striped rods as they came to drink and mate.

122. Josh. 9.

123. He declares that he is on a mission for the king, 1 Sam. 21:1–7.

124. 1 Sam. 21:11–16. When David is brought before King Achish of Gath, he saves his

own life by pretending to be a madman, scratching marks on the doors of his gate, and letting his saliva run down his beard.

125. Gen. 18:12–13.

126. 1 Kings 22:19–23.

127. Potiphar's wife not only pursued the slave Joseph, but—after he had already fled—vindictively accused him of attacking her (Gen. 39:7–18). Jezebel had Nathan convicted on the basis of suborned perjury in order to have him executed (1 Kings 21). Men, too, could also be guilty of this. Laban gave Leah to Jacob after he had contracted to give Rachel (Gen. 34). David had Uriah sent to the front line so that he would be killed (2 Sam. 11), and Amnon tricked Tamar into being alone with him by pretending that she bring him food (2 Sam. 13). All these men have power and status, and used lies and deceit to further extend their own wealth or authority. All these maneuvers are clearly condemned by the Biblical narrative.

128. There has been considerable discussion of the issue of deception. See the articles in Cheryl Exum and Johanna W. H. Bos, eds., *Reasoning with the Foxes: Female Wit in a World of Male Power, Semeia* 42 (1988), with citations to earlier literature, and Susan Niditch, *Underdogs and Tricksters* (New York: Harper & Row, 1987). See, also, note 113.

129. Num. 25:1–2.

130. Judg. 4:17–21.

131. For the Yael story, see chiefly, Susan Niditch, "Eroticism and Death in the Tale of Jael," *Gender and Difference in Ancient Israel,* 43–57; Robert Alter, *The Art of Biblical Poetry,* (New York: Basic Books, 1985), 43–48; Mieke Bal, *Murder and Difference: Gender, Genre and Scholarship on Sisera's Death* (Bloomington: Indiana University, 1988), with copious bibliography. Niditch, like Yair Zakovitch ("Sisseras Tod," *ZAW* 93 (1981): 364–74} sees sexual innuendo in the story. However, both are basing their analyses of the poem in Judges 5, rather than the later prose story in Judges 4. It seems that the poem, which is very early, was conscious of eroticism and gender. The prose story, written during the classic period of Israel and under the influence of monotheism, does not emphasize sex.

132. Beauty begins to be seen as a *power* of women only in the postbiblical period, as is discussed on p. 206. The Book of Esther, commonly held to have been written in the early Greek period, is transitional. It shows a Greek awareness of the "battle between the sexes" and has a heroine who gets into a position of potential power through a beauty contest. When she wants to petition Ahasuerus, however, she relies not on her beauty, but on the traditional use of hospitality and food. The power of beauty is fully realized in the apocryphal book of Judith, in which Judith purposely adorns herself in order to make herself attractive enough to bedazzle the enemy general.

133. For recent discussions of gender, see Helen Lambert, "Biology and Equality: A Perspective of Sex Differences," *Signs* 4 (1978); reprinted in Sandra Harding and Jean F. O'Barr, eds., *Sex and Scientific Inquiry* (Chicago: University of Chicago Press, 1987); also Ivan Illich, *Gender* (New York: Pantheon, 1982); Anne Fausto-Sterling, *Myths of Gender: Biological Theories About Women and Men* (New York: Basic Books, 1985); and Beryl Benderley, *The Myth of Two Minds: What Gender Means and Doesn't Mean* (New York: Doubleday, 1987).

134. For this role of woman as symbol for later Israel, see the next chapter; and for Yael, see Susan Niditch, "Eroticism and Death in the Tale of Jael," in *Gender and Difference,* 52. For Esther, see Sidnie Ann White, "Esther: A Feminine Model for Jewish Diaspora," In *Gender and Difference,* 161–177.

CHAPTER 12    The Wanton Wife of God

1. Hosea is an eighth-century prophet. The marital metaphor is developed in the first three chapters of the books of Hosea. These three chapters form a distinct unit within the book. H. L. Ginsberg has suggested that these chapters are, in fact, the work of an even earlier prophet who lived at the time of Elijah. See H. L. Ginsberg, *The Israelian Heritage of Judaism* (New York: Jewish Theological Seminary, 1982), 97. There is a vast literature on Hosea, as a whole, as well as on these three chapters. A bibliography of much of it can be found in Francis I. Andersen and David Noel Freedman, *Hosea, Anchor Bible* (New York: Doubleday, 1980). More recently, see Helgard Balz-Cochois, "Gomer oder die Macht der Astarte," *ET* 42 (1982): 37–65; Drorah Setel, "Prophets and Pornography: Female Sexual Imagery in Hosea," in *Feminist Interpretation of the Bible,* Letty Russel, ed. (Philadelphia, Westminster, 1985), 86–95, H. Ringgren, in *Ancient Israelite Religion: Essays in Honor of Frank M. Cross,* P. D. Hanson, P. D. Miller, and S. D. McBride,

eds. (Philadelphia: Fortress, 1987); Mary Joan Winn Leith, "Verse and Reverse: The Transformation of the Woman, Israel, in Hosea 1–3," in *Gender and Difference*, Peggy Day, ed. (Philadelphia: Fortress, 1989), 95–108; and Renita Weems, "Gomer: Victim of Violence or Victim of Metaphor?," Semeia 47 (1989): 87–104.

2. For this term and the idiom *znh*, see Phyllis Bird, "'To Play the Harlot': An Inquiry into an Old Testament Metaphor," in *Gender and Difference*, 75–94.

3. This phrase has often been taken literally, to refer to sexual practices in a fertility cult. However, the term occurs within the metaphor, and in human terms the infidelity of this wife signifies the turning of Israel to foreign powers (divine or political).

4. W. L. Moran, "The Ancient Near Eastern Background of the Love of God in Deuteronomy," *CBQ* 25 (1963): 77–87.

5. For Deuteronomy, see Deut. 6:5, 10:12, and 11:1.

6. This may be a step further than the political treaties of the ancient Near East, for the language of jealousy has not yet been found in them.

7. See Exod. 34:14–15; Judg. 2:17; Num. 15:39.

8. In Num. 15:4, this "jealousy" is the reaction of a husband who suspects that his wife has committed adultery.

9. Gershon Cohen, "The Song of Songs and the Jewish Religious Mentality," *The Samuel Friedland Lectures 1960–1966* (New York, Jewish Theological Seminary, 1966) notes the language of jealousy-promiscuity, and suggests that the idea of marriage between Israel and God arose by a Midrashic development from the Decalogue's "you shall have no other gods before me." He, however, was unaware of the ancient Near Eastern treaty material, where "love" is already applied to the treaty relationship. Jon Levenson, *Sinai and Zion: An Entry into the Jewish Bible* (Minneapolis: Winston Press, 1985) claims that *qn'* ("jealousy") must have developed from suzerainty treaties, for the overlord is certainly not willing to share the loyalty of the vassal. The language of *qn'*, however, is not known from the Near Eastern treaties.

10. F. Anderson and D. Freedman, *Hosea*, Anchor Bible, attribute the origin of the metaphor to Hosea's biography. However, it seems unlikely that a metaphor drawn solely from one individual's experience would have so influenced first, Jeremiah (who never married), and Ezekiel (who seems to have had a good marriage). The casual mention by the eighth-century Judean prophet Isaiah that Jerusalem has become a "harlot" (Is. 1:21) may indicate that the parallel between Israel and wife is already in use.

11. It is not often enough noted that women have as great an interest in female chastity codes as men, and are often the greatest policers and enforcers of the code. The dishonor of one makes the other women feel more virtuous by contrast, and makes the men prize the virtue of virtuous women even more. See Maureen J. Giovannini, "Female Chastity Codes in the Circum-Mediterranean: Comparative Perspectives," in *Honor and Shame and the Unity of the Mediterranean*, David Gilmore, ed. American Anthropological Association special publications 22 (1987): 61–89.

12. As Phyllis Trible has shown, the original creation was a creation of equals, and hierarchy did not enter until after the expulsion from the garden. The idyllic love match of the Song of Songs alludes to this story and is clearly paradisiac in the sense of nonhierarchical (*God and the Rhetoric of Sexuality*, Philadelphia: Fortress, 1978), 72–165. For a dissenting view on the original creation, see Pamela Milne, "Eve and Adam—Is a Feminist Reading Possible?" *Bible Review* 4 (1988): 12–21, 39.

13. The Middle Assyrian laws, Law 59.

14. Renita Weems, "Gomer: Victim of Violence or Victim of Metaphor?" *Semeia* 47 (1989): 87–104, addresses the question of the viability of this metaphor today, and therefore holds that—in today's context—the metaphor can incite to domestic violence. This is a far different question from asking whether the metaphor functioned as a paradigm in Biblical thought.

15. Deut. 24:1–4.

16. Num. 5:11–21; see Tikva Frymer-Kensky, "The Strange Case of the Suspected Sotah," *VT* 34 (1984): 11–26.

17. Jer. 3:1.

18. Jer. 3:6–11.

19. Hos. 11:9.

20. Exod. 20:5–6; Deut. 5:9–10.

21. He addresses this female by the feminine singular, without the use of a name. His message is one of reproof, as it always is when he addresses the unnamed female, the Whoring Woman.

22. Jer. 2:2; 2:20.

23. Jer. 2:24; 3:2–5; 2:35; 2:37.

24. Jerusalem: Jer.6:6–8; 13:27; 15:5–6; Judah: Jer. 3:6–13.

25. Drorah Setel, "Prophets and Pornography," understands Hosea to be referring to the land itself, and suggests that any personalization of the land as woman automatically involves an objectification of woman as land and is thus by its very essence pornographic. The image of Zion discussed in chapter 15 shows that such a personification can avoid any pornographic connotation. In the case of the wanton wife, the pornography is in the depiction of the activities, rather than in the characterization of God's partner as female.

26. Hos. 2:12; Jer. 13:27.

27. Ezekiel is not the only exilic prophet to talk about the Wanton. Isaiah 57 also accuses her (in a flashback?), and describes foreign sacrifice and idolatry in the old image of the adulteress setting up her couch on a high and lofty hill, perpetually unable to gratify her lust.

28. Ezek. ch. 22, ch. 23.

29. Ezek., ch. 16

30. For the myth of orgy, see Chapter 13.

31. Vocalizing rēʿayik.

32. The reference seems not to be the inhabitants, who would be ʾohăvayik.

33. Jer. 22:22; cf. 30:14.

34. For this view, see Drorah Setel, "Prophets and Pornography," 86–95.

35. Ezek. 16:34.

36. The woman-image attracts other metaphors drawn from male ideas about women. The bloodiness of women, their "pollution" by blood expresses the pollution of this Whoring Woman, upon whose garments is found the lifeblood of the innocent poor (Jer. 2: 33–34): "It is because of your great iniquity that your skirts are bloodied, your limbs befouled" (Jer. 13:22, reading the Hebrew as nēgōʾalû, an image found in Lam. 1:8–9,17). At the time of destruction, the woman stands revealed in her blood-pollution, like a menstruant (Lam. 1:9–9,17). The final agony of the city is as sharp as the pangs of childbirth (Jer. 13:21).

CHAPTER 13    Asherah and Abundance

1. For this phrase and the forms of local worship, see W. L. Halladay, "On Every Lofty Hill and Under Every Leafy Tree," VT 11 (1961): 170–176.

2. See Baruch Halpern, "Brisker Pipes than Poetry: The Development of Israelite Monotheism," in *Judaic Perspectives on Ancient Israel,* Jacob Neusner, Baruch A. Levine, and Ernest R. Frerichs, eds. (Philadelphia: Fortress, 1987) pp. 77–115; and Mark Smith, *The Early History of God* (San Francisco: Harper & Row, 1989).

3. Exod. 16:32–34.

4. Num. 21:8–10; 2 Kings 18:4.

5. 1 Kings 12:28–29.

6. Josh. 4:1–9.

7. See discussion by W. L. Reed, *The Asherah in the Old Testament,* (Fort Worth: Texas Christian University Press, 1949). For the most recent discussions of Asherah, see Saul Olyan, *Asherah and the Cult of Yahweh in Israel,* SBL monograph ser., (Atlanta: Scholars Press, 1988), and Mark Smith, *The Early History of God.*

8. The verb ntʿ ("plant") used in Deut 16:21 seems to imply a living tree. The other verbs imply a manufactured object: "made" ʿśh (1 Kings 14:15 and elsewhere), "built" bnh (1 Kings 14:23), "set up" nṣb (2 Kings 17:10), hʿmd (2 Chron. 33:19). Note that when Gideon tore down his father's altar to Baʿal, he cut down the asherah, built an altar to YHWH, and used the trees from the asherah to burn a sacrifice.

9. See on this, most recently, H. L. Ginzeberg, *The Israelian Heritage of Judaism* (New York: Jewish Theological Seminary, 1982); the review article by Baruch Levine in *AJS Review* 12 (1987): 143–157; and Baruch Halpern, "Brisker Pipes than Poetry," 77–115.

19. 2 Kings 17:10,16.

11. Rehoboam: 1 Kings 14:23; Hezekiah: 2 Kings 18:4. Saul Olyan observes that Hosea does not argue against the Asherah, even though he condemns the bull images. The only four prophetic passages against this Asherah "show either Deuteronomistic influence or provenance." See Saul M. Olyan, *Asherah and the Cult of Yahweh in Israel,* SBL monograph ser. (Atlanta: Scholars Press, 1988), 1–22 (quotation from page 16).

12. 2 Kings 21:3,7.
13. Exod. 34:13; Deut. 7:5.
14. Deut. 16:21.
15. 2 Kings 23:4–7.
16. For the most recent study, see Walter A. Maier, III, *The Study of Aserah: The Extrabiblical Evidence,"* Harvard University Ph.D. diss., 1984; and Saul Olyan, *Asherah and the Cult of Yahweh.*
17. The *qudshu* figurine is a standing, legs-together, frontally-viewed female whose arms are extended sidewise and upwards. In most cases, she wears a wig known as the Hathor headdress. This type of image became firmly established in the land of Israel in the Middle Bronze Age and continued till Iron I. It is not found during the Israelite period. The classic study of these figurines is by James Pritchard, *Palestinian Figurines in Relation to Certain Goddesses Known Through Literature,* AOS 24 (New Haven: AOS, 1943); for the most recent extensive study of figurines in general, see Urs Winter, *Frau und Göttin: Exegetische und ikonographische Studien zum weiblichen Göttesbild im Alten Testament und in desen Umwelt,* Orbis Biblicus et Orientalis 53 (Freiburg: Universitätsverlag Gottingen, 1983).
18. The initial publication of the Kuntillet ʿAjrud finds is by Z. Meshel, *Kuntillet ʿAjrud: A Religious Center from the Time of the Judaean Monarchy on the Border of Sinai,* Israel Museum cat. 175 (Jerusalem: Israel Museum, 1978). Since then, the amount of scholarship has multiplied enormously. Extensive bibliographies can be found in Walter A. Meier, III, *The Study of Aserah,* 193–194; in a series of articles in *Ancient Israelite Religion,* Patrick Miller, Paul Hanson, and S. Dean McBride, eds. (Philadelphia: Fortress Press, 1987) as follows: Michael David Coogan, "Canaanite Origins and Lineage: Reflections on the Religion of Ancient Israel," 115–124; P. Kyle McCarter, Jr., "Aspects of the Religion of the Israelite Monarchy: Biblical and Epigraphic Data," 137–156; Jeffrey H. Tigay, "Israelite Religion: The Onomastic and Epigraphic Evidence," 157–194; William G. Dever, "The Contribution of Archaeology to the Study of Canaanite and Early Israelite Religion," 209–248; John S. Holladay, Jr., "Religion in Israel and Judah under the Monarchy: An Explicitly Archaeological Approach," 249–302; in Saul Olyan, *Asherah and the Cult of Yahweh;* and in Mark Smith, *The Early History of God.*
19. See the list in J. A. Emerton, "New Light on Israelite Religion: The Implications of the Inscriptions from Kuntillet ʿAjrud," *ZAW* 94 (1982) 2–20, as well as the articles mentioned in the previous footnote. There are some linguistic issues involved. It is hard to read *l' šrth* as "his Asherah" (meaning the actual goddess), because we would not expect a suffix with a proper noun, and no such usage is attested in the Bible. Ziony Zevit has suggested eliminating the problem by reading Ashrata, and taking this to be the name of a Hebrew goddess related to Asherah. See Zevit, "The Khirbet-el-Qom Inscription Mentioning a Goddess," *BASOR* 255 (1984): 39–47. David Noel Freedman has stressed that the *his* is purposeful, to suggest that Asherah now belongs to YHWH rather than to Ba'al; D. Freedman "Yahweh of Samaria and his Asherah," *BA* 50 (1987): 241–249. The use of the suffix may be dialectal (since the inscription comes from the North): moreover, the inscriptions are graffiti and may be no more grammatically exact than modern graffiti. There are drawings on the same storage jar as the blessing which depict a somewhat bovine male and female, and a female lyre player, and these seemed to support that idea that *l(' šrt)h* was an actual goddess and that she and YHWH formed a pair. But more extensive study has indicated that the drawings are from different hands and times than the inscriptions. See P. Beck, "The Drawings from Horvat Teiman (Kuntillet ʿAjrud)," *Tel Aviv* 9 (1982): 3–86.
20. 1 Kings 18:40.
21. See Mark Smith, *The Early History of God,* 89.
22. The association of Asherah with Ba'al may be intended to discredit the cult tree asherah, once the Deuteronomistic authors found this symbol objectionable. S. Olyan, *Asherah and the Cult of Yahweh* and M. Smith *The Early History of God* suggest that Asherah is substituted for Astarte in this story in order to discredit the cult of Astarte, and that this mixing of the two goddesses is what Olyan calls "willful confusion."
23. 2 Kings 23:15. See S. Olyan, *Asherah and the Cult of Yahweh,* 7.
24. 2 Kings 10:18–28.
25. The Book of Chronicles has a tradition that Jehu praised Judah's king Jehoshafat for removing the asherot from the south, but Jehu himself did not try to eradicate the asherah from Samaria (1 Chron., 19:3).
26. Kyle McCarter has suggested that we should rather look for a native Israelite development. We have long known that the Jews living in Elephantine in Egypt in the fifth century B.C.E.

worshiped personified aspects of the temple and of God. These are called *hypostases,* the term for the theological development in which an abstract aspect of God is personified and worshiped as a semi-independent being. In this way, Eshem-bethel, Anath-Bethel, and Anat-yahu at Elephantine are the worshiped personifications of the name and sign of God. The word *ašera* can mean "path, trace." To McCarter, the "ashera" (which he understands as an upright wooden pole) was understood to be the effective presence of YHWH. The similarity of the name of this ashera to that of the Canaanite goddess results from the fact that the Canaanite goddess was also originally a trace hypostatization, in that case that of Yamm, the sea god. But beyond the name, Israel's ashera has nothing to do with Canaan. See P. K. McCarter, "Aspects of the Religion of the Israelite Monarchy," 147–149.

27. This point is made by J. H. Tigay, "Israelite Religions," 174, and note 90. The inscription is found in Moshe Weinfeld, "Further Remarks on the ʿAjrud Inscriptions," *Shnaton* 5–6 (1978–79): 233 (in Hebrew).

28. The major studies are John S. Holladay, Jr., "Religion in Israel and Judah under the Monarchy: An Explicitly Archaeological Approach," in *Ancient Israelite Religion,* 249–299; Jeffrey Tigay, *You Shall Have No Other Gods Before Me,* Harvard Semitic Studies 31 (1986), 91–96; Miriam Tadmor, "Female Cult Figurines in Late Canaan and Early Israel: Archaeological Evidence," *Studies in the Period of David and Solomon and Other Essays,* T. Ishida, ed., (Winona Lake, Ind: Eisenbraun, 1982), 139–173; T. A. Holland, "A Study of Palestinian Iron Age Baked Clay Figurines, with Special Reference to Jerusalem: Cave 1," *Levant* 9 (1977); 121–155.

29. J. B. Pritchard, *Palestinian Figurines;* see also Urs Winter, *Frau und Göttin,* with extensive bibliography.

30. See M. Tadmor, "Female Cult Figurines," 171–173; and W. F. Albright, "Astarte Plaques and Figurines from Tell Beit Mirsim," in *Mélanges Syriens offerts à M. R. Dussaud,* vol 1, (Paris: Geuthner, 1939), 107–120.

31. Though they might have continued through Solomonic times, see J. Holladay, "Religion in Israel and Judah under the Monarchy," 280.

32. See M. Tadmor, "Female Cult Figurines," 171–173; for a catalogue and analysis of those found before 1972, see T. A. Holland, "A Study of Palestinian Iron Age . . . Figurines." For the goddess with the tambourine, see Delbert Hillers, "The Goddess with the Tambourine: Reflections on an Object from Taanach," in *A Symposium on Archaeology and Theology,* a (reprint of *Concordia Theological Monthly,* 41 (9) (Saint Louis: Concordia Press, 1970), 94–107.

33. Depending on the dating of the Lachish strata, the time of the appearance of these figurines in Judah is 720–587 B.C.E. or 610–587 B.C.E.; see J. Holladay, "Religion in Israel and Judah." They may represent a burst of popular piety, deriving ultimately upon old folk traditions that were revitalized with increased commercial contact, and occasioned by the stress of the political developments in the last centuries of Israel's existence.

34. They all ultimately merged in the figures of the Phoenician Tannit and the later Atargatis.

35. William Dever, "Asherah, Consort of Yahweh? New Evidence from Kuntillet ʿAjrud," *BASOR* 255 (1984): 28–29.

36. Drawing in A. Mekhitarian, *Egyptian Painting* (Geneva: Skira, 1954), 38, reprinted in Ruth Hestrin, "The Cult Stand from Ta'anach and Its Religious Background," in *Phoenicia and the East Mediterranean in the First Millenium* B.C., Studia Phoenicia 5, E. Lipinski, ed. (Louvain: Peeters, 1987), 61–77. See also Ruth Hestrin, "The Lachish Ewer and the Asherah," *IEJ* 37 (1987): 212–213. Hestrin also identifies the pillar figurines as three trunks.

37. P. W. Lapp, "The 1968 Excavations at Tell Ta'annek, The New Cultic Stand," *BASOR* 195 (1969): 42–44.

38. Ruth Hestrin, "The Lachish Ewer."

39. J. Tigay, *You Shall Have No Other Gods.*

40. Gen. 49:25.

41. On the issue of whether Israelite Asherah is ever a goddess, opinion is divided. Mark Smith, *The Early History of God,* like Bernard Lang, *Monotheism and the Prophetic Minority: An Essay in Biblical History and Sociology,* The Social World of Biblical Antiquity Series, 1 (Sheffield: Almond, 1983), Patrick Miller, "The Absence of the Goddess in Israelite Religion," *HAR* 10 (1986): 239–248, J. Tigay, *You Shall Have No Other Gods,* and U. Winter, *Frau und Göttin,* before him, do not believe there is ever a goddess intimated in biblical sources. Others, including Freedman, Hestrin, and Olyan, hold that there was an Israelite consort to God. The evidence is very scant, and does not seem to support the notion of a "consort"—at least, not after the eighth century.

CHAPTER 14   Our Father and Our Mother

1. Except in the primeval history, the Bible speaks of Israel rather than of "humanity." When it reflects on the rest of humanity in its relationship to God, it makes clear that it considers Israel the vanguard of humanity, the first to have this relationship with God, but that it considers that the relationship will ultimately be universal.

2. This image has been the subject of some dispute and speculation in recent years. See the discussion of P. A. H. de Boer, *Fatherhood and Motherhood in Israelite and Judean Piety* (Leiden: Brill, 1974); Phyllis Trible, *God and the Rhetoric of Sexuality* (Philadelphia: Fortress, 1978), 31–71; M. Gruber, "The Motherhood of God in Second Isaiah," *RB* 90 (1983): 351–359; John J. Schmitt, "The Motherhood of God and Zion as Mother," *RB* (1985): 557–569; and John W. Miller, *Biblical Faith and Fathering: Why We Call God "Father"* (New York: Paulist Press, 1989).

3. Exod. 4:22–23

4. Deut. 1:31. See also Deut. 8:5, 32:5–6, 18–21.

5. Ps. 89:26–27. So, too, Psalm 2 proclaims God's sonship declaration to David and 2 Samuel 7:14 records the adoption formula for Solomon. For the Davidic dynasty, see Gerald Cooke, "The Israelite King as Son of God," *ZAW* 73 (1961): 202–205.

6. Prov. 3:12. In this way, God acts to punish the house of David (Ps. 89:33; 2 Sam. 7:14) and bring destruction upon Israel.

7. In Jeremiah 3:4–5, 16, the prophet castigates the daughter Israel for turning to God to assure herself that He will forgive her. It is noteworthy that just as mother and father alternate, so do son Ephraim and daughter Bat-Israel. The essential division is cross-generational.

8. Deuteronomy 21:18–21 sees the possibility that parents might want to repudiate a rebellious son, and prescribes that the parents are to go before the elders of the city and declare him stubborn, rebellious, drunk, and gluttonous, and thereupon the men of the city will stone the son to death. This seems harsh, and is an indication that Deuteronomy, which does much to lessen the power of the father, steps in harshly to indicate that there is an absolute end to this lessening of authority. The law also has the social function of protecting aging parents from sons who might abuse them.

9. Is. 1:2.

10. Hos. 11:1.

11. Hos. 11:8.

12. It is in this sense that the metaphor is used in Deut. 32 and Ps. 103.

13. Is. 43:6, 63:16.

14. Is. 46:3–4; cf. Is. 64:7–8.

15. Deut. 32:18. Despite the masculine gender of the verb "birthed you," the verb itself is a term that applies to mothers. The same verb is used when Sarah is said to have birthed Israel in Isaiah 51:2. A similar use of female birthing terms in Moses' complaint to God in Numbers 11:12 implies that God conceived and bore the people, though Moses did not, and it is therefore God's obligation to do something to take care of them.

16. Is. 42:14.

17. God's actions in teaching Israel to walk and feeding him (Hos. 11) and dandling him on the knees (Jer. 31) are what we have until recently considered maternal functions. Similarly, the tenderness and love of God have suggested that the parenthood of God is motherhood, rather than fatherhood. Phyllis Trible has pointed out that the verb used in Jeremiah 31, "my heart yearns for him" comes ultimately from the word for "womb" and translates "my womb trembles for him; I will truly show motherly-compassion upon him." But probably we should not make too much of this. Even though "compassion" (*rḥm, rāḥāmîm*) comes ultimately from "womb" (*reḥem*), the metaphor may no longer be living; males are also said to have (*rāḥāmîm*), as Joseph has for his brother (Gen. 43:30). Furthermore, the semantic development from "womb" to "compassion" took place long before Hebrew, for the Sumerian **arhuš** means both "womb" and "compassion," and male deities are said to be **arhuš . . . sù,** "compassionate," literally "long of womb."

18. Ps. 103:13.

19. Is. 49:15.

20. These parent gods of the ordinary citizen were anonymous minor deities; the parents of the kings were the great gods of the cosmos. Thorkild Jacobsen has argued that this system of personal gods gave rise to the whole idea of gods concerned with the actions and repentance of the worshipper; see Thorkild Jacobsen, *Treasures of Darkness* (New Haven: Yale University Press, 1976), 147–164.

21. Of course, the personal god of major royal figures was a major deity in the pantheon. Even so, this personal deity interceded for the individual with the other gods.

22. See *abbutu epešu* ("intercede"), CAD E *epešu* 2C p. 201 and *abbutu* 4' CAD A 50.

23. For the prophet as intercessor, see Yohanan Muffs, "The Prayer of the Prophets" (in Hebrew), in *Torah nidrešet* (The Interpreted Bible) (Tel-Aviv: Am Oved, 1984), soon to appear in English as "prophetic intercession" in Yohanan Muffs, *Biblical and Oriental Studies* forthcoming.

24. Jer. 31:15.

25. There is one more story involving Rachel in the book of Genesis, but it is not well understood. When Jacob and his family left her father's household, she stole her ancestor-figures, but was forced to bury them as improper to hold once they entered Canaan. Opinions have varied as to why Rachel stole the Teraphim. See A. E. Draffkorn, "Ilāni/Elohim," *JBL* 76 (1957): 216–224; M. Greenberg, "Another Look at Rachel's Theft of the Teraphim," *JBL* 81 (1962): 239–248; M. J. Selman, "Comparative Customs and the Patriarchal Age," in *Essays on the Patriarchal Narratives* A. R. Millard and D. J. Wiseman, eds., (Leicester: Intervarsity 1980), 101–110; and J. Huehnergard, "Biblical Notes on Some New Akkadian Texts from Emar (Syria)," *CBQ* 47 (1985): 428–421.

26. The chief intertextual signal in Jeremiah's vision is the *śâkār* ("reward, payment") which God promises Rachel in return for her lament. This word resonates with echoes of the story of Rachel's quest for a child. Leah's son Reuben found mandrakes, a plant whose root resembles a human baby and was thought to have fertility powers. Rachel wanted these mandrakes, and traded Leah a night with Jacob in return for them. Leah thereupon greeted Jacob that evening with the statement, "You are to sleep with me, for I have hired you (*śākōr śĕkartîkā*) with my son's mandrakes." Leah named the son—to whom she thereupon gave birth—Issachar, for she said "God has given me my reward" (*śĕkārî*). The reward and hire in this story is a son, and the reward which God announces to Rachel in Jeremiah's vision is the restoration of her exiled children.

27. Technically, of course, we could say that Rachel was the grandmother of Ephraim, not his mother. On this matter, however, we should consider the story of the blessing of Ephraim and Manasseh, in which Jacob accepted them as his sons, so that they would inherit equally with their uncles rather than through their father. Juridically, then, they were sons rather than grandsons of the dead Rachel.

28. Gen. 29:24; 37:3.

29. See the discussion of these daughter-figures in the next chapter.

30. The verse "God has created a new thing in the land, a female goes around a man" (Jer. 31:22) has received a great deal of attention recently. It is often seen as the proclamation of a new order attended upon the restoration of Israel, the reversal of patriarchy and the establishment of female dominance. Nowhere else in Jeremiah, or in any of the other prophets, is there any hint of such an idea; and in the context of this poem, it is highly unlikely that Jeremiah would include such a cryptic statement. Verses 21 and 22 play on the sound *šûb,* which is used as the verb "return (to the land)" and in the adjective *mĕšôbēbâ,* applied to Israel-as-girl, meaning "strayer (off the beaten path"). Here too, *tĕsôbēb* ("goes around") is a related concept: what is new is that the restored Israel-girl, instead of wandering all over the place, will henceforth direct all her attention to God. In the mind of the prophet, this is truly "a new thing" in the history of Israel.

31. In this, Rachel is like all the mothers of Israel, particularly the Genesis matriarchs, who bring protection and redemption for their sons, and then disappear. See also J. Cheryl Exum, "You Shall Let Every Daughter Live: A Study of Exodus 1:8–2:10," *Semeia* 28 (1983): 63–82; and J. Cheryl Exum, "A Mother in Israel: A Familiar Story Reconsidered," in *Feminist Interpretations of the Bible,* Letty Russel, ed. (Philadelphia: Westminster, 1985).

32. Jer. 31:15. This inconsolability also resonates with an echo of the Joseph story, for Jacob wept for the absent Joseph, Jacob, like Rachel here, refusing to be comforted (Gen. 37:35).

33. For this aspect of Jeremiah, see Baruch Halpern, "Brisker Pipes than Poetry: The Development of Israelite Monotheism," *Judaic Perspectives on Ancient Israel,* Jacob Neusner, Baruch Levine, and Ernest Frerichs, eds. (Philadelphia: Fortress 1987), 99–100. Halpern describes Jeremiah's "systematic assembly of the assault on hypostatization," but does not notice Jeremiah's use of Rachel or Zion.

34. The figure of *Rachel Imenu,* "mother Rachel," continues to be important in the Rabbinic period and later in Judaism. She is portrayed as the mother-defender of the people, who prays for exiles, for infertile women, and for women in travail. The Midrashic material has been collected by Susan Sered, together with descriptions of pilgrimages to the tomb of Rachel, in her master's thesis for the Hebrew University in Jerusalem.

CHAPTER 15   Zion, the Beloved Woman

1. Zach. 2:11.

2. Amos 5:2.

3. Mic. 4:11; Lam. 1:8, 2:15–16. She also stands like a menstruant whose impurity clings to her skirts (Lam. 1:8–9; Jer. 13:33). The term *nîdâ* in Lam. 1:8 is usually translated "mockery." But despite the spelling, we must see a reference to menstruant (*niddâ*) in light of 1:9, 1:17, and Jer. 13:22.

4. Jer. 8:11, 21–23, 14:17.

5. Jer. 6:2, 6:23, 8:4, 4:17–18.

6. Jer. 4:30–31.

7. Lam. 2:11, 3:48. Lamentations uses several names, all clearly for Jerusalem: Bat Zion (1:6, 2:1, 4, 8, 10, 13, 18), Betulat Bat Zion (nubile Zion girl, 2:13), Bat Jerusalem (2:13,15); Betulat Bat Yehudah (1:15); Bat Yehudah (2:2,5); and Bat Ami (2:11). They do not refer to different figures.

8. Lam. 1:1, 2, 17; 2:18–19; 1:11–16, 8–22.

9. Jer. 9:18, 7:29.

10. Jer. 6:25–26. Although the Masoretes read this passage as though the people are being addressed (in masculine plural), the actual writing in the Bible (the Ktiv) clearly indicates that Jerusalem-woman is being addressed.

11. Jer. 8:18–19.

12. The liturgical poets of the book of Psalms do not use this image, an indication that it was not part of Israelite cultic practices. Zion as a woman does not appear in the Psalms, and the name Zion-girl is only mentioned once (9:14), very casually, as the Psalmist asks for relief from affliction so that he can recite God's praises in the gates of Zion-maid (9:14).

13. These titles have been collected by Aloysious Fitzgerald, "The Mythological Background for the Presentation of Jerusalem as Queen and False Worship as Adultery in the OT," *CBQ* 34 (1972): 403–412. There is, however, no evidence to support his hypothesis that this female city was imagined to be married to the god of the city. See also his follow-up article, "Btwlt and Bt as Titles for Capital Cities," *CBQ* 37 (1975): 167–183.

14. There are other points of similarity between West Semites and Sumerians that diverge from the Akkadian. The discovery of Ebla, a third-millennium city in Syria that had many Sumerian language-texts in addition to a Semitic-language literature, serves to remind us that Sumerian civilization was in direct contact with the West, and that Sumerian and West-Semitic ideas did not always come through the Akkadian prism before they reached each other.

15. The references to the city as "widow" have been studied by Hayyim Cohen, "The widowed City," *JANES* 5 (1973): 75–81.

16. The Book of Exodus, on the other hand, does describe the Exodus as God's judgment upon the gods of Egypt; Exod. 12:12.

17. Mic. 1:11–16.

18. Jer. 18:18–19, 49:3.

19. Egypt: Jer. 46:19, 46:11–12, Damascus: Jer. 49:24; Babylon: Jer. 50:3,13; 51:8.

20. Lam. 4:21–22.

21. Is. 12:6.

22. Ps. 9:12.

23. Is. 8:18.

24. Is. 10:24; 30:10; 33:24.

25. In this, Isaiah was subscribing to an important element of Judean theology, the great attachment of God for Jerusalem. For the development of this Zion theology, see J. R. Roberts, "The Davidic Origin of the Zion Tradition," *JBL* 92 (1973): 329–344, and "Zion in the Theology of the Davidic-Solomonic Empire," *Studies in the Period of David and Solomon: Papers Read at the International Symposium for Biblical Studies, Tokyo, 5–7 December, 1979,* Tomoo Ishida, ed. (Winona Lake, Ind.: Eisenbrauns/Tokyo: Yamaka—Shuppanska, 1982), 93–108, and Jon D. Levenson, *Sinai and Zion* (Minneapolis: Winston Press, 1985).

26. Is. 2:1–3 = Mic. 4:1–3.

27. Is. 8:18, 18:7, 24:13, 14:32, 28:16, 24:23, 4:3–5.

28. Is. 33:20–21.

29. Mic. 4:11, 4:9, 4:10.

30. Who did Micah think would actually go to Babylon? Not the inhabitants, for Micah is not thinking of a Babylonian exile. In the eighth century, when a prophet thought of destruction and exile, he thought of the Assyrians. Moreover, "come to Babylon" is not the language of exile, and the purpose of this voyage is to seek salvation. Perhaps Micah is thinking of a trip by emissaries of the monarchy, sent to negotiate a pact against Assyria with Babylonia, its natural rival. See Henri Cazelles, "Histoire et géographie en Michée 4:6–13," *Fourth World Congress of Jewish Studies Papers,* 1 (1987), pp. 87–89. However, it is not really crucial to know what the prophet thought the practical application of his message would be.

31. Mic. 4:13.

32. See Tikva Frymer-Kensky, "Aššur," *Encyclopedia of Religion,* 1987, 461–462.

33. Much as the Ugaritic war goddess Anat wallows in blood in Canaanite mythic poetry.

34. Jer. 30:12–17.

35. Jer. 51:35.

36. Jer. 31:4–5.

37. Jer. 3:14–16.

38. Is. 40:1, 52:1–9, 40:3–9. Often the phrase *mĕbaśśeret ṣiyyôn* of Is. 40:9 is translated "thou who bringest good tidings to Zion," but the herald is clearly a female, and those to whom the good news is brought are the cities of Judah. When a herald of joy does come to Jerusalem, he is a male, *mĕbaśśēr,* as such heralds usually were, and he comes to announce that God reigns (52:7, cf. 41:27).

39. Mic. 1:16

40. Lam. 4:3, 1:6, 1:6.

41. Is. 49:21, 54:1, 50:1, 41:11, 49:14–20, 54:1–3, 49:22.

42. Is. 54:5–8, 62:34, 62:12, 60:1–16, 62:1.

43. Is. 66:7–8.

44. Is. 66:9–14.

45. Is. 62:5.

46. Is. 62:5.

47. Is. 54:11, 51:16.

48. Her many roles are captured by the many new names that the prophets give her. Ezekiel calls her, "The Lord Is There"; Isaiah, "City of the Lord, Zion of the Holy one of Israel" (60:14), "I delight in her" (Hephzibah), with her land "espoused" (Beulah) (62:4), "Sought out, a city not forsaken" (62:12); and Zachariah renames her, "The City of Truth" (8:3).

CHAPTER 16    Wisdom, Lover of Man

1. Is. 62:5.

2. See Bernhard Lang, *Wisdom and the Book of Proverbs: An Israelite Goddess Redefined* (New York: Pilgrim Press, 1986) and the literature cited there.

3. For this association and further study of wisdom as feminine, see Claudia Camp, *Wisdom and the Feminine in the Book of Proverbs,* Bible and Literature 11, *JSOT* (Sheffield: Almond, 1985).

4. Wisdom will save mankind from the way of evil men (Prov. 1:10–10). To all who follow her, she offers protection and well-being: "He who listens to me will dwell in safety, untroubled by the terror of misfortune" (Prov. 1:33).

5. Delight: Prov. 2:10; material success: Prov. 8:18

6. Prov. 4:5–9.

7. Prov. 8:22–31. There are many possible translations for the word *ʾāmôn,* including "architect" or "craftsperson" (like the Akkadian *ummanu*), or "confidant" ("trustworthy one," from the word *amen*), or "nurse" or "nursling." In the context, "craftsperson" does not seem likely, since wisdom does not claim to have done anything other than delight in God's creation.

8. The verse "The Lord founded the earth by wisdom, He established the heavens by understanding" (3:19) was later (in postbiblical times) taken to mean that Wisdom was an active partner in creating. But the import of this statement is not simply that God likes wisdom, but that she was created. The use of the word *ḥôlāltî* prompted Gerhard Lang to deduce that wisdom was physically born from God. Although it is true that *ḥôlal* is related to the word *ḥyl* ("labor"), the form *ḥôlel* seems to be used as a term for creation without regard for its etymology. Both Israel and the world are said to have been "brought forth" by God, for Israel is told "you rejected the

Rock that begot you, forgot the God who brought you forth" (Deut. 32:18), and the Lord is addressed "before the mountains came into being, before you brought forth the earth and the world, from eternity to eternity you are God" (Ps. 90:2). Even if a mother-goddess image ultimately underlies the metaphor, it seems that all the important creatures can be said to have been "brought forth."

9. This is the basis on which Job is disqualified, first by Eliphaz the Temanite: "Were you the first man born? Were you created before the hills? Have you listened in on the council of God? Have you sole possession of wisdom?" (Job 15:7), and then by God: "Where were you when I laid the earth's foundations? Speak if you have understanding" (Job 38:44).

10. "Since you refused me when I called . . . I will laugh at your calamity and mock when terror comes upon you" (Prov. 1:24–26).

11. Prov. 8:17.

12. Prov. 1:20–21; 8:1–4.

13. Prov: 9:5–6.

14. *ʾîšîm* is an unusual plural of *ʾîš* ("man"). The normal plural, *ʾănāšîm*, can sometimes be a generic term, subsuming women. *ʾîšîm* is used to eliminate the possibility of generic reading. In this context even *bĕnê ʾādām,* which can often mean "human beings," should be understood as "sons of Adam."

15. Prov. 8:30–31.

16. The terms used to denote this woman are *zārâ* and *nokriyyâ*. These are often understood as "foreign" or non-Israelite. It is true that Potiphar's wife was a foreigner, as was Ruth and perhaps Tamar; but, in the context of Proverbs 1–9, these terms refer to someone outside the pale, and outside one's family group and household, rather than a non-Israelite. On this, see P. Humbert, "La femme étrangère du livre des proverbes," *RES* 27 (1937): 49f, and "Les adjectifs *zar* et *nokri* et la femme étrangère des Proverbes bibliques," *Mélanges syriens offerts à R. Dussaud,* 1 (Paris: Geuthner 1939), 259f; and J. N. Aletti, "Séduction et parole en proverbes i–ix," *VT* 27 (1977): 129–144.

17. "I have come out to you, seeking you, and have found you . . . let us drink our fill of love till morning, let us delight in amorous embrace" (7:15–18). Or the woman of folly sits–again, like wisdom–in a doorway or at the height of the town, calling "let the simple enter here . . . stolen waters are sweet, and bread eaten furtively is tasty."

18. Prov. 5:3.

19. Prov. 7:21.

20. The adulterous woman brings death (2:18, 5:5–6, 9:18). No one who touches her will go unpunished (6:29); her lover will die. He may be caught up in the ropes of his sin, and die for lack of discipline (5:22–23); he may meet disease and disgrace (6:33), or he may become subject to the fury of the husband (6:34–35).

21. Prov. 2:16, 7:5.

22. Prov. 5:15–20.

23. See Richard Horsley, "Spiritual Marriage with Sophia," *Vigilae Christianae: A Review of Early Christian Life and Land* 33/1 (1979): 30–54.

24. Sophia has a long history in the early history of Christianity and the Gnostic period. An extensive bibliography is developing on this topic, outside the scope of this book. See Pheme Perkins, "Sophia as Goddess in the Nag Hammadi Codices," in *Images of the Feminine in Gnosticism,* Karen King, ed. (Philadelphia: Fortress, 1988), and the articles in Robert Wilkens, ed., *Aspects of Wisdom in Judaism and Christianity,* (Notre Dame, Ind.: University of Notre Dame Press, 1975). For an interesting modern attempt to incorporate some of this imagery in modern liturgy, see Susan Cady, Marian Ronan, and Hal Taussig, *Wisdom's Feast: Sophia in Study and Celebration* (New York: Harper and Row, 1986).

25. For the effect of this family-orientation on the image of Wisdom, see Claudia Camp, *Wisdom and the Feminine in the Book of Proverbs,* 233–254.

26. For Wisdom as "Woman as Other," see Carol A. Newsom, "Wisdom and the Discourse of Patriarchal Wisdom: A Study of Proverbs 1–9," in *Gender and Difference,* Peggy Day, ed., (Minneapolis: Fortress, 1989), 142–160.

27. Much of this material has been collected by Susan Sered for her master's thesis at the Hebrew University.

28. The fascinating study of Mary is beyond the scope of this book. See Marina Warner, *Alone of All Her Sex: The Myth and the Cult of the Virgin Mary* (New York: Random House, 1976); Geoffrey Ashe, *The Virgin* (London: Routledge & Kegan Paul, 1976); and Michael Car-

roll, *The Cult of the Virgin Mary: Psychological Origins* (Princeton: Princeton: Princeton University Press, 1986).

## Chapter 17    Sex in the Bible

1. For previous studies see A. M. Dubaile, *Amour et fecondité dans la bible* (Toulouse: Privat, 1967), Michael R. Cosby, *Sex in the Bible* (Englewood Cliffs, N.J.: Prentice Hall, 1985); Gerald Larue, *Sex and the Bible* (Buffalo, N.Y.: Prometheus, 1983); Frank Perry, *Sex and the Bible,* (Atlanta, Ga.: Christian Education Research Institute, 1982); Tikva Frymer-Kensky, "Law as Philosophy: Sexuality in the Bible," in *Thinking Biblical Law,* Dale Patrick, ed., *Semeia* (1988), pp. 89–102; Tikva Frymer-Kensky, "Sexuality in the Bible," *Anchor Bible Dictionary,* forthcoming.

2. This, of course, does not mean that ordinary sexuality was approached with a sacral attitude. Mesopotamia was certainly not a sexual paradise, or the Mesopotamian law collections would not have had to contain provisions in the case of rape and adultery. On the other hand, the sacred marriage ritual does give indication of an intellectual climate in which the sex drive had an integral place in the workings of the cosmos.

3. The Descent of Ishtar, rev. 7–10.

4. Exod. 15. This image was joined by the gender-free (or perhaps, partially feminine) image of God as parent, discussed on pp. 164–165, but is never displaced by it. Even in the works of the post-Exilic Isaiah, God is still called "man of wars," and the image of the Divine Warrior remains an important way of conceiving God until the Rabbinic period.

5. Exod. 33:23.

6. The possible exception is Deutero-Isiah's vision of the restoration in Is. 63:4–5 where the verb *bā ʿal* might indicate sexual union. It may, however, only refer to the marital relationship.

7. Prov. 4:8.

8. Exod. 19:15. The sense of Moses' command to Israel is often obscured by the unfortunate male-centered wording of this passage. God is reported as having commanded that the people wash and sanctify themselves and wash their clothes, making preparations for the third day (Exod. 19:10–11). When Moses relayed this to the people, he added his own command, "Do not approach your wives" (Exod. 19:15). By this addition, Moses explains how the people are to prepare for the third day, but he adds his own perspective, suddenly erasing half the people and addressing only the men. It is interesting that the Bible records this as Moses' invention rather than God's; it sheds new light on the Deuteronomic injunction to the people not to add to the laws.

9. 1 Sam. 21:4–5.

10. Lev. 15:16–18.

11. Major impurities lasted a week and were contagious: everyone who came in contact with someone impure in this way would themselves become impure for a day. For a detailed discussion of these issues, see Tikva Frymer-Kensky, "Purity, Pollution and Purgation in Biblical Israel" in *The Word of the Lord Shall Go Forth: Essays in Honor of David Noel Freedman,* Carol Meyers and M. O'Connor, eds., (Winona Lake, Ind.: Eisenbrauns, 1983), 399–414; and Mary Douglas, *Purity and Danger: An Analysis of Concepts of Pollution and Taboo* (New York: Praeger, 1966). My analysis is somewhat different from that of Mary Douglas' classic study in that she does not distinguish between the "impurity" beliefs, which deal with a contagious state which is neither morally deserved nor dangerous to the individual, and Israel's separate set of danger pollutions, a noncontagious state caused by misdeeds which bring the perpetrator into the danger of divine sanction.

12. Menstrual taboos are also to some extent sexual taboos. In Israel, a woman was impure for seven days after the beginning of her menses. During this period, her impurity (as all impurity) was contagious, and could be contracted by anyone who touched her, or even sat where she had sat. Intercourse with a menstruating woman was considered absolutely forbidden, and was sanctioned by the *karet* penalty, which means the belief that one's lineage would be extirpated. The reminder in menstruation of a sexual dimension of existence would not account for the seven-day duration of impurity, however. Another element is present—blood and its associations with death—for contact with death also results in a week-long impurity. It is noteworthy that only intercourse with a menstruant results both in temporary impurity and in divine sanction or *karet*.

13. The positive valuation of marriage is traditional in the ancient Near East. See W. G. Lambert, "Celibacy in the World's Oldest Proverbs" *BASOR* 169 (1963): 63f.

14. Gen. 2:24.

15. Prov. 18:22. For Proverbs, see Daniel C. Snell, "Notes on Love and Death in Proverbs," in *Love and Death in the Ancient Near East, Essays in honor of Marvin H. Pope,* John Marks and Robert Good, ed. (Guilford, Conn.: Four Quarters Publishing, 1987). Snell notes the structural parallel to 8:35 (wisdom speaking): "He who finds me, finds life and gets favor from the Lord."

16. Deut. 20:7, 24:5.

17. Prov. 5:17–18.

18. This concern may be heightened by a desire to combat the example of priestly sexual activity in pagan cults. The whole question of pagan sex cults is very difficult, and is discussed in chapter 18.

19. On the basis of the interpretation of the term *qĕdēšâ* ("holy one") as a cult prostitute, scholars have long argued the existence of sacred prostitution in Israel, which the Bible was trying to stamp out. More recent work has indicated that there is absolutely no evidence that a *qĕdēšâ* was a prostitute, nor that any sexual rites ever existed in ancient Israel (see the discussion in the next chapter). In any event, the wages not to be vowed to the temple are those of a *zônâ,* which everyone agrees is an ordinary prostitute-for-hire, not attached to the Temple.

20. 1 Sam. 2:22–25.

21. Occasionally in these laws, a male is mentioned, which seems to indicate that the law also considers women and their permissible relations, but does not consistently list all of a female's choices.

22. It is hard to know whether the omission of the mother's brother means that the mother's brother and his wife were permitted as being of a different family, or whether they would have been prohibited. A similar question arises with the father's brother's children (first cousins) and with the brother's and sister's daughters. In this case, it would seem that since the father's brother and his wife are prohibited, the brother's daughter must also be, even though it is not mentioned.

23. This was not always so in Israel. In Gen. 20:16, Sarah and Abraham are described as having the same father by different mothers. A similar situation lies behind Tamar's entreaty to her would-be rapist, her paternal brother Amnon, "Speak unto the king, for he will not withhold me from thee" (2 Sam. 13:13). This is not the only instance in which the patriarchal and Davidic narratives differ from later biblical law. Jacob is married to two sisters, which is not allowed in Leviticus. Jacob's and David's sons vie for inheritance position, while according to Deuteronomy, the first to be born is considered the first-born, whatever the wishes of the father.

24. The omission of the daughter in the prohibited relations is another glaring omission. One might argue that since grandchildren are prohibited, children must be also, but one might equally argue that the idea of paterfamilias was still strong enough that the laws could not absolutely prohibit a father's access to his daughter. From the expectation of virginity in unmarried daughters, it is clear that father-daughter incest was neither expected nor encouraged.

25. It is also called *zimmâ* in Exodus 22:11, a term reserved in these laws for incest outside blood kin, applied to mother-in-law, wife's sister, wife's daughter, and granddaughter.

26. In the case of homosexuality, men were more bound than women, since homosexuality was considered a major threat requiring the death penalty (whether real or threatened). Lesbian sex was not a matter of concern.

27. This was not an unusual definition of adultery, and it has been suggested that this unevenness is the essence of male control over female sexuality, and that possibly it demonstrates a desire to be certain of paternity. Within Israel this treatment of adultery is not examined; it is part of Israel's inheritance from the ancient Near East and, like slavery and other elements of social structure, it is never questioned in the Bible.

28. Exod. 22:15–16.

29. Deut. 22:20ff.

30. According to the procedure laid out in Deut. 22:13f., after the accusation, the case was brought before the elders at the gate, and the parents of the girl then produced the sheet to prove that she was a virgin. Once they did this, the man was flogged, fined, and lost his rights to divorce her in the future. Since the parents had plenty of time to find blood for the sheets, it is unlikely that a bridegroom would make such a charge; if he disliked the girl, he could divorce her. If he nevertheless made such a charge, she and her family would have to be very ignorant not to fake the blood.

31. On stoning, see J. J. Finkelstein, *The Ox that Gored,* TAPS 71 (Philadelphia: 1981) 26–29. In addition to the two cases discussed here, stoning is used for the ox that gored a man to death (Exod. 21:12–14), one who lures others into idolatry (Deut. 13:7f.), the disobedient son (Deut. 21:18–21), child sacrifice (Lev. 20:2), sorcery and necromancy (Lev. 20:27), blasphemy (Lev. 24:10f), and violation of the sabbath (Num. 15:32–35), and, by inference, for sedition (Naboth story: 1 Kings 21).

32. Deut. 22:23–24.

33. Deut. 22:25–27.

34. In the sexual uses of the verb, ʿinnâ, there are instances where it means rape: in Judges 19–20, where the concubine in Gibeah was raped to death; in the story of Amnon and Tamar, in which he is said to have overpowered her (2 Sam 13:12–13); and in Lamentations, in which the women of Zion are said to have been raped (Lam. 5:11). But forcible rape is not always the issue. Some cases are ambiguous. In Deut. 22:28–29, a man has taken an unbetrothed girl; he must marry her and not divorce her, because he has illicitly had sex with her. The same scenario is involved in the story of Dinah and Shechem (Gen. 34). There is no indication in the story that Shechem overpowered her. She was not, however, free to consent, and he should have approached her father first. Similarly, the man who sleeps with a menstruant (Ezek. 22:10), or with his paternal sister (Ezek. 22:11), is said to have "raped" her only in the sense of "statutory rape," i.e., that he had no right to have sex with her even if she consented. In Deut. 21:10–13, the verb ʿinnâ seems to imply, not only an absence of force, but a failure of sex. This is the case of a man who takes a captive woman as a wife. She must first spend a month in his house mourning her past; after which, the man can have sex with her. If, however, he does not want her, he must emancipate rather than sell her, for he has "ʿinnâ,-ed" her. That is, he has put her in a situation in which she expected to become his wife, and then has not followed through. The verb does not always have sexual connotations; in nonsexual contexts, it means to treat harshly, exploitatively and/or abusively. Sarah treated Hagar oppressively (Gen. 16:6,9); Laban warns Jacob not to treat Laban's daughters badly (Gen. 31:50). The most common subject is God, who is said to mistreat Israel (Deut. 8:2, 3,16; 2 Kings 17:20; Is. 64:11; Nah. 1:12), David and his seed (1 Kings 11), the suffering servant (Is. 53:4), and individual sufferers (Ps. 88:8; Ps. 89:23; Ps. 119:71, 75; Job 30:11). The most common victim is Israel, which is treated badly by God, by Egypt (Gen. 15:13; Exod. 1:11–13), and by enemies (2 Sam. 7:10; Is. 60:14; Zeph. 3:10; Ps. 94:5; Lam. 3:33).

35. Exod. 22:15–16.

36. Gen. 18–19.

37. Judg. 19.

38. Prov. 6:34–35.

39. Deut. 21:18–21, 22:13–19, 25:7, 21:1–9.

40. For the significance of waṣû, see Chapter 3, note 53.

41. Verse 31.

42. Sumerian Law Fragments, Yale Babylonian Collection 2177, nos. 7 & 8. See *ANET,* 525.

43. Gen. 34:9–10.

44. There is a polemic in the Bible about intermarriage with non-Israelite women. Despite the story of Ruth, which clearly approves of Moabite women, there is often a worry about their ability to influence their husbands to worship other gods (Deut 7:1–5), as reportedly happened to King Solomon. Ultimately, after the return from Babylon, when the community in Israel was small and in danger of being overwhelmed by the other people in the land, the concern for ethnic survival and religious protection resulted in a ban on foreign wives during the time of Ezra.

45. Gen. 1–11.

46. Gen. 6:1–4.

47. On the importance of categories in Israel, see Mary Douglas, *Purity and Danger: An Analysis of Concepts of Pollution and Taboo* (New York: Praeger, 1966); Jacob Finkelstein, *The Ox that Gored,* TAPS 71 (Philadelphia: American Philosophical Society, 1981); Tikva Frymer-Kensky, "Purity, Pollution and Purgation in Biblical Israel," in *The Word of the Lord Shall Go Forth: Essays in Honor of David Noel Freedman,* Carol Meyers and M. O'Connor, eds. (Philadelphia: Fortress, 1983), 399–414; and Tikva Frymer-Kensky, "Biblical Cosmology," in *Backgrounds to the Bible,* Michael O'Connor and David Noel Freedman, eds. (Winona Lake, Ind.: Eisenbrauns, 1987), 233–240.

48. Exod. 22:28; Lev. 18:23, 20:15–16, DT 27:21.

49. Deut. 22:9–11; cf. Lev. 19:19.

50. Lev. 20:13; cf. 18:22. This extreme aversion to homosexuality is not inherited from other Near Eastern laws, though the Sumerian laws consider an accusation of catamy as parallel to an accusation that one's wife is fornicating.

51. Deut. 22:5. Having eunuchs is not considered the same kind of blurring. A eunuch, like people with visible physical defects, could not serve in the temple. But eunuchs were found in Israel, particularly in the royal court (2 Kings 20:17–18; Is. 56:3–4; Jer. 29:2, 34:19, 38:7, 41:16).

52. Lev. 18:28.

53. Num. 35:31–34.

54. Deut. 21:22–23.

55. Deut. 24:1–3; Jer. 3:1–4.

56. Deut. 21:1–9. See Rafael Patai, "The ʿEgla ʿArufa or the Expiation of the Polluted Land," *JQR* 30 (1939–40): 59–69, and Ziony Zevit, "The ʿEgla Ritual of Deuteronomy 21:1–9," *JBL* 95 (1976): 377–390.

57. Num. 5:11–21. T. Frymer-Kensky, "The Strange Case of the Suspected Sotah," VT 34 (1984): 11–26.

58. In Biblical cosmology, the universe is seen rather like a house of cards; if the lines are not kept neat, the whole edifice will collapse, "the foundations of the earth totter."

59. John van Seters believes this a particular motif of the succession history and the Yahwist corpus, "Love and Death in the Court History of David," in *Love and Death in the Ancient Near East: Essays in Honor of Marvin H. Pope,* John Marks and Robert Good eds. (Guilford, Conn.: Four Quarters Publishing, 1987), 121–124. Van Seters also considers the concubine tales of Abner and Rizpah, and Adonijah and Abishag to be instances of this; but he does not sufficiently consider the political, rather than sexual, motivations of these acts. See further J. J. Blenkinsopp, "Theme and Motif in the Succession History (2 Sam. 11:2f.) and the Yahwist Corpus," VT 15 (1966): 44–57, though I agree with Van Seters that in none of these stories is the woman blameworthy.

60. Song of Songs, 8:6–7.

## CHAPTER 18    Sex and the People: The Myth of Orgy

1. The term, "sex cult," comes from Hans Walter Wolff, *Hosea,* Hermeneia (Philadelphia: Fortress, 1974), 14. See also James Luther Mays, *Hosea: A Commentary,* Old Testament Library (Philadelphia: Westminster, 1969), 75.

2. The term is from Max Weber, *Ancient Judaism* (New York: Free Press, 1952) 189; originally published 1918–21.

3. See Helgard Balz-Cochors, "Gomer oder die Macht der Astarte," *ET* 42 (1982): 37–65.

4. A similar conclusion is reached by Robert A. Oden, Jr., *The Bible Without Theology: The Theological Tradition and Alternatives To It* (San Francisco: Harper and Row, 1987), 131–153. Oden, however, does not consider the role of sexual fantasies. He believes that the Bible shares in the accusation of Canaanite cult prostitution (but see the discussion of "sacred prostitution" in this chapter), and believes that both Deuteronomy and modern scholarship have been motivated by a theological desire to denigrate Canaanite religion in order to make biblical religion more distinctive. See also JoAnne Hackett, "Can a Sexist Model Liberate Us? Ancient Near Eastern Fertility Goddesses," *Journal of Feminist Studies in Religion* 5 (1989): 65–76.

5. Robertson-Smith, *Religion of the Semites* (New York: Schocken, 1972), 455, originally published in 1889.

6. James George Frazer, *Adonis, Attis and Osiris: Studies in the History of Oriental Religion,* vol. 1/4 of *The Golden Bough* (London: Macmillan, 1906), 21–25.

7. William Foxwell Albright, *Archaeology and the Religion of Israel* (Baltimore, Md.: Johns Hopkins University Press, 1946), 75–77; Gerhard von Rad, *Old Testament Theology,* vol. 2 (New York: Harper and Row, 1962–65) 141–2, originally published 1957–60; and H. W. Wolff, *Hosea.*

8. Wilhelm Rudolph, "'Praparierte Jungfrauen' (zu Hosea 1)," *ZAW* 75 (1963): 65–73; and Edwin M. Yamauchi, "Cultic Prostitution: A Case Study in Cultural Diffusion," in *Orient and Occident: Essays Presented to Cyrus H. Gordon on the Occasion of his Sixty-fifth Birthday,* Harry Hoffner, Jr., ed., AOAT 22, (Neukirchen-Vluyn: Neukirchener Verlag, 1973) 213–222.

9. 1, 199. Quoted from A. D. Godley, *Herodotus,* Loeb Classical Library (London: Heinemann, 1920).

10. W. Baumgartner, "Herodots babylonische und assyrische Nachrichtens," *Archiv Orientalni* 18 (1950): 69–109.

11. Friedrich Oertel, *Herodots Ägyptischer Logos und die Glaubwürdigkeit Herodots* (Bonn: Habelt, 1970) and O. Kimball Armayor, "Did Herodotus Ever Go to Egypt?" *Journal of the American Research Center in Egypt* 15 (1978): 59–73.

12. Eva Keuls, *The Reign of the Phallus: Sexual Politics in Ancient Athens* (New York: Harper and Row, 1985).

13. Robert A. Oden, Jr., *The Bible Without Theology,* 131–153.

14. For this term, see the forthcoming book by Phyllis Bird, *The Qedeshah in Ancient Israel;* and Joan Goodnick Westenholz, "Tamar, *qedeša, qadištu* and Sacred Prostitution in Mesopotamia," *Harvard Theological Review* 82:3 (1989): 245–266.

15. Deut. 13:18.

16. They were present in the days of Rehoboam (1 Kings 14:24), but were removed by King Asa (1 Kings 15:11), with those still remaining disposed of by his son, Jehoshafat (1 Kings 22:47). Nevertheless, two hundred years later, they were back in the temple itself, and Josiah had to get rid of them (2 Kings 23:7).

17. It is tempting to call this "Canaanite" worship, as do most scholars. However, this religion was not adjoined to an originally pure Israelite religion. On the contrary, Israelite religion grew up in the Canaanite milieu, and this improper cult was probably a native Israelite cult that was outgrown and condemned by the increasingly sophisticated monotheism of the biblical authors. On this, see Baruch Halpern, "Brisker Pipes than Poetry: The Development of Israelite Monotheism," *Judaic Perspectives on Ancient Israel,* Jacob Neusner, Baruch Levine and Ernest S. Friedrichs, eds. (Philadelphia: Fortress, 1987), 77–115.

18. W. von Soden, "Zur Stellung des Geweihten (qdš) in Ugarit," *Ugarit-Forschungen* 2 (1970): 329–338.

19. Mayer Gruber, "The Qadeš in the Book of Kings and in Other Sources," *Tarbiz* 52/2 (1983): 167–176.

20. The interpretation of male prostitute first appears in the Vulgate (translating Deut. 23:8f.) and in the Babylonian Talmud (BT Sanhedrin 55b).

21. As, in fact, does Gruber.

22. Johannes Renger, "Untersuchungen zum Priestertum in der altbabylonischen Zeit," *Zeitschrift für Assyriologie Neue Folge* 24 (1967): 110–88; W. C. Gwaltney, Jr., *The Qadištum and the Ištaritum in Mesopotamian Society,* Hebrew Union College, Ph.D. diss. 1964.

23. 2 Kings 23:7.

24. Johannes Renger, "Untersuchungen zum Priestertum in der altbabylonischen Zeit," ZANF 24 (1967): 110–118.

25. We don't really know who she was, since she is identified only as "Inanna," the goddess.

CHAPTER 19    Gifts of the Greeks

1. The term "Jewish" is used to describe Israel during the period of the second Temple and later.

2. For the early struggle between the "pious" and the Hellenists, see E. Bickerman, *The God of the Maccabees: Studies on the Meaning and Origin of the Maccabean Revolt,* Horst Moehring, tr. (Leiden: Brill, 1979).

3. The foundation works are by Saul Lieberman, *Hellenism in Jewish Palestine: Studies in the Literary Transmission, Beliefs and Manners in the I Century* B.C.E.–*IV Century* C.E. (New York: Jewish Theological Seminary, 1950), Saul Lieberman, "How Much Greek in Jewish Palestine?" in *Biblical and Other Studies,* A. Altman, ed., Philip W. Lown Institute of Advanced Judiac Studies (Brandeis University), Studies and Texts, vol 1 (Cambridge: Harvard University Press, 1962), 123–141. Of note also are Martin Hengel, *Judaism and Hellenism* (Philadelphia: Fortress, 1981), originally published 1974. For a critical review of Hengel, see A. Momigliano, "'Judenthum und Hellenismus' by Martin Hengel," *Journal of Theological Studies,* 21 (1970): 495–499. See, also, the essays in H. A. Fischel, ed., *Essays in Greco-Roman and Related Talmudic Literature* (New York: Ktav 1977). For the most recent overview, see Shaye Cohen, *From the Maccabees to the Mishnah* (Philadelphia: Westminster, 1987), with extensive bibliography.

4. Here, I do not speak from primary sources. My Greek is barely adequate to control the sources cited by others, and I do not independently search the primary texts. I am relying here,

however, on a considerable body of work by serious scholars. Among the earliest were Philip Slater, *The Glory of Hera: Greek Mythology and the Greek Family* (Boston: Beacon Press, 1968), a psychologist, rather than a classicist; and E. K. Lacey, *The Family in Classical Greece* (Ithaca: Cornell University Press, 1968). A very influential study is by Sarah B. Pomeroy, *Goddesses, Whores, Wives, and Slaves: Women in Classical Antiquity* (New York: Schocken Books, 1975). Among the most important of the recent studies is John Gould, "Law, Custom, and Myth: Aspects of the Social Position of Women in Classical Athens," *JHS* 100 (1980): 38–59; Eve Cantarella, *L'ambiguo mallano, Condizione e immagine della donna nell' antichita greca e romana* (Rome: Editori Riunite, 1981); the English version is *Pandora's Daughters: The Role and Status of Women in Greek and Roman Antiquity* trans. by Maureen B. Fant (Baltimore: Johns Hopkins University Press, 1987); M. Lefkowitz and M. B. Fant, *Women's Life in Greece and Rome* (London: Duckworth, 1982); Marilyn Arthur, "From Medusa to Cleopatra: Women in the Ancient World," in *Becoming Visible: Women in European History,* 2d ed., Renate Bridenthal, Claudia Koonz, and Susan Stuard, eds. (Boston: Houghton Mifflin, 1987) 79–105; Sally Humphries, *The Family, Women and Death* (London: Routledge & Kegan Paul, 1983); Aline Roussell, *Porneia: On Desire and the Body in Antiquity* (Oxford: Blackwell, 1988); John J. Winkler, *The Constraints of Desire: The Anthropology of Sex and Gender in Ancient Greece* (New York: Routledge, 1990); and David Halperin, John Winkler, and Froma Zeitlin, eds., *Before Sexuality: The Construction of Erotic Experience in the Ancient Greek World* (Princeton: Princeton University Press, 1990).

5. Respectable Athenian women lived intensely private lives, to a large measure confined to special women's quarters of their homes, coming out in public primarily for weddings, funerals, and festivals. Men spent their days in the public places of the marketplace, the academy, and the gymnasium, coming home primarily to hold banquets (symposia) in the *andron*—the men's hall in their homes. Proper married women were not found at these symposia, at which the men were attended by slaves and *heterae,* women trained to provide chat, music, dance, and sex at these parties. Boys stayed at home with their mothers until they were about seven, at which point they entered the male world. This system created separate spheres of life. The women, left at home, in effect ran the home, controlling it economically and being the major authority to the young child. But the ideal life of the society was participation in the public life of the city, a life to which women had no access except as mediated through the head of their household (father, husband, son). For the wedding, see James Redfield, "Notes on the Greek Wedding," *Arethusa* 15 (1982): 181–201; for separate quarters, see Susan Walker, "Women and Housing in Classical Greece: The Archaeological Evidence," in *Images of Women in Antiquity,* Averril Cameron and Amelie Kuhrt, eds. (Detroit, Mich.: Wayne State University Press, 1983). For the symposia, the pictures on Greek vase paintings collected by Eva C. Keuls, *The Reign of the Phallus: Sexual Politics in Ancient Athens* (New York: Harper and Row, 1985) are an interesting counterbalance to the intellectual impression of symposia conveyed by the philosophical writings.

6. See Marilyn B. Arthur, "Cultural Strategies in Hesiod's Theogony: Law, Family, Society," *Arethusa* 15 (1982): 63–81.

7. Nicole Loraux, "Sur la Race des femmes et quelques-unes de ses tribus," *Arethusa* 11 (1978): 43–87; and J. J. Winkler and G. E. R. Lloyd, *Science, Folklore, and Ideology* (Cambridge: Cambridge University Press, 1983), 58–112.

8. Froma I. Zeitlin, "Cultic Models of the Female: Rites of Dionysus and Demeter," *Arethusa* 15 (1982): 129–153.

9. See the analyses of P. Slater, *The Glory of Hera;* E. C. Keuls, *The Reign of the Phallus;* Page DuBois, *Centaurs and Amazons: Women and the Pre-History of the Great Chain of Being* (Ann Arbor: University of Michigan Press, 1982); and William Blake Tyrell, *Amazons: A Study in Athenian Mythmaking* (Baltimore and London: Johns Hopkins University Press, 1984).

10. F. Zeitlin, "Cultic Models of the Female," 129–157.

11. This is the viewpoint of Philip Slater in *The Glory of Hera,* who described the pathological nature of the Greek family and its reflection in the mythology, and felt that family dynamics caused the gynophobic, narcissistic, Greek male personality.

12. Dorothy Dinnerstein has pointed out in *The Mermaid and the Minotaur: Sexual Arrangement and Human Malaise* (New York: Harper and Row, 1976) that childrearing arrangements in which the female is the sole care-giver to young children leads to both a fear of women and a feeling that they are somewhat less-than-human. If this is true in the precontemporary "normal" Western family, in which fathers have had a minimal role in childbearing, it was certainly even more emphatically the case in the Greek system, in which children were reared only by women until the boys joined the male world at seven.

13. Froma I. Zeitlin, "The Dynamics of Misogyny: Myth and Mythmaking in the Oresteia," *Arethusa* 11 (1978): 149–184; and Marilyn Arthur, "From Medusa to Cleopatra: Women in the Ancient World," in *Becoming Visible,* 79–105.

14. Aeschylus, *Eumenides,* lines 658–661. Translation by Richard Lattimore, in *Aeschylus I: Oresteia. The Complete Greek Tragedies* D. Grene and R. Lattimore, eds. (Chicago and London: University of Chicago Press, 1953), 158.

15. The fear of female sexuality survives in the mask of the Gorgon that Athena wears around her neck, for the Medusa is probably best understood as the *vagina dentata.* In Athens, actual vaginas and pubic areas were kept hairless by depilation.

16. *Eumenides,* lines 737–738. For the various Greek ideas on conception, see Winkler and Lloyd, *Science, Folklore and Ideology,* 58–112. On the implications of the theory of monogenesis (that only the sperm is active in conception and the woman is only the nurturing ground), see Carol Delaney, "Seeds of Honor, Fields of Shame," in *Honor and Shame and the Unity of the Mediterranean,* David D. Gilmore, ed., Special Publications of the American Anthropological Association, 22 (Washington: AAA, 1987), 35. Delaney attributes much of the patriarchal social pattern of the circum-mediterranean to the monogenetic theory of conception. However, the fact that the Greeks also had other theories of conception may indicate that it was patriarchy that influenced the adoption of the monogenesis theory of conception rather than vice versa.

17. Hesiod, *Theogony,* line 591–593, 601. Text translation by Judith Peller Hallett. Quoted from Sarah Pomeroy, *Goddesses, Whores, Wives, and Slaves,* 3. A good selection of misogynist statements can be found in Pomeroy's book and is therefore not repeated here.

18. For Semonides see M. Lloyd-Jones, *Females of the Species: Semonides on Women* (London: Duckworth, 1975), and E. Cantarella, *Pandora's Daughters,* pp. 35–37. Not all the writers of Greece were misogynists: Homer and the Lyric poets give a much happier picture of the relationship between the sexes. Marilyn Archer suggests that their aristocratic outlook made them think it less imperative to control their women. M. Archer, "Early Greece: The Origins of the Western Attitude Toward Women," *Arethusa* 6 [1973]: 7–58.

19. For example, Plato's Timaeus 42. For further on Plato, see David M. Halperin, "Why Is Diotima a Woman? Platonic *Eros* and the Figuration of Gender," in *Before Sexuality: The Construction of Erotic Experience in the Ancient Greek World* David M. Halperin, John Winkler, nd Froma Zeitlin, eds. (Princeton: Princeton University Press, 1990), 257–308.

20. See, initially, Winkler and Lloyd, *Science, Folklore, and Ideology* (1983).

21. According to S. Pomeroy, *Goddesses, Whores, Wives, and Slaves,* 93–119, traditional misogyny is being reexamined in these tragedies. According to E. Keuls, *The Reign of the Phallus,* traditional misogyny is being reinforced. Dorothea Wender, "Plato: Misogynist, Pedophile, and Feminist," *Arethusa* 6 (1973): 75–90, points out that the woman-question is clearly in the wind in the last part of the fifth century.

22. For Greeks on sex, see Hans Licht [Paul Brandt], *Sexual Life in Ancient Greece* (London: Routledge 1932); K. J. Dover, "Classical Greek Attitudes to Sexual Behavior," *Arethusa* 6 (1973): 59–74; K. J. Dover, *Greek Homosexuality* (Cambridge: Harvard University Press, 1978); Michel Foucault, *The Uses of Pleasure: The History of Sexuality,* vol. 2, Robert Hurley, tr. (New York: Random House, 1986).

23. Fr. B7, quoted from Dover, "Classical Greek Attitudes," 59–74; also see John J. Winkler, *The Constraints of Desire: The Anthropology of Sex and Gender in Ancient Greece* (New York: Routledge, 1990).

24. Greek philosophers also wanted to metamorphose and sublimate physical desire, to use sex as a metaphor for knowledge; procreation, for learning. In the Platonic tradition, one could climb the ladder of perfection from erotic attachment to a male (in Plato, erotic attachment to the female did not even get one onto this ladder), upwards to a knowledge of true beauty and spirit, true (disembodied) love. See Evelyn Fox Keller, "Love and Sex in Plato's Epistemology," in *Reflections of Gender and Science,* Evelyn Fox Keller, ed. (New Haven: Yale University Press, 1985), 21–32; Mary O'Brien, *The Politics of Reproduction,* (London: Routledge and Kegan Paul, 1983), 116–139.

25. Ecclesiastes was probably written in the third century B.C.E. and shows influence of and reaction to, Greek ideas. See Martin Hengel, *Judaism and Hellenism* (Philadelphia: Fortress, 1981), 115–129, originally published 1974; and R. Braun, *Kohelet und die frühhellenistische Popularphilosophie,* BZAW 130 (Berlin: de Gruyter, 1973).

26. M. Hengel, *Judaism and Hellenism,* 131–153.

27. For Ben Sira on the subject of women, see Warren Trenchard, *Ben Sira's View of Women: A Literary Analysis,* Brown University Judaic Studies 38 (Chico, Calif.: Scholars Press, 1982).

28. Ben Sira, 42:14.

29. Ben Sira, 25:24. The Christian condemnation of Eve is well known and has been well documented, among others by J. A. Phillips *Eve: The History of An Idea* (San Francisco: Harper and Row, 1984). The Adam and Eve story has been much less important in the history of Judaism. However, in Talmudic times, the same condemnation of Eve and all women is found in the explanation of the special commandments for women. Since Adam was the blood of the world, and Eve caused his death, she was given the precept on menstruation. Since, also, she caused the death of Adam, the pure Challah of the world, and the light of the world, she therefore has the precepts, of taking Challah and lighting Sabbath candles: YT Shabbat 2, 5b, 34; Gen Rabbah 17:7. It is possible that this verse in Ben Sira has been misinterpreted in the light of later commentaries, for which see discussion in chapter 10, note 18. Nevertheless, the generally misogynist tone of Ben Sira is indisputable.

30. Ben Sira 9:7–9, 41:21.

31. For reasons as yet unknown, Gilgamesh has a number of affinities to Greek tales, not the least of which is that the protagonist, Gilgamesh, is semi-divine.

32. For biblical ideas on beauty, see Mathias Augustin, *Der Schöne Mensch in Alten Testament und in hellenistischen Judentum,* (Frankfort-am-Main: Lang, 1983).

33. Shaye Cohen, *From the Maccabees to the Mishnah* (Philadelphia: Westminster, 1987), 43.

34. R. M. Charles, *The Apocrypha and Pseudepigrapha of the Old Testament,* vol. I: *Apocrypha* (Oxford: Clarendon, 1913), 242–247, and Carey A. Moore, *Judith,* Anchor Bible Series (Garden City: Doubleday, 1985), 67–72.

35. Judith 12:20 quoted in translation of Carey Moore, *Judith.*

36. Gen. 6:1–4.

37. 1 En., chs. 6–11 and 106.

38. Chapter 5. See Bernard P. Prusak, "Woman: Seductive Siren and Source of Sin? Pseudepigraphical Myth and Christian Origins," in *Religion and Sexism,* Rosemary Ruether, ed., (New York: Simon and Schuster, 1974), 89–116.

39. 9:2–9, 23:22–6, 25:23–26, 42: 9–14.

40. Testament of Reuben 6:3; Testament of Judah 14:3, 16:1–5.

41. The later commentary, the Gemara, adds that this is because women are "light-headed," meaning that they would not prevent each other from immoral behavior.

42. The Gemara urges that no less than three men be alone with a woman (so that if one had to go to the bathroom, there would still be at least two men with the woman.)

43. David Weiss-Halivni, *Midrash, Mishnah and Gemara: The Jewish Predilection for Justified Law* (Cambridge: Harvard University Press, 1986).

44. BT Qiddushin 81a.

45. This is dramatically different from the one story in the Bible which is even remotely similar: that of the young adulterous wife in Proverbs 7 who comes to invite the young man to a night of love. Her looks are not enough; she has to talk the young man into her bed, assuring him that her husband can cause them no danger and tempting him with the offer of meat and a beautifully perfumed environment.

46. Keth 13b, Y. Keth 1. See also BT Sukkah 53, with discussion by E. Urbach, *The Sages: Their Concepts and Beliefs,"* Israel Abrahams, tr. (Cambridge: Harvard University Press, 1987), 476.

47. BT Qiddushin 80b.

48. BT Qiddushin 39b–40a. See also AdRNA, Judah Goldin, *The Fathers According to Rabbi Nathan* (New Haven: Yale University Press, 1955), 63, for the story of Akiba conquering his impulse.

49. BT Qiddushin 81a.

50. BT Menachot 44a. See also Sifra, Num. 115. The passage is discussed by Warren Zev Harvey, "The Pupil, The Harlot and the Fringe Benefits," *Prooftexts* 6/3 (1986): 259–264.

51. This episode is discussed by M. Herschel Levine, "Three Talmudic Tales of Seduction," *Judaism* 144 (1987): 466–469. It is slightly different from the account in BT Qiddushin 81b and is based on manuscript readings. See the discussion by Yonah Fraenkel, "Remarkable Phenomena in the Text—History of the Aggadic Stories" (Hebrew) in *Proceedings of the Seventh World Congress of Jewish Studies III* (Jerusalem: World Union of Jewish Studies, 1981), 59–61.

52. Women, of course, were considered "light-headed," meaning that they were even more likely to succumb to sexual temptation than the men. There is a story about the great scholar

Beruriah, the wife of Rabbi Meir, in which Meir decided to test his wife's virtue by sending a disciple to seduce her. When she succumbed, she was so mortified that she hanged herself (Avodah Zarah 18b, and particularly Rashi's commentary). Rashi is sometimes suspected of elaborating or inventing this story, perhaps as a caution to his learned daughters not to be complacent in the light of their extraordinary learning. However, the story has ancient roots and is part of the same literary tradition as an episode in the *Life of Secundus* in which Secundus, disturbed by a misogynist's claim that every woman can be bought, returned to his mother's home disguised as a cynical philosopher, and arranged for intercourse with her for fifty gold pieces. When he revealed his identity she hanged herself. See Schwarzbaum, in *Studies in Aggadah and Jewish Folklore* Issachar Ben Ami and Joseph Dan, eds., (Jerusalem: Magnes, 1983), 66–71, as quoted by Herschel Levine, "Three Talmudic Tales of Seduction," 466–469.

53. Judg. 5:27.

54. BT Yebamoth 103a; the explanation of Rashi and Tosephot adds that the purpose of this intercourse was to tire him out so that he could sleep. The phrase "between her feet" is suggestive, and we might infer the possibility that in the earlier poetic account of Yael's deeds, preserved in Judges 5, there might have been a tradition of erotic attraction, at least a hint of double entendre. In the prose account of Judges 4, written during the classical period of Israel, there is no trace of sexuality.

55. BT Sotah 9b.

56. BT Megillah 14a. The Tosephot, medieval commentators, question whether this is not an exaggeration, holding that no man would walk so far because of a thigh. However, their modification is very minor, for they suggest only that we should read that he marched by the light of *her,* i.e., because he was so attracted to her.

57. BT Megillah 15a. The continuation of this passage indicates that not everyone was willing to accept the erotic theory of all womanhood: "Rabbi Isaac said, 'Whoever says "Rahab, Rahab" at once has an issue.' Said Rabbi Nahman to him, 'I say "Rahab, Rahab" and nothing happens to me.' He replied, 'I was speaking of one who knows her and is intimate with her.'"

58. Åke Sjöberg, "Eve and the Chameleon," *In the Shelter of Elyon,* pp. 217–225 (Ahlstrom Av).

59. Bernard P. Prusak, "Woman: Seductive Siren and Source of Sin?," in *Religion and Sexism,* R. Reuther, ed. (New York: Simon & Schuster, 1974), 89–116.

60. There were splinter ascetic groups, such as the Essenes.

61. BT Sotah 48a.

62. BT Yebamot 77a, Gittin 12a.

63. Bereshit Rabba 8:11.

64. Bernadette Brooten, *Women Leaders in the Ancient Synagogue,* Brown University Judaic Studies 36 (Chico, Calif.: Scholars Press, 1982); see, also, Shaye Cohen, *From the Maccabees to the Mishnah.*

65. The extreme position is the vision of Rabbi Dimmi, "Woman was swathed like a mourner, isolated from people and shut up in prison," BT Eruvin 100b. For the situation of women in Greco-Roman times in Israel, see Gunter Mayer, *Die Judische Frau in Der hellenistisch-romischen Antike* Stuttgart, 1987; Judith Romney Wegner, *Chattel or Person? The Status of Women in the System of the Mishnah, Brown University Judaica Series* 19; Leonie Archer, *Her Price Is Beyond Rubies: The Jewish Woman in Graeco-Roman Palestine, JSOT,* suppl. ser. 60 (1990), Leonard Swidler, *Women in Judaism: The Status of Women in Formative Judaism* (Metuchen, N. Jersey: Scarecrow Press, 1976); Judith Baskin, "The Separation of Women in Rabbinic Judaism," in *Women, Religion, and Social Change,* Yvonne Haddad and Ellison Findly, eds. (Albany, N.Y.: State University of New York Press, 1985), 3–18; Theodore Friedman, "The Shifting Role of Women, From the Bible to the Talmud," *Judaism* 144 (1987): 479–488; Leonie Archer, "The Role of Jewish Women in the Religion, Ritual and Cult of Graeco-Roman Palestine," in *Images of Women in Antiquity,* 273–287; Ross Kraemer, "Women in the Religions of the Greco-Roman World," *Religious Studies Review* 9 (1983): 127–139 (with extensive bibliography); Shaye Cohen, "Women in the Synagogues of Antiquity," *Conservative Judaism* 34 (1980): 23–29; and Judith Hauptmann, "Images of Women in the Talmud," in *Religion and Sexism,* 184–212.

66. Arthur Baer, *Philo's Use of the Categories Male and Female* (Leiden: Brill, 1970); and Judith Romney Wegner, "The Image of Woman in Philo," SBL seminar papers, (Chico, Calif.: Scholars Press, (1982), 551–563.

67. Noted by J. Baskin, "The Separation of Women."

68. Peggy Sanday has argued that prior cultural configurations do much to shape human

responses to stressful change, and that if a people's sex-role plan contains male and female principles, the stage is set for mythical male dominance; if the traditional sex-role plan is part of the
"outer" configuration, women will become objects to be controlled: Peggy Sanday, *Female Power
and Male Dominance* (Cambridge: Cambridge University Press, 1981). Both Rabbinic and later
Judaic traditions seem to conform more to what Sanday has described as "mythical male dominance." Sanday's own analysis of Judaism is flawed by a lack of biblical knowledge and an assumption that Israel always had a purely male system.

69. BT Sotah 47a on Mishnah Sotah 9:9.

70. The Christian understanding of sexuality has been the subject of considerable study. See,
most recently, Peter Brown, *The Body and Society: Men, Women and Sexual Renunciation in
Early Christianity* (New York: Columbia University Press, 1988).

## APPENDIX    The Goddesses of Sumer

1. For Inanna, see M-Th. Barrelet, "Les déesses armées et ailées: Inanna-Ishtar," *Syria* 32
(1955):222–260; W. W. Hallo and J. J. van Dijk, *The Exaltation of Inanna* (New Haven: Yale
University Press, 1968); J. J. M. Roberts, *The Earliest Semitic Pantheon* (Baltimore, MD: Johns
Hopkins University Press, 1972), 37–40; Thorkild Jacobsen, *Treasures of Darkness* (New Haven:
Yale University Press, 1976), 135–143; Claus Wilcke, "Inanna/Ishtar," *Reallexikon der Assyriologie* 5 (1976): 74–87; Brigitte Groneberg, "Die sumerisch-akkadische Inanna/Ištar: Hermaphrodi-
tos?" *WO* 17 (1986): 31–46; J. Bottero, "La femme, l'amour et la guerre en Mesopotamie ancienne," *Poikilia: Etudes offertes à J. P. Vernant* (Paris: Éditions de l'École des hautes études en
sciences sociales, 1987), 172f; Rikvah Harris, "The Paradox of Ishtar, Destroyer of Boundaries,"
paper delivered at Rencontre Assyriologique Internationale, Philadelphia, 1988; Jean-Jacques
Glassner, "Inanna et les mes," ibid.

2. For Nintur-Ninhursag, see T. Jacobsen, "Notes on Nintur," *Or.* 42 (1973): 274–298.

3. For Ninissina, see W. Romer, "Einige Beobachtungen zut Gottin Nini(nsina) auf Grund
von Quelle der Ur III-Zeit und der altbabylonischen Periode," *lišan mithurti,* AOAT 1 (1969) 279–
305.

4. As with so many interrelationships of the Sumerian pantheon, the causes for theological
connections are complex. Ninurta of Nippur is closely identified with Ningirsu of Lagash; Ningirsu's mother is Ninhursag. One could, therefore, argue that the equation of Ninlil with Ninhursag
was a result of the conflation of Ninurta and Ninhursag. But the "mother" identification fits
Ninlil, the mother of the many important sons of Enlil.

5. For Nisaba, see W. W. Hallo, "The Cultic Setting of Sumerian Poetry," CRRA 17 (1970),
116–134; Daniel Reisman, "A 'Royal' Hymn of Isbi-Erra to the Goddess Nisaba," *Kramer Anniversary Volume,* Barry Eichler, ed., AOAT 25 (1976): 357–367; and Miguel Civil, "Enlil and
Ninlil: The Marriage of Sud," JAOS 103 (1983): 43–45.

6. Lines 85–87.

7. These epithets are from the hymn, Nisaba and Enki, (Nin mul an-gim), W. W. Hallo,
ed. CRRA 17 (1970), 116–134.

# Index

Abel, 94, 111, 253
Abigail, 129–30, 132–34, 209, 255, 256, 257, 260
Abihu, 101
Abijah, 121
Abimelech, King, 138, 140, 256, 258
Abishag, 130, 255
Abner, 260
Abraham, 98, 100, 101, 194, 247, 273
  civilization's origins and, 108, 113
  relationship with women, 123, 131, 135
  trickery by, 138
Absalom, 121, 261
Abu Salabikh texts, 10, 11, 43, 70
Achish, King, 138, 261
Achsah, 130, 131, 255, 259
Ada, 253
Adad, 88
Adam, 23, 111, 113, 129, 139, 195, 209–10, 217, 249–50, 251, 278–79
  early version of, 108–9
  gender ideology and, 141–42
Adonijah, 130, 258
Adultery
  Assyrian law on, 193
  Bible on, 119, 124, 192, 194, 196–97, 211
Aeschylus, 204, 252
Agade, 62, 65, 233
Agamemmnon, 204
Agricultural fertility, 15, 20, 46, 215; see also Asherah
  in Greece, 215
  in Israel, 89, 90, 91–95, 100, 103, 105–6, 215
  sacred marriage and, 50–57, 247
Agrig, 36
Agushaya Hymn, 30–31, 67, 78
Ahab, King, 128, 156, 157, 260, 261
Ahasuerus, King, 130
Ahijah, 121, 259

Ahimaaz, 261
Ahimelech the priest, 138, 189
Aiah, 122
Akiba, Rabbi, 207–8
Akka, King, 63
Akkad, 2, 172, 222
  fall of, 65–66
  kings of, 61, 62, 64, 65–66
  language of, 5
  marginalization in, 70, 71
  pantheon in, 10–11
  Sumer united with, 60, 65
Akkadian period: see Sargonic period
Alexander the Great, 203
Al-Khansa, 234
Amageshtinanna, 14–15, 38, 39, 40, 234
Amaushumgalanna, 59; see also Dumuzi
Amazons, 204
Ammiditana, King, 236, 242
Ammisaduqa of Babylon, 74
Amnon, 125, 134–35, 141, 197, 262, 273, 274
Amos, Book of, 99, 104, 128, 154, 168, 169, 248
Amram, Rabbi, 208
An, 20, 39, 46, 49, 71, 78, 221, 222, 223, 224, 232, 240
  civilization's origins and, 111
  kings and, 62, 65
  marginalization and, 72, 242
An-anum, god list, 11
Anat, 86, 156, 159; see also Asherah
Anath-Bethel, 266
Anat-yahu, 266
Angels, 106, 218
Anu, 86
Anzu, 232
Apkallus, myth of the, 111
Apocrypha, 206, 210, 214
Apsu, 17, 75
Aratta, 62–63

Aristotle, 205
Ark of the covenant, 154, 155
Aruru, 49, 75, 223; see also Ninhursag
Asa, King, 276
Asalluhi, 71
Asarluhi, 43, 49, 95, 235; see also Marduk
Asherah, 153–61
  description of, 155
  as goddess, 156–58, 159
  notes on, 264–66
Ashnan, 231
Ashrata, 265
Assur, 174–75
Assyria, 2, 155, 182, 193
  kings of, 66
  marginalization in, 76, 78, 79, 80
  Zion's image and, 174–75
Assyrian chronicles, 64
Astarte, 156, 159; see also Asherah
Athaliah, Queen, 122, 126–27, 255
Athena, 179, 204, 277–78
ʾAthirat, 156; see also Asherah
Atrahasis Epic, 74, 75, 87–88, 245
Azag, 15

Ba'al, 5, 86, 127, 151, 244
  Asherah and, 156–57, 158, 160, 265
  as rainmaker, 89–90, 91, 156–57
Ba'al-Peor, 139
Baba, 37, 221, 222, 236; see also Inanna
  childbirth and, 49
  healing and, 39, 223
  sacred marriage and, 52
Babylon, 2, 92, 172, 174, 182, 200
Babylonian exile, 106, 202, 247
Babylonian period, 10, 11, 70, 76
  marginalization in, 74, 76–77, 78, 79, 80
Badtibira, 222
Balags, 37, 43
Bat Ami, 169
Bathsheba, 122, 130, 140, 197, 206, 254, 258
Beer brewing, 32, 33, 35, 40
Belit-ili, 75, 223; see also Ninhursag
Benjamin, 166
Ben Pappi, Rabbi Hanina, 208
Ben Sira, 182, 206, 207, 251, 278, 279
ben Zakkai, Rabbi Yochanan, 211
Beruriah, 280
Bestiality, biblical view of, 193, 195, 196
Beth-Shemesh, 101
Bezalel, 114, 116
Bible, 3, 5, 6, 50, 84, 92, 93, 213; see also specific books of
  on civilization's origins, 108–17: notes on, 249–54
  Greeks and, 205–6, 209–10
  on healing, 95–96
  misogyny absent in, 151

New Testament of, 151, 206
  on procreation, 97–98
  on rainfall, 90, 92
  sexuality in, 140–41, 187–98, 199, 201, 202, 211–12: notes on, 272–75
  women in: see Women in the Bible
Bilhah, 123, 131, 254, 259
Boaz, 137
Bronze Age, 158, 253, 265

Cain, 94, 111–12, 252, 253
Caleb, 130, 131, 259
Canaan, 2, 102, 139, 154, 158, 194
  Asherah and, 156–57, 159
  Israel influenced by, 83
  orgy myth and, 199, 200, 201, 276
  rain importance in, 90, 91
Çatal Huyuk, 92
Cherubim, 154, 155
Childbirth, 23, 24, 49–50, 75, 97, 98, 121; see also Fertility; Procreation
Chosur, 112
Christianity, 1, 213–14, 216, 218
Chronicles, Book of, 265
City goddesses/gods, 9, 10, 12, 62, 223
Civilization, 32–43
  beer brewing and, 32, 33, 35, 40
  biblical account of origins of, 108–17, 249–54
  clothing and, 32, 33, 35, 40
  grain and, 32–33, 34, 35, 110
  learned arts in, 36–44
  notes on, 232–35, 249–54
  surplus storage and, 33–35
Clothing, 32, 33, 35, 40; see also Weaving
Clytemnestra, 204
Covenant, 83, 87, 88, 100–101, 103, 244, 248
Covenant, Book of the, 87
Creation accounts, 72–75
  biblical, 93, 108–9
Cross-dressing, 196
Cultic prostitution, 199, 200–202, 273, 275
Cuneiform law, 83, 113
Cuneiform tablets, 2, 4–5, 200, 229
Curse of Agade, 65, 233, 239

Damascus, 172
Damgalnunna, 37
Damu, 43, 71
Danaids, 204
David, King, 96, 100, 101, 155, 189, 197, 209, 255, 273
  parental metaphor and, 162, 267
  relationship with women, 121, 122, 124, 126, 129, 130, 132–34, 135, 136, 137, 256, 257, 259–60, 261
  trickery used by, 138, 139, 261–62

*Dea nutrix*, 159
Deborah, 127, 254, 256, 258
Decapitated heifer, ceremony of, 196, 245
Delilah, 135–36, 209, 254, 260
Deutero-Isaiah, 99, 149, 218, 272
  parental metaphor used by, 164
  Zion image used by, 168, 175, 176
Deuteronomy, 84, 96, 98, 126, 155, 248,
  264, 273
  on agricultural fertility, 93, 103
  marriage metaphor in, 146
  parental metaphor in, 267
  on prostitution, 201
  on sexuality, 190, 193, 195
Dimmi, Rabbi, 280
Dinah, 194, 232, 254, 274
Dionysus, 204
Divorce, biblical view of, 119, 196, 197,
  273
Domestic women, 22–25
Don Giovanni, 68
Dream interpretation, 38–39, 41, 115
Drought, 90–91, 103–4, 106; *see also* Rain
Dumuzi, 14, 15, 16, 25–26, 231, 232
  laments for, 36, 38, 40, 167
  sacred marriage and, 51, 52–53, 56, 59,
  76, 86, 236, 238
Dynastic period, 33, 59

Ea, 33, 43, 71, 87–88, 235, 244, 246; *see
  also* Enki
  healing and, 95, 97
  marginalization and, 74–75
  warfare and, 67
Eanna, 63, 222, 242
Eannatum, King, 52, 61, 62, 63, 72, 238
Ebla, 10
Ecclesiastes, Book of, 151, 205–6, 243,
  249, 278
Eden, garden of, 109, 111, 129, 250
Egypt, 86, 88, 96, 101, 162, 172, 179, 200
  irrigation system of, 90
  Israel influenced by, 83
  surplus storage in, 115–16
Ehursag of Ur, 61
Ekur temple, 19, 21, 34, 65, 233
El, 5, 86, 157, 244
Eli, 190, 255
Elijah, 89, 90, 121, 131, 156–57, 188, 256,
  260
Eliphaz the Temanite, 271
Elisha, 122, 129, 257, 259
Elkanah, 123
**eme.sal**, 43
En, 241
Enannatumma, 240
Enheduanna, 11, 12, 14, 42, 47, 64, 65, 67,
  79, 235, 240, 241
Enki, 15, 16, 17–18, 19, 20, 22, 23, 26, 27,

28, 31, 33, 142, 221, 222, 223, 230,
  235, 246, 281; *see also* Ea
  civilization's origins and, 110–11
  healing and, 97
  marginalization and, 71, 72–74, 241
  nature and, 46
  Ninurra absorbed by, 43, 71
  place in pantheon, 10
  reproduction and, 48–49
  sacred marriage and, 55
  warfare and, 66–67
Enki and Ninhursag Myth, 15, 16, 17, 22,
  23, 26, 48–49, 72
Enki and Ninmah Myth, 15, 17, 19, 20, 49,
  72–74, 222
Enki and the World Order, 27, 49, 231,
  234, 238
Enkidu, 30, 33, 142, 206
Enlil, 15, 16, 19–21, 20, 29, 34, 38, 39, 46,
  86, 221, 222, 223, 224, 229, 230,
  231, 281
  childbirth and, 49–50
  civilization's origins and, 111
  kings and, 60, 65–66, 77, 241
  marginalization and, 71, 72, 74
  place in pantheon, 10, 12
  procreation and, 48
  as rainmaker, 91
  sacred marriage and, 55
Enlil, Hymn to, 49–50
Enlil and Ninlil Myth, 16, 48, 223
Enmebaragesi, 79
Enmenanna, 64
Enmerkar and the Lord of Aratta Epic, 41–
  42, 62–63, 238
Enoch, 111, 207, 250, 251, 252
Enosh, 112, 254
Ensuhkeshdanna, King, 63
Enuma Elish Myth, 16–17, 66, 71, 74–75,
  76, 244
Ephraim, 163, 166, 167, 267, 268
Er, 123, 124
Ereshkigal, 28, 46, 50, 235
Eridu Lament, 37
Esarhaddon, King, 75
Esau, 136–37, 140, 261
Esther, 130, 254, 262
Euhemerus, 112
Eunuchs, 274
Eve, 23, 111, 113, 129, 139, 209–10, 217,
  250, 251, 252, 278–79
  conflicting interpretations of, 109–10
  gender ideology and, 141–42
"Ewe and Grain," 23, 32, 110, 245
Exodus, Book of, 88, 89, 95, 96, 98, 99,
  101, 102, 269
  on agricultural fertility, 91
  on civilization's origins, 113–14
  on sexuality, 191, 192

Exodus, the, 93, 122, 269
Exorcism, 43, 70
Ezekiel, Book of, 101, 188, 260
    marriage metaphor in, 144, 149, 150,
        151, 264
    on pollution, 102, 245
    Zion image in, 270
Ezra, 261

Fara texts, 43, 70
Father-god, 18
Female figurines, 158–60, 161, 266
Fertility, 47, 75, 199; see also Agricultural
    fertility; Childbirth; Procreation
Flood, biblical account of, 94, 102, 104,
    113, 216
Furies, 204–5

Galas, 43, 67
Gatumdug, 49
Gehazi, 96, 257
Gemara, 207, 279
Gender
    changes in, 35, 43
    ideology of, 30–31
    significance of division in, 12–13
Genesis, Book of, 23, 94, 166, 194, 195,
    209, 214
    on agricultural fertility, 90, 93
    on civilization's origins, 108–9, 113, 250,
        251
    parental metaphor in, 268
    on procreation, 97–98
    on women, 122–23, 126, 128–29, 136
Geshtinanna, 36, 167
Gibeonites, 138
Gilgamesh Epic, 30, 33, 79, 142, 206, 223,
    232, 235, 242, 243, 279
    dream interpretation in, 38, 41
    Inanna in, 59, 61, 63, 77, 78, 236
God, 1, 100–107, 216–17, 243–44; see also
        Marriage metaphor; Parental metaphor;
        Zion
    asexuality of, 188–89, 197
    Asherah and, 153, 154, 156–58, 160,
        161, 264, 265, 266
    childbirth and, 97, 98, 121
    darker side of, 101–2
    goddess attributes absorbed by, 5, 86–87
    healing and, 95–97, 100
    increasing power of, 84–85
    procreation and, 95, 97–98, 100
    as rainmaker, 89–91, 92–93, 95, 98, 100,
        103–4, 156–57, 215, 248
    unexplained acts of, 100–101
Godwomen, 14–31
    domestic image of, 22–25
    gender ideology and, 30–31

    nondomesticated image of, 25–29
    notes on, 229–32
    queenly wife image of, 19–22
Grain, 32–33, 34, 35, 110
Great Matriarch Hymn, 223
Greece, 68, 127, 200, 202, 203–12, 216,
    217–18
    misogyny in, 205–6, 210, 213, 278,
        279–80
    nature and, 215
    notes on, 276–81
    Wisdom-Woman in, 179
Gudea, King, 38, 49, 52, 54, 72, 236
Gudea Temple Hymn, 52
Gula, 36, 221
    childbirth and, 49
    healing and, 39, 43, 71, 95, 223

Hagar, 122, 123, 131, 254, 274
Haggai, 99, 106
Hammurabi, King, 76–77, 239
    laws of, 28, 232
Hamor, 194
Hannah, 98, 123, 127, 254
Hathor, 160
Haya, 39
Healing, 39, 43, 71, 89, 223
    God and, 95–97, 100
he-gál, 50, 55
Hephaistos, 112
Heracles, 204
Herodotus, 200
Hesiod, 203, 204, 205, 252
Hezekiah, King, 153, 154, 155
hili, 63
Hittite culture, 67, 113
Hiyya, Rabbi, 208
Holofernes, 206
Homer, 278
Homosexuality
    biblical view of, 193, 195–96, 273, 275
    Greek view of, 68
Hosea, Book of, 99, 104, 153, 154, 166,
    199, 248, 260
    Asherah and, 264
    marriage metaphor in, 144, 145–46, 147,
        148, 149, 150, 262, 263, 264
    on pollution, 102, 245
Huldah, 255
Huwawa, 243

Iabal, 253
Ibbisin, King, 239
Iddin-Dagan, King, 52, 53, 223, 237, 240
Idolatry, 94, 196
Inanna, 14, 49, 58–69, 142, 174, 212, 221–
    22, 223, 231, 232, 233, 242, 276,
    281; see also Baba

civilization's origins and, 110–11
as daughter, 16
gender ideology and, 30
laments and, 36, 37, 38
love and, 68–69
marginalization avoided by, 71, 77–78, 80
nature and, 46, 47, 235, 236
as nondomesticated woman, 25–29
notes on, 237–41
place in pantheon, 12
sacred marriage and, 51, 52–55, 56, 57, 58–59, 62, 76, 86, 236–37, 238, 240, 247
sexuality and, 47–48, 68, 187–88, 222
warfare and, 66–67, 222
Inanna, Exaltation of, 47
Inanna, Hymn to, 52, 53
Inanna, king and, 52
Inanna and Ebih Myth, 28, 42, 65, 66, 231, 240
Inanna and Enki Myth, 110–11, 222
Inanna and Her Self-Praise, Hymn to, 240
Inanna and Sukalletuda Myth, 28
Inanna–Ninegalla Hymn, 28, 232
Inanna's Descent to the Netherworld, 28, 38, 47
Incantations, 39, 43, 49
Incest taboo, in Bible, 124, 190–91, 196
Inninsagurra Hymns, 42, 64, 65, 240
Intermarriage, biblical view of, 194
Iraq, 2, 3, 4, 10
Iron Age, 158, 159
Irra, 86
Isaac, 98, 100, 101, 138, 261
relationship with women, 122, 131, 136, 259
Isaac, Rabbi, 280
Isaiah, Book of, 104, 128, 188, 272
marriage metaphor in, 263, 264
parental metaphor in, 267
Zion image in, 168, 172–73, 174, 177, 179, 269, 270
Ishbi-irra Hymn, 39
Ishhara, 48; see also Inanna
Ishkur, 46
Ishtar: see Inanna
Ishtar, Hittite hymn to, 67
Isin dynasty, 10, 11, 61, 72, 76, 223, 236
Isis, 160
Israel, 2, 3, 5–6, 83–99, 216; see also Asherah; Bible; God; Marriage metaphor; Parental metaphor; Zion
agricultural fertility in, 89, 90, 91–95, 100, 103, 105–6, 215
civilization origins in, 108, 113–14, 115–16
fall of, 84, 102
female figurines in, 158–60, 161, 266

Greek influence on, 203, 205–6, 211, 213, 276
incest taboo in, 124, 190–91, 196
monogamy in, 125, 190
monotheism origins in, 83–84, 85
notes on, 243–47
orgy myth and, 199, 200–201, 202, 276
pollution concept in, 94–95, 102, 106, 196, 245
sexuality and, 189–90, 272
Issachar, 268

Jabal, 111
Jachebed, 255
Jacob, 98, 100, 101, 140, 166, 194, 257, 261, 273, 274
relationship with women, 122, 123, 124, 126, 131, 135, 136–37, 259, 262
trickery used by, 138, 139
Jael, 255, 256
Jehoahaz, 157
Jehoshafat, King, 265, 276
Jehosheba, 122, 255
Jehu, 157, 265
Jephunneh, 259
Jeremiah, Book of, 104, 153, 217, 248–49, 258
marriage metaphor in, 144, 149, 151, 263
parental metaphor in, 166, 167, 267, 268
on pollution, 102, 245
Zion image in, 168, 169, 170, 171, 172, 175
Jeroboam, King, 96, 121, 154, 255, 256, 259
Jerusalem, 76, 202; see also Zion
Jezebel, Queen, 123, 126–27, 156, 254, 262
Joab, 129, 258
Joash, 122
Job, 249, 271
Jonathan, 126, 261
Joseph, 98, 115–16, 166, 209, 262, 268
Josiah, King, 153, 154, 155
Jubal, 111
Jubilees, Book of, 251
Judah, Rav and Rab, 208
Judah (city)
Asherah in, 155
fall of, 84, 102, 169, 171
female figurines in, 159, 266
marriage metaphor and, 149, 150
Zion image and, 169, 171, 176, 270
Judah (person), 123, 124, 201, 254, 257
Judaism, 1, 214, 216; see also Bible; God; Israel
Judea, 203
Judges, 126, 158
Judith, 206, 262

Kārēt, 134
Ki, 46, 71, 222, 223, 241
Kings, 50–57, 58–69; see also individual
    kings; Sacred marriage
  disappearance of divinity complex, 76–78
  as gods, 59–60
  notes on, 237–41
  as sons of gods, 60–62
Kings, Book of, 155
Kish, 62, 63, 79, 222
Knesset Israel, 183
Korah, 134
Kubatum, 42, 51
Kullab, 62
Kuntillet Ajrud, 156, 157, 158

Labab, 166
Laban, 122, 136, 138, 261, 262, 274
Lagash, 35, 51–52, 71
"Lahar and Ashnan"; see "Ewe and Grain"
Lamashtu, 28, 78, 232, 242
Lamech, 111, 112
Lamentation over the Destruction of Nip-
    pur, 38
Lamentation over the Destruction of Sumer
    and Ur, 37, 38
Lamentation over the Destruction of Ur, 37,
    38
Lamentations, 17, 36–38, 39, 41, 43, 115,
    116, 167, 233–34
Lamentations, Book of, 170, 171, 176, 269,
    274
Larsa dynasty, 10, 11, 61, 72, 76, 236
Leah, 122, 123, 127, 138, 166, 254, 257,
    262, 268
Learned arts, 36–44
Leprosy, 96, 246
Lesbianism, 196, 273
Levirate, 123
Leviticus, Book of, 102, 190, 193, 195, 196
Lipit-Ishter, King, 39
Lisin, 40
Lot, 100, 124–25, 193, 247
Love, Inanna and, 68–69
Ludingirra, 16, 35
Lugalbanda, 59, 61, 63, 77, 223, 229, 232,
    238, 240
Lugal-e Myth, 15, 19, 223
Lugalzagesi, 233
Lukurs, 51
Lulal, 27
Lysistrata, 204

Maacah, 127, 255
Ma'at, 179
Maimonides, 234
Malachi, 99, 106
Male gods, 5–6, 86, 89, 187, 188; see also
    individual gods

Mami, 74
Manasseh, King, 155, 268
Manna, 139, 154
Manoah, 98, 255
Marduk, 43, 85, 86, 95, 235, 244, 246; see
    also Asarluhi
  healing and, 97
  marginalization and, 74, 75–76
  as rainmaker, 89, 91
Mareshah, 176
Marginalization, 66, 70–80
  of mother-goddesses, 71–75, 242
  notes on, 241–43
Mari, 80
Marriage, 67, 119, 190; see also Sacred
    marriage
Marriage metaphor, 144–52, 169, 197
  notes on, 262–64
Marriage of Sud, 19–20, 21, 223
Medea, 204
Medusa, 278
Meir, Rabbi, 207, 280
Menstrual taboos, 193, 272
Mephibosheth, 255
Merab, 255
Mes, King, 236
Mesilim, King, 238
Meskiaggasir, King, 238
Mesopotamia, 4, 50, 68, 91, 95, 110–11,
    115, 272
  archeological excavations in, 2
  gender ideology in, 30
  irrigation system of, 90
  Israel influenced by, 83
  kings of, 60, 63–64, 65
  legal system in, 113, 119
  marginalization in, 70, 71, 75, 77, 78–
    79, 80
  orgy myth and, 201–2
  overpopulation in, 97, 246
  pantheon in, 10, 11–12
  parental metaphor in, 165
  sacred marriage and, 52, 55
  unification in, 11
Metis, 204
Micah, Book of, 255, 270
  Zion image in, 168, 172, 173, 174–75,
    176
Micaiah, 138, 260
Michal, 122, 126, 136, 209, 255
Midrashim, 183, 247
Miriam, 96, 254, 258
Mishnah, 207, 210
Misogyny
  biblical absence of, 151
  in Christianity, 214
  in Greece, 205–6, 210, 213, 278, 279–80
Moab, 125
Moloch, 127, 196

Monogamy, 79, 125, 190
Monotheism, viii–ix, 1–6, 105, 106, 117, 202; *see also* Radical monotheism
abstract quality of, 144, 153
anthropocentricity of, 107
notes on, 229
origin of, 83–84, 85
as revolutionary concept, 88–89
women and, 142–43
Moses, 96, 101, 154, 188, 255, 259, 267
guilt-producing tactics used by, 131–32
relationship with women, 121, 122, 130, 134, 136
trickery used by, 138
Mot, 86
Mother-goddesses, 15–19
agricultural fertility and, 92
biblical mothers compared with, 122
God vs., 97, 98
marginalization of, 71–75, 242
Murder, Israelite view of, 94
Mylitta, 200; *see also* Inanna

Nabal, 132, 133, 134, 209
Naboth, 123, 128
Nabu, 76, 86
Nadab, 101
Nahman, Rabbi, 280
Nammu, 16, 46, 71, 73, 222, 242
Namrat, 37
Nanna, 12, 20, 42, 222, 235
laments of, 38, 233, 234
place in pantheon, 9
Nanše (Nanshe), 35, 37, 38–39, 222–23, 230, 234
Naomi, 124, 137, 254, 258
Naram-Sin, King, 61, 64, 65, 236, 239
Narru, 75; *see also* Enlil
Nathan, 261, 262
Nature, 45–57
notes on, 235–37
sacred marriage and, 50–57
Neo-Sumerian period, 10, 11
Nergal, 46, 235
Netherworld, 15, 20, 28, 36, 38, 46, 50
New Testament, misogyny in, 151, 206
Nimrod, 112
Ninazu, 20, 111
Ninegalla Hymn, 28, 232
Ningal, 37, 38, 240
Ningig, 51
Ningirim, 36, 43, 70–71, 233
Ningirsu, 52, 221, 222, 229, 230, 236, 238, 281
Ningishzida, 55
Ningizzida, 55
Ninhursag, 20, 22, 23, 26, 223, 229, 230, 236, 238–39, 281; *see also* Ninlil; Ninmah; Nintur

childbirth and, 49, 50
kings and, 60
marginalization of, 71–72
as mother, 15, 16, 17, 18
procreation and, 48–49
Ninimma, 22, 72
Ninisinna, 36, 43, 221, 223, 233, 235
childbirth and, 49
healing and, 39, 95
laments of, 37
Ninkarrak, 39
Ninkasi, 33
Ninkurra, 22, 72
Ninlil, 15, 16, 27, 28, 48, 223, 224, 229, 230, 233, 281; *see also* Ninhursag; Sud
place in pantheon, 12
as queenly wife, 19–22
Ninmada, 111
Ninmah, 20, 49, 222, 223, 230; *see also* Ninhursag
marginalization of, 72–74
as mother, 15, 17–18, 19
Ninmehussa Hymn, 64
Ninmenna, 223; *see also* Ninhursag
Ninmesarra Hymn, 42, 64–65, 67
Ninmug, 27
Ninmulangim, 233
Ninnisiga, 22, 72
Ninshubur, 37, 38, 52, 54
Ninsun, 38, 59, 77, 223, 229, 238
Nintinugga, 36, 39, 49, 221, 223, 233
Nintu, 19–20, 49, 238–39; *see also* Sud
Nintur, 16, 49–50, 223, 281; *see also* Ninhursag
Ninurra, 33, 35, 43, 71
Ninurta, 15, 19, 20, 46, 55, 223, 229, 230, 281
Nisaba, 19, 20, 27, 179, 223–24, 233, 281
civilization's arts and, 33, 34, 36, 39–40, 41
marginalization of, 71
procreation and, 49
sacred marriage and, 55
Nisaba and Enki Hymn, 281
Noah, 94, 97, 112
Noiada, 255
Nondomesticated woman, 25–29
Nudimmud, 75, 246; *see also* Ea
Numbers, Book of, 196, 267
Numushda, 37
Nunbarshegunu, 224, 230; *see also* Nisaba
Nungal, 34, 36, 49, 233

Oholiab, 114
Old Testament: *see* Bible
Onan, 123–24
*Oresteia*, 204

Orestes, 204
Orgy myth, 199–202
    notes on, 275–76
Origen, 109
Othniel, 259

Paganism, 1, 2, 3, 86, 112
    agricultural fertility and, 91
    sexuality in, 187
    women in, 118
Pandora, 109–10, 205, 252
Pantheon, 9–13
    notes on, 229
Parental metaphor, 162–67
    notes on, 267–68
Patriarchy, 79, 120, 126
Patristic texts, 151
Pederasty, in Greece, 205
Penina, 123, 127, 255
Pentateuch, 83, 119, 146, 244
Persian period, 218
Personal gods, 9–10
Phallic power, 73
Pharaohs, 115, 121, 122, 133, 138, 140,
    197, 260
Philo, 112, 210, 214, 253–54
Phoenicia, 157
Plato, 205, 214, 278
Plow my Vulva, 52–53, 54–55
Pollution concept, 94–95, 102, 106, 196,
    245
Polyandry, 79
Polygyny, 79
Polytheism, 1, 5, 6, 86, 89
    agricultural fertility and, 92
    shifts of power in, 87–88
Potiphar's wife, 141, 209, 255, 260, 262,
    271
Prisons, 34–35
Procreation, 19, 47, 89; see also Childbirth;
    Fertility
    God and, 95, 97–98, 100
    male role in, 48–49
Prodicus, 205
Prometheus, 110, 252
Prostitution
    biblical view of, 123, 130, 190, 191, 257
    cultic, 199, 200–202, 273, 275
    Inanna identified with, 29, 48, 67, 232,
        241
Proverbs, Book of, 122, 193, 261, 279
    Wisdom-Woman in, 179, 180, 181, 182
Psalm 2, 267
Psalm 29, 84
Psalm 65, 248
Psalm 67, 248
Psalm 68, 89
Psalm 74, 101
Psalm 82, 85, 106

Psalm 89, 101
Psalm 93, 84
Psalms, 146, 269; see also individual psalms
Pseudepigrapha, 210
Puah, 122, 133, 255
Pythagorean system, 203

Qudshu, 156
Queenly wife, 19–22

Rachel, 98, 122, 123, 127, 166, 167, 233,
    234, 254, 257, 262, 268
    strategies used by, 131, 138, 259
    as Wisdom-Woman, 183
Radical monotheism, 106, 154, 155, 217–
    20, 244–45
Rahab, 136, 209
Rain, 46, 215, 222
    God and, 89–91, 92–93, 95, 98, 100,
        103–4, 156–57, 215, 248
Rape, 21, 29
    biblical view of, 192, 194, 274
Rashi, 279, 280
Rebekkah, 98, 122, 126, 140, 254, 257,
    260
    strategies used by, 131, 136–37, 138, 259
Red Sea account, 96
Rehoboam, King, 155
Reproduction: see Procreation
Reuben, 151, 207, 268
Rim-Sin, 79
Rizpah, 122, 255
Rome, 211, 214
Ruth, 123, 124, 137, 141, 254, 258, 261,
    271, 274

Sabbath, 183
Sacred marriage, 58–59, 62, 86, 92, 187,
    202, 223, 236–37, 238, 240, 272
    agricultural fertility and, 50–57, 247
    marginalization and, 76, 77
Saltu, 31, 67, 142
Samaria, 150, 157, 160
Samson, 98, 135–36, 209, 255
Samuel, 89, 98, 132
Sanchuniaton, 112, 254
Šara, 27
Sarah, 98, 122, 123, 140, 206, 254, 267,
    273, 274
    civilization's origins and, 108, 113
    sexuality of, 197
    strategies used by, 131, 138
Sargon, King, 11, 12, 42, 63–64, 66, 79,
    239
Sargonic period, 10, 60, 64, 77, 78
Satan, 210
Saul, King, 89, 122, 126, 127, 132, 133,
    136, 189, 209

Secundus, 280
Semen, 48–49
Semites, 10, 11, 80
Semonides of Amorgos, 205
Septuagint, 260
Seraphim, 188
Seth, 112
Sexuality, 63, 92, 203
  in Bible, 140–41, 187–98, 199, 201, 202,
    211–12: notes on, 272–75
  Inanna and, 47–48, 68, 187–88, 222
  Talmud on, 207–9
Shara, 33, 71
Shechem, 194, 274
Shekhinah, 183
Shelah, 124
Shifrah, 122, 133, 255
Shulgi, King, 52, 61, 237
Shulgi X Hymn, 52, 53, 237
Shu-Sin, King, 42, 51
Sillah, 253
Silulim, 20
Sippar, 9
Sisera, 127, 139, 209, 255
Sodom, 100, 124, 150, 193
Solomon, King, 104, 116, 122, 123, 130,
    255, 258, 274
Song, 39, 115, 116
Song of the Plowing Oxen, 38
Song of the Sea, 188
Song of Songs, 147, 197, 202, 243, 263
Sophia, 182, 218, 271
Stele of Merneptah, 172
Stoning, 192
Sud, 19–20, 21, 29, 223; see also Ninlil;
    Nintu
Sukalletuda, 28, 231
Sumer, 5–6, 92
  Akkad united with, 60, 65
  archeological excavations in, 2
  civilization in, 32–44, 110–11, 113, 114–
    15, 116
  female imagery in, 172
  kings of, 59, 66
  language of, 5, 10, 11, 37, 43
  marginalization in, 71, 79
  mother figures in, 121
  pantheon in, 9–13
  Wisdom-Woman in, 179
Sumerian period, 36
Summa alu, 68
Surplus, storage of, 33–35, 55
  in Israel, 115–16
"Šurpu," 23
Syncretism, 10, 67
Syria, 80, 200

Tabernacle, 115, 173
Talmud, 207–9, 210, 211

Tamar, 123–24, 141, 197, 201, 254, 255,
    257, 262, 271, 273, 274
  strategies used by, 134–35, 136, 137
Tammuz, 76, 127; see also Dumuzi
Tauutos, 254
Tebel (mixing), 191, 195
Temple, destruction of, 155
Ten Commandments, 146, 149
Ten Plagues account, 96, 101
Teraphim, 268
Testament of Reuben, 151, 207
Testaments of the Twelve Patriarchs, 207
Theodicy, 100, 106
Theogony, 204
Theseus, 204
Thutmosis III, 160
Ti'amat, 17, 71, 75–76
Tithing, 106
Torah, 114, 146–47, 182, 183, 209
Tosephot, 280
Tower of Babel, 113, 217, 250
Tubal-Cain, 111
Tukulti-Ninurta, King, 77, 242
Tyrian documents, 156, 157

Ugaritic texts, 201
Umma, 71
Umul, 73
Ur, pantheon in, 9, 12
Urash, 222; see also Ki
Uriah, 262
Ur III dynasty, 37, 42, 223, 230, 236
  kings of, 60–61, 63, 65
  marginalization in, 77, 79, 80
  pantheon in, 10, 11, 229
UrNammu, King, 36, 236–37, 239–40
"UrNammu's Death," 42
Uruinimgina, King, 79
Uruk dynasty, 51, 52, 60, 62–63, 222
Urzababa, King, 63
Uttu, 16, 18, 26, 28, 49, 72, 231
  as weaver, 22–25, 27, 33
Utu, 9, 12, 26, 231, 238
Utuhegal, 236
Uzzah, 96, 101

Vagina dentata, 68, 278
Vashti, 255
Vassal Treaties, 75
Venus star, 46
Virginity, biblical view of, 190, 192, 273
Virgin Mary, 30, 183, 271
von Rad, Gerhard, 20

Warad-Sin, 79
Warfare, 66–67, 222
Water purification, 43
Weaving, 22–25, 26–27, 33

Wisdom literature, 118, 211
Wisdom of Ben Sira, 206, 251
Wisdom-Woman, 179–83
  notes on, 270–71
Wise Woman of Abel, 129, 132, 255, 256
Wise Woman of Tekoa, 132, 134, 255, 260,
  261
Wolff, Hans Walter, 200
Women in the Bible, 118–43; *see also* God-
    women; Wisdom-Woman
  beauty and, 140, 206
  evil, 126–27
  gender ideology and, 140–43
  household authority and, 129–30
  lack of solidarity and, 127
  as mothers, 121–22, 123–25
  notes on, 254–62
  powerlessness of, 125–26
  strategies used by, 128–40

  as wives, 122–23
Writing, 3–4, 39–40, 41, 42, 59, 115

Yael, 139, 209, 262, 280
Yamm, 266
YHWH: *see* God
Yohanan, 210

Zabalam, 222
Zachariah, 99, 270
Zelophehad, 130, 134, 255
Zephaniah, 175
Zeresh, 255
Zeus, 203, 204
Zilpah, 254
Zion, 179, 182, 183, 211
  as beloved woman, 168–78
  marriage metaphor and, 149, 169
  notes on, 269–70
Zipporah, 255
Zulummar, 75; *see also* Ea